PREFACE

Britain's relationship with the Europ[ean Union is of] bewildering complexity surrounded [by] misinformation. Pro-Europeans and Euro-sceptics seek only to promote their own committed views at the expense of objectivity and even honesty. In contrast, this is a book designed to inform rather than influence, and to explain the issues in terms ordinary mortals can understand.

The author, Dr. David Winn, a recent but very mature graduate in law, provides a comprehensive analysis of Britain's involvement with the European ideal right from its inception. He explains the problems Britain faced in deciding to join and negotiating terms, and in accepting the Maastricht Treaty as well as how the rivalries, and disagreements with its European partners developed over the years.

The decisions and motives of all Britain's politicians are examined, and placed within the context of an evolving Europe. Dilemmas of the present involving the single currency, the expansion of the EU to include states formerly under the influence of the Soviet Union, and the far reaching constitutional conference currently in progress are thoroughly described in a balanced and analytical manner.

The book is concerned with questions of law, government, the constitution and national sovereignty as well as practical issues of politics, and economic and social benefits. It provides a wealth of background information and fascinating snapshots of individuals and their often colourful opinions.

Finally, and most importantly, this book will not tell you what to think about Britain and the EU, but after reading it you will know precisely why you think it.

BRITAIN v EUROPE

David Winn

Futuro Publishing Ltd

BRITAIN v EUROPE

Copyright © David A. Winn LL.B., Ph.D.
The author asserts his rights
in accordance with Sections 77 and 78 of the
Copyright Designs and Patent Act of 1998

ALL RIGHTS RESERVED

NO PART OF THIS BOOK MAY BE REPRODUCED IN ANY FORM,
BY PHOTOCOPYING OR BY ANY ELECTRONIC OR MECHANICAL MEANS,
INCLUDING INFORMATION STORAGE OR RETRIEVAL SYSTEMS,
WITHOUT PERMISSION IN WRITING FROM BOTH THE COPYRIGHT
OWNER AND THE PUBLISHER OF THIS BOOK.

ISBN Number
0-9545139-0-8

Cover Illustration by Hannah Byford
Printed & bound in the UK by Tandem Press
www.tandempress.co.uk

First Published June 2003 by
Futuro Publishing Ltd.
140 Ashley Crescent
London SW11 5QZ

INTERNET

This book may also be used as a gateway to much more extensive information via the internet. In particular many of the politicians referred to earlier in the book will appear to most readers as little more than names on a page. However many of these characters have their own fascinating stories which could not be included within the book. It also includes extensive links to further sources of information, biased or otherwise. These may be all accessed via the website as shown below.

Throughout the book the symbol ⁿ❂ has been used to indicate that additional information will be available via the site. However, it will also be used to post updates and additional reports as the rapidly moving developments regarding enlargement, the Euro, and the New Constitution appear, as well as any necessary corrections.

Finally it is hoped to include comments from readers. Contributions will be welcome from anyone wishing to make corrections, to shed light on or dispute any of the arguments made within the book, or to generally contribute to the overall debate.

Internet Site: http://www.BRITAINvEUROPE.co.uk

Reader Section Access Code: BvE01*****

BRITAIN v EUROPE

CONTENTS

	PAGE
INTRODUCTIONS: Constitutions - Britain v Europe	
PART I : Britain	
Rule of Law	1
Evolution of the Constitution	2
Hereditary Monarchy	3
Judicial Abuse	6
The British Solution	7
The Role of Parliament	9
The Role of the Courts	12
PART II: Europe	16
Constitutional Failure	17
Modern Constitutions	
Germany; Austria France; Italy; Benelux;	19
Spain; Portugal; Greece;	24
Finland; Scandinavia; Ireland.	27
New Members	34
No Thank You	35
Part III: Introducing the European Union	37
1. Was Churchill a European?	
Early Federalism	39
The Churchill contradiction	40
Council of Europe	42
2. Britain at a Loss after the War	
Labour Govt on the World Stage	44
Marshall Plan & NATO	45
3. Europe Strikes Back	
Monnet & Schumann	49
Britain on the Fringe	50
Britain v European Coal & Steel Community	52
A. The First Community	56
4. Back & Forth in Defence	
European Defence Community	59
Western European Union	61
5. Britain's Dose of Reality	
Legacy of Greatness	63
The Suez Canal	64

6. Conception of the Common Market
        Absent from Messina   67
        Agonising Britain   68
            B. The European Economic Community
                    Preamble   73
                    Functions   74

7. Britain Losing its Way
        France after Suez   78
        Collapsing Circles   79
        De Gaulle's Common Market   81

            C: European Institutions
                    Overview   82
                    European Parliament   83
                    Council of the European Union   83
                    European Commission   84
                    European Court of Justice   85
                    Consultative Bodies   87
                        ECOSOC   87
                        Committee of Regions   88
                    Organisational Scrutiny   89
                        Ombudsman   89
                        Court of Auditors   90
                    Financial Institutions   90
                        European Central Bank   90
                        European Investment Bank   91

8. About Turn! Halt!
        Road to Isolation   92
        Economy v Sovereignty   93
        Negotiate of Not   95
            D: The Law of Europe
                    Legal Digression   98
                    Primary Legislation   98
                    Secondary Legislation
                        Regulations   99
                        Directives   99
                        Enforcement   99

9. Forces Gather & Grow
        Adversarial Politics   103
        Macmillan v Gaitskell   104

10. Second Time Around
        Wilson's Conversion   107
        The Road is Still Blocked   110

11. The Power of de Gaulle
        Empty Chair   112
        Ambassador Soames   115

	E: European Law Applies	
	Direct Effect	117
	Indirect Effect	123

12. Preparations & Hurdles
    Hague Summit 127
    Fishy Conspiracy 130
    Edward Heath 131

13. Negotiations Background
    Political Convergence 134
    Acquis Communitaire 136
    Swallow the Lot
        F: National Law v European Law
            Supremacy 143
            Conclusion 146

14. Negotiations Tactics
    Much Ado 147
    Tactical Success 150

15. Negotiations Results
    Tariffs & Trade 153
    Commonwealth Sugar 154
    New Zealand Butter 154
    Community Finance 156
    Fisheries 157
    Summary 158
        G: The Law and the Treaty of Rome
            Treaty Making Powers 160
            The Treaty of Rome 162

16. The First Battl
    The Tactics of Edward Heath 166
    Defeating Parliamentary Opposition 168
        H: The European Communities Act 1972 173

17. Let The People Decide
    Referendum? 176
    New Terms 180
    Campaign and Result 184
        I: EU Law Arrives in Britain
            Entry of EU Law 190
            Establishing the ECJ 194

18. Thatcher, The European
    Thatcher – Battling With but For Europe 197
    Towards a Single Market 202
        J: The Single European Act 208

19. The Lady WAS for Turning
    Accelerating Europe 211

Halting at Bruges		213
Battle for ERM		215
K:	EU Law in UK	
	Commission Enforcement	219
	New Rules of Interpretation	222
	British Courts v UK Government	228
	Judges & Politicians in Proportion	232

20. Battle of Maastricht
    A New European Treaty? 238
    In the ERM 239
    and Negotiationg Maastricht 240
    Back From Re-Election 242
    ERM Ejection 244
    The Battle for Maastricht 246

L:	New Vision of Justice	
	New Role for the ECJ	249
	Adding a Few Words	250
	Changing a Few Words	252
	Adjusting an Old Concept	253
	Stopping a Few Changes	256

21. Major Trials
    Battling Eurosceptics 259
    BSE 266
    EMU 267

M:	The Cows Come Home	
	Defenceless Britain	271
	Protection Required?	273
	BSE	274
	Foot and Mouth	279

22. Labour Revival
    Realignment – Kinnock & Smith 280
    New Labour 282

23. Blair's New Government
    A New Bank for England 285
    A New Social Chapter 285
    Meeting Minds at Amsterdam 287
    But, No further on EMU 290
    No Further on Tax 294
    Euro Elections 298
    Re-Grouping at Lisbon 299

N:	The Sky's the Limit	
	Ever Expanding Competence	302
	Open Skies - For the Commission	305
	Single Street Market	307

24. European Stumbles.
    Sacking the Commission 311
    Romano Prodi 317

Corruption Tackled		318
O: Driving the Forces of Integration		
Power and Politics		321
Power Behind Politics		327
Power Without Politics		330
Rescue by Subsidiarity		332

25. Council Control
Austria 337
Nice 339

26. Surfing the European Waves
Employment/Social Affairs 346
Enlarging the Budget/ CAP Reform 352
P: Enlargement
Politics of the Club 357
Joining the Club 361

27. Rising Tides
Defence / Foreign Policy 367
Justice & Home Affairs 373

28. Stemming the Flood
Sovereignty of Parliament 380
Scrutiny by Parliament 381
The Parliament of Scotland 384
Constitutional Scrutiny 385

29. Economics (Trade & Investment)
Trade Performance 388
Overseas Investment 391

30. Economics (Stability, Growth, & Euros)
Safety in Numbers 397
The Famous Five 399
Will Britain Join? 404
Better Off Out? 406

31. Towards 2004
The Final Step 408
Convention on the Future of Europe 413

The Europe of our Children and Grandchildren 418

Acknowledgements 423

Appendix 1: Competence of the European Commission 425

INDEX 431

Constitutions – Britain v Europe

INTRODUCTION: Part I - Britain

The Rule of Law
It is central to the modern concept of government, common to all Western democracies that the entire country lives under the "Rule of Law." The exact meanings and implications of this simple phrase have given rise to countless articles, essays and studies of its precise meaning and significance. However, its most important aspects can be conveniently summarised by a few famous quotations.

The seventeenth century English judge, Thomas Fuller stated, "Be you never so high, the law is above you." This phrase was repeated by Lord Denning when, in delivering a House of Lords judgement in 1975, he insisted that the Secretary of State for Education had exceeded his ministerial power in directing a newly elected Tameside Borough Council to implement a comprehensive education policy. In other words, even the government is subject to the rule of law. The early president of the United States, John Adams, had explained the principle that people should live under a "Government of laws, not of men," as he incorporated the phrase into the first constitution of Massachusetts. In a similar vein, Theodore Roosevelt also explained the concept. "No man is above the law and no man is below it: nor do we ask any man's permission when we ask him to obey it." Of course, some countries have a stronger sense of obedience to the law than others, and in Britain the "law of the land" generally is held in great respect. People may occasionally feel unfairly treated after marginally exceeding the speed limit, but they still tend to hold the law in higher regard than the politicians who made it. This is why the control of the process of making the law is so important.

In England the constitutional writer A.V. Dicey described the "Rule of Law" in two principles. Firstly, "No man could be punished or lawfully interfered with by the [state] authorities except for breaches of law." In other words, all government actions must be authorised by law. Secondly, "No man is above the law and everyone, regardless of rank, is subject to the ordinary laws of the land."

Clearly society benefits from the stability and predictability stemming from the rule of law, and from its application as a restraint on government power in general. It provides powerful institutional resistance to a government's natural tendency to increase its discretionary powers even to the level of arbitrariness. Moreover according to the International Commission of Jurists in Delhi in 1959 the function of the rule of law, is "not only to safeguard and advance civil and political rights of the individual in a free society, but also to establish social, economic, educational and cultural conditions under which his legitimate aspirations and dignity may be realised." But, having established that the concept of the rule of law is of such importance it is necessary to understand how such requirements can operate in practice and how an appropriate balance between the interests of the state and the individual can be maintained. This is the realm of constitutional law.

Evolution of the Constitution
A constitution is defined as the entire body of rules which determines how the people of a nation organise their government. It defines how a government is formed, specifies and limits a government's power with respect to individual citizens, and determines what procedure is necessary to change it. The rules describe the various institutions of the State, define their duties, powers and relationships, how they interact together and to whom they are accountable. A constitution is intimately connected with the concept of law, but at the same time represents a higher version of law beyond the reach of everyday government and transient political pressures. Subjection of the ruling authorities to restrictions on the extent of their power represents the peoples' protection against tyranny. Thus the history of all European constitutions represents an account of each country's transition from the absolute rule of kings, to the democracies of today. Parliamentary systems emerged, usually violently, as a mechanism for reflecting the ultimate sovereignty of the people over their own systems of government.

In contrast to most other States, the United Kingdom has a constitution which has developed continuously, gradually, and mostly peacefully over a period uninterrupted since 1066. More significantly, it is not to be found written down in a single or even a collection of documents, but depends on a mixture of law and powerful convention. For a large part of this history the constitution involved a description of the powers of the King, which varied according to the personalities involved, and the interaction between the monarch's military forces and financial power and that of his barons, or later ministers. It is clear though, that even a monarch who claimed and exercised absolute power was unable act without some support from individuals such as nobles and of some military power to enforce his decisions, and this structure, however it was formed, always required money which ultimately comes from the labours of the people or from external conquest. Thus in any realm there was always some balance which had to be found between the different levels of the structure. Tensions or conflicts of interest within the system, although they were occasionally resolved in a violent or coercive manner, had to be balanced in some way in order to develop a sufficient degree of consent for society to survive. The human desire for peace and stability in everyday life ensured that a particular structure of sufficient initial power to establish itself, quickly attained a recognised legitimacy which guaranteed its survival. The body of rules evolving as a result of this process is called the constitution.

The formation of a constitution results from a complex interaction between social, political and economic forces. However Britain has one other important characteristic differentiating it from its neighbouring states. It has never suffered the discontinuity of a foreign invasion. In Europe such traumatic events have frequently imposed sudden and often drastic changes on a particular country, even though practical aspects of daily rural life may not have been affected unduly after the violence had subdued. People had often become willing to transfer their allegiance to a new lord of their local manor, and ultimately to a different King who was even more distant from their ordinary lives than governments are today. Individuals were appointed by the successful invader to key positions, usually within the existing governing structure, and life continued mush as before. Frequently however, and especially after many years of stability, the sense of legitimacy felt by the people was translated to a sense of loyalty towards their established monarch or his family and thus a national identity grew to be intimately connected with the monarch. This sense remains today in the eight monarchies of Europe, especially in Britain where the Queen is seen as a symbol of national unity and identity among all those who consider themselves British, even among those who are of a republican persuasion.

Hereditary Monarchy

A hereditary monarchy, with its clearly defined and accepted rules of succession contains an inherent protection against disruption in times of transition. Thus, although the history of English and Scottish monarchs contains many examples where the transition became violent and unpredictable, the system evolved into a controlled and defined mechanism where succession is now defined in law, in advance, as part of the transition to a constitutional monarchy. Although the hereditary principle is regarded by some as outdated and anti-democratic the certainty of succession guarantees that rivalry within the royal family can no longer descend to the seeking of support from external parties. Since succession cannot be traded for future political favours the monarchy is permanently insulated from the short term influences of professional politicians. It is this independence which enables the monarchy to function, paradoxically, as the ultimate guarantee of democracy in Britain and in the other European monarchies. In the days of intensive and relentless media interest in the minutiae of the royal family's private life, and amid a general public distrust of privilege even if coupled with duties, it is easy to overlook this role as the actual protector of democracy which has successfully operated several times during the present Queen's reign.

The government of the day is referred to as Her Majesty's Government, and all government powers are exercised in the name of the Crown. The Queen is nominally the head of the judiciary, the head of the armed forces, is required to assent to any Act of Parliament before it can have legal effect, and is even head of the church. This would represent an enormous power for any individual of whatever public standing, but the curious feature is that exercise of any of this power is limited by powerful conventions which render the powers irrelevant in any but the most exceptional circumstances. The monarch will act only on "Advice" tendered by, usually an elected politician accountable to Parliament, and both willing and able to take the responsibility for the action "Advised". Thus the royal assent to an Act of Parliament has not been withheld since 1707. Even during times of constitutional crisis or during a transition of government the monarch still depends on Advice, even though Advice from alternative parties may be sought.

The important feature is that in all normal circumstances the nominal holder of government's sovereign power does not in practice exercise any of this power at all, but merely holds reserve powers. These can be used only to ensure the continuing legality of government. The Queen does however retain a constitutional right "to be consulted, to encourage and to warn," which leads to the curious convention of weekly audiences with the Prime Minister. This means that she is not entirely divorced from the daily reality of politics. In addition, she ultimately possesses the power to force the government either to submit to the verdict of Parliament or to submit itself to the verdict of the people at a forced general election.

Of course this is all a rather fortunate result of earlier turmoil. In England Charles I inherited the belief of his Scottish father James I (or VI of Scotland), in the "divine right" of a king to rule as he saw fit, and without constraints of an established law. He was, after all, born into that position by a positive act of God, and believed that, "The King protecteth the law, not the law the King." Similarly in France Louis XIV believed that "Le Loi, c'est Moi." Both monarchs attempted to exercise unrestricted personal power, and although Charles I was beheaded for his pains the French guillotine did not perform similar service until Louis XVI was perpetuating the same philosophy one hundred years later. However whereas in France a republican form of government was instituted, the earlier English revolution failed to establish sufficient legitimacy under Oliver Cromwell and his successors, and the monarchy was restored in 1660 with Charles II.

It was only 25 years later that Charles' brother, James II again caused a confrontation with Parliament. Although crowned in the protestant ceremony James was a practising catholic. This was accepted as a private matter until he asked Parliament to remove laws which prevented catholics from holding public office. Eventually he attempted to repeal those laws by proclamation and open rebellion began. James was soon forced to flee the country and was deemed to have "abdicated" by vacating the throne. According to the "Convention Parliament" which sat to resolve the crisis, James had been subverting the constitution, breaking the contract between King and people, and violating the country's fundamental laws. He had been attempting to "govern by a despotic power unknown to the constitution and inconsistent with it" contrary to the oath he swore at his coronation. This was actually a radical concept in Europe at the time introducing an almost contractual relationship between the monarch and the people which still remains. The result in 1688, was that the Convention Parliament offered the throne to William of Orange and his wife Mary, who was James II's protestant daughter. Both were grandchildren of Charles I. The condition for bestowing the Crown was acceptance of a document known as the "Bill of Rights" which defined the future relationship between monarchy and Parliament, and established a purely protestant succession.

Judicial Abuse of Power

James II's "abuse" of his royal power illustrates the essential elements necessary for despotism or for avoiding it and so deserves closer examination. James had proved adept at manipulating an immature and not yet independent legal system for his own ends, using assumed powers both to <u>create</u> and to <u>enforce</u> new "laws". In this way he was attempting to assume complete control of government policy, with the aid of a compliant judiciary.

In the aspect of the law dealing with individuals' behaviour, now known as criminal law, the greatest threat of injustice comes from arbitrary enforcement proceedings, and the greatest threat to democracy comes even today when these are used for political ends. Use of the judiciary by a king as a political weapon had been known since the 15th century and under Henry VIII when the "Star Chamber" in Westminster had been used for arbitrary proceedings against opponents by the king and/or various councillors before its abolition by Parliament in 1641. A new example was to appear early in the reign of James II when a rebellion led by the Duke of Monmouth was defeated in the last pitched battle to take place on English soil at Sedgemoor. Many rebels were brought to "justice" in trials known to history as the Bloody Assizes. Under the infamous judge, Lord George "Bloody" Jeffreys, around 300 rebels were hanged, even though many had pleaded guilty under a promise of mercy. Some 800 were transported and many more were imprisoned or cruelly whipped. Judicial power proved to be more important than any generally accepted legality. On this occasion the result was a definite shift in the balance of state power towards the King, which gradually and with increasing confidence, he was able to extend to other spheres of government. Later, the drafters of the US Constitution were acutely aware of the danger of excessive judicial power illustrated by these failings in England. Judicial power could have a great potential for centralisation but it could also become a powerful engine of oppression if it was unchecked. The need for such "checks and balances" was particularly acute in the context of the federal or multi-layered system of government which they were designing.

James II's increasing control over the legal process demonstrates the much wider implications involved, as he wielded assumed legal powers in order to implement his own policies with regard to religion. The power of the king to grant a dispensation from a particular statute in a specific case, or to suspend a statute when the interest of the state so required had long been regarded as a necessary legal safeguard, despite its potential for abuse. In one particular case a compliant judge had upheld James' misuse of this prerogative power against the law preventing catholics from holding offices. This encouraged the King to completely circumvent the will of Parliament by issuing a Declaration of Indulgence. While nowadays, people might support James' actions as an example of promoting religious freedom people at that time were more afraid of religious oppression, and James was seen as trying to force catholics into important offices. In France a century of religious tolerance had recently been destroyed as Louis XIV revoked the Edict of Nantes. Tens of thousands of protestants fled to England, and many feared that James was becoming a serious threat to Protestantism itself, despite his position as head of the protestant church. He countered the murmurings of discontent by establishing a new Court of High Commission even though this completely contrary to statute. He even then formed a separate army of some sixteen thousand troops, commanded by many catholic officers which was soon encamped on Hounslow Heath as a threat to Londoners.

This last British example of misuse of prerogative power shows how important a role the law should have in constraining the executive and administrative powers of the government, and in ensuring that day to day decisions accord with a direction which today would be democratically decided. It also illustrates the danger of compliant judges being used to achieve selective enforcement of laws for political ends, and demonstrates the utility of having a military force available as an ultimate deterrent of dissent. Thus, the pervasive power of the law has been, in the history of most countries, both a benign protector of society and an irresistible tool of oppression.

The British Solution

Recognition of these dangers, and acceptance of the solutions defined in the Bill of Rights by the new joint monarchs William III and Mary II formed the basis of the constitution which continues to exist in Britain today. Neither the later 1707 Act of Union of England with Scotland, which combined the two Parliaments, nor the recent establishment of a new Scottish Parliament altered the fundamental principles. These are that the different spheres of state power should operate separately and independent of central control – a concept followed in constitutions throughout the democratic world. So, in Britain the resulting constitution can be summarised as follows:

1. Parliament is the supreme legislative authority.

The creation of laws (including those laws defining government policy, and those concerning taxation) requires consent of "The Queen in Parliament"; namely the House of Commons, the House of Lords, and the Royal Assent, and Parliament is itself subject to democratic control by the people.

2. The Executive (and administrative) Branch of the government is separate from and accountable to Parliament, and responsible for acting in accordance with the law of Parliament.

3. The Judicial Branch is separate from the executive and the legislative, with individual judges under a duty to enforce the laws of Parliament in a rational and impartial manner, and to follow rules of precedent..

4. Ultimate control of military forces is separated from the executive.

5. The monarch is the central source of state authority and legitimacy, now constrained by the need to act only on "Advice" and by the contract of the coronation oath.

Thus although there have been many changes to details such as electoral rules and franchise, and matters concerning each branch of government, the modern constitution of Britain can be said to date from 1688, even though several transitions had yet to be completed. The office of Prime Minister had yet to appear with independent authority and this still enabled forceful or even wayward monarchs eg. George III, to exert excessive influence particularly in foreign policy. However the concept of the purely constitutional monarch emerged as the logical response to the democratic aspirations of the people and the separation of executive authority was completed.

This means that the monarchy today can remain an important symbol of national continuity, lending support to the public view that the constitution has gradually evolved and adapted through such events as the signing of the Magna Carta and the English Revolution in a sequence unbroken since the Norman Conquest of 1066. This lends an immensely powerful sense of legitimacy to and respect for the country's system of government. It is difficult to argue that today's constitution is perfect.

However, the system essentially invented in 1688 has allowed for considerable but always legal changes in the political system which have withstood numerous crises ranging from economic collapse to world wars, and social changes resulting from industrial revolution and the rise and fall of a world wide empire. It has commanded the general and enduring, though occasionally grudging support of the people while continually providing them with effective protection against any form of dictatorship or despotism.

The Role of Parliament

Numerous examples exist in history where political power has been obtained by use of military force and retained by repression, overriding any of the theoretical constraints and protections provided by a constitution. Carefully devised and well established mechanisms for ultimate protection of the Rule of Law have failed in the face of military superiority, and in circumstances of domestic turmoil. Constitutions which are purely written have been ignored; and those with a designated human protector have failed due to that individual's weakness or a lack of means or support for maintaining opposition. However, such emergencies apart, the Rule of Law is continuously maintained, and government power rests on its accepted legal base, which in turn means its legitimate power to *create* and to *enforce* the laws of the land.

Most commentators would agree that sovereign power of the state belongs ultimately to its people and is exercised on their behalf and according to the Rule of its Laws, by its government. Different roles, duties, functions and rules may be assigned to a Head of State, however both in Britain, and in other European countries, the fundamental principle is one of government by Parliamentary democracy. The executive of the government is responsible to Parliament which possess a right and duty to scrutinise any actions of the executive branch and to call ministers to account when necessary. In turn Parliament is accountable to the people through electoral rules, and thus the constitutionally elected Parliament is effectively responsible for the exercise of the country's legal sovereignty.

The orthodox view of this Parliamentary sovereignty was described by the Victorian constitutionalist A.V. Dicey.

> "The principle of Parliamentary sovereignty means nothing more nor less than this: namely, the Parliament thus defined [The Queen in Parliament] has, the right to

make or unmake any law whatever; and, further, that no person or body is recognised by the law of England as having the right to override or set aside the legislation of Parliament.

A law may, for our present purpose, be defined as 'any rule which will be enforced by the courts'. The principle, then, may be looked at from its positive side, be thus described: any Act of Parliament, or any part of an Act of Parliament, which makes a new law, or repeals or modifies an existing law, will be obeyed by the court. The same principle, looked at from its negative side, may thus be stated: there is no person or body of persons who can, under the English constitution, make rules which override or derogate from an Act of Parliament, or which (to express the same thing in other words) will be enforced by the courts in contravention of an Act of Parliament."

From this understanding follow the three fundamental rules of Parliament's sovereignty in Britain, although later sections of the present work will describe how these principles have been modified:

1) Parliament, as the supreme law making body, may enact laws on any subject matter.

While obviously there are serious limitations regarding the practicality of some measures which could be considered, this means that there are no legal restrictions. There are nevertheless some Acts of Parliament which effectively entrenched in the system for political reasons. As an example consider the Scotland Act of 1998 which established the Scottish Parliament. Formally this derives its authority from Westminster, under the acts of Union in 1706/7. However it is politically inconceivable that the powers of the Scottish Parliament could be removed.

2) No Parliament may be bound by a predecessor or bind a successor

This is a logical deduction from the requirement of supremacy. It means that today's Parliament is able to repeal any law enacted by a predecessor, whatever attempts may have been made to entrench it. Clearly, when Parliament explicitly states such an intention the law will remain clear but on some occasions Parliament inadvertently passes a statute to some extent in contradiction of an earlier one. This leads to the concept of "implied repeal" whereby the later statute is regarded as repealing the original measure. However questions still arise since even constitutional measures are enacted by Act of Parliament, and should not be contravened by simple administrative Acts. Thus, a concept of some higher level of Act of Parliament has been developed by the courts, limiting at least implied repeal where Acts such as the Act of Union, The European Community Act and to a lesser extent, the Human Rights Act are concerned. This was illustrated by the recent case of the "Metric Martyrs".

3) No person or body may question the validity of Parliament's enactments.

In the seventeenth century the eminent judge Coke stated that judges were entitled to use the Common Law of England, developed over generations of judicial practice, to control and judge void any Act which is "against common right or reason, or repugnant or impossible to perform." However since 1688 the explicit supremacy of Parliament has prevented any such action, giving precedence to statues over the concepts of common law. Thus the courts will enforce any law passed according to the established procedure. This meant that courts were denied any means of reviewing Acts of Parliament. Interestingly the courts developed means of reviewing acts by the executive branch. For example, in the case of *Associated Provincial Picture Houses Ltd. v Wednesbury Corporation (1948)* the court decided that authorities acting under statute could only be regarded as acting legally, and thus under the terms of a particular statute if their decision was "reasonable", which included taking appropriate matters into consideration, and avoiding bad faith or dishonesty. A court would intervene if an authority's decision "was so unreasonable that no reasonable authority could have made it." No such limitation can be applied to a Parliamentary Act.

Finally it should be noted that the law is not entirely composed of Acts of Parliament. Frequently an Act will include a procedure under which new regulations or conditions may be introduced, subordinate to the Act, but an integral part of it. The Act will define the procedure required to introduce the new measure, the most common being a Statutory Instrument. Every year there are many more Statutory Instruments than Acts of Parliament usually prepared by the ministry concerned for operating the Act. Usually the relevant will require that the Instrument is "laid before Parliament", and will come into effect unless the House votes against it. The important point is that the entire procedure uses Parliament's unlimited legislative authority to delegate some of this power, to some other body, usually a ministry, in a particular area and as a matter of administrative convenience. All such secondary legislation must conform to the requirements of the main Act or its validity may be challenged in the courts. Another example of non-Parliamentary legislation is local authority bye-laws. Local authorities have a delegated authority to enact regulations for the "good rule and government" of their local area, and for " the prevention and suppression of nuisances" therein. Such laws are authorised by the Local Government Act and usually require public notice and ministerial consent. Theoretically even legislation of the Scottish Parliament derives its legal basis from the Westminster Parliament under the Scotland Act.

The Role of Judges

The function of the courts is to ensure that law passed by Parliament permeates the entire country and governs the relationships between individuals and institutions throughout the land. It provides the mechanism for enforcement of the laws created under Parliamentary authority by adjudicating between disputes as they arise, or in criminal cases by ensuring that individuals have the necessary protection against arbitrary or unjustified state actions and sanctions. Naturally this presents an enormous potential for abuse which is largely contained by ensuring the independence of the judiciary. Protection for individual judges, and both organisational and procedural mechanisms isolate courts both from the executive and legislative branches of government as well as from political interference.

At an individual level a judge's security of tenure has been protected since 1700 under the Act of Settlement. Other than for incapacity, judges can only be removed from office by the Queen following an "Address" presented to her by both Houses of Parliament. This last occurred when a judge was sacked for embezzlement in 1830.

Organisational separation is effective but not quite so robust. It is obvious that in any integrated or hierarchical structure even separated organisations have to meet at some point. However, in most constitutions the judicial branch would not normally combine with others except at Head of State or the Parliamentary level. In this respect Britain is slightly different since while the Queen is the nominal Head of the Judiciary and all Justice "flows from the Crown" the actual head of the judiciary is the Lord Chancellor. Although this figure has limited effect on actual judgements of specific cases he is a Minister within the government's Cabinet, he acts as

Speaker of the House of Lords and does remain a senior a Law Lord able to influence judgements binding on lower courts in his own right. He therefore occupies a curious role in all three branches of government. Although several conventions are aimed at minimising any conflict of interest (eg. when speaking for the Government in debate, he removes himself from the Woolsack, the Speakers seat), he cannot therefore be regarded as politically independent.

Further protection is provided by court procedures. An important feature of any court judgement is that it must be fully reasoned. Thus anyone may read the explanation behind a particular judgement, and may identify any fallacy deficiency within it. Therefore if the decision involves for example, some questionable interpretation of the law, the case may be submitted to a court at the next higher level for reconsideration. British law provided that the House of Lords was the highest court of the land, where the actual meaning of the statute would be finally defined. Of course then, if Parliament objected to this final statement of the law, it retains the option of changing or rewording the statute to ensure that the courts conform to its actual will.

Publication of the courts' reasoning is an important aspect of the system. Of course this enables any interested party to obtain a definitive statement of some aspect of the law at a particular time. However it is also important to provide consistency within the judiciary. This is the main reason for the courts' duty to follow strictly, any line of reasoning which has been established in a judgement of a higher court. A court at a lower level will examine and decide two aspects of the dispute before it. First it will examine all the relevant circumstances of the case and make a judgement as to the "facts" of the case. Then it will decide how the law applies to those particular facts using established rules of interpretation and the lines of reasoning previously determined. Thus "precedent" is regarded as a central feature of the process within a court hearing, and lawyers will always site numerous "authorities" to argue that their case is exactly the same as, or quite different from a particular case decided at a high level. This has frequently meant that the law was not finally determined until it had been fully examined in an actual case, it must be an *actual* case, in the House of Lords. This has led to development of an entire system of English "common law" which provided judicial authority *solely* from earlier precedent sometimes going back for centuries. Murder for example, remains a common law offence.

Interestingly, and unusually another feature of the court reporting system is that whenever a decision of the court is not unanimous, the report will include the reasoning of the dissenting judge. While of no value at all to the party who lost the case, such judgements can provide a valuable insight into the development of the law, and occasionally appear as the early stages of a shift in judicial opinion.

In deciding a case the court's determination while guided by precedent must "interpret" the law and in doing so is bound to follow several important rules. The fundamental objective, following the judges' duty to follow the law, is to ascertain the "Intention of Parliament". The first, and most important assumption is that this has been expressed primarily by the words of the statute itself. This leads to judgements which consider most carefully the *exact* meanings of words, and the precise effect of a sentence's grammatical structure. One example is the case of *Whitley v Chappell* (1868) where the offence of impersonating another person in order to vote was held not to cover impersonating dead people, because they are not entitled to vote. Where such analysis reveals ambiguity a "Mischief rule" is used to identify, from the statute, which "mischief" Parliament intended to address and the remedy it intended. Similarly where use of ordinary meanings of words would lead to an absurdity a secondary meaning may be adopted, and anomalies amounting to injustice may even be avoided by adding words of "*necessary* implication" but such cases are exceedingly rare. Britain is fortunate in that its judges, ever sensitive to accusations of attempting to make law themselves, have dutifully avoided any decision which could be interpreted as usurping the constitutional role of Parliament.

One quotation exemplifies the attitude prevalent throughout the judiciary regarding their duty of obedience to Parliamentary will. Refusing a claim that a statute was contrary to international law, Judge Ungoed-Thomas J in the case of *Cheney v Conn* (1968) said, "What the statute itself enacts cannot be unlawful, because what the statute says and provides is itself the law, and the highest form of law that is known in this country. It is the law which prevails over every other form of law, and it is not for the court to say that a parliamentary enactment, the highest law of this country, is illegal." This respectful attitude had spilled over from Parliament to the executive branch using reasoning that the government was responsible to Parliament. However in the case of *Council for the Civil Service Unions v Minister for the Civil Service* (1985) the House of Lords confirmed that decisions even by Ministers of State could be reviewed by the courts to ensure their legality. Lord Diplock explained that decisions could be challenged on grounds of illegality, (ie. the decision-maker did not correctly understand the law that regulated his decision-making power and/or did not give effect thereto), its procedural impropriety (where there was failure by the executive or administrative tribunal to observe the appropriate procedural norms) or its irrationality (if the decision was so outrageous as to be outwith the bounds of the rational). Thus individuals in the government itself were brought within the rule of law.

Of course judges are capable of mistakes, and often become involved in controversy, so attracting media interest. Similarly judges often appear under the public gaze when particular decisions are being criticised, and this leads to frequent comments that judges are old fashioned and failing to move with the times, or are generally "out of touch." Frequently such criticism is necessarily true since judges are not empowered to adjust laws in accordance with public feelings, nor can they consider political or journalists' opinions in their interpretation of the law. In addition, the long experience that senior judges must bring to the law, and the powerful ethos of precedent is accompanied by a powerful sense of tradition, and a natural restraining factor counter- balancing the politicians' tendency to react immediately and hastily to some situation temporarily in the news. In fact, reading judgements from senior judges reveals a remarkable capacity for objective and detached evaluation of competing factors. In varying degrees they display an extraordinary sensitivity to the effects of their decisions not only on the parties before them but also to their wider responsibilities in society. An excellent example applying until the Human Rights Act imposed its statutory system was illustrated by the courts' powerful use of the common law to enforce individual rights. Thus, so far, judges in Britain with their shared commitment to their duty and their obedience to the will of Parliament have performed admirably the functions assigned to them by the constitution, and within the coherent body of constraints formed by the rules of interpretation and of precedent.

Constitutions – Britain v Europe

INTRODUCTION: Part II – EUROPE

Those in Britain fearful of the changes being brought about by membership of the European Union have occasionally lamented that Britain was throwing away "One thousand years of (constitutional) history." The previous section shows that this is an exaggeration. However it remains true that none of Britain's European partners can boast a comparable period of constitutional stability and continuity. Just as those who have never experienced war are said never to fully appreciate peace, the benefits of a system of government which allows even drastic change in policies and its membership while still protecting its people against abuse of power remain undervalued until they are lost.

The history of Europe is one of the often turbulent transition from numerous absolute monarchies to stable systems of democracy under which individual rights are protected by the state and from the state. Political leaders are given control of state powers but are nevertheless prevented from introducing measures which undermine the rights of their citizens. Nowhere has this transition been easy and rarely was it free from violence. Moreover it frequently resulted in replacement of an autocratic monarch with another form of tyranny and it is remarkably recently that dictatorship can be said to have been eliminated in Europe.

A very brief survey of the recent history of the present EU member states illustrates the constitutional turmoil which many of them have experienced over a very recent period. It is no wonder that several countries viewed the European Union as a haven for the peace and stability for which their people yearned. Many countries, having regarded their nations as somehow diminished by their internal turmoil, or their lack of democratic independence came to view membership of the EU as a symbol of international acceptance. This can also be seen clearly in the newly independent states of Eastern Europe where joining the EU has become a matter of national prestige. Local politicians are able to proclaim their success in transforming their countries to the long envied levels of Western Europe, and perversely may even boast that they are now able to give up their newly won sovereignty to the European Institutions. There is a sense of achievement and pride that their country had "come of age" within the community of nations and can now be regarded as an "equal" partner with their prosperous neighbours. Even several existing members sought to join the European Union as a means of enhancing the political security of their nation and saw membership as enabling them to entrench democracy and respect for human rights. Few British politicians would have believed such a haven of protection was necessary for Britain, and those few other countries which had grown accustomed to political stability would have similar reservations. Britain thought it was merely joining a common market.

Constitutional Failure

The history of most European countries has not been fortunate. The violent overthrow of the French monarchy, one hundred years after the settlement in England provides a telling example of the dangers of discontinuous constitutional change. The political vacuum caused by the removal of the centralising power produced political turmoil with intense and violent rivalry between various parties in a struggle for power. The result was the appearance of the strongest individual of his time Napoleon Bonaparte. This actually provided many benefits. Imposition of his codification of laws, which remains the basis of French law today, added to his "firm" leadership and legacy of efficient administration provided France as well as some other territories administered by Napoleon, with the basis for future stability. However at the same time he used his military strength and consequent popularity to adjust the constitution to his liking, until he was proclaimed Emperor of France in 1804. The concept of monarchy was hard to remove from the popular imagination. Napoleon then stated his intention "to build a federation of free peoples in a Europe united under a liberal government," and set about this by attacking and conquering as many European countries as he could manage. He was indeed forming nations based on the "rule of law", but only providing that it was his law, and that it remained firmly in his hands. War raged across Europe until his defeat at Waterloo in 1815.

History indeed shows that almost any form of constitution can remain stable in the absence of external danger, and when periods of prosperity distract the people from any deficiencies it may have. But, in times of national emergency or crisis a constitution is tested and regrettably many have failed the test with devastating results. The most extreme example dates from the end of World War I when Germany was rebuilding under the Weimar Constitution. This appeared as an enlightened document with extensive guarantees of civil liberties in an explicit declaration of basic rights. The president and the parliament (Reichstag) were directly elected by universal suffrage, the president appointed the Chancellor to head the government and ministers were responsible to the Reichstag. Finally, in order to protect against a possible recalcitrant government there were reserve powers available to the president in the advent of an emergency, defined in Article 48.

In the early 1930's Germany was exposed to economic depression like much of the world but with crippling war debts and weakened coalition governments unable to undertake any decisive economic corrections Germany was suffering more than other countries. In 1930 when growing public discontent caused the collapse of an unstable coalition government President Hindenburg invoked Article 48 to appoint Heinrich Bruning as Chancellor. Bruning used presidential decrees to govern while the Reichstag remained too divided to re-assert its authority. Strident nationalism was appearing, fostered by increasing public unrest.

In April 1932 Hindenburg was re-elected as president. Two months later, again invoking Article 48, he replaced Bruning as chancellor with a right-wing friend Franz von Papen. Bruning still enjoyed the "confidence" of the Reichstag, so Hindenburg dissolved it declaring that it "no longer represented the will of the people." This incident illustrates how allowing unrestricted power of the Head of State to appoint the Head of Government can suddenly create a constitutional danger.

Although at this moment there was a perilous concentration of power in the hands of Hindenburg the situation appeared to be a satisfactory response to a constitutional emergency caused by a paralysed parliament. The elections Hindenburg correctly ordered for July gave sufficient seats to von Papen, but only providing he retained the support of the largest party in the Reichstag, the Nazi Party. As leader of the largest party Adolf Hitler had demanded to be made Chancellor, but Hindenburg refused. But in November, when elections reduced the seats of the Nazis and increased those of Communists, von Papen was forced to step down. Hindenburg and his followers did not trust his successor, Kurt von Schleicher, so the President intrigued with von Papen to appoint a "puppet" Chancellor, effectively controlled by the President above, and a Vice-Chancellor, von Papen, below. Hitler was appointed Chancellor by perfectly legal and constitutional means.

In February 1933 the Reichstag was burnt down. Hitler immediately blamed the Communists and issued an emergency decree under Article 48 to deal with the Communist "threat", and proceeded to arrest many of their leaders. Another general election in March was held against the background of anti-communist fear and nazi propaganda coupled with vast demonstrations and open displays of violence all creating the impression of an unstoppable power. Remarkably the people still refused to give Hitler a majority; and he received no more than 44% of the popular vote. However, he decided to prepare an Enabling Act, entitled "A Law for Removal of Distress from People and Reich", giving him "emergency" power to rule by decree for four years. The Reichstag was opened after a truly massive state ceremony replete with powerful German national symbolism, attended by all leaders of the state, armed forces and church, all parties separately cajoled into accepting a compromise with Hitler which he could later forget. Then, when sitting, the Reichstag needed a certain persuasion to pass his Enabling Act.

The first round of persuasion comprised a set of promises that presidential powers would remain intact, the Reichstag respected, and independence of the component states preserved – neither the first nor the last such promises to be completely ignored. Secondly, the deputies entered by passing solid ranks of black-shirted SS troops encircling the building, and inside found corridors lined with brown-shirted SA troops. Having removed all communist deputies, and imprisoned several other opponents this atmosphere of intimidation proved sufficient. The required vote was recorded, leading to jubilation of the huge waiting crowds. The old President Hindenburg, theoretically submitting to the "will of Parliament" was relegated to a symbolic inconvenience until his death in 1934 removed even this completely ineffective restraint. Hitler had already begun to construct an entirely new state structure, the Third Reich, under cover of unchallengeable legality which lasted until all organs of state power were under his personal control.

After the War a new federal constitution was imposed by the allies, and ratified in Germany in 1949. Government operates with powers distributed in a defined manner between the separate States (Länder) and the federal centre. The Federal Government comprises two houses of parliament, the Bundestag and the Bundesrat (the upper house with Länder representation); a Federal Constitutional Court, and a Federal Presidency. The executive is headed by the Chancellor, described as "the captain of the ship of state", who is appointed by the President after winning a vote in the Bundestag. His Cabinet of autonomous Ministers are appointed by the President on the binding advice of the Chancellor. With this structure democracy and the Rule of Law quickly returned to Germany and the country gradually regained respectability to play a leading role in the EEC even before its re-unification with the communist East Germany following the collapse of the Soviet Union.

Austria

The Austro-Hungarian Empire and the Habsburg monarchy was brought to an end with the First World War and a new Republic was created in 1920. Essentially the same constitution remains in force today with a directly elected President, appointing the Chancellor of the government. A dual chamber Parliament comprises the directly elected lower chamber or Nationalrat, and the upper Bundesrat which includes representatives of Austria' nine regional states. However this was by no means a smooth and continuous process from the beginning and even today with a much a wider spread of political views than found in much of the rest of Europe the coalitions necessary to form government often experience serious polarisation of opinion.

The new Republic of Austria in the 1920's was suffering incredible divisions. The predominant one was between a staunchly conservative rural population and urban socialists. There were also many groups who had favoured a union with Germany, which had been prevented by the victorious allies, and numerous border disputes arose from the perceived arbitrariness of the country's creation. Worse still, there were several paramilitary forces formed, usually with sympathies to particular parties. In an atmosphere almost of impending civil war the Christian Socialist Chancellor, Engelberg Dollfuss became increasingly authoritarian. Unrest continued to increase and in 1934 a socialist general strike was put down with the use of the army and their artillery used against workers' apartment blocks. With no pretence of following the constitutional rules, opposing political parties were simply abolished, and Parliament was dismissed. Three months later Dollfuss himself was assassinated in a failed nazi coup. His successor Schuschnigg attempted to preserve his countries independence by friendship with Mussolini but this failed when Hitler formed an Italian alliance. Isolated Austria was unable to resist Hitler's "Anschluss" or union with Germany. Both Chancellor and President resigned as invasion eliminated Austria as an independent nation.

After the War Austria reinstated its constitution but found itself a buffer between the West and the Soviet Blocs throughout the Cold War. This convenient neutrality lasted until the collapse of communism. Then, in 1995 Austria was free to join the EU, and so began bitter internal struggles which enabled it to meet Maastricht criteria and join the Euro on schedule.

France

Although Hitler was the most extreme example it is generally true that constitutions remain vulnerable to forceful characters, particularly where strength is an admired quality, and such vulnerability is particularly exposed when emergencies can be used to invoke reserve constitutional powers. France offers a more recent example when for ten years after the late 1950's France's General de Gaulle used emergency powers resulting from the war of Algerian independence to change the French Constitution. He obtained these powers in a perfectly legal and constitutional process, but this was not to last. Gradually he increased presidential power at the expense of Parliament, with partisan appointments of ministers and dismissal of any dissenting parliament; instituting special courts for trying political crimes "against the State", and taking personal charge of the armed forces ignoring the constitutional necessity of taking ministerial advice. Much of the written constitution was thus being ignored, and with Presidential control of the media and widespread public support of de Gaulle's policy regarding Algeria, there was little opposition. Thus de Gaulle was simply strong enough to ignore the constitutional constraints and real French democracy disappeared until well after his death. One writer dismissed the written constitution as a mere treaty "provisionally settling the allocation of power to suit the victors in a political struggle." It was therefore partisan, and not endowed with any sense of permanence and in consequence each regime suffered from a fragile legitimacy. The prime objective of constitutionalism, that policies could change and governments could change while the system itself remained constant, was simply not operating.

De Gaulle was succeeded as President by Georges Pompidou, and then by Valeri Giscard d'Estaing. It should be noted that under the French constitution, dating from 1958, most executive authority is vested in the directly elected presidency, who is also the commander in chief of the armed forces, and guardian of the Constitution. Clearly the weakness exploited by General De Gaulle still exists. The President chairs the Council of Ministers which he appoints on the advice of his Prime Minister. Parliament, responsible for legislation, comprises the National Assembly which is directly elected, and the upper Senate comprising regional representatives.

In 1981 Francois Mitterand was elected as France's first Socialist president, but the right-wing Jacques Chirac was elected as Prime Minister in the legislative elections of 1986. This was an example of the famous French "co-habitation" caused by the two highest offices in the land having opposite party affiliation. It can be regarded either as a source of paralysis or an important check on the powers of the separate branches of government. This example of co-habitation lasted until Chirac was elected President in 1995. Chirac was subsequently embroiled in a serious corruption scandal, but achieved re-election and hence continuing immunity in 2002 largely because his opponent in the run-off was the extreme right-wing Jean-Marie Le Pen.

Italy

The modern state of Italy dates from its unification under the royal house of Savoy in 1870. After the First World War a former socialist, Benito Mussolini was trying to take political advantage from the ensuing turmoil using public demonstrations of support to exert his influence. He had formed a political party, the Fascists, and announced that "either the government will be given to us, or we will seize it by marching on Rome." The march on Rome did occur and the government fell. Mussolini refused to co-operate with the customary negotiations aimed at forming a coalition and was eventually asked by the King to form the government himself. The King, fearful of actual civil war, and under threat of being replaced on the throne by his cousin, failed to withdraw support from Mussolini even as he changed laws to control the electoral system, and then began to construct separate state apparatus, including a private army, under his personal control. A prominent opposition leader was murdered, but calls from the opposition for the King to dismiss were ignored partly in response to the new balance of power, and partly because the protestors were republican. Opposition was then banned and a new constitution with two heads, one of which could be ignored, was implemented.

The Italian role in World War II ended when, supported by the allies, Mussolini was captured by King Victor Emmanuel III. However a referendum in 1946 abolished the monarchy and a new constitution was instituted in 1948. It defined the legislative branch as comprising a directly elected Chamber of Deputies and a Senate comprising regional representatives. The President is elected in a joint session of Parliament comprising both houses, and thereafter acts as the central source of state power, on the advice of a responsible minister. Just three years after adoption of this constitution Italy became a founder member of the European Coal and Steel Community, and then of the European Economic Community.

Since the war Italy has suffered more than its fair share of political turmoil. A former Prime Minister, Aldo Moro, was murdered by left-wing fanatics; bombing campaigns were conducted by right-wing extremists; corruption scandals and alleged Mafia links have tainted nearly all politicians, including the current figures, extending even to some convictions eg. for bribery. Numerous political parties and regularly shifting alliances have produced a remarkable fifty-nine governments since the War. However the constitution remained successfully intact until it was updated in 2001, devolving considerable regional autonomy in fields such as taxation, environment and education to each of Italy's twenty regions.

The Benelux Countries

The Netherlands became an independent country, again, following the defeat of Napoleon. More recently the country suffered considerably from German occupation while its royal family and former government took refuge in England. Resistance remained within the country even though it was often punished by execution of hostages. The Dutch people also suffered real hardship, many approaching starvation during the battles leading to liberation. Afterwards though, the country rapidly returned to normality, and soon became a beacon for liberal and stable democracy, and for enthusiastic European co-operation. Under the current constitution of 1983 the monarch appoints and acts on advice of Ministers who control the executive in a Council of Ministers. Legislation requires consent of both the directly elected chamber, the upper chamber and royal assent. Queen Juliana was succeeded by the present Queen Beatrix in 1980.

The Kingdom of Belgium dates from its declaration of independence from the Netherlands in 1830. It remained intact until King Leopold was forced to surrender to German forces in 1940. Ten years later the Belgian people voted for return of the monarchy but serious rioting and strikes resulted in Leopold's son Baudouin assuming the throne in 1951 until his death and succession by his brother as Albert II in 1993. Belgium was a founder member of the EEC, but in 1958 formed a complete economic union with the Netherlands and Luxembourg. The present constitution dates from 1993, when the country was divided into three almost autonomous regions Flanders, Wallonia and Brussels. For a relatively small country the government structure is remarkably complicated. The legislative branch of the Federal Government comprises a House of Representatives, a Senate and the King, who appoints ministers and acts on advice. In addition there is a "Community Level" structure, a body of representatives of the three regions, and a body representing the different linguistic interests of the country. This was really only the latest response of a central administration to the continuing friction between the French and Flemish parts of the country. It is interesting to note that after operation of the constitution for only three years, parliamentary control in the area of the state budget and social security was effectively suspended. The Prime Minister obtained the power to control such matters by royal decree so that emergency measures could be passed which would ensure that Belgium was able to meet the Maastricht qualifying criteria for joining the Euro.

The small Grand Duchy of Luxembourg has had a chequered history having been part of several European empires. Its modern independence as a constitutional monarchy under a Grand Duke (currently Henri after abdication of his father Jean in 2000), dates from 1867, interrupted by occupations in both World Wars. It has long supported economic union, and has remained an enthusiastic supporter of the European ideal ever since joining its original founders.

Spain

Although Spain had remained neutral during the first World War it still suffered economic turmoil in the aftermath. Government corruption was widespread and political turmoil necessarily followed, reaching a climax when Spain's army was defeated in its colony of Morocco. In 1923, King Alfonso III ruling under a constitution dating only from 1876 and anxious to respond to popular demands for government reform while damaged by scandal at court, appointed General Primo de Rivera as head of government. The constitution and the civil rights protected by it were immediately suspended and dictatorship, tacitly supported by the weakened monarchy grew until republicans won elections in 1933 and the King abdicated. Five years later Spain was suffering a full scale Civil War, which resulted in military dictatorship under General Franco. Excesses of this government including murder and violent persecution of Franco's political opponents, led to Spain being ostracised by the United Nations until 1955.

In the 1960's economic growth and industrialisation was producing increasing expectations and industrial unrest. Political conflict between liberalising (Opus Dei) and fundamentalist (Falangist) factions under Franco produced alternating policies which gradually eroded his fragile support. The regime survived until Franco's death in 1975 when the monarchy was restored under King Juan Carlos, and a new constitution ratified by the people in 1978.

Under this present constitution the King of Spain acts as the central source of state authority including its military and judicial aspects, and acts under the advice of the President of the Government or a competent Minister. Legislation is approved by the Cortes comprising the Congress of Deputies and the Senate and subject to royal assent. The constitution was challenged only three years after its adoption in a new attempt at military coup but this produced shock rather than support and was quickly defeated. Then, in 1986 Spain joined the EEC.

Portugal

In the early 20th century the established Portuguese monarchy suffered by assassination of King Carlos, and abdication of Manuel II in a revolution. Weak government continued until military officers took control. Dr. Antonio Salazar, the successful Minister of Finance seized power from this group in 1932 and instituted a "New State" constitution. This provided Salazar with an authority for a personal dictatorship which lasted beyond his death. The government he formed strove to avoid the undermining influence of industrialisation and prosperity, and he obstructed any moves towards reforms similar to those being undertaken in the rest of Europe. Eventually the regime was attempting to shield its people from reality in a country almost closed off from the world. Of particular importance to Portugal was its colonial empire which was required to purchase produce from Portugal, thus creating a dangerous dependence for the mother country. Increasingly desperate and debilitating attempts to resist independence movements from the colonies led to serious discontent within the armed forces. After Salazar's death, his successor Caetano attempted some cautious liberalisation in several areas, using the inventive slogan, "renewal in continuity". However the main result of this was to awaken political opposition, and after some attempts to reverse his policies and continue the colonial struggles a war-weary nation was relieved that Caetano fell to a military coup. The date of April 25, 1974 is still celebrated in Portugal. A leftist military junta governed the country for two years while political parties emerged and organised, and then a new constitution was approved in 1976.

This document, designed as a socialist blueprint includes a comprehensive description of protected individual rights, and enshrines the principles of separation of state powers. It defines the powers of a directly elected President as the central state power advised by the Council of State. The Assembly of State of directly elected deputies promulgates legislation. The executive government is the Council of Ministers with the Prime Minister appointed by the President after receiving advice of the Assembly, and Ministers appointed on the Prime Minister's advice. The Azores and Madeira remain integral parts of the Republic. Modifications to the constitution, including an allowance for referenda, were seen as necessary to accommodate developments in the EU which Portugal had joined in 1986, only ten years after emerging from dictatorship.

Greece

In the 19th century a monarchy was imposed on the people of Greece by the Great Powers of the time being Britain, France and Russia. The Danish prince, becoming George I of the Hellenes, (grandfather of the present Duke of Edinburgh) took ten years to accept the restraints required by a constitutional monarch but the beginning of the new century saw defeat in a war with Turkey, serious economic stagnation and political paralysis. In 1922 a military junta seized power and King Constantine I abdicated. A republican constitution was introduced but the governments failed to quell political turmoil which was worsened by worldwide depression. A referendum in 1935 led to restoration of the monarchy. In an effort to provide order within the country the King appointed General Metaxas as Prime Minister, and unwisely, was persuaded to suspend several articles of the constitution on the pretext of countering a communist inspired general strike. This immediately led to a new dictatorship which lasted until the Axis powers occupied the country, and the King, George II, fled to Egypt.

After the War the monarchy was restored again, but George died to be replaced by his brother Paul. A constitutional settlement led to an unstable tripartite leadership of monarchy, military and parliament. At last economic growth and progress was being achieved, but, as elsewhere this led to increased expectations, and demands for greater freedoms which theoretically already existed in the constitution. Lack of progress in this direction coupled with rumours of intrigue and corruption provided an opportunity for another military coup in 1967, leading to the dictatorship of the "Colonels".

The latest military regime was tolerated despite its reputation for brutal repression, but the economic crises such as oil pricing during the 1970's prevented expected economic progress. Then, in the aftermath of a crisis over Cyprus which almost led to full scale war with Turkey the Colonels, the regime was overthrown by the Commander of the Military Police. He, in turn, gave way to democratic opposition led by Karamanlis who then led a "Government of National Salvation". A referendum rejected the restoration of the monarchy of Constantine II, and a modern constitution was rapidly approved by government majority in 1975. In fact the main opposition parties had protested that the new constitution reinforced the executive at the expense of a marginalized parliament, and that the powers of the president were excessive, particularly with regard to sweeping powers available "in case of a serious disturbance or of manifest threat to public order and to the security of the state from internal dangers." However it did include protection for fundamental rights, and recognised an institutional role for political parties. In any event there was no means of rejecting it.

In 1980 Karamanlis was elected President and in 1981 Greece joined the EEC. At the same time a general election produced the first socialist government, of the PASOK party, led by Papandreou, producing also the first example of a Greek co-habitation. Despite occasional railing of Papandreou against NATO and against the EEC he was gradually tamed and a viable modus vivendi was achieved between them. Then in 1986 a revision of the constitution to remove the extreme presidential prerogatives, and to strengthen the role of Parliament was accepted, producing a level of democracy in Greece comparable with that of its European partners. Several changes of government and shifts in policy have since been achieved without a Greek drama.

Finland

The people of Finland have spent a large part of their history under the control of their neighbours Sweden and Russia, but have still managed to maintain their own distinctive identity. They last escaped formal Russian domination after the Russian revolution when Finland was able to declare its independence. During the Second World War Finland attempted to remain neutral but was drawn in when it was attacked. As punishment for fighting the USSR Finland was forced to pay reparations and later to spend many years in "friendship" with the Soviet Union. The country was both dependent and independent throughout the Cold War. Although it was free to trade under agreements negotiated with both the EEC and with Comecon countries it was not until 1989 that the Soviet Union recognised Finnish neutrality. The final collapse of the Soviet Union freed Finland from its neighbour's influence and the country immediately applied for membership of the EEC, joining in 1995.

Scandinavia

Absolute monarchy in Denmark was first brought under legal control following a constitution of 1849 which produced a separation of powers, including independence for the courts, and a dual chamber parliament directly elected by every man over thirty who was neither a servant nor a convicted criminal. It also included a number of individual rights such as freedom of expression and assembly which extended to public assistance and free education.

During the First World War, in which Denmark remained neutral, universal suffrage in a voting system of proportional representation was introduced, and between the Wars social democratic governments gradually developed a Welfare State. In 1939 Denmark signed a non-aggression pact with Germany, and was invaded a year later. Limited autonomy was removed in the face of Danish resistance and the country was governed by decree until the end of the War.

Work on a new constitution began but was hindered by the need for general support, and did not succeed until 1953. This document strengthened the protection of human rights and political freedom, introduced a single chamber parliament, the Folketing, and limited the powers of the monarch, (King Frederik IX until he was succeeded by his daughter Queen Margrethe II in 1972). Denmark included the Faroe Islands and Greenland which were subsequently given self government. The present Queen has no political power but retains the functions of appointing members of the government according to the party situation in the Folketing, the appointment of judges, assenting to legislation and retains a right to government consultation. All royal acts are performed subject to Advice. The Constitution includes an interesting approach to the surrender of powers to supranational institutions in that if a 5/6 majority is not achieved in the Folketing, a referendum must be held. This enabled the Danish people to approve membership of the EEC in 1973, to accept the

Single European Act in 1986, to reject and accept the Maastricht Treaty in 1992 and 1993, and to reject membership of the Euro in 2000. In addition an ordinary Act can be challenged after the approval of the Folketing if 1/3 of its members object, in which case a referendum is held.

Sweden operated under a constitution dating from 1809, which provided for the monarch to adopt the constitutional duties as in Denmark, governing in partnership with the Riksdag, and which include the classical version of the separation of state powers. However subsequent monarchs frequently exercised personal power over the government and it was not until 1918 that Gustav V finally accepted the modern role of the monarchy and the supremacy of the democratic process. This was in response to a dramatic incident in 1914 when the King was at odds with his Liberal government. While the government had come into power partly promising disarmament, the King wanted an immediate strengthening of the armed forces. A Farmers' Rally of 30,000 assembled in support of the King listened to his defence of royal prerogative in his "Courtyard Speech" at the Royal Palace in Stockholm. He dissolved the Riksdag and ordered new elections, but had actually precipitated a widespread call for the introduction of republic. Resolution of the crisis was postponed by the start of the First World War, but afterwards elections were won by left wing parties and Gustav was forced to accept the reduced role already assigned to him under the constitution.

Sweden was relatively unaffected by World War Two. It was forced to allow transit of German troops to Norway until 1943, but otherwise remained independent and attracted many fleeing refugees from both Denmark and Norway. In 1950 Gustav was succeeded by his son Gustav VI Adolf, who became a popular monarch scrupulously fulfilling his duties until his death in 1973. Largely because of this there was little enthusiasm for removing the monarchy in the 1975 constitution designed although a considerable reduction in its power was agreed. The present Carl Gustaf XVI is limited to purely ceremonial duties opening the single chamber Riksdag annually and receiving foreign dignitaries. He no longer possesses the reserve powers common to other monarchies, although he does retain the right to be kept informed by the Prime Minister, and convenes special Cabinet meetings as required. The Prime Minister is appointed by the Speaker of the Riksdag and to transfer powers to a new government it is the Speaker who convenes the special session of the Cabinet before the King.

Norway never became a member of the EEC. Despite its geography and a closely connected history with Sweden and Denmark it has remained distinct, and also prosperous in part because of the vast oil reserves discovered in the North Sea in the 1970's. It was in 1905 that Norway's Parliament, the Storting, proclaimed that the union of the Crowns of Norway and Sweden was dissolved and that Norway would be henceforth completely independent from Sweden. In effect the King of the Union was deposed and the now vacant throne of Norway was offered to Carl a Prince of Denmark, who took the title of King Håkon VII. Thus the monarchy was clearly a creation of the written Norwegian constitution and subject to its terms.

In common with Denmark state authority is vested in the King, although it is exercised on advice of Ministers. Despite this some vestiges of prerogative power remain as illustrated in 1928 when the King appointed the country's first Labour government, contrary to the advice tendered by the outgoing government.

In 1939 Norway had declared its neutrality but was invaded anyway the next year. The Germans demanded the appointment of a new Prime Minister, Vidkun Quisling, to head a puppet government. The King made a statement to the government. "The decision is yours. But if you choose to accept the German demands, I must abdicate. For I cannot appoint Quisling as Prime Minister". Thus the appointment was refused, the King fled to London and Quisling had to proclaim himself head of the government. Suffering widespread resistance Quisling was forced to introduce martial law which lasted until German defeat and the return of the King. The constitution remains in force with Olaf V succeeding in 1957 and Harald V since 1991.

Norway rejected membership of the EEC in a referendum of 1972, leading to the resignation of the government, and again did so in 1994 by a similar margin of around 5%. Norway remains a member of EFTA, giving it conditional access to European markets, but now at a heavy price.

Ireland

In the early 19th Century Ireland had been united with England and Scotland, and had proportionate representation in the Westminster Parliament. However at a time when Britain was concerned with rapid industrialisation and building its empire, the rural economy of Ireland and the separate requirements of its people were neglected both by government and by powerful landowners within the country. Major rebellions resulted from dissatisfaction in 1848, and 1867 and although they were dealt with harshly, calls for Irish Independence never abated.

The first Bill aimed at granting this independence was defeated in the House of Lords, but was replaced with reforms aimed and meeting other Irish demands, and another such Bill also defeated in 1893. Later, after Asquith had curtailed the power of the Lords to veto bills passed by the Commons in 1911 a Home Rule Bill was again introduced. This was now fiercely opposed by the largely Protestant north and a real threat of civil war appeared whichever way the decision was to fall. The First World War interrupted the process but in 1916 Irish Nationalists seized the General Post Office in Dublin in the Easter Rising. The British quickly quelled the disturbances but executed its leaders to the outrage of much of Ireland. In 1918 members of the party *Sinn Fein* won 83 out of the 106 Irish seats in the Westminster Parliament but instead taking these seats they formed a new Assembly of Ireland, the Dail Eireann. This Assembly then elected Eamonn de Valera as President of the Irish Republic, and started with the building of a new state structure. Although the British responded with military repression traditional tactics were unable contain the disruption caused by the IRA, and independence now appeared inevitable to many in Britain. In a dispute which continues today fervent opposition from Ulster meant that partition of Ireland seemed the only logical possibility, and Prime Minister Lloyd George began to push for it. In 1921 the Anglo-Irish Treaty was negotiated, and ratified by the Dail by 64 votes to 57, although many politicians on all sides felt it represented a betrayal. The treaty established the Irish Free State as an independent dominion of the British Crown, with the six northern provinces having the option of remaining as an integral part of the United Kingdom.

Despite an immediate civil war with hundreds of casualties the Irish Free State survived until 1937 after De Valera, heading the Fianna Fail party, had spent years gradually reducing British influence. The really independent Republic of Eire was proclaimed. The problem of Northern Ireland remains a source of bitterness today with enduring intransigence on both sides of an insoluble dilemma. Terrorist activity from the IRA resurged in the 1970's, but was matched with opposing violence resulting in numerous casualties among innocent civilians. This remained the prime obstacle to cordial relations between the British and Irish governments until real dialogue led to the Anglo-Irish agreement of 1985. The "peace process" continued in 1993 with the Downing Street Declaration which offered dialogue regarding the province in exchange for renunciation of violence and in 1998 this led to the Good Friday agreement which provided for political co-operation, renewed government from the Stormont Parliament and a mechanism for disarmament of terrorists on both sides of the community. Regarded as the only, even if continually lengthening route to a permanent peace this continues as the basis for continuing dialogue hopefully towards a lasting peace.

The constitution of 1937 begins with an unusual preamble:

> "In the name of the Most Holy Trinity, from Whom is all authority and to Whom, as our final end, all actions both of men and States must be referred, We, the people of Ireland, humbly acknowledging all our obligations to our Divine Lord, Jesus Christ, Who sustained our fathers through centuries of trial, Gratefully remembering their heroic and unremitting struggle to regain the rightful independence of our Nation, And seeking to promote the common good, with due observance of Prudence, Justice and Charity, so that the dignity and freedom of the individual may be assured, true social order attained, the unity of our country restored, and concord established with other nations, Do hereby adopt, enact, and give to ourselves this Constitution."

This is a clear example of the catholic influence of the constitution which included provisions to prohibit divorce and abortion, although specific references protecting the catholic church were removed in 1973. Divorce was not permitted until an amendment of 1996 and only then in very limited circumstances, while abortion remains unconstitutional unless required to save the life of the mother. It is interesting that the prohibitions relating to abortion were amended in response to the European Court which, while allowing the basic prohibition on grounds of it being a national view of a fundamental right, prevented the imposition of restrictions to travel, and the provision of information relating to abortion services. Measures disrupting the operation of the single European market were not to be permitted.

The constitution itself provides for a directly elected President who had usually been a former politician. However the present holder of the post, Mary McAleese had a legal, University and broadcasting background. She is the first President to come from Northern Ireland, replacing in 1997, Mary Robinson who had been a law professor and senator, and who left the job to become UN Commissioner for Human Rights. Formally the President holds the powers to appoint the Prime Minister, Taoiseach, nominated by the Dáil, the ministers as advised by the Taoiseach, as well as judges, and military officers on the advice of the government. The supreme legislative authority is the Oireachtas comprising the President and the two houses of parliament the Dáil Éirann and the upper house the Seanad Éirann. Both houses are directly elected, but candidates for the Seanad are nominated by several interest groups within society such as Universities, cultural, industrial, organised labour. The President summons or dissolves the Dail and enacts the laws passed by it, on advice, and is the nominal head of the armed forces. Presidential intervention on critical matters, or referral of a government Bill to the Supreme Court to ensure it is not "repugnant to the constitution" is authorised after consultation with the "advisory" Council of State. This body comprises ex-officio members such as the Taoiseach, the Chief Justice, and the speakers of both houses of parliaments, former holders of state office, and several members nominated personally by the President.

A referendum is required for any constitutional change and several of these have resulted from EU membership. Thus membership of the EEC was approved in 1972, the Single European Act in 1987, ratification of the Maastricht Treaty in 1992, and the Treaty of Amsterdam in 1998. The Treaty of Nice was rejected by voters in 2001, but they were persuaded to change their opinions in October 2002. It is interesting to note that although major changes still require ratification at every step, Ireland has one of the few constitutions which grants explicit supremacy to decisions of the EU. The Irish have shown little fear of European intrusion and enthusiastically accepted membership of the Euro zone. In fact Ireland has proved one of the major beneficiaries of the Union, having received generous subsidies and development grants, and has consequently achieved a marked reduction in their traditional economic dependence on Britain.

New Members of the Union

There are marked differences even between the three Baltic States of Estonia, Latvia and Lithuania, let alone between the other countries formerly under control of the Soviet Union namely Romania, Bulgaria, Hungary, Czech Republic and Slovakia, and Poland. All of these have fascinating histories which cannot be mentioned here because of space. However it is their common and recent national escape from communist oppression which is most relevant here. All emerged with their national identities intact, and an enthusiasm and optimism regarding their future which is unknown in the West. Consequently, in just ten years all have made remarkable progress towards building their own democratic systems, and free market economies using the benchmarks of EU membership as targets to guide their national transformation. The impressive achievements of them all have not been without difficulties. The rate of progress and the levels of resistance have varied considerably from country to country, but the trend has been established and with EU assistance all are confident of a rapid rise in their peoples' prosperity.

Finally, but by no means least are those two Mediterranean islands of Malta and Cyprus. Malta was a crown colony of the British Empire since 1814 and in the Second World War earned the George Cross from King George VI for their heroic resistance to the Axis forces. The island had its own legislature since 1921 but gained self-government after the war. Plans for an actual union with Britain foundered and Malta became fully independent in 1964, proclaiming itself a republic under Don Mintoff's Labour Party. Mintoff engineered a "non-alignment" of the country which involved special relations with Libya and with several communist states but this phase passed and after the mid 1980's Malta's path towards Europe appeared. An application to join the EEC was made in 1990, but shelved when Labour won an election in 1996, and then revived when the Nationalist Party won in 1998. Hesitancy regarding membership was said to be resolved in March 2003 when 53% of the population approved membership by referendum.

Membership of Cyprus has proved more controversial. The island was annexed from Turkish rule under the collapsing Ottoman Empire in 1914, but in the 1950's Greek Cypriots began a guerrilla war against the British aiming for unification with Greece. The Turkish community was violently opposed to any such move. In 1959 Archbishop Makarios was elected president and a year later independence was granted under a new constitution which both communities had agreed. Violence between the communities erupted when Makarios attempted to modify power sharing arrangements and UN peacekeepers arrived in 1964. Ten years later Greece's military junta backed a coup against Makarios, but Turkish troops landed in the north of the island to protect the Turkish community. Since then the island has been divided. At time of writing efforts to re-unite the island have failed despite efforts by the UN and in particular its General Secretary, Kofi Annan. Without reunification only the Greek Cypriot part of the island will gain membership of the EU.

No Thank You

To close this section we refer to a remarkable country in the geographical centre of an expanded Europe, surrounded by EU members but remaining detached and fiercely independent. Such neutrality has been a feature of Switzerland for almost two hundred years. The country even avoided participating in the two World Wars. Much of this is due to the sheer importance of their banking system to much of the world. However some credit must also be due to the country's unique system of government. Its mere description evokes from the imagination a vision of conventional politicians throughout Europe scornfully and derisively dismissing the practicality of such an idealist system. Nevertheless the Swiss concept of direct democracy has thrived and persisted, as a lesson to the world.

Switzerland's modern history dates from its formation after the defeat of Napoleon in 1815. Then in 1874 its unique system of direct democracy was applied to the federal level of government. The country has seven million inhabitants, divided into twenty six cantons (which have their own constitutions), and a total of around three thousand communes. The constitution distributes powers at the different levels of this hierarchy. The executive comprises seven ministers, elected by Parliament one of which becomes "president" as first among equals, but only for one year when another is chosen. The country has been governed by the same four party coalition since 1959. However what is really unique is the public participation in government decisions. Any law being proposed by the government will be put to the people in a referendum if a petition of fifty thousand signatures is obtained. Thus every year there are two or three referendums with several such government decisions presented to the people for their approval. The main effect has been a remarkable development at all levels in the arts of compromise, as authorities are forced to adopt a consensus most likely to meet with approval. Moreover referendum campaigns are conducted with an openness and honesty of debate unknown in most of Europe. The citizens even approve their own level of taxation. There is no opposition party, no presidential veto, and no party discipline.

Switzerland's legendary neutrality is of such an extent that it was only in 2002 that the people narrowly agreed that their country could join the United Nations. In trade the country has been rather more liberal, joining the European Free Trade Association when it was founded in 1959. It also joined the Council of Europe in 1963, but neither of these organisations pose any threat to national sovereignty or freedom of action. Thus membership of the EEC and EU has seemed a remote possibility and even when EFTA was partly merged with the EU in creation of the European Economic Area, Switzerland refused to join. In recent years the government has actually supported joining the EU, explaining that Switzerland has common interests and common values with Europe. As recently as 2001 though, the voters decided that this was insufficient and refused permission for talks even to begin.

All this is not to say that Switzerland is isolated or immune from political pressures from the rest of the world. Its revered banking system was shaken to its core by pressures responding to accounts held by victims of the Jewish Holocaust. Similarly worldwide pressure to combat international crime and terrorism continues to make its mark on traditional Swiss policy, and approval for Swiss soldiers to participate in peacekeeping missions abroad caused serious soul-searching against the sacrosanct concept of neutrality. Even so the success of this political system in preserving a confederation which speaks three languages (French German and Italian, with a minority Romansch), has undeniably created unequalled stability with both peace and prosperity. Faced with the prospect of the fundamental changes which membership of the EU would require the verdict of the people remains clear. No thank you.

INTRODUCTION

PART III: INTRODUCING THE EUROPEAN UNION

The previous sections of this introduction serve as somewhat lengthy descriptions of the historical journeys each of the present Member States have made towards the New and emerging Europe, setting into context the changes to be described later. They describe how in addition to the natural diversity among the peoples of Europe with their marked differences in language and customs, and their different routes to a modern democracy, there remain very important differences in the way their governments have been run. In joining the European Union each has been required to adjust many aspects of their society, with varying degrees of success. The formation of Europe has not only been about the creation of a simple trading bloc or a "Common Market" but has required an integration of all these traditions and the construction of a new legal order across the continent in order to attain the aims defined in the original Treaty of Rome.

This book proceeds to describe exactly what changes the European Union has introduced into the systems of government throughout Europe during its evolution, and in particular how Britain has adapted or has been forced to adapt to the resulting challenges. A much fuller understanding of what has actually happened can be gleaned from the parallel account of how political opinion developed within Britain and its establishment. Consequently the book is organised into two separate threads which merge towards the end, as described in the Contents pages. The problems of successive governments and of individual politicians in handling the British dilemma are described in detail in order to explain fully where Britain stands today on the issues of the moment.

Britain in particular now stands before two momentous decisions. Pressures will remain on both sides of the question regarding adopting the single currency and the proposed Inter-Governmental Conference of 2004 is intended to define a constitution for a European Union expanded to 25 Member States. The decisions soon to be taken are likely to determine the status of Britain for at least a generation. The following chapters describe the background necessary for a full understanding of all these issues.

Chapter 1: Was Churchill a *European*?

Early Federalism

Even before the end of the Second World War in 1945 there was a growing awareness that the future would need to be different. The Great War in 1914-18 had been thought of as "a war to end all wars", but this failed to produce a secure settlement to the historic enmity between France and Germany. Hitler had jolted everyone's thinking out of the gentle pacifism of the 1930's. The world had emerged from severe economic depression, gradually becoming optimistic and internationalist. An idealism emerged which changed perceptions of the world but made people generally slow to notice and slower to recognise the looming dangers of Nazi Germany.

In Britain ideas which today would be described as "Federalist" had become perfectly respectable, promoted by a political party known as Federal Union, which in 1940 had more than 10,000 members, and supported of course by many idealists, but also by many serious and influential figures of the time. One of these was Winston Churchill who, as early as in 1930 was earning his living writing for magazines. He argued both a political and economic case for forming a United States of Europe, "to appease obsolete hatreds and vanished oppressions". He admired the underlying dynamism of the American economy with its respect for science and its industrial organisation and saw the single market and unifying government of the USA as the model for a future Europe.

It seems remarkable to many Euro-sceptics today that such a stalwart, such a totally loyal and patriotic Briton could actually have been in favour of a constitutionally united Europe. Surely, Churchillism did not mean support for the abolition of the monarchy and Britain subjected to government from the continent! No, it didn't. His article states that in Britain "we have our own dream and our own task. We are *with* Europe but not *of* it. We are linked but not comprised. We are interested and associated but not absorbed." Thus began a contradictory or at least confused vision of Britain's role in Europe which continues to this day.

Even during the war Winston Churchill although intimately concerned with the survival of Britain itself in his management of the war effort, and central in the daily demands of national politics was still considering the long term future of the continent. In December 1940 he foresaw a Europe comprising five single powers – Britain, France, Italy, Spain and Germany with four confederations covering the rest of Europe meeting in a "Council of Europe" with a separate judiciary and economic council to *settle currency questions* and with power to deal with any breach of the peace. Two years later, writing to his Foreign Secretary, Anthony Eden, he continued to discuss a united European family with minimised barriers to a common continental market and with unrestricted travel. Later in a 1943 broadcast he counselled preparing for "the largest common measure of the integrated life of Europe that is possible, without destroying the individual characteristics and traditions of its many ancient and historic races." The horrors of war were encouraging a purpose and a vision of the future not just summarised by his famous "V"ictory sign, but including a structure to ensure permanent continental peace.

The Churchill Contradiction

To the surprise of the world Churchill lost the General Election immediately after victory. Swiftly he moved on to the European stage. After the widespread slaughter of the war, the emphasis had changed to rebuilding and the emerging European leaders, well aware that new solutions were required to prevent future wars, were highly receptive to Churchillian oratory delivered by the hero of his time.

In the University of Zurich in September 1946, to the astonishment of his eminent audience he called for work to begin on the United States of Europe, centred around a partnership between France and Germany. At a time when Germany had just been occupied and divided by the victorious allies and Churchill himself had that year described the threat from communism by introducing the phrase, "Iron Curtain", this was a proposal of extraordinary vision. It nevertheless contained two important limitations. Firstly it did not contain his earlier ideas of *supreme* judiciary and economic council since the first step was formation of a Council of Europe as a forum for association of sovereign governments. Secondly, it did not include Britain. He said, "Britain and the Commonwealth, mighty America, Soviet Russia must be friends and sponsors of the New Europe, and must champion its rights to live and shine". It does not seem to have occurred to Churchill in this speech that his proposed destiny for Europe should include Britain. The potent symbolism of a United States of Europe meant little more than a new Franco-German partnership.

Churchill's image as the Great European continued with an address in the Albert Hall in April 1947 entitled "Let Europe Arise". However, within the evangelical zeal, the thread of British separation from Europe continued. "We shall allow no wedge to be driven between Great Britain and the United States of America, or be led into any course which would mar the growing unity in thought and action, of the English-speaking nations, spread so widely about the globe, but joined together by history and by destiny." Even so, the movement towards European Unity expanded culminating in an extraordinary assembly in The Hague, in May 1948, known as the first Congress of Europe.

Churchill, as the keynote speaker, made the objectives clear:-

> "It is time indeed that that voice should be raised upon the scene of chaos and prostration, caused by the wrongs and hatreds of the past, and amid the dangers which lie about us in the present and cloud the future. We shall only save ourselves from the perils which draw near by forgetting the hatreds of the past, by letting national rancours and revenges die, by progressively effacing frontiers and barriers which aggravate and congeal our divisions, and by rejoicing together in that glorious treasure of literature, of romance, of ethics, of thought and toleration belonging to all, which is the true inheritance of Europe, the expression of its genius and honour, but which by our quarrels, our follies, by our fearful wars and the cruel and awful deeds that spring from war and tyrants, we have almost cast away."

and implications were not ignored:-

> "Mutual aid in the economic field and joint military defence must inevitably be accompanied step by step with a parallel policy of closer political unity. It is said with truth that this involves some sacrifice or merger of national sovereignty. But it is also possible and not less agreeable to regard it as the gradual assumption by all the nations concerned of that larger sovereignty which can alone protect their diverse and distinctive customs and characteristics and their national traditions all of which under totalitarian systems, whether Nazi, Fascist, or Communist, would certainly be blotted out for ever."

but although the Congress included and encouraged many European federalists present the involvement of Britain remained ambiguous.

Council of Europe

Three months later France proposed the creation of the Council of Europe, which first met in Strasbourg in August 1949 under its first president, the Belgian federalist Paul-Henri Spaak, and under the guidance Churchill as its first hero who made another grand and uplifting speech. Churchill saw the Council of Europe as a "European Unit" in the newly formed United Nations but was primarily interested in promoting the mood and feeling of Europeanism, and development of a European voice with worldwide influence. However his inspiring but nevertheless vague oratory did not include governmental machinery or formulae aimed at specific objectives. Glossing over the lack details or of a clear and defined plan, the committed European federalists nevertheless followed Churchill's philosophy, but in a direction he didn't advocate. He had provided the impetus but left others to find the policies.

One policy immediately following the enthusiasm generated by this meeting of the Strasbourg Assembly was for the creation of a European authority with real supra-national political character with limited functions but with real power. Real obstruction from the Council's ministers was led by British Prime Minister Bevin. He was in a position to ignore the support of the proposal from British Conservatives, and so prevented any dilution of national government control. He also opposed and prevented discussion of any matter deemed to fall within the remit of the OEEC, the United Nations or anyone else appropriate. Political aspirations of this new body were thus killed off right from the start, eventually leaving only a Court and Commission of Human Rights to administer the new European Convention.

From this point Churchill's enthusiasm for the European project gradually waned, as did much of the energy of the great but aging figure. He was still an important voice in support of Britain's position in the *world*, but was more involved in domestic politics. Indeed when he again won an election in October 1951 he appeared simply to ignore the first steps to formal co-operation (or integration) which had by then just begun. The electorate, with little exposure or understanding of the latest European steps, had shown no interest and had no knowledge of a new plan for Europe from Robert Schumann. Churchill, despite his vocal advocacy in opposition, becoming more concerned with global politics and in countering Soviet oppression, simply ignored the possibility of joining the European project. Thus, whatever your point of view, here passed Britain's first opportunity to participate in European integration.

Chapter 2: Britain at a Loss after the War.

Labour Government on a World Stage

For present purposes two important threads, the political and the emotional, determined the British reaction to embryonic European integration after the War. The feeling of relief at a hard won victory and an anticipated end to all the personal sacrifices of wartime living led to public euphoria which masked the harsh reality that Britain was to become.

In reality the British economy had been devastated by the War, with one quarter of national wealth having been lost. Export trade had dropped to below one third of pre-war levels and financial reserves had been seriously depleted. The famous economist, John Maynard Keynes who negotiated with great difficulty an emergency American loan of £3.75 billion, contrasted the ease with which financial problems during the war had been solved with the "financial Dunkirk" which Britain now faced. Ministers did not dare to reveal to the average Briton, Keynes' warning that a "greater degree of austerity would be necessary than we experienced at any time during the war." Neither did Ministers themselves, engaged in a historic project to build a welfare state, choose to face the implications of the true economic position.

Defeat had produced much more dynamic economies than had victory, and while industrial production in Britain rose by 30% between 1947 and 1951, the equivalent growth in Germany was close to 300%. The British economy remained second only to that of the United States, but with a Labour Government limiting incentive by promoting wealth re-distribution and high taxation, it was clear to any reasonable analyst clear that Britain's long term economic power was in relative decline. One of the very few such analysts was Sir Henry Tizard, the Chief Scientific Advisor to the Ministry of Defence. He said, "We persist in regarding ourselves as a Great Power, capable of everything and only temporarily handicapped by economic difficulties. We are not a Great Power and never will be again. We are a Great Nation, but if we continue to behave like a Great Power we shall soon cease to be a Great Nation."

British society was totally oblivious to any such heresy. It was vastly more comfortable to believe that Britain's destiny had been enhanced and her inherent strength increased by recent victory. The empire, although itself being transformed to a Commonwealth, was still a source of strength and advantage rather than a burden. There was a sincerely held belief that through their inner strength, and dogged determination it was the British that won the war. National pride prevented any questioning of the greatness of Britain, and obscured the new economic and political reality of a changed world. Politicians of all shades absorbed this prevailing mood and perpetuated its associated myths.

The Prime Minister immediately after the war was Clement Attlee but probably of more influence regarding our relations with Europe was his Foreign Secretary, Ernest Bevin founder of the Transport and General Workers Union. Interestingly he had persuaded the Trade Union Congress to vote for a United States of Europe three years before Churchill's 1930 article, and as another 1930's federalist his new Prime Minister Attlee had argued for an international body with rights and authority superior to that of individual states. "Europe must federate of perish." This policy continued after the war with these senior politicians ready to join a sovereign world government.

This vision never hampered the Labour Government's ability to deal with the realities of foreign policy and practical diplomacy. One aspect of this dream, the forging of a socialist alliance with the Soviet Union, soon fell to a harsh realisation that communism was not amenable to peaceful partnership. Political developments in the Soviet sphere of influence, culminating in the invasion of Czechoslovakia in 1948 and the outbreak of the Korean War in 1951 prevented any such co-operation, and pushed Britain back towards the western alliance.

Marshall Plan and NATO

Bevin, although starting his Foreign Office career with a wide internationalist outlook became an important figure in strengthening even further British ties with USA. In 1947 when the US Secretary of State proposed a massive programme of economic aid for European recovery Bevin worked to add specific actions to the vague intentions, thus creating what became the Marshall plan. This was a massive American programme of economic aid valued at US$13 billion, between 1948 and 1952. Eventually it was shared among sixteen nations of Europe with Britain receiving $3.2bn, France $2.7bn and Germany $1.4bn. However in the early stages of negotiations Soviet Foreign Minister Molotov walked out of discussions denouncing the proposals as "economic imperialism", and rapidly ensured that the satellite countries such as Czechoslovakia and

Poland also declined to participate. The Plan therefore resulted in strengthening the division of Europe.

Molotov's description was undoubtedly accurate. Political objectives were high on the list of American motives following President Truman's doctrine advocating worldwide containment of the spread of communism. Substantial resources were allocated to influence public opinion by promoting the benefits of the American way of life. American economic interest was another important factor. The USA was experiencing a massive but unsustainable trade surplus, while the weakness of its European customers looked likely to produce a sharp fall in international trade. The Marshall plan was thus presented as a benefit to the donors as well as recipients.

From the viewpoint of the British Government's policies it was fortunate that Bevin had taken a central role in organising the European response to the initially vague proposals. One key requirement of the Marshall Plan was that Europe would form a customs union which represented a standard, free-trader solution to the inefficiencies of separate markets. However the British regarded creation of a barrier-free single market as a threat to its Commonwealth trading arrangements. Inevitable weakening of these links would lead to disintegration of the "Sterling Area", (deposits of mainly Commonwealth countries who held their national resources or reserves as pounds in London), and might spell the end of Britain as an independent world power. In addition, although Bevin himself had supported ideas of a single market because of its potential economic benefit, the prevailing models involved creation of a supra-national co-ordinating body. This was perceived as infringing on areas of national sovereignty, and was thus completely unacceptable. Bevin's key role enabled him to ensure that European free trade, supervised by the intergovernmental Organisation for European Economic Co-operation (OEEC) was eventually in accordance with a British and minimalist model. The Belgian federalist Paul-Henri Spaak was prevented from running the organisation

Secondly, in Europe, Bevin proposed in a Churchillian speech of 1948 the formation of the Western Union including the "spirit and machinery" of international cooperation. Designed to unite "trade, social, cultural and all other contacts", and described as a "spiritual union of the West" it led to the signing of the Treaty of Brussels.

This original proposal had revived federalist supporters mostly residing in Europe, and supra-national ideals were widely discussed. Even

Prime Minister Attlee conceded that Britain was "prepared with other powers, to pool some degree of authority". This time Britain could not, "stand outside Europe and regard her problems as quite separate from those of her European neighbours." Nevertheless the government was forced to consider the political realities resulting from the various pressures within the Labour Party, and the public influence exerted by Churchill. So when it came to detailed negotiations those concerned with British interests felt threatened by formal mechanisms for economic co-operation, arguing that while committed to co-operation, Britain was opposed to *institutions* of co-operation. British policy determined that not one particle of power should be removed from national governments and so the Permanent Consultative Council which resulted was a much diluted version of the European Parliament originally proposed.

Thus Britain, then the most powerful nation in Europe, believed the balance of its interests laid elsewhere and instead of fostering and nurturing European integration used its influence to sabotage these early steps. The final Brussels Treaty, while including many of the emptied proposals, really concentrated on joint defence arrangements with France, Belgium, the Netherlands and Luxembourg. Many subsequently regarded this as the first real and then missed opportunity for Europe as a whole.

At the same time though, Bevin was acutely aware of continuing European weakness and was instrumental figure in the formation of the North Atlantic Treaty Organisation in 1949. NATO was a major Atlantic expansion of co-operation in defence formed in the Western Union and saw the return of American troops to Europe, seen as protectors of an uneasy and fragile peace. Essential as this was, it added a quite different dimension to the ideals of Western Union and again diverted Government attention away from much closer, purely European co-operation. Britain had essentially exchanged a potential leadership role in European political development for that as an Atlantic bridge.

It is arguable that against the background of a potential or emerging Soviet threat, obtaining the substantial American commitment to Europe was of greater benefit to the continent as a whole than would have been the integration of weaknesses proposed by European federalists. Nevertheless the effect was to distance Britain from Europe and to prevent any committed involvement in European integration.

These developments can be seen as necessary in the mood of foreboding which emerged at this beginning of the Cold War, when fear of nuclear weapons concentrated leaders minds on unprecedented dangers only seen at Hiroshima at the end of the war. However, Britain's position can be better understood remembering its lingering legacy of greatness. Britain's role in the world had been described by Churchill as the intersection of three circles representing the Commonwealth, the United States, and Europe. Policy, resulting from this definition was always to remain at this intersection. Towards the end of the war and shortly afterwards Britain had occupied the third seat at the table of world powers with USA and USSR, as typified by the famous meeting at Yalta between Churchill, Roosevelt and Stalin. But Britain was clearly no longer in the superpower league. Thus, as the two superpowers polarised the world, Britain was left very much a junior partner on the Western side.

Bevin's considerable achievements with the Marshall Plan and with NATO encouraged the prevailing image of Britain at the centre of these three circles, and contributed to continuing self-deception of Britain as a permanent global power. Certainly nobody at the Foreign Office understood the fundamental contradiction between the worldwide political influence they were required to maintain and the real economic situation. Britain simply could not possess the resources required to support its ambitions. The result was that no thought was ever given to prioritising any of the competing interests within the different three circles, and Britain continued to ride all horses. Britain was supporting the economic recovery of Europe, but was obstructing and preventing political co-operation which could threaten British perceived pre-eminence in Europe. The dilution of economic reforms integral to the Marshall Plan and of the political co-operation in the Treaty of Brussels were the last successes of this strategy. The Europeans had understood Britain's real motives.

Chapter 3: Europe Strikes Back

Monnet and Schumann

Britain had successfully controlled the European agenda but had certainly not silenced the voices advocating federalism, nor satisfied those quietly supporting it. The road to integration had been diverted by formation of the Western Union. Therefore a new route had to be found by the believers in integration. Two such figures were soon to orchestrate an impressive political manoeuvre, seizing a historic initiative – Jean Monnet and Robert Schumann.

Jean Monnet was a professional diplomat, born in Cognac, who had worked in Britain but extensively in America. He was an "international civil servant", never more and often less than an official, but with unrivalled contacts which he ceaselessly used to promote his vision of a politically united Europe. He was both a covert activist and a practical visionary who over the years built an impressive reputation among numerous fervent supporters as well as among horrified detractors. In 1940 after the fall of France to Nazi occupation he had persuaded both Churchill and General de Gaulle of the merits of Anglo-French Union, and he continued in this belief and more after the war when the two statesmen had moved on. The Council of Europe was a long way from Monnet's dream of a politically united Europe, and his time for orchestrating a decisive step in his preferred direction was nigh.

His partner, Robert Schumann, had become the French Foreign Minister, after a background categorised as German until he was thirty-two due to his origin in Alsace-Lorraine, on the ever fluid border between France and Germany. His parents were French, but he spoke French with a German accent and had even been conscripted into the German army during the First World War. He was not the type of man who could be a politician today. He was a quietly, modestly spoken bachelor and scholar with deep catholic convictions and expert knowledge of philosophy and theology. But, his importance in the present account was that due to origins he understood the significance of coal and steel.

The proposal formulated by Monnet involved nothing less than a complete fusion of the coal and steel industries of France and Germany (and of any other countries wishing to participate). These industries, forming the fundamental materials for industrial economies, were to be controlled by a separate organisation. Both countries had recent experience of the fundamental strategic importance of these industries determining their ability to conduct war, but now they were not only to lose control, but to surrender sovereignty over these industries to an authority transcending the individual nations. A new formal and legal community, controlled by French and German citizens but accountable only to this High Authority would be created.

Schumann's support of this plan did not stem from any integrationist ideal. France was alarmed by the rapidity of German's post-war recovery. He was aware that steel production would be cheaper in Germany, and both the British and the Americans were quite happy to allow Germany to continue increasing production levels, thus incidentally but definitely and inevitably damaging French industry. German domination of these strategic materials was definitely a development to be avoided. In addition the plan offered the very positive, historical result of a Franco-German permanent reconciliation with neither nation possessing the resources necessary for a future war. Despite earlier French reservations regarding German inclusion among nations, Schumann became the sponsor of the plan.

Monnet also had little difficulty selling his plan to the West German Chancellor, Konrad Adenauer. The Federal Republic was a newly formed nation, still divided into zones of foreign occupation, vulnerable as the front line between Moscow and Washington and needing to complete its period of national rehabilitation. Monnet's scheme represented an ideal opportunity to remove suspicions of any future threat, and would enable Germany to play a more equal role in the Western system, once again a respectable nation. Adenauer was soon a strong supporter.

Britain on the Fringe

Monnet had always predicted that Britain would oppose his plan, and knowing of Britain's proven ability to frustrate the intentions of continental politicians kept his scheme from hidden from the British, even though they were Europe's largest producer of coal and steel. An unlikely partner in this conspiracy of silence for a short time was the American Secretary of State Dean Acheson. When Schuman first explained the scheme to him Acheson was sceptical, thinking that this could indicate the beginnings of a European cartel which could threaten American manufacturers. However his opinion was quickly reversed when he considered the security and political benefits for Europe. Acheson was a supporter - but sworn to secrecy.

For a short time this was an embarrassing secret for Acheson to keep from his friends in Britain. He had indeed very friendly relations in London, and had always discussed European issues openly and with a large measure of agreement. He was at lunch with Bevin at the same time that the Cabinets in Bonn and Paris were giving their approval to the scheme. Shortly afterwards, when the French ambassador had turned up to inform Bevin about the imminent announcement, Acheson kept his appointment with Bevin to find him in a towering rage about being deliberately kept in the dark.

After Shumann had held his press conference and described his plan to transform the future of Europe, the parties concerned became apologetic to Britain who was invited to join the scheme. Over the next few days British anger subsided and led to a pragmatic Government debate, very much like many others to come, on British participation in European integration against the background of an agenda it had lost control.

One important factor was the pride of the Labour Government in recently nationalising the British coal and steel industries. Having taken these strategic industries under state control, could the Government really pass control over to an external organisation? This would conceivably allow Europeans to reduce the size of Britain's steel industry without regard to economic effects in Britain. It might well lead to greater political "co-operation" in this area. The idea represented a serious threat to both economic and thus political sovereignty, and if Britain entered it would be difficult to retrace its steps if the effects were not liked. A decision to enter appeared, for practical purposes, irreversible.

Strengths and weaknesses, opportunities and threats were considered right across Government departments. The Foreign Office considered the diplomatic progress which would result. France had always appeared reluctant to allow Germany to return to the Western fold, yet here was an ideal device to achieve exactly that. However their main conclusion was that anything more than "consultative association" would indeed prove irreversible – an inherently undesirable condition. They also proposed, with an early example of "spin", that Britain should be wary of criticising this already popular plan, and should stress the positive benefits of the Atlantic community rather than an unwillingness to become committed to Europe.

The Treasury considered that British industry would remain viable whether in or out of the Monnet-Schumann plan but warned of opposing, longer term potential threats. "Out" of the scheme, improved efficiency of continental industry would threaten British markets; "In" the scheme, the industry could face harmful re-organisation, or harmonisation of working conditions. Ironically it was Harold Macmillan who, in a Commons debate made this point most clearly. " One thing is certain and we may as well face it. Our people are not going to hand to any supranational authority, the right to close down our pits or steelworks. We will allow no supranational authority to put large masses of our people out of work in Durham, in the Midlands, in South Wales or in Scotland."

Both departments agreed that these basic industries had significant effects on the rest of industrial production and the economy. Giving up control of these would therefore limit freedom of action in an increasing number of related areas. Loss of control of essential industries implies an inevitable step towards political federation, and increasing loss of national independence. Monnet himself was reported to have admitted to senior civil servants that the objective was to set up a European federal structure. Such a suggestion was never reported in official British records. However Monnet did admit that surrender of sovereignty over a wide and strategic field was involved and was in fact a pre-requisite to participation in negotiating "details" such as how pricing, production and management decisions would be reached. With the largest such industry the price of entry was correspondingly greater for Britain, but the emphasis on prior acceptance of principles showed that the proposal was indeed primarily political.

A period of subtle diplomatic wrangling ensued with the French appearing to encourage Britain to participate in the negotiations, and with both parties trying to bridge a verbal gap insisting on the principle of accepting the High Authority as a precondition for participation. Finally though the gap remained and the decision making process which then faced the country illustrated clearly the *British Dilemma* which continues to this day.

Britain v The European Coal and Steel Community

This was also the first occasion of many to come that a European question with primarily a political purpose had been posed in the guise of an economic and industrial proposal. Since then political steps which would in themselves be unacceptable have been implemented by default, and approved only by diversion of attention to the less emotive, commercial aspects of the proposal.

This time though, the political considerations dwarfed any ideas regarding coal, steel and industry as a whole. The young, Kenneth Younger standing as a proxy Foreign Secretary at this crucial stage for an ailing Bevin had considered consequences carefully but privately. He was unable to decide whether success or failure of the scheme would be in Britain's best interests. He thought that ultimate failure of the plan would lead to French and German humiliation and would set back the hopes of European peace; but it would also lead to serious American displeasure and British culpability. With thoughts to be echoed by British politicians in years to come, he was also afraid of the effects on Britain in the event of the scheme ultimately proving successful. The policy being recommended clearly amounted to little more than procrastination, and by failing to participate from the start Britain would greatly reduce any chance of influencing the future shape and direction of the Community. Later, he concluded that Britain's discussions regarding the Schumann plan represented a serious failure in foreign policy.

France, particularly in the form of Schumann himself really did want the British to participate, even though Monnet himself probably didn't. Germany was also pressing Britain to join. The Italians were pressing Britain to stop quibbling over details. The Foreign Minister, Count Sforza famously advised that it was "the music and not the words which counted". The Dutch had also agreed to participate, achieving acceptance of a condition that they might not ultimately accept the High Authority – precisely the same position as Britain occupied outside this group. With such support for British participation as well as Europe's strongest industry it seems remarkable that Bevin did not have confidence in Britain's ability to (re-)negotiate from inside the final negotiations.

Many voices from future British politics supported the plan during the main Parliamentary debate. The young Lieutenant-Colonel Edward Heath, recently returned from Germany and impressed with the pace of their economic recovery made his maiden Parliamentary speech in support of the plan. He had admitted that his interest in the Schumann plan was "governed *entirely* by political considerations", and feared that Britain's best chance in twenty years of shaping European future was being thrown away. In the House he described the plan's supra-national aspects as an objective rather than a principle which should not be feared by Britain, and warned that, "By standing aside from any discussions we may be taking a great risk with our economy – a very great risk indeed." So, even at this early stage in his career, Heath was already employing economic arguments to support as political objective.

Julian Amery, a traditional supporter of colonial and Commonwealth interests thought that British Imperial interests, "dictate our participation in these talks". Similarly, a young Quintin Hogg thought that the Commonwealth would only survive if Britain joined Europe. He regarded supra-nationalism as envisaged by pooling resources and the High Authority was desirable despite the short-term shock to a proud people. Friendly poses and constructive attitudes were an inadequate response to the opportunities available. David Eccles who later became a Cabinet Minister thought that refusal to talk would be "utterly incomprehensible" to the millions in Europe who feared another war, and encouraged participation in a Schumann plan arranged where members acted not as national delegates but as Europeans.

Finally, the shadow Foreign Secretary, Anthony Eden said that the plan must not be allowed to fail. It was in Britain's interest and within Britain's capacity by talking, that the plan succeed. It should not be seen as an assault on sovereignty but as a fusion, merger or extension of sovereignty, and that acceptance of European federation was not an integral part of the plan. He said that Britain should indeed be prepared to enter discussion leading to formation of a body whose decisions would be binding on the government, "providing we were satisfied with the conditions and safeguards." Clearly these could only be decided during negotiations.

Despite all these pressures, warnings, and thoughtful, well-considered and coherent opinions, the Foreign Office and the Treasury finally defined the question to be decided as whether or not Britain should immediately commit itself irrevocably to a European community. The Foreign Office could not recommend such a commitment. Neither could the Treasury, largely because of its open-ended nature, and because future collaboration would still be possible if Britain remained outside. That was how the Cabinet was ultimately advised, and that is what it agreed.

The Monnet/Schumann plan was therefore implemented, setting limited and specific objectives as steps towards the long term political objective of European Union. The preamble to the Treaty spoke of Europe was to be built through practical achievements which will "create real solidarity" and establish "common bases for economic development". The community created was to constitute "the basis for a broader and deeper community among peoples long divided by bloody conflicts" and foundations were to be laid "for institutions which will give direction to a destiny henceforth shared". Thus, the Treaty establishing the European Coal and Steel Community (ECSC) was signed in Paris on April 18, 1951 by France, Germany, Italy, The Netherlands, Belgium, and Luxembourg; the Community to be headed by none other than Jean Monnet.

Chapter A: The First Community

The scope of this first Community is revealing mostly for the way in which expansive and extravagant wording of the preamble to the treaty reflecting its lofty inspiration contrasts with the actual and somewhat mundane substance to the proposal which was to integrate two strategic industries. While Britain was reading the words of the Treaty, and particular the details of the numerous articles defining the institutions and their powers, the preamble itself was a clear warning that much more was designed to follow and a clear example of the Count Sforza's "music."

PREAMBLE from the
TREATY ESTABLISHING
THE EUROPEAN COAL AND STEEL COMMUNITY

THE PRESIDENT OF THE FEDERAL REPUBLIC OF GERMANY, HIS ROYAL HIGHNESS THE PRINCE ROYAL OF BELGIUM, THE PRESIDENT OF THE FRENCH REPUBLIC, THE PRESIDENT OF THE ITALIAN REPUBLIC, HER ROYAL HIGHNESS THE GRAND DUCHESS OF LUXEMBOURG, HER MAJESTY THE QUEEN OF THE NETHERLANDS,

CONSIDERING that world peace can be safeguarded only by creative efforts commensurate with the dangers that threaten it,

CONVINCED that the contribution which an organized and vital Europe can make to civilization is indispensable to the maintenance of peaceful relations,

RECOGNIZING that Europe can be built only through practical achievements which will first of all create real solidarity, and through the establishment of common bases for economic development,

ANXIOUS to help, by expanding their basic production, to raise the standard of living and further the works of peace,

RESOLVED to substitute for age old rivalries the merging of their essential interests; to create, by establishing an economic community, the basis for a broader and deeper community among peoples long divided by bloody conflicts; and to lay the foundations for institutions which will give direction to a destiny henceforward shared,

HAVE DECIDED to create a EUROPEAN COAL AND STEEL COMMUNITY.....

Bearing in mind the fundamental objective of the founders was to prevent individual nations from using these industries to wage war on each other, there is a definite logic to the proposition that the creators of the ECSC indeed intended a permanent limitation to the sovereignty of the nations concerned. The institutions within the new structure would be completely pointless if a powerful nation was still able to exert control. Therefore the entire industries were to be completely and permanently removed from the jurisdiction of national governments. The law applicable to those industries was no longer the law of each nation, but the law as defined in the Treaty. In other words, with regards to the coal and steel industry, the law of the Treaty was to take precedence over any national law.

This was summarised in a European Court judgement relating to the ECSC, quoted by Prof J.H.H. Weiler:

> *"The Treaty rests on a derogation of sovereignty consented by the Member States to supranational jurisdiction for an object strictly determined. The legal principle at the basis of the Treaty is a principle of limited competence. The Community is a legal person of public law and to this effect it has the necessary legal capacity to exercise its functions but only those."*

This is actually a radical departure for the concepts of international law. The Court was saying that the Treaty had created a new type of legal order, which was no longer dependent on the former concepts of international law. This older, established legal order continued to respect national sovereignty. International treaties were expressions of contractual agreement between nations, accepting that their sovereignty would be exercised in a particular manner, and would be subject to adjudication which would be respected by all parties. The law of the Community was simply to take formal precedence in each Member State.

With limited application to a particular industry, and a recognition that such administrative matters would be decided jointly, the legal conclusion above was hardly noticed, and where it was, its significance was not appreciated. But, large oaks grow from small acorns, and in years to come politicians would themselves be taken by surprise at the extent of the power of this new order.

This period in the birth of European jurisprudence created other novelties which became of increasing importance after the ECSC had combined its institutions with the those of Economic Community under the Merger Treaty of 1965. In the case known as *Fedechar (Fédération Charbonnière de Belgique v High Authority of the European Coal and Steel Community.* Case Number 8-55). The case resulted from a Belgian challenge regarding the High Authority's power over pricing policy. The Court stated:

> *"The rules laid down by an international treaty or a law presuppose the other rules without which that treaty or law would have no meaning or could not reasonably and usefully be applied. It results from article 8 of the treaty that the high authority enjoys a certain independence in determining the implementing measures necessary for the attainment of the objectives referred to in the treaty."*

This argument was subsequently used as the starting point for defining the Court's ultimate responsibility. In *Fedechar* the Court decided that the High Authority, (later replaced by the Commission), should have every power necessary for achieving its objectives as defined in the Treaty, whether or not these were specifically granted by the Treaty. In due course the Court was to justify many of its own decisions on a similar basis. Necessary "Implied Powers" would be employed in order to fully achieve the objectives of the Treaty. In addition such arguments imply the primacy of those objectives themselves. This led to use of a so called "purposive construction" whereby judges would interpret legislation to comply with its original purpose almost irrespective of its actual wording. Of course this contrasts with the traditional British practice of considering only the words of a statute as the considered intention of Parliament. Moreover, a serious and unrecognised consequence also followed from this philosophy because the purposes of the Treaties themselves were defined in the preamble. Thus, while British lawyers and politicians particularly would see the expansive language of the preamble as vague and as mere rhetoric, later it was used as a reference point to justify an ever broadening scope of powers to be claimed under the Treaties.

Chapter 4: Back and Forth in Defence

A European Defence Community

Despite the expansive words and vision of Churchill in preceding years, there was no move towards Europe after his victory in the General Election of October 1951. Despite the heavy criticism of Labour's rejection of the Schumann plan, there was no move to join the ECSC. Despite Anthony Eden's warnings against British isolation from Europe, his appointment as Foreign Secretary heralded no change whatsoever in British policy. From this is becomes clear that the political leaders in both parties really continued to believe in Britain's continuing global role. They no doubt considered that Britain remained "greater" than Europe, and had no real wish to help in the building of a separate continental power. Europe was simply not important, and it was not in Britain's interest to help it become so.

Britain had of course a stronger, historical sense of national identity, leading to a belief that nationalism was the basis of government and could not be abandoned. This in turn led to the conviction to be repeated by many politicians during the evolution of European institutions, that the scheme simply would not work. Speaking at Columbia University in January 1952, Eden explained to the Americans that joining a European federation was something Britain knew in its bones that it could not do, since it violated "the unalterable marrow" of the British nation.

Maintenance of a special relationship with the United States and of an Atlantic Alliance against communism was an important objective of British policy. Successive American administrations were encouraging European integration, hoping for a particular leadership role for their closest ally, Britain, which would enhance their influence in the developing Europe. Conversely the view in the Foreign Office was that broader participation in Europe would dilute Britain's unique position of influence in Washington.

Against this background appeared a new proposal from Paris, the Pleven Plan for a European Defence Community. Ironically this idea grew from Churchill's address to the Strasbourg Assembly in August 1950, when he called for a combined army in Europe under unified command which would provide a message of peace to the whole world and provide for future protection of the "House of Europe". Under the Pleven plan military forces would serve under a European Minister of Defence, subject to "European democratic controls", and working in co-operation with USA and Canada. However, with Churchill back in power this protector quickly became labelled a "European Army", which could not conceivably be trusted to protect Britain.

The ensuing debate in Britain, again largely unnoticed, did produce for the first time, again of many to come, a public disagreement from within a Cabinet. A staunchly pro-European Minister, David Maxwell-Fyfe announced in Strasbourg that Britain would allow no genuine method (of implementation) to fail through lack of examination. He thought he was expressing British agreement in principle for formation of European defence forces. He was therefore surprised when on the same day in Rome, Anthony Eden announced that no British forces would be committed to such an army. Thus, to the annoyance of the other European members Britain brusquely excluded herself from the EDC. European nations now had a precedent of working without Britain so the plan did not only progress, but expanded to encompass the political aspects of control.

The Treaty establishing the European Defence Community was signed, subject to ratification, and seen as providing a framework for risk free German rearmament, now possible because of the industrial binding effects of the ECSC. Like the ECSC the EDC was supra-national in nature, but it was more openly federalist since it proposed only a temporary or transitional administration pending creation of a true confederate structure. The treaty itself required the EDC Assembly to prepare proposals for a directly elected assembly and definition of its powers.

Without waiting for the EDC Treaty to come into force the Consultative Assembly of the Council of Europe intervened to suggest that basic principles of the supranational authority be defined immediately. The Foreign Ministers of the ECSC Member States asked the Assembly of the ECSC to adjust its membership in accordance with EDC requirements and produce the proposals required. Under considerable influence from Monnet, this led rapidly to a draft treaty for creating a European Political Community, with aims covering human rights, common security, co-ordinated foreign policy and a common market. This organisation would comprise a bicameral legislature, a Council of National Ministers, a Court of Justice, and an Economic and Social Council, all financed by contributions from national members and Community Taxation.

The British sat aloof but despite the establishment's evident disdain for European integration, must have been perturbed or at least bewildered by the speed and scope of these developments. However it was important to remember that these far reaching political proposals has been built up on the basis of the EDC which Germany, Italy, and the Benelux countries had quickly and enthusiastically ratified. In France though opposition had appeared against the rearmament of Germany, the distancing of France from its British ally, and for exposing the French armed forces to supranational control or threat of dissolution. A remarkable alliance of Gaullists, Communists, Socialists and Radicals in the French National Assembly voted against ratification. The entire structure collapsed.

Western European Union
The Americans had from the start been strong supporters of the Pleven Plan with President Eisenhower noting that Churchill appeared to be living in the past, and resistant to new ideas. On the other hand Britain was suspicious that creation of a more powerful military force in Europe might enable the Americans to withdraw or at least reduce their military commitments in Europe – a definitely undesirable consequence. Relations across the Atlantic, a cornerstone of British policy began to feel shaky, under a shadow of blame for the failure of the proposals. Therefore, the American displeasure at British refusal to co-operate, threatening to lead Secretary of State Dulles to an "agonising re-appraisal" of US foreign policy, galvanised Eden into an inventive rearguard rescue meeting the ostensible objectives of the plan if not the political aspirations behind it.

Within weeks Eden engineered the agreement of a replacement plan for European defence, this time based on an extension of the Western European Union. From the British, but also the French perspective this had the critical constitutional advantage of being an "international" as opposed to a "supra-national" body. National governments retained the ultimate control. British troops would not be commanded by a French or German general. This allowed agreements regarding the rearmament of Germany to proceed, satisfying the main American objective. Paradoxically Eden then agreed, in parallel with American guarantees, that British troops would be committed to Europe for seventy years, in quantities that would have been more than adequate for EDC participation. British troops would indeed remain under British control but Britain accepted the condition that they could not removed from Europe without the consent of the Western European Union allies.

It is interesting to note that this unprecedented military commitment was subject to very little discussion within Britain. Commentators have used this as the first example of a recurring British strategy in proposed participation in European ventures. Suggestions not liked are attacked as being unrealistic, unworkable or ultimately as an assault on the British constitution, its traditions or simply its national interest. In contrast, proposals regarded as favourable, expeditious or simply unavoidable for practical political or economic reasons are presented as trivial, insignificant and with negligible constitutional or economic effect; a mere administrative convenience, hardly worth mentioning. Moreover it is not only British politicians who have regularly used such mis-descriptions to divert attention from otherwise controversial measures. Generations of Eurocrats to follow quickly learned the convenience of disguising anticipated, expected and even desired effects of their proposals from sceptical observers.

Chapter 5: Britain's Dose of Reality

A Legacy of Greatness

As we look back fifty years to the politicians of that time, it is instructive to look further back to see the view which those people had of their own contemporary history. From the present it is difficult to comprehend just how important the British Empire had become. At the end of Queen Victoria's reign almost one-quarter of the world's population lived in areas coloured red on the map. During her long reign Victoria had seen Britain transformed as the industrial revolution, supported by trade in raw materials from the colonies and exports of manufacturing goods worldwide. In 1880, a remarkable 23% of the world's manufacturing output was in Britain, dwarfing the 15% contribution of the United States. Similarly, while Bismarck's army was forming a German empire on the continent the British Prime Minister Disraeli showed a distinct lack of interest. "England has outgrown the continent of Europe. England is no longer a mere European power, she is the metropolis of a great maritime Empire."

However this dominance was unsustainable as the benefits of industrialisation spread from their origin in Britain to Europe and USA. Throughout the 20th century economic growth certainly continued in Britain, even after the damaging and vastly expensive victories of the two World Wars, leading to Macmillan's famous quotation that "You've never had it so good." However competing countries had by then caught up. Already by 1910 the USA per capita level of industrialisation had exceeded Britain's, but more importantly, the *rate* of growth exceeded Britain's and continued to do so. Later, in the 1950's British growth was around 2.7% per year compared to 4.6% in France and 7.8% in Germany. By 1958 the size of the German economy was to exceed that of Britain. Therefore it had been easy for a detached observer to see, for a long time, that Britain's economic power was in rapid *relative* decline. Moreover, even if economic growth had continued more impressively, power would have necessarily been diluted as other countries developed their own roles on the world stage. Just as Britain could no longer afford to continue spending 9% of its gross domestic product on defence, no longer could it maintain the defence commitments necessary to support a role as an independent world power.

Detached observers of the type to make such an observation were rare in Britain at this time, with suggestions of waning influence simply contrary to the political consensus and perceived wisdom. Public opinion was still based on a historical view of Britain, and both politicians and most high level civil servants retained the view of British destiny taught in the public schools of the era. The fact that reality had sharply diverged from this comfortable view became clear to all concerned only after the "Suez Crisis" of 1956.

The Suez Canal

Frequently described as the last gasp of independent colonialism these events coincidentally united France and Britain in a plot which was to shatter illusions on both side of the Channel, albeit with contrasting consequences. Both countries were struggling to maintain colonial interests against the background of communist agitation, and more subtle American opposition to the remnants of colonialism. The French were fighting rearguard actions in Indo-China, and engaged in a viscous war in Algeria; while Britain was trying to hold off insurgents in Cyprus, Kenya and Malaya. At the height of the cold war events in Egypt did not command a great deal of attention.

The focus of the crisis was the Suez Canal which had been built by the French in the 1860's, and which was owned and operated by the Suez Canal Company, itself owned by Britain and France. Britain maintained defence forces under an Anglo-Egyptian treaty of 1936, which Britain enforced in 1951 after Egyptian renunciation. Nevertheless the growing strength of Egyptian nationalism, leading to the expulsion of King Farouk in 1952, persuaded Britain to renegotiate and to withdraw troops by 1956. A new leader Colonel Gamal Abdel Nasser emerged from the military who had taken control of the country and in 1956 he was elected, unopposed, as President.

Instability in the Middle East was reaching a new level of intensity. The newly formed state of Israel, founded only in 1948, had fought off combined armies of Arab states and the Soviet Union was courting Arab influence by actively supporting nationalist groups. Nasser added to this a prominent pro-Arab, anti-western activism which involved support for anti-government forces for example in Algeria and especially against Israel.

American interest did not become decisive until Nasser signed an arms supply agreement with communist Czechoslovakia. The Secretary of State, John Dulles, reacted by withdrawing an American offer to provide much of the finance for Nasser's key project, the construction of the Aswan dam.

Britain, the other main partner in the funding plan had no choice but to follow suit. In retaliation Nasser shocked the world with his announcement in July, just after the last of the British troops had left. The Suez Canal Company would be nationalised with immediate effect. Problems with financing the dam would, he predicted, be solved with the canal tolls (on Western shipping).

In London, Prime Minister Anthony Eden was scandalised by this development and riding a wave of popular indignation, ordered plans for a military invasion of Egypt. In the weeks that followed, an alliance with France formed as a result of their common interest. However warning voices also appeared. The Foreign Office advised that as a sovereign power Egypt was fully entitled to nationalise property on its territory, providing suitable compensation was made. There was no legal justification for military intervention. More seriously, Roger Makins, the British Ambassador in Washington repeatedly and emphatically warned that the United States would oppose any use of force.

Ostensibly the next event was an Israeli invasion of the Sinai peninsular which began to advance towards the canal. Britain and France demanded withdrawal of both sides and as such apparent diplomatic initiatives were ignored, immediately announced a joint invasion force, to preserve the strategic value of the canal from the two combatants, and to maintain freedom of navigation. It was not admitted for many years that there was in fact secret agreement with the Israelis to start their action and thus provide the justification for the Anglo-French operation, aimed not only at wresting control of the canal, but also at the removal of Nasser in an earlier example of a "regime change" objective.

British and French airborne forces rapidly occupied Port Said, and the Egyptian air force was quickly decimated. There is little doubt that militarily the invaders were fully capable of seizing complete control of the canal zone. However, diplomatic forces then combined to force a quite different result.

In Washington President Dwight Eisenhower was appalled by the joint invasion. In his view this was likely to destabilise even further the precarious balance in a highly strategic region, and encourage Soviet support for disruptive "liberation" movements throughout the world. With the background of the nuclear arms race, he was also acutely aware that Soviet support which had been offered to Nasser indicated a serious risk that the situation could escalate into a super-power confrontation, which he was more than anxious to avoid. Finally to be considered, was the ingrained American distaste for a blatantly colonialist or imperialist venture.

Cease-fire resolutions proposed by the USA at the UN Security Council were swiftly vetoed by the UK and France which were both permanent members. Consequently the USA took the issue to the UN General Assembly where the veto did not apply, and where the scale of international criticism took both France and Britain by surprise. The Soviet Union in particular found a powerful opportunity to orchestrate attacks on western imperialism and deflect criticism of its own brutal invasion of Hungary. The UN did indeed order a cease-fire and largely as a result of efforts from the Canadian Lester Pearson also agreed the UN's first neutral "peacekeeping" force which would itself guarantee the future security of the canal. Compliance with the UN resolution was eventually achieved but not through British respect for this newly operating international order. Unprecedented public criticism from its closest ally, and threats of Soviet involvement were also not decisive.

The key figure in the Cabinet back in London was Harold Macmillan, the Chancellor of the Exchequer, who had previously used very strong language in support of Britain's military adventure. His was the most spectacular loss of nerve. Directly responsible for maintaining the sterling area he knew that in September sterling reserves had fallen by £20 million, and by a further £30 million in October. Macmillan then reported that in the first week of November after just days of battle a further £100 million had fled London vaults. Flight from sterling looked as though it would accelerate, precipitating a currency collapse. Requests for American financial assistance were curtly refused. Macmillan advised the Foreign Secretary, Selwyn Lloyd, that "in view of the financial and economic pressures, we must stop", and similarly begged the Cabinet to surrender. Britain had little choice but to accept humiliation. The invaders were ordered to halt and await the UN intervention force.

Chapter 6: Conception of the Common Market

Absent from Messina

In 1955 Anthony Eden had replaced Winston Churchill as Prime Minister, and had won a subsequent general election. Harold Macmillan became Foreign Secretary, R.A. Butler the Chancellor of the Exchequer. Collectively the Cabinet was concerned with domestic issues such as a series of damaging dock strikes or traffic congestion in Park Lane, and imperial issues such as the guerrilla warfare then raging in Kenya. As was customary, Europe attracted very little attention.

In Europe, Jean Monnet was shortly to resign from his high profile job as head of the European Coal and Steel Community, to resume his role of influence and manipulation, this time in the shadows. However two powerful figures were central to the next step in European integration. The first was the Belgian Foreign Minister, Paul-Henri Spaak, whom the British had vetoed as Chairman of the Organisation for European Economic Co-operation on account of his federalist tendencies. The second was a man whose short spark of influence of history was about to change Europe, the Dutch Foreign Minister J. W. Beyen.

Ministers of the ECSC were due for a routine meeting in Italy. At that moment the Italian Foreign Minister was pre-occupied with electioneering in Sicily. Therefore the meeting was arranged, to the aggravation of several delegates, not in Rome, but in the small and little known town of Messina. High on the agenda was a proposal crafted by the smaller nations of Belgium, the Netherlands and Luxembourg, which was so disturbing to the larger nations that they were reluctant to discuss it at all. The preamble to the document invited participants to agree that "it is necessary to work for the establishment of a united Europe by the development of common institutions, the gradual fusion of economies, the creation of a common market and the gradual harmonisation of... social policies." For discussion, remained the best methods which might be used to bring about these expansive and comprehensive aims.

The rest of the meeting was spent discussing whether several separate "Communities" covering individual economic sectors should be created; or whether a complete customs union, the approach favoured by Beyen, would be preferable. Finally, it was agreed that a whole series of studies would be set up under the direction of Spaak, with panels of experts to decide the practicality in areas such as railways, power etc.; customs union involving common internal tariffs and an external customs barrier; and possible harmonisation of social laws and monetary policy.

In contrast to the surreptitious launching of the Schumann plan, wide support for this Beyen Plan was canvassed right from its early stages. In fact Spaak had discussed the draft outlines of the plan with the British government before the Germans, French and Italians. British officials quickly decided that the proposals were woolly, and vague but knowing instinctively that they should be opposed immediately tried to estimate the likely results. They soon concluded that there was little support on the continent for further moves towards integration, the actual proposals were a mess, and that progress expected following the Messina meeting should be expected to be restricted to the verbal. In any case the French could never become sufficiently disciplined to accept trade proposals contrary to their narrow national interests. All in all, the subject was not even sufficiently significant to warrant involvement of the politicians.

The actual decisions and the communiqué from Messina were greeted, where they were noticed at all, with a lack of interest which was surprising considering the far-reaching suggestions which were now to be studied. Even Monnet, who had not by then been converted to the cause dismissively judged Messina as a "timid step towards the making of Europe" likely to end in mere co-operation between nations. Proposals had removed mention of High Authorities to avoid early rejection by those sensitive to issues of sovereignty such as Britain, but also France. Thus the French Foreign Minister, Pinay, was thinking on the lines of organisations with the power of decisions, but subject to national unanimity and so remaining intergovernmental in nature. It quickly became apparent that despite Britain's continuing unconstructive reputation all European countries wanted Britain to join. So, the question which arose was, although this time free from troublesome pre-conditions, the same one as had recently caused such intense feelings. "Shall Britain participate in these discussions?"

Agonising Britain

The first political involvement was from Chancellor of the Exchequer Butler who today would be described as an extreme Euro-sceptic. Perhaps Europe was considered to be primarily an economic matter because it was the Treasury which maintained the committee responsible for monitoring European events which might affect Britain. In addition, the new Foreign Secretary, Harold Macmillan, happened to be in San Francisco, so the Treasury was the first department to consider Britain's response. Butler's first reactions to the reports concerning Messina was that the proposals were very weak and uninteresting. Shortly afterwards he suffered a visit from Beyen, whom Butler disliked intensely, but who was nevertheless stressing persuasively the need for Britain to participate. Soon, after suitable evaluation, the considered Treasury view appeared. Messina was inspired by political motives, and included highly suspect economic plans. A common market was unacceptable to Britain, but there could be no objections or threat if Europe should decide to form one. There was an argument in favour of participating at talks, since by making clear opposition to any supranational basis Britain could guide the Six towards acceptable forms of co-operation. However participation would only be recommended through observer status and not Ministerial or high ranking official presence. The Foreign Office concurred.

Macmillan, on his return, contributed a more positive attitude. If there could be a version of Europe which Britain could join, she had to be present in order to shape it in this formative period. Greater influence would be exercised with proper participation. Both Ministers involved, Butler and Macmillan, were therefore tasked to accept Beyen's invitation. Macmillan, after softening Butler's draft by replacing "precluded" (from joining a common market) with "special difficulties" in such a proposal, sent the reply to Europe. It would clearly be seen as a very constructive response heralding a reasonable and positive approach to the forthcoming negotiations.

In order to support Britain's participation in the negotiations departments across Whitehall were conducting a series of studies parallel to those organised by Spaak. However the sectoral studies paled into insignificance when the implications of the proposed common market were considered. In fact the Treasury had previously studied the consequences to Britain of a European customs union and had concluded that the economic benefits it would bring Britain, would exceed the probable loss from abandoning Commonwealth trading preferences. Now, this study of trading prospects, commercial policy, taxation, labour and capital movements was repeated and the Treasury economists again produced the conclusion that British participation in a European common market would represent a long term benefit to the country.

Economics however, proved to be the least important criterion in determining British policy, despite the ostensible discussions asking simply whether the proposal was good for British trade and business. Again the most important aspect concerned the effects on sovereignty and the need for a supra-national body. Because of this Britain was to remain implacably opposed to the scheme.

Despite Macmillan's earlier intervention in favour of real participation the negotiations opened in Brussels chaired by the Belgian Foreign Minister Spaak, with Germany represented by its Foreign Minister, France by very senior officials, and Britain by an under-secretary from the Board of Trade, Russel Bretherton. Bretherton, although a very competent and highly regarded character with notable personal presence, was fully afforded the respect due a national representative, but was never regarded as an equal by the Europeans. More importantly he remained under the control of the President of the Board of Trade, Peter Thorneycroft, who was attempting to guide the negotiations remotely in the days before instant communications. Bretherton almost immediately reported back that the Spaak committee was showing firm determination to implement the Messina proposals, and that a customs union was in principle already agreed. Thus he would almost certainly be unable to fulfil his brief to "steer Spaak Britain's way".

Here it became clear that the position Britain has sought, to participate in talks without pre-conditions or obligations and with no commitment to any final result, was not so beneficial as had been imagined. Officials were well aware of the potential "sucking in" effect of participation. It is actually difficult to address particular points during meetings without conveying a presumption of commitment to the result. Bretherton himself quickly sought greater flexibility in his negotiating remit. Even if not initially convinced he had come to believe that Britain could obtain real benefits from the unfolding events. He believed that if he could express British acceptance for participating in a common market "in principle" he could then use his collaborative attitude and the regard he had established among the delegates to steer negotiations Britain's way. He may not have realised, initially, that this principle was in fact the real stumbling block. He was therefore instructed not to imply that we would join, even if all our points were met. Therefore Bretherton was obliged to repeat Britain's position that a new institution was unnecessary and would only duplicate the work of the existing (multi-national and inter-governmental) body, the OEEC. He certainly knew that the economic logic in support of this argument would have no effect on the negotiations which he had already reported really concerned a predominantly political project. British participation therefore continued as presence but without influence.

Back in London the considered, final view began to crystallise as it was realised that Britain would not succeed in preventing the appearance of another and wide-ranging "High Authority". As frequently seen in the politics of complex decisions the result was not presented as an objective balance of the competing forces and opinions. Outweighed arguments, not in accordance with the final position, are simply re-written with a different conclusion, in order to avoid assisting any opponents with useful facts or providing them with the opportunity to re-weight the relative importance of the various factors. The Treasury committee first involved in the Messina proposals produced the final assessment. Membership of the Common Market would weaken Britain's relationship with the Commonwealth; Britain was a world power and would suffer from the Common Market's restricted effect on free trade; membership would lead to further integration or federation which would not be acceptable to the public and; British industry could no longer be protected against European competition.

Back in Brussels Britain tiresomely repeated its position that the whole project was unnecessary, but this time adding another recurring feature of British responses – denial. Tradition states, although with disputed accuracy, that Bretherton made his famous dismissal of the European project. "Gentlemen. You are trying to negotiate something you will never be able to negotiate. But, if negotiated, it will not be ratified. And if ratified, it will not work." There was little reason for continuing participation and Bretherton did not attend subsequent meetings.

Voices of criticism for this decision, often coloured with hindsight, have since appeared to summarise the verdict of history. Collectively Britain's political classes were suffering from an acute lack of foresight. At the time Bretherton, was still warning within his department that Britain had underestimated the political will behind the ideas of Messina and was stressing the dangers of a purely negative attitude. A dissenting judgement also appeared from the Federation of British Industries who had sent Peter Tennant for talks in Europe. He returned puzzled by the government's view that the scheme was impractical and idealistic, and he found little evidence of a doctrinaire commitment of supra-nationalism in the style of Monnet. Two of his observations in particular deserve mention. Firstly he characterised the British attitude as "lurching between belligerence and indifference". Secondly, commenting on British uncertainty, he suggested that the perceived advantages and disadvantages appeared to cancel out thereby producing inactivity, which he regarded as an unacceptable response to an emerging reality. He reported the subsequent view of British industry that Commonwealth trade would inevitably decline in its relative importance, and that we should not exclude ourselves from developments in an area responsible for a 20% and rising proportion of our trade. Finally, he warned that these trends would force Britain, to face entry in ten of fifteen years time, on terms dictated by founding members.

Decisions though had already been taken, and the pretence of British participation in negotiations had ended. Without British involvement the Spaak committee produced a comprehensive report early in 1956, and in March 1957 the Six countries signed up for an "ever closer union of the peoples of Europe", with the Treaty of Rome.

Chapter B: The European *Economic* Community

Preamble

Although not meriting much attention at the time, and certainly not in Britain, it is the preamble to the Treaty of Rome which really defines the potential scope of the document, and the organisation it creates. It may be regarded as lacking in precision, but in the thoughts of its creators its glorious ambiguity provided sufficient flexibility to support future construction of a massively diverse supranational administration. This impressive introduction to the Community is followed by a description of the institutional structure which over subsequent years, was built on the strength of it.

**PREAMBLE from the
TREATY ESTABLISHING
*THE EUROPEAN ECONOMIC COMMUNITY***

HIS MAJESTY THE KING OF THE BELGIANS, THE PRESIDENT OF THE FEDERAL REPUBLIC OF GERMANY, THE PRESIDENT OF THE FRENCH REPUBLIC, THE PRESIDENT OF THE ITALIAN REPUBLIC, HER ROYAL HIGHNESS THE GRAND DUCHESS OF LUXEMBOURG, HER MAJESTY THE QUEEN OF THE NETHERLANDS,

DETERMINED to lay the foundations of an ever closer union among the peoples of Europe,

RESOLVED to ensure the economic and social progress of their countries by common action to eliminate the barriers which divide Europe,

AFFIRMING as the essential objective of their efforts the constant improvements of the living and working conditions of their peoples,

RECOGNISING that the removal of existing obstacles calls for concerted action in order to guarantee steady expansion, balanced trade and fair competition,

ANXIOUS to strengthen the unity of their economies and to ensure their harmonious development by reducing the differences existing between the various regions and the backwardness of the less-favoured regions,

DESIRING to contribute, by means of a common commercial policy, to the progressive abolition of restrictions on international trade,

INTENDING to confirm the solidarity which binds Europe and the overseas countries and desiring to ensure the development of their prosperity, in accordance with the principles of the Charter of the United Nations,

RESOLVED by thus pooling their resources to preserve and strengthen peace and liberty, and calling upon the other peoples of Europe who share their ideal to join in their efforts,

DETERMINED to promote the development of the highest possible level of knowledge for their peoples through a wide access to education and through its continuous updating,

HAVE DECIDED to create a EUROPEAN COMMUNITY ....

Functions

As with the ECSC it is difficult to read the above and to conclude that the Member States were simply aiming to build a free trade area or a Common Market. Clearly the intention behind even the original Treaty goes very much further. The actual document has grown with several amendments and additions since 1956 and now comprises over 300 Articles, 2 Annexes and 34 Protocols. It begins with a more detailed description of the actual tasks the EEC is to perform, and it should be remembered that none of this includes the European Union which is the subject of a separate treaty. The following extracts show how the objectives of the EEC have involved since its inception and show the current extent of its objectives.

The original statement of the actual objectives of the European Community defined in the Treaty of Rome is indeed recognisable as a Common Market:

> Original *ARTICLE 2*
> *The Community shall have as its task, by establishing a common market and progressively approximating the economic policies of Member States, to promote throughout the Community a harmonious development of economic activities, a continuous and balanced expansion, an increase in stability, an accelerated raising of the standard of living and closer relations between the States belonging to it.*

The current version indicates the much more ambitious aims of the EEC with further details extracted from the two subsequent articles. As a further indication of the evolution of the Community those purposes which are in common with the original definitions are printed in bolder type:

> *ARTICLE 2*
> *The Community shall have as its task, by establishing a common market and an economic and monetary union and by implementing common policies or activities referred to in Articles 3 and 4, to promote throughout the Community a harmonious, balanced and sustainable development of economic activities, a high level of employment and of social protection, equality between men and women, sustainable and non-inflationary growth, a high degree of competitiveness and convergence of economic performance, a high level of protection and improvement of the quality of the environment, the raising of the standard of living and quality of life, and economic and social cohesion and solidarity among Member States.*
>
> *ARTICLE 3*
> *1. For the purposes set out in Article 2, the activities of the Community shall include, as provided in this Treaty and in*

accordance with the timetable set out therein:

(a) **the prohibition, as between Member States, of customs duties and quantitative restrictions on the import and export of goods, and of all other measures having equivalent effect;**

(b) a common commercial policy;

(c) **an internal market characterised by the abolition, as between Member States, of obstacles to the free movement of goods, persons, services and capital;**

(d) measures concerning the entry and movement of persons as provided for in Title IV;

(e) **a common policy in the sphere of agriculture** *and fisheries;*

(f) **a common policy in the sphere of transport;**

(g) **a system ensuring that competition in the internal market is not distorted;**

(h) **the approximation of the laws of Member States to the extent required for the functioning of the common market;**

(i) *the promotion of coordination between employment policies of the Member States with a view to enhancing their effectiveness by developing a coordinated strategy for employment;*

(j) **a policy in the** *social [employment] sphere comprising a European Social Fund;*

(k) the strengthening of economic and social cohesion;

(l) a policy in the sphere of the environment;

(m) the strengthening of the competitiveness of Community industry;

(n) the promotion of research and technological development;

(o) encouragement for the. establishment and development of trans-European networks;

(p) a contribution to the attainment of a high level of health protection;

(q) a contribution to education and training of quality and to the flowering of the cultures o the Member States;

(r) a policy in the sphere of development cooperation; **the association of the overseas countries and territories in order to increase trade and promote jointly economic and social development;**
(t) a contribution to the strengthening of consumer protection;
(u) measures in the spheres of energy, civil protection and tourism.
2. In all the activities referred to in this Article, the Community shall aim to eliminate inequalities, and to promote equality, between men and women.

ARTICLE 4
1. For the purposes set out in Article 2, the activities of the Member States and the Community shall include, as provided in this Treaty and in accordance with the timetable set out therein, the adoption of an economic policy which is based on the **close coordination of Member States' economic policies***, on the internal market and on the definition of common objectives, and conducted in accordance with the principle of an open market economy with free competition.*
2. Concurrently with the foregoing, and as provided in this Treaty and in accordance with the timetable and the procedures set out therein, these activities shall include the irrevocable fixing of exchange rates leading to the introduction of a single currency, the ECU, and the definition and conduct of a single monetary policy and exchange-rate policy the primary objective of both of which shall be to maintain price stability and, without prejudice to this objective, to support the general economic policies in the Community, in accordance with the principle of an open market economy with free competition.
3. These activities of the Member States and the Community shall entail compliance with the following guiding principles: stable prices, sound public finances and monetary conditions and a sustainable balance of payments.

Chapter 7: Britain Losing its Way

France after Suez

Although Britain had yielded to American pressure, forcing France also to abandon the seizure of Suez and had thus suffered unprecedented humiliation, it was several years before the implications became fully understood in Britain. In Paris, the consequences were more immediate. Negotiations regarding the formation of the common market were nearing completion but the French remained hesitant about the whole project for the same reasons that were preventing British participation. There had been a real chance that France would not ultimately join. The Suez fiasco changed feelings by demonstrating the powerlessness of the two major European powers in the face of determined American opposition, and suggested to wavering Frenchmen that France could only regain a position of power and independence only through European unity. France therefore intensified its commitment to the negotiations and pressed hard and successfully to shape the union in the way France would most benefit. This meant that the remaining French colonial empire would be protected by inclusion and incidentally, that agricultural support for French farmers would become a key feature.

On the domestic and colonial scene France was about to suffer dangers dwarfing the effects of Suez, in that area where domestic and colonial aspects were almost inseparable – Algeria. Algerian and French communities had become interwoven not only in many areas of Algeria, but also in many areas of France. Therefore containment of forces for independence became almost impossible as the political struggle turned to violence. Most of the French army was already fighting in Algeria and terrorist attacks soon became frequent in France itself. Within the government, the political tradition which led to government by coalition led to numerous internal plots and intrigues. Ministers were actively plotting against the Prime Minister, and frequently concealed actions from cabinet colleagues. Civil servants similarly concealed information from Ministers. Critical newspapers were closed under emergency powers, as panic spread within the government and Algerian dissidents were arrested without trial and reportedly tortured.

These events led to an open police revolt, followed by government resignations and changes, and eventually even a military conspiracy codenamed "Operation Resurrection", which made real progress towards an actual military coup. Another active body of landowners, fascists, students etc in the "Committee of Vigilance" also plotted formation of a new government supporting Algérie Française. A general strike, and rioting supported by paratroopers who had been called into quell the violence, added to a real sense of impending anarchy.

In May 1958, the cult wartime figure General de Gaulle intervened. He persuaded the leaders of "Resurrection" to suspend their final blow, and gained support from the Committee of Vigilance. The French President was forced to ask de Gaulle to form an emergency government and to accept de Gaulle's conditions. Thus, just six months into the life of the EEC the constitution of the French Fourth Republic itself fell and General de Gaulle dictated a new constitution for his Fifth Republic, providing extensive powers to a President – the position de Gaulle was soon to attain.

Collapsing Circles

Back in Britain the Suez crisis immediately ended the political career of Anthony Eden, who in British tradition shouldered the blame for the British humiliation. This meant that Harold Macmillan who had actually been more responsible or even more guilty than most of his colleagues was able to emerge, without an election, as new leader of the party, effectively with a clean sheet. The new Prime Minister however, despite his pro-European leanings was not inclined to change the main decision of his predecessor regarding Europe. In fact, during the collaboration with France leading up to Suez, the feelings of common interest with France had grown much stronger. French politicians had used this opportunity to press Britain to continue with the negotiations again, and had even promised to make matters easy for Britain. Eden, having taken the decision before showed no interest in this suggestion. Nor did Macmillan afterwards. It was simply too soon to understand what had really happened.

Gradually it became impossible for Britain not to see accurately the new international landscape, but immediately after Suez the vision of Britain in the centre of the intersecting circles of Atlantic alliance, Commonwealth relations, and Europe still remained. Priority was actually given to repairing the damage caused to the "special" American relationship, despite the obvious conclusion that this could never be a relationship of equals. Britain had shown itself unable to follow a course of action against American opposition. This particular circle would appear to have faded.

The preservation of the Sterling Area, achieved by sacrifice of a right of independent action in Suez, was still not perceived in London as a remnant of faded power. Instead, it was an indication that world power remained, albeit somewhat diminished. Nevertheless harsh economic realism ensured that some adjustments to policy were made relatively quickly. Extensive defence cuts reduced commitments East of Suez, and incidentally upset France with diluted commitment to the Western European Union. Within the Commonwealth decolonisation which had stopped after Indian independence in 1948, resumed. Britain no longer showed any sign of resistance to independence for Nigeria, Tanganyika, Uganda, Cyprus etc. Colonialism was clearly at an end, even if not everybody had noticed. For Macmillan, who in 1952 had suggested that forging the Commonwealth into an economic unit as powerful as the USA and USSR was Britain's only alternative, illusions or delusions of empire had faded by 1958. This circle of destiny for Britain was fast disappearing.

Despite these fundamental weaknesses in defining Britain's future position in the world, the innate and deeply ingrained resistance to ceding sovereignty to Europe prevented Macmillan from turning decisively towards the continent. During his earlier years in politics he had always been on the European side of the debate, but he still could not bring himself to embrace a continental partnership as defined by Monnet and his heirs. He supported a European ideal, but not the one being negotiated. Before his promotion from the Treasury he had made one final attempt to steer the Europeans from their chosen path.

His plan was to form a European Free Trade Area which would include all the trading advantages Britain sought, but none of the political disadvantages it feared. There would be no internal tariff barriers to trade, but no restriction on a member's external tariffs. This would enable Britain to preserve its Commonwealth advantages. Moreover this plan would be purely industrial and would not involve agriculture at all. At this time, even before Suez, Macmillan's fear was that of a world "divided into a Russian sphere, an American sphere, and a united Europe of which we are not a member". His ambition with his EFTA plan was that it would bind the Six to the other less integrationist nations of Europe within an even larger internal market.

The British proposal was received mainly with irritation by the Six who had spent so much political energy negotiating a quite different organisation. It was never going to deflect the Six from the goal they now had in their sights. As Prime Minister Macmillan continued promoting EFTA, still fearing that a Common Market and not a free trade area would come into being. This was a result to be avoided "at all costs" since it would lead to German domination and put Britain in a very bad position indeed. So despite understanding the importance of Europe to Britain he could still not sever his thoughts from the other objectives.

De Gaulle's Common Market

The Common Market came into being on 1st January 1958, and after a few months General de Gaulle appeared, in control of France. De Gaulle had always opposed sacrificing national sovereignty to Europe and could well have prevented France from proceeding had he become President earlier. Instead, he felt forced to regard the project as too late to change. Instead and by way of compensation he initiated a ruthless policy of promoting solely French interests in any area. Meanwhile, Macmillan saw another opportunity. He felt that the appearance of De Gaulle gave him an important opportunity because of their common wartime background and in particular because of Macmillan's personal intervention in support for De Gaulle at earlier critical periods. De Gaulle though had moved on. At their disastrous meeting Macmillan essentially begged de Gaulle to give up the Common Market system, almost to the embarrassment of the unbending President. Macmillan had introduced an argument to be heard many times in later years that a European union with too restrictive binding forces contained the seeds of internal war, contrasting with the project's ultimate aim of permanent European peace. In contrast, De Gaulle, secure with his own vision of French interests, could see no such threat.

De Gaulle soon decided simply to stop any further discussions aimed at adding any EFTA dimension to the new Common Market. Britain's initiative was rejected. Europe needed to concentrate on its agreed agenda. Instead EFTA came into being entirely separately with Britain, Norway, Sweden, Denmark, Austria, Switzerland and Portugal. Now Macmillan, no less than the rest of Britain, had to face the future which he summarised memorably. "For the first time since the Napoleonic era the major continental powers are united in a positive economic grouping, with considerable political aspects, which though not specifically directed against the United Kingdom, may have the effect of excluding us both from European markets and from consultation in European policy". The third circle had moved on, and without Britain.

Chapter C: European Institutions

Overview

While Britain was still in agonising indecision the founders of the Common Market moved forward with their grand European project. Here we digress from this historical account of the depressing debate and describe how the Six were intending to achieve the objectives their treaty had defined. In this section are described the institutions which the Treaty of Rome founded for this purpose, and the ways in which the organisation has developed since then until the present time.

First though, and stepping back from the detail, it is important to notice that from its inception the organisation was to be endowed with government-like authority within its limited areas of competence. However, although including those aspects of power typical of an independent state, these different branches were not separated in the same way as the legislative and executive branches of a constitutional government would be. There is an independent the judicial function, but executive powers are distributed between the Commission and the Member States' Governments, while legislative power is distributed between the Council (of national ministers), the Commission, and the European Parliament. A dauntingly complex system of binding procedures and checks and balances aimed at preventing centralisation of power has evolved. Clearly the organisation is very much more than a group of national representatives meeting to co-operate on matters of common interest. Therefore it cannot be described as an "intergovernmental" organisation. It is certainly a unique and "supranational" organisation which quickly developed a life of its own and in many cases transformed itself, almost un-noticed, from the servant of its original creators to their master.

At the centre of the decision making process is the "institutional triangle" of Commission, Council and Parliament (originally described as the *Assembly*) which broadly represent the interests of the Community itself, the Member States, and the people, respectively. The fourth institution created in the original treaty was the Court of Justice. Subsequently several other subsidiary bodies have been created. The most important of all these bodies is described below.

1. The European Parliament

Since 1979 the European Parliament has been directly elected by the citizens of Europe for a period of five years. It usually sits in Strasbourg with occasional sittings in Luxembourg where its Secretariat is based. All national political parties are represented, and within the Parliament are grouped according to their broad political affiliations rather than their nationality.

Over the period of its history its powers have gradually increased. In many areas of Community competence it now enjoys real legislative powers whenever the treaty requires legislation to be concluded according to the co-decision procedure. Other procedures such as co-operation, consultation or merely assent provide lesser roles for scrutiny of legislation, but even in these cases Parliamentary involvement is compulsory or else the resulting legislation may be judged invalid by the European Court.

Parliament also shares authority for the Community Budget with the Council after it is drawn up by the Commission and exercises a democratic supervision of the Commission and other institutions. Appointment of Commissioners must be approved by Parliament which subsequently has the right of censure of the whole Commission only.

2. The Council of the European Union.

Originally known as the Council of Ministers this is the main decision making body of the EEC and later the EU. It comprises Ministers of the Member States, authorised to bind that government in the relevant field. Its composition depends on the subject matter of the time eg. for an agricultural agenda, it is the Agricultural Ministers who meet. It shares legislative authority with Parliament, with assistance from the Commission. Decisions within the Council originally required unanimity, with each Member State effectively gaining a veto against any decision deemed to affect one of its "vital" interests. However more and more areas of policy came to require a "qualified majority" of votes. Each Member had an agreed number of votes, broadly proportional to its size Eg. at present Germany, France and UK having 10 votes, Finland, Denmark and Ireland 3 votes. An act would be adopted if 62 votes were cast in favour.

The *European Council* is actually a separate body comprising the Heads of each Government which now meets normally twice a year, under a rotating Presidency of the Council. This provides the strategic direction for development of the entire European Union, including the EEC. In recent years it is this body which has grown in importance as the ultimate means of obtaining the political consensus necessary for advancing with particular proposals, and at the highest level necessary in order to resolve frequent deadlock at ministerial level. It possesses a particularly important role in those areas outside the competence of the EEC and actually within EU competence eg. foreign and defence policy.

There is an interesting inherent contradiction in the meetings of the Councils. On one hand ministers are expected to work in a spirit of European co-operation. Ministers from the most loyal supporters of European ideals eg. Netherlands, have little difficulty in doing exactly that. However the Ministers are also present, representing their nation and therefore expected to protect and advance their own national interests. Indeed they are usually responsible to their own national parliaments for doing exactly this. Therefore many ministers, and not only French ones, openly promote national interests over a competing Community interest. When the possibility of majority voting is considered this really implies that the Council functions in the same way as a superior and very select parliamentary body.

3. The European Commission

The European Commission today comprises approximately 18,000 staff, headed by twenty Commissioners nominated by the Member States. Each Commissioner is appointed for five years, subject to Parliamentary approval. Despite their national origins each swears an oath to act only in the interests of the Community, and not to accept influence of instruction from a national government. This is an important duty which has not always been regarded seriously by both Commissioners and "their" national governments who naturally will decide on re-appointment. Each Commissioner is assigned a specific responsibility relating to a particular area of policy by the President and his two Vice-Presidents. They are assisted by directors-general of twenty five Directorates-General in that number of different policy areas, each responsible to the relevant Commissioner. An individual Commissioner may be dismissed by the European Court after essentially a conviction for misconduct, and the European Parliament has the right to dismiss the Commission but only in its entirety.

The role of Commission President is of considerable importance. He chairs the full meetings of the Commission, represents the Commission at Council meetings, and often represents Europe as a whole at international summit meetings. The personality of the President has thus become important with the most forceful characters having provided a powerful driving force for determining the entire direction of Community development. Thus at various times in its history the Commission has been regarded as an embryonic European government, as a background motivator for European integration, or in its darker days, as a mere civil service staffed by poorly regarded "Brussels Bureaucrats."

The most important role of the Commission is that of "Guardian of the Treaties" defined in the treaties as ensuring the proper functioning and development of the common market. Its duty according to the Treaty is to:

> *- ensure that the provisions of this Treaty and the measures taken by the institutions pursuant thereto are applied;*
> *- formulate recommendations or deliver opinions on matters dealt with in this Treaty, if it expressly so provides, or if the Commission considers it necessary;*
> *- have its own power of decision and participate in the shaping of measures taken by the Council and by the European Parliament in the manner provided for in this Treaty;*
> *- exercise the powers conferred on it by the Council for the implementation of the rules laid down by the latter."*

It therefore initiates and drafts all legislative proposals, has executive responsibility for implementing Community policies, and represents the Community in international negotiations within Community competence. In order to ensure proper operation of the Treaty it monitors, investigates and challenges Member States who are not correctly meeting their obligations under Community law in an almost judicial role and will refer such cases to the European Court as "prosecutor" to ensure enforcement.

4. The European Court of Justice (ECJ)

The fourth institution defined in the original Treaty of Rome is the Court whose duty is to "ensure that in the interpretation and application of this Treaty, the law is upheld." This is a curious phrase, central to the role of the Court, which has been the subject of much academic debate. It appears to say that the treaty must not break the law, but fails to specify exactly which "law" is being referred to. Instead the phrase is taken by the Court as meaning that the treaty itself is "the law", and that the Court has the final word in its interpretation. Judges from the English school of literal interpretation may regard this as an unduly stretched interpretation of the words. They argue that quite different wording would have been used, and would actually have been necessary if this had been the actual intention. Even so, the Court has decided and this is the now accepted meaning of the phrase.

The ECJ comprises fifteen judges, currently one from each Member State, who are appointed for a six year term, which is staggered to avoid replacement of all judges at the same time. Their independence must be "beyond doubt" and they must possess "the qualifications required for appointment to the highest judicial offices in their respective countries or who are 'juriconsults' of recognised competence." Thus some states have appointed academics instead of practicing judges. The judges are supported by eight Advocates General who are essentially legal advisors to the Court. Their analysis and "opinion" presented to the Court is highly "persuasive" and usually followed.

It is important to note a number aspects of ECJ decisions. Firstly, judgements presented in Court are closely reasoned, but there is no formal obligation to accept the "precedent" from their previous rulings. It will be seen later that this has provided an important means for gradually developing the law in response to changing circumstances. This is a process similar to that of the English common law, but whereas in England judges would struggle to "distinguish" the present case from its predecessors, European judges may simply disregard a previous ruling, even failing to explain any change in law which their decision implies. In contrast, the House of Lords making such a departure is obliged under its Practice Statement of 1966 to explain fully the reasons for any such departure from its own precedents. Despite this the European Court has always regarded consistency in the law as an important objective, and particularly across national boundaries. The requirement for "uniform interpretation" of European law has actually been extended and used to justify the ECJ's close and definitive control over interpretation of its provisions.

It is also apparent that the ECJ's process of interpretation itself is entirely contrary to British tradition. Instead of giving primacy to the actual words of a statute European judges seek to divine the intention behind these words. On occasions this has even extended to changing the "natural meaning" of the wording. Meanings applicable from this "purposive" construction may be derived both from descriptions within the legislation, and from the judges' experience regarding the intentions of the entire Treaty itself, including those described in the Preambles. Finally, one other characteristic is that there is always an odd number of judges sitting and judgements of the court are determined by majority voting. But, there is no provision for any dissent on the bench, and the British tradition of publishing a minority conclusion or of explaining alterative reasoning is unknown.

Since 1989, the ECJ has been assisted by the Court of First Instance. This court, introduced to reduce much of the workload on the ECJ has its own jurisdiction applicable to actions brought by individuals or companies rather than institutions, although its judgements may be subject to ECJ appeal on points of law.

5. Consultative Institutions

In their legislative or policy making capacity the Council and the Commission are advised by two bodies each entitled to consultation. The aim is to provide a greater voice within the European Union structure to various the sections or organisations of the people across the continent. It is an attempt to introduce a wider level of democracy within the Union, but unfortunately few people are aware of the bodies concerned, and their real influence seems limited.

a) The Economic and Social Committee.

Founded by the original Treaty of Rome, ECOSOC is a consultative body now of 222 members across the Community representing broad sections of society including trade unions, employers, farmers, craftsmen, consumer groups etc. Committee members are nominated for appointment by the Member States, in numbers broadly proportional to the nations' sizes. Thus 24 members are from the four largest countries, 12 from the next six, 9 from Denmark, Finland and Ireland, and 6 from Luxembourg. They work in their own countries establishing links with the organisations they represent, and travel to Brussels for their meetings. These are organised into three main groups – Employers, Workers and Various. In addition the Committee is divided into six sections eg. Agriculture; Employment & Social Affairs, etc. It elects a president and two vice-presidents for two year offices, and each section has president and a bureau. Members may meet in ad hoc sub-committees and convene study groups, assisted by experts in order to prepare their opinions.

The Committee prepares opinions on matters referred to it by the Commission, the Council or the European Parliament. Occasionally they are requested to produce exploratory opinions which are broader and more reflective variants needed when the institutions is planning action in a new policy area. Otherwise the opinion will refer to specific measures en route to becoming legislation. In addition the Committee may provide opinions on its own initiative on any issue it considers of interest.

The system does provide an opportunity for those groups to be affected by proposed legislation to assess its effects in advance and gives them an opportunity to suggest amendments. The majority of EC legislation can only be passed validly after such an impact study by ECOSOC has been received, and this ensures wide consultation on the majority of legislative proposals. There is however no legal obligation on the legislative bodies to follow its advice.

b) The Committee of Regions

This committee dating from the Maastricht Treaty, also comprising 222 members nominated by Member States and is designed to represent all regional or local interests across the Community. These may be representatives of local or regional governments or of major cities. Members are allocated to one of six Commissions covering areas such as Territorial Cohesion Policy; Sustainable Development; European Governance. A Bureau comprising a president and 35 members and leaders of political groupings within the Committee organises the activities, with administrative support provided by a secretariat-general.

The aim is that regional points of view may be expressed as an integral part of the legislative process. Therefore, on topics of direct relevance to regional and local authorities the Commission and Council is obliged to consult the Committee. However it frequently consults on other matters and the Committee is authorised to act on its own initiative. It is closely involved in topics involving regional policy and structural funds; transport; public health; education, youth and culture; environment.

The committee has also gained a theoretical responsibility to safeguard the principle of "subsidiarity" under which decisions should only be taken at the level most appropriate. Thus the Community is in principle prevented from interfering in those matters which are more appropriately dealt with at a national or a local/regional level, and the Committee of the Regions is a voice which consistently says so. However, as a counterbalance to the Community's overall centralising tendencies the Committee is decidedly underweight. It poses little threat to the central establishment. Moreover national governments frequently interpret attempts by a local government to influence policy directly within Europe as by-passing and thus undermining their own authority. Indeed regional governments have been known to relish attempts to circumvent policies of national governments of differing political persuasion by appealing to Europe, unaware of the risk of jumping from the frying pan into the fire.

6. Organisational Scrutiny

There is a very real sense in which the institutions of the EU scrutinise each other to ensure consistency of policy, and conformance with the law. The European Parliament in particular has a critical role in scrutinising the activities of the Commission even though its ultimate powers are somewhat limited. Similarly the ECJ has ultimate responsibility couple with ultimate power to ensure that institutions comply with European law. However there are two separate organisations designed to identify shortcomings within the institutions.

a) The European Ombudsman

Many European countries have an ombudsman employed as a central point for individuals to make complaints regarding the way they have been treated by any government department. The European Ombudsman is elected by the European Parliament, and reports to Parliament in a similar capacity. Operating from Strasbourg, he is entitled to investigate any complaint relating to "maladministration" within Community institutions who are obliged to co-operate. However, his role in Europe is less powerful than in some Scandinavian countries since his main influence is limited to persuading and cajoling institutions to correct any errors or failings, or to reconsider their decisions. As a last resort he will publish a critical report, leaving it to Parliament and the institutions themselves what action, if any, will be taken.

Most complaints have involved a lack of transparency in decisions made by the Commission and the Ombudsman frequently refers to the obligation under the Treaty that decisions should be taken "as openly as possible." He also intervenes on cases of access to information, cases of discrimination, and infringements of basic rights, and introduced a code of conduct for good administrative practice

b) The Court of Auditors

The Court of Auditors was established in 1977 as an overseer of the budgetary arrangements then being made. However, it was not until the Maastricht Treaty that it became an independent institution in its own right. It operates from Luxembourg and comprises 16 members who must be qualified and experienced auditors within the Member States. The Members elect a President for a term of three years.

The main role of the Court is to monitor the legality and regularity of all Community income and expenditure, ensuring sound financial management and transparency. It employs around 550 staff divided into various groups. Most of the Court's work is concentrated on the European Commission even though around 90% of Community expenditure is managed by national authorities. Over many years the Court produced many reports highlighting discrepancies and failings in financial management sometimes amounting to fraud. Gradually the Commission has been addressing such concerns, most recently under the control of the British Commissioner Neil Kinnock and his Anti-Fraud office.

7. Financial Institutions
a) The European Central Bank

The formation of a central bank and a common currency was nothing more than a distant dream to the original signatories of the Treaty of Rome. So much was this so that for many years British politicians remained content to ignore it as a fantasy. Meanwhile much of the rest of Europe progressed towards this objective often falteringly and over many years until Euro notes and coins appeared in 2001.

It is important to note that for many years monetary policy across the European Union was *co-ordinated* by all the national central banks working within the European System of Central Banks (ESCB). The twelve members of the Union joining the Euro system formed a separate organisation, headed by the governors of the participating central banks, to manage the new currency, and the European Central Bank (ECB) itself. The highest decision making body in the ECB is the Governing Council. This comprises the national governors assisted by members of the Executive Board, comprising the President, Vice-President and four other members all appointed by accord of the Heads of Government of the participating Members. There is also a General Council which includes the governors of the non-participating members, contributing to the Banks co-ordination role.

Later sections will describe the measures taken to ensure the political independence of the ECB, and to protect from influence exerted by any politician, national government, or community institution. Even the European Council has no right to interfere the in implementation of monetary policy. The main objective is the maintenance of price stability which the ECB interprets as controlling consumer price inflation to less than 2%. Thus the role involves controlling the Euro money supply essentially according to monetarist principles. In addition it is responsible for the setting of interest rates, as well as preserving the value of the Euro, physically holding the official reserves of each Member State, and issuing the banknotes.

b) The European Investment Bank

The European Investment Bank was founded by the Treaty of Rome to aid achievement of the Union's objectives by funding projects that, "promote European integration, balanced development, economic and social cohesion, and development of an innovative, knowledge-based economy." It operates as an investment bank owned by Member States as shareholders, and managed by a Board of Governors, a Board of Directors and a Management Committee. It is financed solely by raising capital on the financial markets, and is operated on a non-profit basis. It finances projects directly, and for smaller projects through around 180 banks across Europe acting as intermediaries.

Under its statutes the EIB operates autonomously within the Union, making decisions based solely on the merits of the proposals, providing they meet specified criteria relating to the area of economic activity, while giving preference to the most disadvantaged regions. Special mechanisms were put in place to allow funding for the present applicant countries, and projects have been funded to support sustainable development in developing countries. Finally the EIB is the majority shareholder, (with the Commission and other financial institutions), in the European Investment Fund, founded in 1994. This is a venture capital and financing guarantee facility to support Small and Medium-sized Enterprises, and development of early-stage technology oriented companies.

Chapter 8: About Turn! Halt!

A Road To Isolation

Returning to the British dilemma of the 1960's reveals a sense of unrealism, and contrasts starkly with the optimism of European building process described above. The people of Britain showed no signs of concern or even realisation that circumstances alone, or the short-sightedness of their political leaders had destroyed the basis of their country's future standing in the world. Commentators of the time had failed to produce any such interpretation of current events, and without such media information, nobody was able to step back and obtain a clear view of Britain's true place in the world. In fact, and as usual, few were interested in doing so. People continued their daily lives with cautious optimism despite national economic problems which were seen as the government's problem. As the "swinging sixties" began people lived with an overall contentment although mixed with an often uneasy feeling that the world and its traditional values was changing. Responsibility for greater thoughts had been passed to leaders without any comprehension that these were, in the words of the Victorian poet Matthew Arnold, "Wandering between two worlds, One dead, The other powerless to be born."

Macmillan's discomfort at losing the battle to prevent formation of the Common Market and his realisation that it became impractical to disrupt the plans of the Six, crystallised as a new fear of British isolation. Nervous voices began to appear, questioning the established policy in the light of its unforeseen but now predicted consequences. This gradual change in perception began at an official rather than a politician level. A report despatched to London from the embassy in Bonn summarised the fear which was soon to prevail. Unless a workable understanding between EFTA with a population of 90 million, and the EEC with a population of 170 million, could be reached, (despite de Gaulle's closure of this avenue), Britain faced disaster. With the EEC economy growing rapidly our position would change from the biggest market and second largest exporter of manufactured goods to Europe, to a member of a second eleven scattered around an increasingly powerful United States of Europe. The consequences of UK exclusion are much more serious to the UK than to Europe, and we must stop believing or even hoping that the Six would ever allow access to their markets, while permitting our agriculture and Commonwealth trade to be excluded.

Economy v Sovereignty

Papers also began to appear from the Treasury. "It cannot be compatible with either our political or our economic interests….. to drift on indefinitely on the basis of a divided Europe, with the United Kingdom linked to the weaker group." An Atlantic Free Trade Area was impractical, and the Commonwealth was not a realistic alternative since it dependent primarily on the strength of Britain. Despite such forthright criticism of current strategy politicians were not ready to receive a proposal for actual membership. Recommendations were sought with less emotive wording. "Association" was not strong enough to convey how far Britain's attitude needed to change. Consequently, EFTA should now strive for "Near-identification" with EEC policy.

Despairingly, Macmillan received this proposal. Realising the weakness of his position his attention again shifted to what would have to be given up:- Control of tariffs; Commonwealth preferences and thus relations; independent agricultural support; sovereignty. The thoughts appeared that "near identification" was hardly different from full membership and that perhaps it was time to end "our traditional policy of remaining aloof from Europe". Macmillan had recently been in South Africa, referring to the "winds of change blowing through imperial Africa". He was realising that the same winds had reached Britain, bringing increasingly gloomy clouds over Downing Street. Talks with Khruschev to produce international détente which Britain had heavily promoted, had collapsed in disarray, adding to the sense that Britain's world of certainties had crumbled. Macmillan's diary of July 1960 summarised a new, depressing view of Britain "caught between a hostile America, and a powerful, boastful empire of Charlemagne – presently under French but inevitably in future under German control".

A more detailed analysis of the practical effects of membership began, led by Treasury officials. Specific advantages were identified and positive interpretations of obstacles began to appear. Membership of a successful EEC might "change our concept of vital UK interests". Participation in majority voting in the Council of Ministers could be seen as a "guarantee rather than a destroyer of British influence".

Numerous papers were produced covering different aspects of British trade, and probable effects particularly relating to Commonwealth partners. New Zealand butter, Rhodesian tobacco, Caribbean sugar, wood pulp, aluminium etc. were all considered in fine detail. The economic case for entry became clearer, and the case for "association" with the EEC, including concessions in some areas of Commonwealth trade gradually emerged as the government objective.

The issue of sovereignty which had previously blocked all such thinking did not disappear. The Lord Chancellor reported the legal opinion to the minister now responsible for relations with Europe, Edward Heath. Signing the Treaty of Rome, and passing the necessary legislation would amount to a loss of sovereignty in three respects. First, Parliament would surrender some of its functions to a Council of Ministers which could by majority vote make regulations which could become the law of the land despite Parliamentary opposition. Second, the Crown's treaty making power would in part be transferred to an international organisation, bypassing Britain's traditional safeguard of requiring parliamentary approval. Third, British courts would sacrifice some of their independence by becoming subordinate in some respects to the European Court of Justice.

The issue of sovereignty was therefore well known and realised at the time, although to sensitive to be discussed in public. Later, detailed debate concerning the real meaning of sovereignty was to become common. For example, was it meaningful to remain "sovereign" despite having no influence on markets on which the country depended? At this time however it simply appeared that other influences seemed more significant. In France for example, General de Gaulle was maintaining his fiercely nationalist response to EEC activities and was effectively paralysing the political aspirations sought by the Five. At home, British farmers had organised a powerful and vocal lobby aimed at preserving their interests, and in the Commonwealth powerful voices from Canada and Australia were ensuring that Britain remained aware of its wider obligations. Thus in May 1961 Macmillan reported to the House of Commons that there would be no question of entering the EEC without giving the farmers and the Commonwealth what they wanted. Loss of sovereignty and undermining of the constitution were less urgent objections than food and empire. These could be overlooked rather than faced, as arguments concentrated on more practical safeguards to trade. The prize of a large and expanded market for British goods could be compared to the risk of industrial decline outside. The political cost would be better ignored, as a distraction from the economic argument. The knowledge that the EEC was primarily a political venture was a fact which the government, and Macmillan in particular would prefer not even to think about, let alone pronounce upon.

Negotiate or Not?

Some support for the British predicament had been heard from European capitals. Chancellor Adenauer of Germany had suggested a purely economic association as a first step, and both Italy and the Benelux countries supported concessions in order to encourage ultimate British membership. However in Paris the view was made perfectly clear. The Commonwealth and the EEC represented two *alternative* economic systems which could not be combined. Britain could not expect any special treatment for Commonwealth preferences, nor could she expect to sustain the cheap food prices that resulted from them. Britain would certainly not be allowed to change the Treaty of Rome.

Despite this clear message from France, and despite the established, uncompromising policy which De Gaulle routinely employed in European matters, Macmillan took a new but tentative step towards Europe. Negotiations would begin, but not on an application to join; simply on whether satisfactory terms could be negotiated to justify such an application. In announcing this decision to the Commons Macmillan was reserved and hesitant, striving to strike a "delicate balance". Considering the forthcoming discussions he could not suggest that joining was so beneficial and advantageous that Britain could accept any terms. Nor could he convey to the Six that it was almost inconsequential whether Britain joined or not.

It was not until a year later that Macmillan started any serious attempt to prepare public opinion for possible entry to the EEC. A leaflet was produced explaining that the government was taking "the most fateful and forward-looking policy decision in peacetime history". "Economic opportunities would greatly outweigh the risks"; A Britain detached from Europe would mean inflicting permanent injury on our common cause." "In the past as a great maritime power, we might give way to insular feelings of superiority over foreign breeds", but now "we have to consider the state of the world as it is today and will be tomorrow, and not in terms of a vanished past."

Nowhere could be read Lord Home's earlier comments to the House of Lords as Foreign Secretary that the "Treaty of Rome would involve considerable derogation of sovereignty", not confined to economic areas, and that consequences would be "different in kind from any contract into which we have entered before". Instead was introduced the new concept of "pooling sovereignty". "In renouncing some of our own sovereignty we would receive in return a share of the sovereignty renounced by other members." The obligations would not alter the position of the Crown, "nor rob Parliament of its essential powers, nor deprive our Law Courts of their authority in our domestic life". The case for "internal influence" also appeared, as mitigation for accepting the EEC's ultimately political goals. "As a member, Britain would have a strong voice in deciding the nature and the timing of political unity".

Thus we see for the first time two recurring themes of Britain's relations with Europe. Firstly, the failure to commit Britain to commit herself to the project at an early stage led to a serious negotiating penalty following the eventual decision. Secondly the domestic political situation, encouraged the contradictory position used by most British leaders following Macmillan that the issue was of fundamental importance to British interests, but would nevertheless have minimal effects on British independence and self-determination etc. Two variations to the traditional description of politics as "the art of the possible" seem to fit the British attitude. John Kenneth Galbraith suggested that "Politics is not the art of the possible. It consists in choosing between the disastrous and the unpalatable." Then in an early advocacy of spin, Otto von Bismarck said, "Politics may be the art of the possible, - but it may also be the art of ignoring, overlooking or diverting attention from discordant facts."

So in Macmillan's mind the objective was the preservation of some vestige of Britain's power and avoiding becoming isolated, but the price of loss of sovereignty was not to be mentioned, and the means were to be presented as an economic end in themselves and described as little more than an elaborate, and not terribly interesting commercial transaction.

The details of these mere commercial matters were negotiated in excruciating detail by a British team under the leadership of Edward Heath. Discussions were frequently difficult because lobbies representing every product were able to promote their own interests which the British then had to discuss separately with the Six. Moreover there was always an understandable reluctance from the Six to dismantle deals which they had previously negotiated amongst themselves also frequently with great difficulty. Nevertheless excellent progress was made between autumn 1961 and January 1963. By this time all sides believed they were very close to a complete deal. Nobody had considered the earlier warnings from France.

It was clear that General de Gaulle's France had come to dominate EEC proceedings, and had successfully blocked the discussions with the other five regarding progress towards political integration. Moreover most of the agreements subsequent to the Treaty of Rome, for example regarding the common agricultural policy had been achieved only by meeting all French objections. In hindsight it was clear that France would not have welcomed any shift of power within the community. Actually, de Gaulle was in principle opposed to the Common Market ideal itself, and to him, its only acceptable future laid under French domination. Moreover de Gaulle's personal doubts regarding Britain's willingness to commit itself to a European future had not changed. These reservations concerning Britain's historical baggage were even heightened when Macmillan negotiated the Polaris missile supply contract with President Kennedy in Bermuda. Even personal discussions between the two men revealed stark differences. Shortly after the Cuban crisis Macmillan met de Gaulle who argued forcibly that Britain would need to reduce its dependence on its Atlantic alliance if it wanted to be taken seriously as an EEC applicant.

French domestic politics also played a role. Late in 1962 de Gaulle had struggled to win important changes to the constitution in a very closely fought referendum. Then the Gaullist party won a majority in the National Assembly, and de Gaulle's power became effectively absolute. So, on 14th January, 1963 President de Gaulle made his announcement, not on the excruciating details still being tediously discussed but on the very principle of British membership. His statement to his famous press conference summarises the position he would enforce and the EEC would take.

"Non".

Chapter D: The Law Of Europe

Legal Digression

At this point in the narrative Britain's drift towards Europe is brutally halted, and De Gaulle's virtual but largely benevolent dictatorship of France has yet to gain its full strength. Just as De Gaulle is poised to disrupt the embryonic law of Europe, we examine how this was intended to operate under the terms of the Treaty of Rome. As described above the institutions of the triangle interact according to several different procedures to create the law and the details of these various processes are of a complexity beyond even summarising in the present work. Instead it is important to note some unique features of the new supra-national legal system which quickly developed a life of its own, soon leaving behind De Gaulle's disruption as a mere aberration in Community development.

Primary Legislation

The British constitution, like most others, makes a clear distinction between *primary* legislation which is an Act of Parliament and *secondary* legislation which comprises orders or regulations made separately but under the authority of the Act. Both have legal force and will be upheld by the courts, but primary legislation having been properly debated and directly approved by Parliament is granted a higher level of respect. Traditionally this meant in Britain that a court could not challenge any primary legislation, but could challenge any secondary legislation found not to be in accordance with the Act itself. The legal scheme created by the Treaty of Rome has the same distinction. In this case all the foundations of Community Law were defined in the treaty itself. This included procedures to be used for amending the treaty. Therefore amendments, or supplements in the form of a new treaty, have been made enacted having been negotiated in an intergovernmental conference (IGC), formally and unanimously agreed, and then ratified by all the Member States in accordance with their own constitutional requirements. Thus the primary legislation of the European Union today is defined in the texts of the Treaty of Rome (now known after its amendments as the EC Treaty or TEC); the Maastricht Treaty (properly known as the Treaty on European Union or TEU); with amendments incorporated from the Treaty of Amsterdam of 1997, and the Treaty of Nice in 2000. The currently progressing IGC is likely to propose a complete revision of these documents.

Secondary Legislation

Under Article 249 of the TEC the European Institutions may use secondary legislative powers to carry out their tasks. In doing so it is essential that the legislation includes a statement describing the source of authority under which it is enacted. Thus a specific Treaty Article, referring to the subject matter of the proposed measure will be used to provide the necessary "legal base." Failure to do so correctly will result in annulment of the measure should it subsequently be challenged in the ECJ. There are two main types of such legislation:

a) Regulations

According to the Treaty, "A regulation shall have general application. It shall be binding in its entirety and directly applicable in all Member States." Thus legislation correctly passed, should take effect in each Member State without further action and will achieve uniformity of the law throughout the EC.

b) Directives

Again the Treaty states, "A directive shall be binding as to the result to be achieved, upon each Member State to which it is addressed, but shall leave to the national authorities the choice of form and methods." Thus although Member States are free to devise their own way of implementing the directives in national legislation they are obliged to ensure the achievement of the directive's objectives usually by a specific date. This form of legislation allows a certain flexibility and is most often chosen where the objective is one of harmonisation.

Enforcement

One aspect of the enforcement of Treaty provisions is their correct observance by all the Community institutions. The authority of the European Court of Justice to annul incorrectly characterised secondary legislation was mentioned above. This authority extends to a right to challenge and annul any Community measure which has a legal effect, whether on grounds of a lack of competence, a procedural infringement, or a breach of one of the general principles of Community law. It also extends to a general judicial review of either actions, or failures to act, by various institutions. Thus the ECJ has an important role in ensuring all Community institutions respect the Treaty.

More generally, it is obvious that rules and regulations can rapidly become pointless if they cannot be effective enforced, and the Treaty of

Rome included novel solutions to this aspect of law. Firstly there was a general obligation on Member States to co-operate, as they were already agreeing to do by signing the Treaty. This was expressed in Article 10:

"Member States shall take all appropriate measures, whether general or particular, to ensure fulfilment of the obligations arising out of this Treaty or resulting from action taken by the institutions of the Community. They shall facilitate the achievement of the Community's tasks.
They shall abstain from any measure which could jeopardise the attainment of the objectives of this Treaty."

This duty of compliance is complemented by Article 211 under which the Commission is charged with the task of ensuring "the proper functioning and development of the common market." This duty is expanded by Article 226 which authorises the Commission to investigate the failure of any Member State to fulfil its Treaty obligations, and if necessary under Article 227 has discretion to call the Member to account before the European Court of Justice. Losing the subsequent case would mean that the Member was held, "in breach of its Treaty obligations." In the extreme event of a Member still refusing to comply there exists a further sanction for exacting a financial penalty on the errant state, possibly recurring until full compliance is achieved.

It has never been clear to what extent the original Member States intended to be formally bound by this general statement in all its ramifications. Ever since the foundation of the Community Member States have attempted to avoid particular obligations which they found distasteful for one reason or another, even though in most cases they would have approved the measure before it became the law of Europe. Many States appeared to believe that the political authorities within the Community would remain supreme, with national leaders resolving such matters by negotiation. While accepting that the Community was to operate within a rule of law this did not imply any loss of control nationally. This reasoning was actually consistent with international organisations. The rules of international law were essentially contracts between individual states, which could be modified by agreement or even broken. Another example was the enforcement provisions of the European Court of Human Rights which provided for informal but usually effective enforcement of Court judgements. Ministers of offending countries were individually called to account by their peers in

Council of Europe meetings. Many commentators have also commented that the ECJ was modelled on the French Conseil d'Etat which is the country's highest administrative court. This was designed to ensure that all areas of the French government would adhere to the law. It was certainly accepted that European institutions with extensive executive powers should be subject to a policing mechanism to ensure compliance with the law and the founding treaties. But, existing administrative courts in Europe certainly had no right to question any national legislation. If anything, this was a prohibition stronger in countries such as France than it was with Britain's common law. Was the court of the EEC really intended to be different?

The Court itself had no hesitation regarding the answer to this question. In 1986, in its judgement of *Parti Ecologiste "Les Verts" v European Parliament* it stated:

> *"[The Community] is based on the rule of law, inasmuch as neither the Member States nor its institutions can avoid a review of the question whether the measures adopted by them are in conformity with the basic constitutional charter, the Treaty."*

This explicit statement confirmed that the ECJ would indeed have the right to review secondary legislative measures, and added that such review could extend to measures enacted by the Member States.

There is also, within Treaty of Rome itself, one article suggesting that this court was indeed intended to be different. This is Article 234 (formerly 171), which provides the innovative concept of a "preliminary reference" procedure from a national court. It allows the ECJ to provide a ruling on the interpretation of the Treaty, or the validity and interpretation of secondary legislation when requested to do so by a national court which has before it a case involving an issue of Community law. The ECJ does not actually judge the case before the national court but it provides in an appropriate form an answer to the question of legal interpretation before it. This usually decides the case in the national court. It is said that this provides for uniform application of Community law right across Europe, as logical and appropriate for a true Common Market.

This novel legal development has two remarkable facets. Firstly the implication is that Community law was actually to be enforced directly by the national courts, despite the lack of a statement to such effect. The ECJ was therefore never intended to be just a body concerned only with administration within the institutions, nor was it to function as a remote referee in intergovernmental disputes. Secondly national courts were to be guided, or probably bound under the duty of national co-operation in Article 10 to follow the rulings of the ECJ. What seems most surprising is that for a matter of such importance and for two propositions of such novelty within the judicial systems of all the Member States, the Treaty itself remained silent. These propositions can only be *deduced* from the very fact of Article 234 as described above. However, this simple deduction was to serve only as a starting point. Later digressions from the political history will describe the extensive legal order which the ECJ proceeded to construct on the basis of this single result.

Chapter 9: The Forces Gather and Grow

Adversarial Politics

Courtroom dramas are often the closest that most people come to the legal system. However this does create a general familiarity with the traditional English procedure based on the adversarial system. Its early justification came from a famous quotation by Lord Eldon in a case in 1822 that, "Truth is best discovered by powerful arguments on both sides." Thus the two opposing sides present the best arguments they can construct in the most effective and convincing manner they can devise for dispassionate decision by judge or jury. Law students frequently contrast this with the inquisitorial system prevalent in continental legal systems. This alternative philosophy calls for a much more active role for the judge. In the most extreme example a French examining magistrate will determine which witnesses are called and will proceed to cross examine them himself.

The same adversarial thinking has permeated British political thinking for a similar length of time. Her Majesty's Loyal Opposition perpetually argues against policies introduced by the governing party. Opposing views are therefore presented to the public who will in due course have the opportunity to elect the party with the selection of policies which most appeals, or in which they have developed the most confidence. Thus on any particular issue the public is almost invariably presented with the opposing opinions of for or against. Reflecting this, the BBC interprets its required political neutrality so that any innocuous government announcement will be followed immediately by an opposition comment. In contrast the private media remains free to slant its reporting in favour of whichever viewpoint its editors determine.

Britain's electoral system also contributes to this pervasive polarisation of opinion. Throughout the 20th century the two-party system was entrenched and the so-called "first past the post" election method produced alternating majorities in Parliament. Voting systems based on one of the numerous varieties of proportional representation are criticised in Britain for producing uncertainty in government, with the Italian example of numerous governments in fifty years after the war. Outside this extreme however participating parties, by trading their policies on a priority basis, do manage to form a workable consensus based on policies in many European countries.

Clearly Parliament itself is an important arena of conflict disguised as debate. Rather than a forum for an honest exchange of views it has always appeared as a gladiatorial stage of battle for competing ideas which serves to reinforce division rather than resolves issues. Any politician found to be influenced by his opposition to the point of adjusting his view would be treated to a torrent of abuse and criticism, and lasting damage to a political career. Party whips exist to ensure obedience rather than dispassionate evaluation.

Macmillan v Gaitskell

It is interesting to realise that polarisation of opinion regarding Europe had not been prevalent at the time of Macmillan's Common Market application. The subject was far from high in the list of public concerns. The backward looking fears of membership weighed heavily in Macmillan's early thinking and in that of his predecessors. Nevertheless there remained a considered view that even though the world might indeed be changing the horrors, treacheries, betrayal of history, and depletions of national sovereignty, were certain and intolerable consequences of joining Europe. It was not necessary to argue for an alternative role, simply a compelling necessity to avoid the route of membership. Even supporters of membership were aware that resolving the issue involved a judgement of balance in the important factors. The Commonwealth mattered even to European supporters, and few challenged the prevailing view that the weakening of Commonwealth links would mean the end of "honour and self interest." Even so views of the Commonwealth did vary with Conservatives regarding it as a remnant of imperial influence, and Labour seeing an opportunity for an "international and multi-racial partnership" in the world. This explains the universal outrage which resulted from US Secretary of State Acheson's comment that "Great Britain has lost an empire, but not yet found a role." In any event it is clear that at this time no body of opinion had formed which urged bold and vigorous or even unambiguous activity and diplomacy aimed unequivocally at entry to Europe.

The Labour opposition led by Hugh Gaitskell had its own overriding objective – to defeat the Conservatives in election. Failure to achieve this in 1959 meant that Gaitskell's political future now depended on the next election. He would not get another chance. His position, typified the difficulties of a modern party leader. Entry to the Common Market was opposed on both extremes of the party; by right wing "Little

Englanders" and by left wing "pro-Soviets" for entirely incompatible reasons. Therefore to maintain a party balance Gaitskell was forced into arguments centring on the "terms of entry", and to avoid questions regarding principles.

In fact Gaiskell's true view of Europe was probably neutral. Statements on both sides of the argument were made by him, indicating a rejection of dogma and extremism and a weighing of the factors of economic output, balance of trade, food prices, invisible earnings, Atlantic alliance. He regarded the economic arguments as balanced roughly 50:50, and in heated arguments with Monnet himself and later with Spaak he rejected the ideas of "faith" in the European ideal, and of the inevitability of political union. At the same time he was aware of the "risk of becoming nothing more than a little island off Europe. We shall be dwarfed politically by the Six." He avoided comment as to whether Europe would enable enforcement of or impeding of socialist policies. However, it would appear that Europe was not an important matter in Gaitskell's overall view, even amounting to "boring".

It is possible that Gaitskell's attitude this resulted from indecision and continuing British uncertainty but the issue was definitely seen as a distraction from his role of simply opposing the government. His overriding doubt gave no opportunity to demonstrate passionate and principled leadership. The labour party was clearly concerned by Britain's persistently poor economic performance, and it was inherently hostile to imperial illusions. However the luxury of opposition allowed it to advocate aggressively a general "modernisation", while opposing with equal vigour any significant change to the status quo. Similarly while understanding the weakness of the Commonwealth as a focus for British destiny he nevertheless advocated an effective veto for Commonwealth governments over Macmillan's entry terms. Criticism and opposition has never needed to be consistent.

Thus both leaders were struggling rationally towards a reasoned definition of Britain's future, honestly trying to balance the conflicting signals and pressures. Even in 1961 trade with Europe was already bigger than that with the Commonwealth, and the risk from internal tariff free Europe was readily predictable. But in the August 1961 Commons debate opposition remained solid, albeit with politeness and balance. One of the best examples came from Derek Walker-Smith who saluted the sense of Christian purpose animating the aims and aspirations of the Six, and carefully examined economic arguments, but he wanted to know whether sovereignty really needed to be sacrificed for economic benefits. He pointed out fundamental differences between Britain and the "detritus of the Holy Roman Empire", with their collective evolution looking to share a whole range of practices with themselves but not with us. He thought it was deeply wrong to disregard such weighty historical traditions as subsidiary to an economic arrangement of convenience. "There are considerations which go beyond those of the counting house".

Balance and reason however, is not the stuff of political leadership. Sentiment, exaggerated to passion which overshadows reason, is needed to exercise suitable eloquence and display a noticeable personal charisma. Therefore, to the amazement of his colleagues, Gaitskell found himself making a highly divisive, anti-Common Market speech at the 1962 Labour Party Conference in Brighton. "Would we necessarily, inevitably be economically stronger if we go in and weaker if we stayed out? – NO". "Is it true that by going in we should become more prosperous? – NO". Joining the Common Market "would mean End of Britain as an independent European state. It means the end of a thousand years of history." "Could Britain as a mere *province* of Europe behave as a mother country to series of independent nations? – sheer nonsense." The Common Agricultural Policy was "one of most devastating pieces of protectionism ever invented" The proposed treatment of Commonwealth partners was "astonishing and odious". Then after these almost inflammatory comments he remembered his balance. "I still hope profoundly that there may be such a change of heart in Europe as will make [future entry] possible."

The British dilemma over Europe therefore advanced from a subject of reasoned, if emotionally based debate, to an item of political contest, even though it was still nowhere near the top of the agenda. Gaitskell was still able to accuse Macmillan of applying to the Common Market as a "diversion from domestic difficulties; aimed at election success and restraining opponents in his party." Or, of "Smashing relations (with Australia) for personal political advantage". A rising Harold Wilson joined in, "If there has to be a choice we are not entitled to sell our friends and kinsmen down the river for a problematical and marginal advantage in selling washing machines in Dusseldorf." Gaitskell's balanced view had truly emerged as the rallying point for opposition to membership. Gaitskell, despite his preparatory thinking had cast himself as the first "euro-sceptic".

Chapter 10: Second Time Around

The Conversion of Harold Wilson

Behind the public, political scenes other important forces were slowly but inexorably gathering. Of critical importance was the evolution of thinking in the usually younger areas of the Foreign Office. It is clearly easy to argue with the benefit of hindsight that at the time of the Schumann plan the civil service failed to provide the dispassionate analysis which the country really required at that time. However the Foreign Office dutifully shifted its official view in line with Macmillan's slowly forming, European policy. In fact there were several officials who had become committed to Britain's future in Europe, and who had begun to exert their own brand of gentle influence on the developing political thought.

The records reveal the influence and long term determination of several individuals. The highest ranking was Con O'Neill who was appointed head of the UK delegation to the European Communities after the De Gaulle veto and who eventually led and recorded in fascinating detail all aspects of the final negotiations. Secondly was John Robinson, a brilliant, medium ranking official who had specialised in the European issue, energetically maintaining contacts throughout the Six, and keeping alive the belief in Britain's European destiny, irrespective of the wavering tides of political opinion. During the final negotiations it was said that he "knew everyone, understood everything, foresaw everything, and did everything." The quality of the intelligence and analysis he provided amazed politicians and colleagues alike, almost as if he had bugged their offices. However the important point is that he was by no means a dispassionate observer. He was an able, energetic and devious operator whose every action was aimed at getting Britain into the Common Market. Thus, although the Foreign Office overall had not been totally converted to the pro-European cause, those responsible for Europe were those most committed, and those most capable of getting Britain in.

In the political field the dilemma of Europe, when it was discussed at all, remained low key. It hardly featured in the general election of October 1964. Harold Wilson who become leader of the Labour party following Gaitskell's death defeated by a narrow margin Sir Alec Douglas-Home who had himself succeeded Macmillan. "Thirteen years of Tory misrule" had been Wilson's laconic and memorable theme. Wilson had inherited an anti-European position but again the interests of party unity prevented any principled position. Ambivalence had become a prerequisite of party unity, and in this area Wilson was a real master. Moreover, particularly where Harold Wilson was concerned, no opportunity for effective criticism could be sacrificed for the sake of stated policy. For example, before becoming leader Wilson had mercilessly ridiculed Macmillan after the veto. "Being naked in the conference room is one thing. Naked and shivering in the cold outside while others decide our fate is an intolerable humiliation".

So political convenience demanded that the subject of the Common Market was removed from any area of controversy and discussion. For this purpose a new tactic was invented which appeared to remove the controversy to an academic, and entirely rational and uncontroversial level. This was achieved by the defining of five entirely reasonable and sensible "Conditions" which would need to be fulfilled before the Party would support Common Market Entry. These tests were: suitable and binding Commonwealth safeguards; freedom to pursue independent foreign policy; honouring pledges made to other members of the European Free Trade Association (EFTA); the right to plan the British economy; and acceptable guarantees for British agriculture.

In other areas the Labour Party manifesto contrasted the gloomy reality under a Conservative government by painting a picture of optimism approaching the poetic. "The Labour Party is offering Britain a new way of life that will stir our hearts, re-kindle an authentic patriotic faith in our future and enable our country to re-establish itself as a stable force in the world today for progress, peace, and justice." Its own reality in government was to prove somewhat similar to that being criticised. But, as a newly appointed government the enthusiastic, optimistic and energetic leaders began with a ambitious and revivalist domestic agenda involving wholesale economic reforms on the basis of a "National Plan", designed to end Britain's notorious "Stop-Go" economic cycles. Europe, which was dedicated to (internal) free competition and opposed to state controls became even more of an irrelevance.

Reports were still appearing from Con O'Neill these could be safely ignored. His warnings of Europe's continuing and "inexorable process of adding little by little to the corpus of intra-Community decisions, doctrines and commitments has brought further divergence" remained a constant but background irritation. It had always been understood, at least by the Six that the Treaty would continue its directed evolution and every year saw not only serious studies regarding proposed collective policies, but also saw progress on real, substantial agreements and serious further surrenders of national sovereignty in terms of the decision making process. O'Neill and his colleagues never stopped warning that continuing delay in entry meant increasing difficulty, and increasing cost of the eventual result.

The European sections at the Foreign Office continued to exert their polite and respectful influence towards their own long term objectives, warning against the negative impressions being communicated by too strident emphasis on the five "conditions", and continually striving to rebuild European bridges. Thus in January 1966 when Wilson and his Foreign Secretary ordered a discreet review of the economic impact on Britain on the current European policies, the proponents of entry in the political background were well prepared with their arguments. A humiliating failure to deal with white supremacist Unilateral Declaration of Independence in Rhodesia had also recently started to lead Wilson into criticism from all sides of the Commonwealth, further damaging any natural tendency he felt towards the old traditions. Continuing economic weakness was also forcing a reluctant Wilson to withdraw further from Britain's remaining worldwide commitments. As previous leaders had seen, options for the future were in short and reducing supply.

It was against this background that Ministers received a timely report from Con O'Neill in Brussels. "For the last twenty years this country has been adrift. On the whole it has been a period of decline in our international standing and power. This has helped to produce a national mood of frustration and uncertainty. We do not know where we are going and have begun to lose confidence in ourselves." Although phrased as the country O'Neill was certainly aware that he could easily have used the same words to describe the government. He continued. "Perhaps a point has now been reached when acceptance of a new goal and a new commitment could give the country as a whole a focus around which to crystallise its hopes and energies." He concluded, "Entry into Europe might provide the stimulus and target we require."

This sentiment undoubtedly struck a chord with the uncertain Prime Minister who himself was personally feeling adrift and buffeted by events he could neither foresee and colleagues he could not control. Whatever the merits of the proposed objective there were considerable advantages to his standing in the country.

The Road is Still Blocked

Wilson had already begun to prepare the ground for his shift, knowing of the considerable opposition certain to appear even within his own cabinet. One common tactic had already been detected by Barbara Castle who recorded in her diary that Wilson had "already succeeded in guiding us to discussion on the details, which is more effective than anything else in making principles less important." Then, by October 1966 he had managed to persuade his cabinet to authorise a secret, exploratory mission for himself and his new Foreign Secretary, George Brown, to tour the European capitals. Then Wilson started to prepare public opinion with a reasonable, objective and certainly non-doctrinaire approach to the opportunity. "Given a fair wind, we will negotiate our way into the Common Market, head held high, not crawling in. Negotiations? Yes. Unconditional acceptance of whatever terms are offered us? No."

During the European tour itself, to be known as "The Probe", some new arguments or at least slants were advanced. Wilson proposed greater technological co-operation as a counter balance to the American domination increasingly feared in many capitals. There was also a novel if contrived description of British history, as resulting from early English invasions and the Norman conquest, and hence demonstrating true European roots. Our "kith and kin" had now been relocated from the Commonwealth to Europe.

However, a more important effect was that the very fact of the tour had convinced the public that the Labour government supported entry in principle, and Wilson's statements had encouraged that view despite cabinet dissent. Afterwards, Wilson explained to his colleagues how much had been achieved during the tour and finally a new formal application was reluctantly agreed in May 1967.

This time argument was more widespread and intense, with debate raging in most sections of the country. A deeply opposed consensus in the city, in industry and in the media began to lean towards the feeling that entry was a probable necessity. Sovereignty appeared in the debate, but was dismissed by the Chancellor of the Exchequer, James Callaghan, who appeared to have been converted to the European cause. He recalled his own experiences in government of finding practical restraints on his own dealings in financial, economic and political matters, no doubt echoing the discoveries of his recent predecessors. "International factors have such an effect", he argued, "that nations are not free to make their own decisions."

Little did he realise how true these were to become in the traumatic Sterling devaluation the following year. He concluded, "The argument about sovereignty is rapidly becoming outdated."

This period of debate was also unusual compared with those to come, and with Macmillan's for that matter, in that it was conducted with relative honesty. Wilson explained that the EEC's agricultural policy would increase food prices by 10 – 14%, that the overall cost of living would rise by 2.5 – 3.5%, and that effects on the balance of payments would be negative. He accepted these hard predictions from opponents on economic grounds, but omitted some of their harsher conclusions that the enormous increases in food prices would lead to uncontrollable wage inflation so that nothing could justify British membership. Instead, Wilson predicted that the temporary economic pain would lead to increasing exports and a higher rate of growth, as well as providing Britain with a place in the larger political world.

Parliamentary approval for a formal application was sought, and obtained with one of the largest majorities ever seen: 488 to 62. However, in a sign of things to come 35 Labour MP's had voted against the government, and over 40 abstained. Then, in Paris, one week after the Commons' overwhelming approval, President de Gaulle sympathised with Britain's obvious movement towards Europe, but spoke of the dangers of "destructive upheaval" and the "complete overthrow of equilibrium" which would result if Britain joined, and of the weakness of sterling resulting from its unsustainable pretensions as a reserve currency.

Despite many cordial preparations throughout the European capitals, and despite Wilson's tactical mixture of determination and his suggestions of retaliatory threats in the event of rejection, De Gaulle never budged. International currency markets intervened and soon forced a humiliating devaluation on the government and De Gaulle added a disdainful lecture to his second veto. The Common Market was incompatible with everything that mattered in Britain: its relationship with the USA, and its Commonwealth; its agricultural policies; its currency and international indebtedness. He wished to see Britain "one day make her choice and accomplish the enormous effort that would transform her." But, "a vast and deep mutation" would have to be effected.

Chapter 11: The Power of General De Gaulle

Empty Chair.
Back in Europe the developments had not been as entirely smooth as reports such as those from Con O'Neill had been suggesting – largely because of General de Gaulle. His central views regarding the greatness, prestige or merely the best interests of France were well known. Coming to power one year after the Treaty of Rome, he had continually sought to mould the Common Market to French requirements, while rejecting measures which might infringe French sovereignty. Such opinions became even more pronounced after de Gaulle's changes to the French constitution increased his power. "When I want to know what France thinks," he stated, "I ask myself."

Although his fears regarding loss of sovereignty were close to the traditional British feelings his desire for broader co-operation was made apparent in 1961 & 2. He proposed the "Fouchet Plan" which involved much greater integration, to include common foreign and security policies, as well as expanded economic co-operation. However the controlling body was to be a strictly inter-governmental organisation to be given authority over the existing EC structures. Since this was a complete reversal of the principles of supra-national principles of the Treaty of Rome, the Five were less than impressed. Although France had consistently argued that European unity was essential to balance the existing American dominance smaller partners in particular were becoming more wary of French, especially of de Gaulle domination. One Italian diplomat stated, "The best boss is he who is richest and furthest away." Nevertheless it was the Dutch who eventually caused the rejection of Christian Fouchet's ambitious plans. It is interesting to speculate that this vision of European integration would have been much more acceptable to those British opponents preoccupied with the issue of sovereignty, a fact which de Gaulle could not have overlooked. De Gaulle could therefore have supported British entry and enlisted British support for this internal but fundamental reform. However, other interests were, if anything more important to the General.

Despite failure to change Europe's direction, it remained in France's interests to co-operate. De Gaulle believed that a customs union would induce French industry to increase its productivity with access to a larger market. However of more importance was the Common Agricultural Policy. French farming was vulnerable to the higher competitiveness of

North American or British Commonwealth agriculture, and at that time around one-quarter of France's working population was employed in agriculture. There was in addition a growing surplus of French production which needed a wider European market. Therefore a preferential agricultural policy was essential and its entrenchment a major objective. The European Commission had been mediating the Common Agricultural Policy in the "general interest" which included consumers, and aiming towards a market-oriented, externally open, narrowly defined and centrally administered system of support with low support prices. But, in the face of French insistence on protection the final policy was for high subsidies, high prices, strong external protection, universally applicable but with decentralised administration.

This major defeat for the first president of the Commission, Walter Hallstein, eventually led to a major crisis in 1965. Hallstein believed that de Gaulle was temporarily vulnerable politically, when an agreement regarding financing of the Common Agricultural Policy was required, in the run up to a presidential election. He mis-calculated that De Gaulle would need to avoid losing support of French farmers and therefore he connected agricultural reform measures with proposals to increase the supra-national powers of the Commission, particularly in the sensitive budgetary field. De Gaulle though was no seasoned diplomat afraid to jeopardise good, harmonious relations by escalating a disagreement from a dispute into a fight. So, in response to this "attack" on his national interests de Gaulle ordered the withdrawal of all French representatives from Community institutions. Since these were before the days when majority voting was possible this effectively called a complete halt to all community development. France was in effect blackmailing its partners and appeared willing to sacrifice the EC itself rather than compromise its national interest.

This French "empty chair" policy lasted from July 1965 till January 1966, when it was resolved by a totally pragmatic but dubious Luxembourg Accord. Its main provision was that, contrary to the legal position defined in the Treaty of Rome, any member state was entitled to "veto" any policy deemed to be contrary to its vital national interest. The Rule of Law had just been seriously undermined, but the European Commission and even the European Court of Justice were no match for a determined and ruthless national adversary – then. In any event, the result was that the EEC could again move forward.

Ambassador Soames

General de Gaulle had never been afraid of causing offence in his protection of French interests. His veto of British entry in 1963 had caused a serious, but only temporary stir among the Five partners. By comparison, his 1967 veto caused barely a ripple, except in London. Despite his unrivalled dominance in Europe events would show that he remained dissatisfied with the principles of the Treaty of Rome no less than when he had become President.

The most curious incident, illustrating his profound dissatisfaction, occurred after the second veto, when the British pro-European forces had, despite French rejection, gained a general but cautious and grudging acceptance that Britain's future was in the EEC. While economic upheavals, then the Vietnam war, and the social developments of the late sixties were holding attentions elsewhere in government the Foreign Office was quietly strengthening its European deployments. One critical figure was again John Robinson, who was recalled from Brussels to become a leading voice in the "European Economic Organisations Department". By 1968 he had transformed this into an unashamed European Integration Department. Another was Christopher Soames, a broad and gregarious Conservative politician, married to Winston Churchill's daughter, who, to almost universal surprise was appointed by Foreign Secretary George Brown as ambassador to Paris. It was hoped that this man would enable Britain to get to know and influence De Gaulle more effectively than it had managed in the past.

Frustratingly to the British, it took some months to arrange the first meeting. De Gaulle had been in no hurry, but then the conversation which followed over a lunch was a source of controversy and denial for many years. Since that time it has emerged that the General described a new kind of Europe which he wished to see created. This would be of wider membership, but cover more areas of policy with a particular emphasis on joint defence, and most importantly it would be shorn of its supra-national aspects. National sovereignties would be restored. He proposed secret negotiations between Britain and France, which would lead to a new grand plan to be launched by the British and which France would support.

This radical proposal was so unexpected, but also of such critical importance that the Soames' staff at the embassy prepared a summary which they sent to de Gaulle's office for verification. French officials were also uncertain, but nevertheless confirmation was received from the Quai d'Orsay, the French Foreign Ministry. There could be no doubt that the General had indeed proposed a conspiracy which would lead to the destruction of the EEC in its present form.

To those remaining opposed to loss of sovereignty in Britain this proposal would have represented an ideal opportunity to reconstruct a wide ranging but intergovernmental Europe, on the lines Britain had supported since the Schumann plan. The existing EEC threatened an excluded Britain with serious and increasing economic damage. Its destruction would allow active participation in all schemes for co-ordination of policy without its constitutional and supranational implications. Clearly it would have encountered fierce opposition from at least the smaller members of the EEC, and it was certainly doubtful whether a practical proposal could really have been produced. Nevertheless, its potential for resolving all of Britain's entrenched conceptual difficulties would suggest that at least exploratory discussions would have been in Britain's best interest.

Emphatically, this was not the view held by John Robinson at the Department for European Integration. To him it was an obvious proposal to wreck the existing basis of Europe of which he was a long-standing and committed supporter. It was a serious threat to his ambitions, and it had to be stopped. He therefore warned that the proposal was not actually offer to help get Britain into Europe, (as required by government policy), but instead it would destroy any chance of Britain forming the necessary alliances with the Five. Conspiring with France against the EEC which we were applying to join would later be construed as treachery, while a refusal would be presented to the Five by France as British refusal to discuss a constructive role in Europe. Robinson and his supporters presented de Gaulle's suggestion as a cunning trap, adding afterwards that their own duty lay in pursuing a policy which had been widely debated and which enjoyed broad support. They had to protect ministers from this "potentially fatal distraction" and to help them resist "the temptations of plausible but inadequate alternatives".

Coincidentally Wilson was due to meet with the West German Chancellor, Kurt Kiesinger in Bonn, so the question as to whether the Soames conversation should be mentioned required an urgent answer. Wilson's view was that further talks with De Gaulle would seem appropriate. He saw no obligation to mention the matter to the ally whose support was most needed in the European campaign. Nor did he see any benefit in simply telling tales, or in expressing a moral disapproval of De

Gaulle's plot. He also thought that a betrayal of De Gaulle's confidence was itself distasteful. The Foreign Office and the Cabinet Secretary, led by Robinson had other ideas, and these had been pressed forcefully on the current Foreign Secretary, Michael Stewart. Serious arguments took place on the journey, and in the embassy that evening. Eventually Wilson relented and on the following day disclosed to Kiesinger the outline of the Soames conversation in as casual a manner as he could muster. Obviously the response in Bonn was far from casual.

Meanwhile, Robinson had implemented a second string to what can only really be regarded as his sabotage. The Foreign Office had prepared a briefing document to ensure that the meeting with Kiesinger had gone their way. To Wilson's fury this was a complete account of the incident, complete with suitable analysis and interpretation. Worse, it had already been circulated to all relevant departments and embassies, "to keep them in the picture". Naturally, this rapidly became a very serious embarrassment to the French. Relations with France sank, and sank further when the Foreign Office briefed journalists on the Soames original memo. "De Gaulle's Secret Offer: Scrap Six" the headline read.

De Gaulle's power was not to last much longer. In May 1969 he ordered a new referendum to reform the constitution which he had unnecessarily defined as a personal vote of confidence. When this was lost, he resigned and retired.

Chapter E: European Law is Directly Applicable

Direct Effect

Writing in 1981 in the American Journal of International Law the author Eric Stein produced a famous article summarising of the development of European Law which is being examined here:

> "Tucked away in the fairyland Duchy of Luxembourg and blessed, until recently, with benign neglect by the powers that be and the mass media, the Court of Justice of the European Communities has fashioned a constitutional framework for a federal-type Europe."

One fascinating feature of the law is that it often develops most dramatically as result of some trivial event and a relatively minor dispute. Such a case occurred in the Netherlands shortly after the Treaty of Rome came into force, when a small Dutch importer of chemicals from Germany objected to an increase in the duty it was charged by Dutch customs. In fact rates of duty under the Dutch regulations had not in themselves increased, but the authorities had reclassified a particular chemical, ureaformaldehyde, and this resulted in a higher charge to the importer. This small and unknown company was to become famous in all legal circles.

Opening in a normal Dutch tribunal the company Van Gend en Loos claimed that this represented an increase in duty which was prohibited under Article 25 (then numbered 12) of the Treaty which stated, "Member States shall refrain from introducing between themselves any new customs duties on imports or exports or any charges having equivalent effect, and from increasing those which they already apply in their trade with each other."

The Dutch tribunal decided to refer the matter to the European Court of Justice under the preliminary reference procedure of Article 234, and asked two questions:

> *a) Whether article 12 of the EEC Treaty has direct application within the territory of a member state, in other words, whether nationals of such a state can, on the basis of the article in question, lay claim to individual rights which the courts must protect;*
>
> *b) In the event of an affirmative reply, whether the application of an import duty of 8% to the import into the*

> *Netherlands by the applicant in the main action of ureaformaldehyde originating in the Federal Republic of Germany represented an unlawful increase within the meaning of article 12 of the EEC Treaty or whether it was in this case a reasonable alteration of the duty applicable before 1 March 1960, an alteration which, although amounting to an increase from the arithmetical point of view, is nevertheless not to be regarded as prohibited under the terms of article 12;*

The famous case of *Van Gend en Loos v Nederlandse Administratie der Belastingen*; ECJ Case Number C26/62, began.

The government of the Netherlands, supported by that of Belgium immediately challenged the jurisdiction of the ECJ. They submitted that any alleged infringement of the Treaty could only be submitted to the Court under Articles 226/7, ie. at the suit of the Commission or another Member State. Referring to the usual tenets of International Law they argued that the Treaty gave rights and obligations between nation states themselves, by means of contractual relations arising under the Treaty. It had no effect on the rights of individuals, or companies.

The ECJ replied,

> *"The objective of the EEC Treaty, which is to establish a common market, the functioning of which is of direct concern to interested parties in the community, implies that this treaty is more than an agreement which merely creates mutual obligations between the contracting states. This view is confirmed by the preamble to the Treaty which refers not only to governments but to peoples. It is also confirmed more specifically by the establishment of institutions endowed with sovereign rights, the exercise of which affects member states and also their citizens. Furthermore, it must be noted that the nationals of the states brought together in the community are called upon to cooperate in the functioning of this community through the intermediary of the European Parliament and the economic and social committee."*

This paragraph should be examined carefully. Firstly it asserts that the Treaty is more than an international agreement because it is of direct concern to interested parties in the community. This is curious. Does the Court really suggest that States cannot agree amongst themselves measures which may affect their citizens? Secondly it asserts that Community institutions have "sovereign rights", even though this concept cannot be found within the Treaty. Similarly the fact that nationals are elected to a European Parliament would not appear to affect the legal rights of a national government. Thus, even on a generous interpretation, these starting points appear not to reflect the level of logical rigour which lawyers would expect a matter of such importance to command.

The judgment proceeds,

> "The task assigned to the court of justice under article 177, the object of which is to secure uniform interpretation of the treaty by national courts and tribunals, confirms that the states have acknowledged that community law has an authority which can be invoked by their nationals before those courts and tribunals."

Article 234, previously 177, indeed does give the Court a right to interpret Community legislation, and it is a small step but a step nevertheless to imply that securing uniform interpretation by national courts is *the object* of the Court. However the Treaty definitely did contemplate Community law being invoked in national courts, otherwise this article would not have been included. Therefore this part of the judgement must be regarded as correct. Then, *starting from this point*, the statements above would appear to become more reasonable, and the Court's statements can then be regarded as a coherent summary of the Treaty's intention.

Just to emphasise what this means, the Court's judgement continues,

> "The conclusion to be drawn from this is that the community constitutes **a new legal order of international law for the benefit of which the states have limited their sovereign rights,** albeit within limited fields, and the subjects of which comprise not only member states but also their nationals. Independently of the legislation of member states, community law therefore not only imposes obligations on individuals but is also intended to confer upon them rights which become part of their legal heritage. These rights arise not only where they are expressly granted by the treaty, but also by reason of obligations which the treaty imposes in a clearly defined way upon individuals as well as upon the member states and upon the institutions of the community."

This conclusion was at the time, astounding to constitutional lawyers throughout the Community. It reversed the accepted presumption of international law that any international legal obligation is only concerned with the results to be achieved and is directed solely to the national governments themselves. Its proposition is essentially that because the signatories of the Treaty had intended their national courts to follow the interpretation of the ECJ the Member States have limited their sovereign rights. This was revolutionary enough, but the Court hadn't finished. The judgement proceeds to explain how this conclusion affects the interpretation of the then Article 12.

> *"The wording of article 12 contains a clear and unconditional prohibition which is not a positive but a negative obligation. This obligation, moreover, is not qualified by any reservation on the part of states which would make its implementation conditional upon a positive legislative measure enacted under national law. The very nature of this prohibition makes it ideally adapted to produce direct effects in the legal relationship between member states and their subjects.*
>
> *The implementation of article 12 does not require any legislative intervention on the part of the states. The fact that under this article it is the member states who are made the subject of the negative obligation does not imply that their nationals cannot benefit from this obligation*
>
> *In addition the argument based on articles 169 and 170 of the treaty put forward by the three governments which have submitted observations to the court in their statements of case is misconceived. The fact that these articles of the treaty enable the commission and the member states to bring before the court a state which has not fulfilled its obligations does not mean that individuals cannot plead these obligations, should the occasion arise, before a national court, any more than the fact that the treaty places at the disposal of the commission ways of ensuring that obligations imposed upon those subject to the treaty are observed, precludes the possibility, in actions between individuals before a national court, of pleading infringements of these obligations.*

> *A restriction of the guarantees against an infringement of article 12 by member states to the procedures under article 169 and 170 would remove all direct legal protection of the individual rights of their nationals. There is the risk that recourse to the procedure under these articles would be ineffective if it were to occur after the implementation of a national decision taken contrary to the provisions of the treaty.*
>
> *The vigilance of individuals concerned to protect their rights amounts to an effective supervision in addition to the supervision entrusted by articles 169 and 170 to the diligence of the commission and of the member states*
>
> *It follows from the foregoing considerations that, according to the spirit, the general scheme and the wording of the treaty, article 12 must be interpreted as producing direct effects and creating individual rights which national courts must protect."*

Finally the Court proceeded to the actual second question, which was the real substance of the dispute. It suggested that the actual question concerned classification of products, and that this was outside ECJ jurisdiction. However it suggested that the correct question concerns whether an increase in duty caused by re-classification contravened Article 25 (12). This was a matter of Community law, and the interpretation to be given to the concept of duties. It concluded that where the same product became subjected to a higher rate of duty, it was of no importance how the increase came about, it was still an increase and therefore it was contrary to the article. Whether or not, as a matter of fact, there had been an increase in the duty applied, was a matter for the national court, and this national court would be called upon to issue the judgement in the case, based on its assessment of the facts, and the guidance of the ECJ regarding the above interpretation.

Thus, with the *Van Gend* case in 1962, the first pillar on which European law depends was formed. **European law applies directly within Member States, and the duty on them to co-operate in achieving Community objectives includes national courts which must apply Community provisions.**

Since then a number of details have emerged to complete the doctrine. Firstly the *Van Gend* case referred only to Articles of the Treaty and then, only subject to three conditions. The article must be clear, or sufficiently precise before it is capable of direct effect. It must be unconditional, and thus not dependent on a decision of another body. Finally it must not be subject to further implementing measures. Thus where the Treaty indicated that the Community should create implementing Regulations the Article itself was not directly effective.

Regulations themselves were described in the Treaty itself as "directly applicable in all Member States," (Article 249, ex 189). However since 1970, (in the case of Franz Grad) the doctrine of direct effect was held to apply to Regulations again providing the above criteria could be met. The doctrine was extended slightly further in 1972, when in *Commission v Italy* (Case 39/72) the Commission won its referral under Article 226 complaining that Italy had failed to implement milk supply regulations. The ECJ suggested that Italian practice of directly transposing the wording of Community Regulations into Italian law was itself a default since it brought into doubt the legal nature of the provisions. Stronger rebukes followed in *Fratelli Variola v Italian Finance Ministry*, (Case 34/73) when the ECJ stated, "No procedure is permissible whereby the Community nature of a legal rule is concealed from those subject to it."

However the effect of Directives remained uncertain until 1978. It should be remembered that while Directives may be designed to provide particular rights or duties to citizens or companies the exact method of providing these remains at the discretion of each Member State. Thus in the case of Ratti the Court determined that the concept of direct effect could not be invoked before the date for implementation had passed. The national government was obliged to take certain measures, but not before the agreed date. Afterwards however, any failure to produce the required measures represented an impermissible deprivation of the rights of their citizens.

Next, in a British case of 1984, a Miss Marshall brought a case against her employer, the Southampton and South West Area Health Authority, attempting to enforce rights emanating from the Equal Treatment Directive. On reaching age 62 she had been dismissed from her position as senior dietician since she had passed normal retirement age for women. The industrial tribunal held that this was not contrary to English statutes regarding sex discrimination since the matter concerned normal retirement ages. The Court of Appeal referred the matter to the ECJ, asking whether the facts revealed an act of discrimination contrary to the

Equal Treatment Directive, and whether Miss Marshall could rely on the Directive even though English law at that time did not provide the remedy she sought. The ECJ replied that while individuals (including individual companies) could not be regarded as obliged to comply with a Directive because no legal measure had been directed towards them, national governments had agreed to implement appropriate measures by signing the Treaty. Therefore it would be unjust if governments were allowed to benefit from their own failure to meet their obligations. Therefore it is only reasonable that Directives should be enforceable against the State, and Miss Marshall won her case.

One final brick in the construction of the doctrine was completed in the 1989 case of *Foster v British Gas*. Regional and local authorities had already been regarded as part of the State, and even the Chief Constable of the RUC had been held to be an "emanation of the State", and thus directly subject to the terms of a directive. In *Foster*, the ECJ broadened considerably its definition of what would be part of the state for purpose of direct applicability of Directives. It would include, any "organisations or bodies which were subject to the authority or control of the State or had special powers beyond those which result from the normal rules applicable to relations between individuals." British Gas was part of the State.

Indirect Effect

One of the principle objectives of the ECJ has always been to enforce the consistent and uniform application of European Law across all its internal boundaries. It was a principle derived not from any wording within the Treaty but from deduction by the ECJ that this was merely a logical consequence. The principle as with others encountered little attention from politicians let alone opposition. No doubt national politicians were occupied with concerns of their own, and were reluctant to interfere even though the ECJ was gradually creating an unprecedented concentration of power in an organisation notably less accountable than the highest courts in any of the individual Member States. After all, it was said, even in the face of real and unexpected activism from the ECJ, the court was merely upholding the rule of law.

One of the earliest expressions of this fundamental principle occurred in an otherwise obscure case of *Walt Wilhelm v Bundeskartellamt* in 1968. This included the statement,

> "The binding force of the Treaty and of measures taken in application of it must not differ from one State to another as a result of internal measures, lest the functioning of the Community system should be impeded and the achievement of the aims of the Treaty placed in peril."

The case of Marshall described above was later seen as a significant weakening in the effectiveness of directives since their direct effect was limited, even though broadly interpreted to "emanations of the state". In later case, also involving Miss Marshall, the then Advocate General van Gerven suggested that this limitation should be abandoned by the ECJ on the grounds that such a distinction militates against the coherence and uniformity in application of Community law. Similarly in a 1992 case *Dori v Recreb,* Advocate General Lenz suggested that the legitimate expectations of citizens of the European Union were that Community law would apply uniformly and consistently throughout the territory of the Union. Such expectations were not compatible with a doctrine which resulted in a variation in the protection of rights conferred under Community law depending on whether or not the person against whom such protection was sought was a public or a private body. However in neither case was this advice heeded by the ECJ since presumably in a majority decision, the distinction was maintained. Instead the Court chose to rely on another discovery of intentions which it divined within the text of the Treaty, to prevent Member States from defaulting on their duty of complete compliance with Directive objectives.

This risk of such failure in implementation was considerably reduced following a case of 1983, after two qualified social workers Sabine von Colson and Elisabeth Kamann were refused staff appointments at an all male prison, in one of the German states, Nordhein-Westfalen. Because of the risks the employers perceived to be directly connected with duties of staff within the prison, lesser qualified male candidates were employed in preference to the two ladies. This was soon judged to be contrary to the Equal Treatment Directive (75/207/EEC).

The problem arose because the German government, in its implementation of the Directive had not included sufficient sanctions to ensure effective enforcement, and was duly criticised for this when the case of *Von Colson & Kamann v Land Nordheim-Westfalen* (Number 14/83) reached the ECJ. Member States were reminded that the duty under Article 10 to take all appropriate measures "to ensure fulfilment of its obligations...resulting from action taken by the institutions of the Community," extends to the nations' courts and therefore that sanctions must be made available to the courts which would provide an effective deterrent against non-compliance. The Court stated:

> *"Although that provision leaves Member States to choose the ways and means of ensuring that the Directive is implemented, that freedom does not affect the obligation imposed on all the Member States to which the Directive is addressed, to adopt, in their national legal systems, all the measures necessary to ensure that the Directive is fully effective, in accordance with the objective which it pursues."*

The judgement therefore went further than simply dealing with the case at hand, dealing generally with the situation where a national government had not completely, (or correctly) implemented a Directive in its national law. Under such circumstances:

> *"National courts are required to interpret their national law in the light of the wording and the purpose of the directive in order to achieve the result required by the third paragraph of Article 189* [achieving the directive's results]"

This concept whereby Community provisions would be applied indirectly as law by means of interpretation was not fully developed until a judgement of 1992 in the case of Marleasing SA v La Comercial Internationale de Alimentation SA. In this case the Spanish government had not introduced any legislation at all to implement several requirements in a Directive relating to public limited companies. The ECJ replied to the referral from the Spanish court, insisting that the Spanish law *as a whole* be interpreted to give effect to the Directive. This was a serious stretch of the very concept of interpretation implying that it does not apply merely to particular provisions, and it proved seriously controversial in the legal profession, and particularly in Britain. There was however, one escape route. A small phrase from the Von Colson judgement describing the courts duty to interpret, "in so far as it is given discretions to do so under national law," was used to counter this idea in national courts. These then tended to interpret their national law merely "as far as possible" to in accordance with the directive.

This small gap was not filled by the ECJ until 1993. A group of employees in Italy had been made redundant when their employer became insolvent. In the case of *Francovich and Boniface v Italy*, they complained that under a Community Directive, whose date for implementation had already passed, they should have been entitled to compensation for the arrears in their wages which had been lost. However the Italian government had made no attempt to introduce any measures to implement this Directive, and there was no domestic statute which could have been interpreted to give it any effect. Consequently Italy was held by the ECJ, to be in breach of its Treaty obligations.

The Court then went a small but significant step further. They explained that in this case the Directive was designed to confer new rights on individuals, that the nature of those rights were made perfectly clear by the provisions of the Directive, and that the Italian government was directly responsible for the loss caused to the individuals. Therefore the government's duty to uphold Community law means that the individuals must be entitled to sue their national governments in their local courts and obtain suitable compensation. It was not only the Italian government which was taken by surprise. There was after all, no such suggestion within the wording of the Treaty and no national government which had remotely contemplated such a result. There was nothing in international law even similar. The judges had simply invented (or discovered within the intentions of the Treaty) a new concept of State Liability. This was indeed a new legal order.

Thus, although a Directive may not be directly effective, it is still necessary for a national **court** to implement its measures to the extent that its national government has failed to do so, using whatever tools of "interpretation" may lie within its discretion, bearing in mind its prime duty to uphold Community Law. If the national government fails to introduce the appropriate measures it is responsible to its own citizens for any resulting damages. Responsibilities of national authorities with regard to both Regulations and now Directives cannot be evaded.

The European Court of Justice had spoken. "European Community Law is Directly Applicable in Member States," either one way or another.

Chapter 12: Preparations and Hurdles

Summit at the Hague

The retirement of General de Gaulle and his replacement by the Gaullist Georges Pompidou did not create an instant change in French policy, even though Pompidou was known to be less against British entry than his predecessor. As President he still had the interests of France foremost in his mind.

In the EEC though, the Five saw the departure of de Gaulle as end of an era characterised by stagnation and a great opportunity to renew progress towards integration across several policy areas, including expansion. President Pompidou soon found himself pressed to soften opposition to British entry and to allow commencement of formal discussions with the applicants which included Ireland, Denmark and Norway. This renewed eagerness for British entry gave France the opportunity to achieve an important objective denied by the Five in the 1965. They insisted on an agreement to secure permanently the arrangements for financing the Common Agricultural Policy. Earlier in the year the existing system had caused serious friction between France and Germany when the latter, suffering economical difficulties the opposite of Britain's had been forced by the markets to revalue the Deutschmark. Agricultural prices which had always been central to the French interest, became a very sore point of discussion. The solution offered to France was that financing would no longer depend on contributions from each Member State but would be levied centrally. The Community would therefore have its financing available automatically and independently of national governments, and would allocate a grossly disproportionate amount of its funds to the support of farmers. In addition the European Parliament would be given increased budgetary powers. Back in London officials were regarding this development certainly as a significant increase in the cost of Britain's entry and with occasional suspicion that this was precisely the purpose of the measures. They however, were mere observers.

The scheme was approved at a Summit Meeting of EEC Heads in The Hague in December 1969, held well before such summits of heads of government became a regular, routine occurrence. The communiqué was expansive in praise of the Common Market achievements, and in its description of the revitalised community objectives. The meeting was to act as a springboard for the next stages in EEC evolution. The decisions taken included uncontroversial measures such as formation of a European University, technological co-operation particularly in the Atomic Energy Community, but also a number of policies which if widely known in Britain would have been political dynamite, striking fear into the hearts of opponents of federalism. The following extracts illustrate these points.

3. Over and above the technical and legal sides of the problems involved, the expiry of the transitional period at the end of the year has, therefore, acquired major political significance. Entry upon the final stage of the Common Market not only means confirming the irreversible nature of the work accomplished by the Communities, but also means paving the way for a united Europe capable of assuming its responsibilities in the world of tomorrow and of making a contribution commensurate with its traditions and its mission.

4. The Heads of State or Government therefore wish to reaffirm their belief in the political objectives which give the Community its meaning and purport, their determination to carry their undertaking through to the end, and their confidence in the final success of their efforts.

8. They reaffirmed their readiness to further the more rapid progress of the later development needed to strengthen the Community and promote its development into an economic union. They are of the opinion that the integration process should result in a Community of stability and growth. To this end they agreed that within the Council, on the basis of the memorandum presented by the Commission on 12 February, 1969, and in close collaboration with the latter, a plan in stages should be worked out during 1970 with a view to the creation of an economic and monetary union. The development of monetary co-operation should depend on the harmonisation of economic policies. They agree to arrange for the investigation of the possibility of setting up a European Reserve Fund in which a joint economic and monetary policy would have to result.

13. They reaffirmed their agreement on the principle of the enlargement of the Community, as provided by Article 237 of the Treaty of Rome. In so far as the applicant States accept the treaties and their political finality, the decisions

> taken since the entry into force of the treaties and the options made in the sphere of development the Heads of State or Government have indicated their agreement to the opening of negotiations between the Community on the one hand and the applicant States on the other. They agreed that the essential preparatory work could be undertaken as soon as practically and conveniently possible. By common consent, the preparations would take place in a most positive spirit.
>
> 14. As soon as negotiations with the applicant countries have been opened, discussion will be started with such other EFTA members as may request them on their position in relation to the EEC.
>
> 15. They agreed to instruct the Ministers for Foreign Affairs to study the best way of achieving progress in the matter of political unification, within the context of enlargement. The Ministers would be expected to report before the end of July 1970.

This was a remarkably clear statement from a new generation of leaders of the Six that its *political* objectives are those which give the Community its meaning and purport. Thus, the integrationist dreams of the Founders of Europe had not changed or even faded. The economic aspects of the Community were merely secondary, whatever views were being expressed by supporters and detractors in Britain. The British public, having been told repeatedly of European idealism, might not even have recognised the statement as a description of true intent, and of the real meaning behind the European Community. Fortunately though, for Britain's leaders and opinion formers, very few even noticed the statement and even fewer still realised it could have been a warning of the direction their politicians were really leading, knowingly or not. Instead British politicians remained free to promote more comfortable discussion of the pros and cons of the Common Market, while simply ignoring the political objectives of its masters.

One point which was to become especially important point was the repetition of the essential pre-condition for entry negotiations – candidate states must accept the political finality of the Treaty, *and* _all_ subsequent decisions. This enormous and expanding body of legislation, regulation and agreement, later to be described as the *"acquis communitaire"* had to be completely accepted in principle – first. While there would be negotiations there would be no question of re-negotiations of anything already decided by the Six.

A Fishy Conspriracy

The Community's insistence on unconditional acceptance of everything they had agreed among themselves was then used to produce an additional opportunity to benefit the Six. It was a proposal which later had a political effect vastly disproportionate to its minor economic scope, and even threatened last minute failure of the subsequent negotiations: - a Common Fisheries Policy.

The Treaty of Rome had envisaged a Common Fisheries Policy, but despite the expiry of the general transition period to the Common Market, there was little interest among the Members for deciding one. It was not even until May 1969 that the Commission had formulated any proposals and these had immediately been blocked by France, opposed to the requirement of common access by all community vessels to national waters. However, in recent years the French government had been investing heavily in shifting the emphasis of its fishing fleets from inshore to distant water fishing. A more expansive view was in order.

The Germans, Belgians and especially the Dutch had also shown a marked lack of interest in the subject. This was explained by one Dutch official, "the Dutch inshore waters were so poor that they had neither expected, nor so far experienced, any influx of foreign vessels". In contrast foreign fishing vessels always wanted to fish in British rather than in other continental waters. The British industry was summarising, "the waters within our own fishing limits are teeming with fish, whereas there are none at all within the fishing limits of the present Community countries." Official statistics had also defined the issue more clearly. Aggregate landings of in the EEC amounted to 2.2 million tons and in the four applicant countries to 5.4 million tons.

Therefore, on the very day that negotiations on British Membership opened, the EEC decided on a Common Fisheries Policy, based on the principles of a common market for fish, but also, much more controversially, of common access to all European fishing grounds and areas. Geoffrey Rippon, the leader of the British team diplomatically described this as a "coincidence", but few observers doubted the opportunistic objective of the Six, even though many doubted whether they would really manage to agree the details.

Thus, the price of British entry had gradually increased not only as a result of the initial divergence and the natural development of EEC policies, but in this instance also as a result of the deliberate attempts by the Six to increase benefits to themselves from anticipated British membership.

The Rise of Edward Heath

British policy however, long and slow in formation, had now apparently settled and was not to be abandoned as a result of issues which amounted to details hardly worth mentioning or reporting. Harold Wilson had repeatedly made it clear that despite rejection, the objective of British policy remained entry to the Common Market and he had appointed George Thomson as Minister for Europe. After de Gaulle's departure, organised lobbying in the capitals of the Six began again. Government priority though soon had to be shifted to the forthcoming general election. This time entry into Europe had emerged as a minor election issue, and had been included in the Labour manifesto. Similarly, the Conservatives were undertaking to negotiate – "no more, no less", but were also seen as supporting entry. Therefore "Europe" produced little public debate and the issue was well down the list of the electorate's concerns. Dissent within the parties was also sufficient to encourage the low-key approach on both sides. Again Wilson included an apparently honest assessment of the downside of entry suggesting effects even worse than before. Food prices would increase by 18-26%, cost of living by 5%, and balance of payments worse by anything from £100M to £1,100M. The party policy nevertheless was that membership was a long term benefit "providing the terms were right". Wilson was confident of winning the election and had discussed a cabinet reshuffle aimed at intensifying the campaign to attain entry. Then, to the surprise of most people in the country he lost the June 1970 election to the Conservative, Edward Heath.

It is interesting how the history of politics often produces appropriate men appearing at key times. Heath had become leader of the Conservatives in 1965 after defeating Reginald Maudling who did not believe at all in losing sovereignty for a benefit to trade, even if the benefit were proven. The candidate's European credentials were of course known but these were of little interest to the Conservative party which was concerned with domestic policy issues, and with selecting a personality most likely to defeat Wilson. Thus it was almost an accident that Britain now found that it had a Prime Minister with a commitment to

Europe approaching the zealous, and who regarded entry as his country's destiny and his life's mission.

From his early career Heath had a supporter of European integration in the style of Monnet. He supported the Schumann plan, describing its objective as creating a European Germany in contrast to a German Europe, but knowing that this was intended as merely the first step to complete political integration. From the time of his maiden speech in the Commons Heath retained this unwavering conviction.

He had participated in Macmillan's negotiations with a notably greater commitment than his hesitant leader. On the first day he said, "We recognise (our application) as a great decision; a turning point in our history, and we take it in all seriousness." Neither was he deterred by de Gaulle's veto. "We are part of Europe by geography, tradition, history, culture and civilisation. We shall continue to work.... in Europe for the true unity and strength of this continent."

On becoming Prime Minister, Heath was impressed to find the detailed campaign plans for entry as well as the extensive preparatory work which had continued within the civil service, after the previous negotiations. In addition the now established, key "Europe" supporters in the Foreign Office remained active and needed little by way of mobilisation. Therefore Heath was able to continue with Wilson's plans and timetable and so, in July 1970 the real negotiations could begin.

Domestic obstacles to the Heath nirvana remained. Not least of these was public opposition. In April opinion polls had indicated that only 19% of the population supported entry and over 50% opposed even participation in talks. Public opinion, although clear on the subject was not however dogmatic or even firm, especially considering that the subject was not regarded as terribly important. Heath was of course undaunted and proceeded to deal with this inconvenience with a single-minded determination using whatever arts of politics he could devise or adapt. The end was certainly sufficiently important to justify the means.

Not least among the opposition was Her Majesty's Treasury. To them, the enormous costs of the Common Agricultural Policy meant that there was no longer any question of balancing the costs and the benefits. Losses by way of contributions, price increases, and adverse balance of payments far outweighed any conceivable advantages. However this was not a time for reasoned assessment, or balanced evaluation. The Treasury reports were simply ignored. They certainly could not be allowed to prevent Heath's white paper from stating unequivocally that entry on the terms offered would be beneficial to the economy. Full Steam Ahead!

Chapter 13: Negotiations for Entry - Background.

Climate Change / Political Convergence

Formal negotiations for entry to the EEC began in Luxembourg on 30th June 1970. In legal and diplomatic terms these were in response to the British application of 1967, which had been "left on the table". But in those few years the political climate had been transformed. French opposition in principle had now evaporated, and in many ways the decision to proceed with expansion had already been taken by President Pompidou at The Hague summit. In contrast to the situation in 1967 negotiations were opening under excellent auspices.

Some months had been required for the Communities to establish their negotiating positions, and the French, not forgetting their national interested, had obstructed this process by refusing any commitment until the details of the Agricultural Policy had been ratified. Gaullist "extremists" remained prominent in French politics, and many of them had hoped that this could deter undesirable entrants, ie. Britain. The General himself, still enjoying widespread support and fearful influence had remained a potential threat. Critical pronouncements from that quarter with their possible devastating effect had still needed to be avoided, until he died in November 1970. However, over the course of the negotiations Pompidou gradually removed opponents of his reversed policy. Pompidou's Prime Minister for 10 months after De Gaulle, M. Couve de Murville, who had been a highly skilled and determined opponent of British entry, disappeared from office. The Foreign Minister, M. Debré was moved to the Ministry of Defence and while less involved in the talks became gradually resigned to their success. His replacement, M. Schumann, had been in favour of British entry from the start.

Politics elsewhere in Europe had also moved in favour of enlargement. The West German Chancellor, Dr. Kiesinger may have been in favour of British entry but he was totally unwilling to risk harmonious Franco-German relations, which to him were a clear and unquestionable priority. His replacement in October 1969, Herr Willi Brandt, could also not afford to damage relations with France but he adopted a more balanced attitude with much greater support for enlargement and a practical sympathy for British positions. A third domestic change worked in favour of the British when Signor Colombo became Italian Prime Minister. He had already been one of Heath's important contacts, and had been helpful in earlier negotiations. Subsequent Italian support became influential during the negotiations because of his leadership.

Back in Britain the political climate had also shifted. Sharp divisions had appeared between "for" and "against" with little sign of a real middle ground despite the insistence of all political leaders on a "balance of interest" or a "provided the terms are right" approach. Significantly, suggestions that we could reform the EEC into the preferred type of institution ie. intergovernmental, had now been recognised as illusory and had vanished. Perversely this also led to rejection of any proposal involving objectives less than full membership, even if this would provide the economic benefits which all parties said they were aiming to achieve, while avoiding the constitutional complications feared.

It is interesting to compare responses to a cautious proposal after the first veto, for "association" as an alternative to membership which would amount to a trading arrangement free of political or constitutional implications. This was the vision which Britain really sought for Europe and had led to the formation of EFTA. However, in his time Macmillan rejected any idea of "association" or "near-identification" as producing the same problems regarding agriculture and Commonwealth preferences without any internal influence on the direction of the policy itself. "All the duties and none of the say." At the same time Edward Heath had also rejected the suggestion, but for quite different reasoning, emphasising the unfairness of the scheme to the existing members. "Having failed to persuade Europe to adopt free trade," he said, "a mere association would seek all the advantages of the internal market but without its obligations." After 1968 and the second veto, measures proposed by the Benelux countries, and later Italy aimed at bringing closer to Europe by expanding the competence of the Western European Union were blocked by France, but a scheme for a "commercial arrangement" emanating from Germany and endorsed by an official opinion of the Commission was rejected by Britain, because it would "compromise the aim of full membership".

Thus it appears that membership of the EEC had gradually become an aim in itself, almost irrespective of its cost, and either disregarding or simply not considering as important all the causes of the previous years' agonising, nor even the benefits that were quoted as justifying the application. It is even difficult to argue that the economic benefits were so obvious that other factors were overshadowed, since the Treasury had predicted that the economic effects were detrimental. Opposition was certainly lively, but the two main political leaders were committed.

Wilson, of course, was known for his pragmatism rather than his principles. But it was entirely plausible that Edward Heath sincerely believed in the Monnet vision of the United States of Europe, and in Britain's part within it. "Considerations of the counting house" could be regarded as secondary.

This point of view was explicitly stated by many politicians. For example one Conservative MP, Sir Anthony Meyer said in the Commons, "Frankly, I do not think it depends on the terms at all. I believe it would be in the interests of this country to join the EEC whatever the terms." Similarly, Lord Crowther, speaking in the Lords said, "You do not haggle over the subscription when you are invited to climb aboard a lifeboat." Nevertheless haggling there was to be.

Acquis Communitaire

Behind the political scenes the supporters of integration were now well organised and thoroughly prepared. To them, the previous years had represented a succession of missed opportunities, and Britain was lucky to have another chance before divergence between Britain and the EEC had become simply too great. In contrast to the previous negotiations, the right personalities were falling into place, and external events were now moving propitiously. Membership had become simply an overriding imperative whose time had come. "What mattered was to get into the Community and thereby restore our position at the centre of European affairs which, since 1958, we had lost. The negotiations were concerned only with the means of achieving this objective at an acceptable price."

Legally, the expansion of the Communities was governed by the then Article 237 of the Treaty of Rome,

"Any European State may apply to become a member of the Community. It shall address its application to the Council whose decision, after the opinion of the Commission has been obtained, shall be unanimous thereon.

The conditions of admission and the adjustments to this Treaty necessitated thereby shall be the subject of an agreement between the Member States and the applicant State. That agreement shall be submitted for ratification by all the contracting States in accordance with their respective constitutional rules.'

However, although this Article provided for revisions to the Treaty, any such discussion was regarded by the Six as prohibited for practical political reasons. Thus the communiqué of the Hague summit modified the conditions as follows: They reaffirmed their agreement on the principle of the enlargement of the Community, as provided by Article 237 of the Treaty of Rome. *"Insofar as the applicant states accept the treaties and their political finality, the decisions taken since the entry into force of the treaties and the options made in the sphere of development the heads of state or government have indicated their agreement to the opening of negotiations between the Community on the one hand and the applicant state on the other."* They agreed that the essential preparatory work could be undertaken as soon as practically and conveniently possible. By common consent, the preparations would take place in a most positive spirit.'

In other words, it was a precondition of negotiations that the "Acquis Communitaire" be accepted without reservations. This was taken to mean that *everything* which had been agreed by the Communities, (ie. including the ECSC and Euratom), had to be endorsed, accepted and made binding on the candidate country. It was described by a German official as representing an almost inconceivable flood of European legislation, amounting to over 13,000 pages. Starting from the Treaties it was to include any amendments, annexes or protocols and any agreement, regulation, enactment, or policy made in any form by any of the institutions, even if not published, up until the time of joining. This was a remarkable, all encompassing requirement, which was made fundamental and which was subsequently repeated as the starting point for any future membership negotiations.

Two main reasons have been quoted as explaining the necessity of complete acceptance. Firstly, it is clear that almost all of the decisions previously taken by the Six represented an often laboriously negotiated compromise between the conflicting interests of the members. Allowing the same points to be re-opened would mean a repeat of previous arguments, with a significant change in the balance of interests. Hardly any policy would survive intact, and the Communities would essentially be starting from the beginning. Therefore it was essential for the existing members not to risk losing any advantages previously gained. Secondly, the creation of a minor exception could be used to undermine other policies of greater importance. Agreeing a concession in response to a strong case on an unimportant point can set a dangerous precedent by making it more difficult to resist, as a matter of principle, a similar argument on a more important issue.

Therefore, although many of the Community measures were regarded as unpalatable, it was quickly recognised in London that acceptance could not be avoided. The first requirement for discussions to begin was therefore described in the famous phrase, "Swallow the lot, and swallow it now".

Swallow the Lot !

This Britain immediately undertook to do. In the 1967 negotiations the opening statement of George Brown included the following commitment:

> "I begin with the Treaties. They, and particularly the Treaty establishing the European Economic Community, are the pillars of the Community structure. We accept all three Treaties, subject only to the adjustments which are required to provide for the accession of a new member, for example our participation and voting in the Communities' institutions, and our contribution to its financial expenditure. I shall come in a moment to the particular issues on which we seek satisfaction but let me say at once that, subject to this. Her Majesty's Government accept without reserve all the aims and objectives of the three Treaties and will implement them.
>
> "I will go further. We recognise that the Community is a dynamic organisation which has already evolved and will continue to evolve. If it is to be true to the spirit of the Treaties which established it, the Community's institutions will develop and its activities will extend to wider fields beyond the activities covered by the existing provisions of the Treaties. We believe that Europe can emerge as a Community expressing its own point of view and exercising influence in world affairs, not only in the commercial and economic but also in the political and defence fields. We shall play our full part in this process. Indeed it is the realisation of this European potential which has, above all, aroused our desire to join the Communities. As a member we shall accept whatever responsibilities the evolving Community may decide to assume and we shall join as eagerly as other members in creating new opportunities for the expression of European unity."

Other extracts emphasise that Britain also possessed the necessary political qualifications;

> "The European Communities are developing on an economic base. But we in Britain, no less than the present Members of the Communities, do not see the issues only in economic terms. The balance of economic advantage for us is a fine one. Some of the most decisive considerations for us have been political."
>
> "We are aiming at something far more than material prosperity. We see this leading to a greater political purpose for Western Europe. And if that purpose is to be realised, Britain must share it. We want, as soon as we can, to develop really effective political unity with our fellow West Europeans."
>
> "And above all that unity requires a common purpose and outlook, and a will to work together. We have already given assurances about this, and what I have to say today will confirm them. The fundamentals of the Communities will remain unaffected, for we shall be accepting precisely the same treaty aims and obligations in letter and spirit as yourselves We aim to create with you a unity which will be all the greater because it will be built on the rich diversity of achievements and characteristics of European peoples who share a common purpose and a common resolve for peace."

The intervening years and a change of government revealed no detectable change in British policy. In his opening statement to the 1971 Conference, Anthony Barber included the following: -

> "Both Mr. Heath, in a speech last month, and the previous British Government have made it clear that we accept the Treaties establishing the three European Communities and the decisions which have flowed from them. I confirm that this is the position of Her Majesty's Government, subject to the points to which I now turn.
>
> The list of questions which we wish to see covered in negotiations remains the same as those put forward by the previous British Government in July 1967. For Euratom and

> the European Coal and Steel Community we seek only a very short transitional period. Adaptation to the obligations of the European Economic Community will clearly require more time than that. And it would be unrealistic not to face up to the fact, at the outset, that there are some very difficult problems to be solved. Our main problems, as you know, concern matters of agricultural policy; our contribution to Community budgetary expenditure; Commonwealth sugar exports; New Zealand's special problems; and certain other Commonwealth questions.
>
> The position which the previous British Government took in July 1967 was, of course, subject to developments in the Community in the meantime. Fisheries policy may prove to be one such development."

The response of the Communities was less dogmatic than its insistence on complete acceptance of existing decisions would have suggested. It revealed a recognition that some flexibility regarding the acquis communitaire would actually be required before Britain would be able to join, and defined the principles which would apply. On his last day as President of the Council of Ministers, M. Pierre Harmel set out the rules in his opening address to the conference in Luxembourg, including the following:

> "The rule which must necessarily govern the negotiations is that the solution of any problems of adjustment which may arise must be sought in the establishment of transitional measures and not in changes in the existing rules."
>
> "The object of the transitional measures will be to allow for the adjustments which prove to be necessary as a consequence of the enlargement. Their duration must be restricted to that required to achieve this aim. As a general rule, they must incorporate detailed timetables and must commence with an initial significant mutual tariff reduction on the entry into force of the accession treaties.
>
> "The transitional measures must be conceived in such a way as to ensure an overall balance of reciprocal advantages. [ie. Adequate synchronisation of the progress of freedom of movement of industrial goods with the achievement of the agricultural common market].

> "The enlarged Community must be ready to continue its policy of association, both as regards the existing associated African and Malagasy states and for the benefit of the independent African countries of comparable structure and level of development which request association; but the possible extension of the policy of association should not lead to a weakening of relations with the present associated states."

In addition there was an important condition that nothing would be left over for settlement after the candidates had entered the Community.

The wider political aspects to the conference were also not to be neglected. Harmel had started with a brief account of the history of integration:

> "The Council of Ministers is well aware that it is performing at a happily chosen moment, one of the fundamental acts which mark Europe's march towards its unification. A march, the first step of which was taken 24 years ago. This was on 19 September, 1946, at Zurich. The ruins of our old continent had hardly ceased smoking when Winston Churchill, the first to do so, spoke there of reconciliation. We must, he said, re-create the European Family, and provide it with a structure which could well be christened the `United States of Europe'."

He proceeded to summarise the achievements in integration from the Schumann plan onwards, and emphasised common aims concerning but at the same time going beyond the economic progress expected. Political objectives as defined in The Hague summit were reverently quoted. Finally, in contrast to the British position aimed at playing down differences he offered a more realistic assessment of the scale of the problem:

> "The task which awaits our negotiators is vast; the problems which they will have to solve are numerous and complex. But their efforts, and ours, will be sustained by a common political will to spare no effort to reach agreement in the shortest possible time. [The] Community will do everything in its power to achieve this end."

Negotiations were indeed detailed and complicated, but negotiators themselves were aware that ultimately they were peripheral and secondary. The fundamental question was political, and was to be answered by France.

Was France ready to admit as a partner a potential rival? And was Britain at last ready to act primarily as a *European* country? This was ultimately decided by President Pompidou, his mind only being finally made up at a private summit meeting with Edward Heath. This would determine whether "satisfactory" terms would ever be offered by the Community. Thus the decision had an important element relating to personality, including factors such as Heath's pro-European background, and his personal friendship with the man who became Pompidou's private secretary, M. Jobert. Many observers believed afterwards that Wilson would not have been able to show sufficient conviction to convince Pompidou.

Chapter F: National Law v European Law

Supremacy

Sometimes the principle of the Rule of Law enables an ordinary individual to stand up against the might of an entire national administration, sometimes on an issue of great principle and sometimes in settlement of merely mundane dispute. In a historic mixture of the two the citizens of Europe are indebted to a Mr. Costa of Milan who refused to pay his electricity bill and thus created the second pillar upholding the entire edifice of European Law. Mr. Costa had previously been a shareholder in the electricity company and the Italian government had passed laws which nationalised the entire industry. This, Mr. Costa argued, was contrary to the statutes of European Law, and hence ENEL (Ente Nazionale per l'Energia Elettrica) was illegally constituted and hence unable to enforce payment. The Italian government argued in court that since nationalisation had occurred after Italy's Ratification Act had incorporated European Law, the Italian court was obliged to apply the later domestic statute in precedence to European Law. The Italian court referred this question of conflict to the ECJ, in *Costa v ENEL* Case No 6/64, and judgement was delivered on 15th July, 1964.

First the Court repeated their earlier conclusions that the Treaty of Rome was unlike any previous international treaty, and again emphasises that Member States have transferred specific powers to the Community:

> *"By contrast with ordinary international treaties, the EEC treaty has created its own legal system which, on the entry into force of the treaty, became an integral part of the legal systems of the member states and which their courts are bound to apply.*
>
> *By creating a community of unlimited duration, having its own institutions, its own personality, its own legal capacity and capacity of representation on the international plane and, more particularly, real powers stemming from a limitation of sovereignty or a transfer of powers from the states to the community, the member states have limited their sovereign rights and have thus created a body of law which binds both their nationals and themselves."*

The judgement continues, using the Courts assumed authority to use not only the words of the Treaty, but to divine the purpose within the spirit of the Treaty:

> "The integration into the laws of each member state of provisions which derive from the community and more generally the terms and the **spirit** of the treaty, make it impossible for the states, as a corollary, to accord precedence to a unilateral and subsequent measure over a legal system accepted by them on a basis of reciprocity. Such a measure cannot therefore be inconsistent with that legal system. The law stemming from the treaty, an independent source of law, could not because of its special and original nature, be overridden by domestic legal provisions, however framed, without being deprived of its character as community law and without the legal basis of the community itself being called into question."

Therefore the ECJ speaks, with a historic conclusion from the above premises:

> **"The transfer by the states from their domestic legal system to the community legal system of the rights and obligations arising under the treaty carries with it a permanent limitation of their sovereign rights."**

Under English law, and that of most European countries the concept of "implied repeal" would have been applied. A later statute would be regarded as taking precedence over an earlier one, and in effect repealing the earlier measure. The ECJ here makes it more than clear, that no such concept can be applied at least in a national context, to any measure of European law. The Court again refers to its obligation to ensure the uniformity and effectiveness of European law, and states that any other decision in this case would have meant that European statues would become "merely contingent" on and could be "called into question" by national acts. This was not acceptable since European obligations were intended to be "unconditional." The direct applicability of regulations as quoted in Article 249 would be meaningless if States were entitled to negate it by enacting subsequent and inconsistent legislation.

Surprisingly it was not until March 1978 when the final nail in the coffin of resistance was forced into place again against Italian opposition. The issue concerned the imposition of veterinary inspections fees on meat being imported from France. The importing company Simmenthal spA., argued that the measure constituted a "measure having an equivalent effect to a quantitative restriction" on imports contrary to Article 28 concerning the free movement of goods. In fact the Italian court had already found in favour of the company but the Finance Administration appealed. This court found that there was a conflict between the Community legislation and the Italian regulations which would need to be resolved by the Italian constitutional court, but referred the issue to Europe.

In Case Number 106/77 *Amministrazione delle Finanze dello Stato v Simmenthal spA* the ECJ emphasised that:

> *"The direct applicability of Community law means that its rules must be fully and uniformly applied in all the Member States from the date of their entry into force and for so long as they continue in force. Directly applicable provisions are a direct source of rights and duties for all those affected thereby, whether Member States or individuals; this consequence also concerns any national court whose task it is as an organ of a member to protect the rights conferred upon individuals by Community law.*
>
> *Any recognition that national legislative measures which encroach upon the field within which the Community exercises its legislative power or which are otherwise incompatible with the provisions of Community law had any legal effect would amount to a corresponding denial of the effectiveness of obligations undertaken unconditionally and irrevocably by Member States pursuant to the Treaty and would thus imperil the very foundations of the Community.*
>
> *A national court which is called upon, within the limits of its jurisdiction, to apply provisions of Community law is under a duty to give full effect to those provisions, if necessary refusing of its own motion to apply any conflicting provision of national legislation, even if adopted subsequently, and it is not necessary for the court to request or await the prior setting aside of such provisions by legislative or other constitutional means."*

Thus the ECJ held that national courts must uphold the provisions of European law against ANY conflicting statute of national law, immediately, and without consulting a superior court even if the issue is one of constitutional impact which would otherwise require interventions of a constitutional court.

Conclusion

The combination supremacy with the concepts of direct and indirect effects described above ensures that a Community Directive will be enforced throughout the EU, by national courts irrespective of the actions or inactions of national parliaments. Furthermore when combined with the doctrine of supremacy it becomes clear that these parliaments have become irrelevant as far as Directives (and Regulations) are concerned. According to the ECJ they no longer possess power to change any part of such measures.

Of course the ECJ made it clear that the voluntary limitation of national sovereignty implied by these conclusions applies only in limited fields. These areas were defined by the original Treaty, as indicated in an earlier section. They may be listed as follows:

Measures establishing the Common Market
(Customs Union, Free Movement of Goods, People,
Services, & Capital; Commercial Policy; Competition)
Measures implementing common policies
(Agriculture, Transport)
Equal Pay without discrimination based on sex.

Many other articles, particularly those of Title III concerning Social Policy contain several, broadly described objectives. For example the original Article 117 states that Member States "agree upon the need to promote improved working conditions and an improved standard of living for workers." Such generalities could clearly not imply any intention to create legally binding agreements, even though they could and did later form the basis of binding Regulations. Only the equal pay requirement could be construed in this way since under this Article 119, "Each Member State shall....ensure and subsequently maintain the application of the principle that men and women should receive equal pay for equal work." and this imperative is followed by definitions. Consequently although the principle of direct application was of enormous importance its scope was indeed limited, and therefore its emergence created little impact.

Nevertheless the European Court of Justice had spoken again. **"European Community Law is Supreme over ANY national legislation, and must be immediately enforced by a national court."**

Chapter 14: Negotiations – Process and Progress.

Much Ado

The details regarding the accession negotiations of 1970 have been recorded in remarkable, exhaustive detail by the leader of the British delegation at official level, Con O'Neill. This dossier provides a comprehensive account of all aspects of these discussions including negotiating objectives and tactics on all sides, analysis and resolution of each critical issue, results from each significant meeting, the conduct and attitude of each participant and a review of the successes, failures and mistakes. Only the briefest summary is included here.

The 1967 "Conference between Member States of the European Communities and other States which have applied for membership of the Communities" had by 1970 become .the "Conference between the Communities and the States which have applied for membership of the Communities". Perhaps this was the result of a small but significant shift in constitutional thinking contending that now the Community had its own separate identity, and was not merely an organisation of separate states. Alternatively it may have been a purely tactical response to the realisation that last time Britain had frequently succeeded in dividing the Six. In either event this time the Six had felt that the "Community" should be negotiating.

This consensus among the Member States had several curious consequences for procedure from their side, since although the Six wanted the "Community" to conduct the negotiations none of them were ready to delegate any responsibility. This was particularly apparent in the formal meetings. It rapidly became the rule that only the President spoke for the Community side. O'Neill relates how the permanent representative of The Netherlands once ventured a few words when not in the chair. He was roundly chastised by the French and the rule was never to be broken again. Nobody else spoke from the Community side unless a few words were invited by the President. O'Neill also remarked, almost with humour, that their insistence that they spoke only with one voice meant that they couldn't speak at all until they had decided among themselves what the voice was to say. This meant that dialogue was impossible. Very frequently the British would withdraw while the Community reaction was decided, and if reference to governments was required this could take months. Thus all the formal meetings tended to be remarkably short. O'Neill suggests that not one of the meetings between the leader of the British delegation, Geoffrey Rippon and his ministerial counterparts lasted more than one hour. Another aspect also became clear very quickly. The Commission, although voicing the collective opinion was not to speak on its own account, or for the benefit of the conference of two sides, but as a servant of the Six Member States. It was also, at first anyway, not permitted to communicate directly with the British except for matters of "information or clarification".

Another consequence of the Six's difficulty in negotiating with a single but dependant voice was that the Community never took the initiative in proposing solutions for a given issue, and were reduced to reacting to, or negotiating on the basis of, an agenda or a specific proposal submitted by the British side. However, every eventual agreement was formally recorded as a response to a final community proposal resulting from a summing-up. They could not say the first word, so they were that much more keen to have the last one.

In fact this tactic did not, according to O'Neill, serve the community well. The British side was very well organised, and lobbying through the various embassies, and through ministerial and other unofficial contacts was very closely co-ordinated. Thus one negotiating tactic was used on a number of occasions when the expected Community position was not likely to be acceptable. This especially arose when the French were pressing a hard position and the Five were inclined to concede simply in order to make progress. In order to avoid this and so as not to present Britain as obstructive, pressure was exerted to influence particular delegations aimed at preventing the consensus from being reached. "If we were unlikely to get a reasonable proposal we wanted the crisis on each subject to be within the Six rather than between the Six and ourselves". Frequently the British still managed to divide the Six. According to O'Neill this certainly helped us "in representing ourselves as seeking, not so much our own protection and advantage, as Community solutions to Community problems."

Thus to a large extent the British were able to control the agenda, if not the progress, which was more effectively controlled by the French. This allowed judicious selection of the issues, and careful thought given tactically to the optimum time for raising each one. For example, it was felt that although the contribution to the Community budget was critical, early concentration on mere monetary matters would not create a suitably positive environment of co-operation, and would detract from our ability to demonstrate our true commitment to broader European ideals. Similarly some issues were deliberately neglected until near the end, so that they would be regarded as peripheral to important issues already resolved, and the negotiating process itself would have gathered it own momentum towards completion. Relatively small issues which could raise important issues of principle could be best left to a final clearing up exercise. One example was the decision which enabled the Channel Islands and the Isle of Man to maintain access to the Common Market, without the treaties or the acquis communitaire applying to them. Obtaining such access effectively without membership would have been unthinkable in the initial stages.

The British had also determined and the Community agreed, that negotiations should proceed in parallel on the various issues. This meant that although the overall attitudes of co-operation were important in the background, and the overall balance of compromise under scrutiny, there were few instances of benefits of one issue being traded for advantages in an unrelated area. The most important exception to this occurred during the critical summit between Edward Heath and President Pompidou, May 1971. Amid the pomp and ceremony of a formal visit extensive private talks were conducted between the two men, aimed at removing the major obstacles remaining in the negotiations. This meeting was very successful in repairing Anglo-French relations and in removing any remaining fears of the two parties. However in the present context the important point was that there was to be a definite trade-off between the final New Zealand solution and the British budgetary contribution.

Control of the agenda was by no means complete, and of serious concern had been the fact that some Community policies were still developing in the normal course of Community business. The most important of these was the Common Fisheries Policy which had only just been introduced but had not been defined. This was contentious because theoretically at least candidates, were required to accept all policies as they were up until the time of joining, even if they were still forming during the negotiations. For the candidates this was regrettable but generally a necessary price to be paid. Fisheries though, was of critical importance especially to Norway who proposed participation in the Community discussions regarding formation of the policy. This idea that a non-member could participate was seen as heretical by the Six, and treated with derision. Instead there were separate discussions between the Six and each candidate. Although these eventually had the same formative effect on the policy they made this issue the most hotly disputed, and the last to be resolved. It also led to Norway eventually deciding not to join.

Tactical Success

According to O'Neill the overriding strategic objective was to sign a satisfactory Treaty of Accession by the end of 1971, so that full membership would begin on 1st January 1973. This date was chosen to suit the government's broader political objectives, giving sufficient time for membership to be established and operating satisfactorily before the next general election. Working back for this date it was decided and agreed with the Six to work towards resolving all the most important issues by the summer of 1971. The British were well aware that their need for this relatively rigid timetable would be reflected as a tactical disadvantage. They knew that the French in particular would be guided by an understandable intention to squeeze every advantage out of the British desire for early progress. No doubt they calculated that by going slow initially they could induce the impatient British to make concessions.

O'Neill recalls how extraordinarily well informed his delegation was regarding the attitudes and negotiating positions. Embassies in the Six capitals constantly provided important background details, while friendly delegations amongst the Six kept Britain informed. This was also due, in no small measure to John Robinson whose long appointment in Brussels now bore fruit. It was said that during the negotiations he "knew everyone, understood everything, foresaw everything, did everything". The briefing dossiers he produced on the thinking of the French or other negotiators were as though "he bugged their offices".

Other tactical considerations were determined by the public openness of the talks. Disputes or developments within the Community very rapidly leaked and became public knowledge. It became impossible to conceal anything, particularly something which was discussed at a formal session. Consequently the handling of the Press became of considerable importance. Every time therefore, the British released Press briefing papers to ensure that their version, in preference to an unfavourably slanted or simply garbled version, became available immediately. Of course private discussions were still possible in the corridors outside the formal conference, with the aim of resolving a particular issue before the Press had an opportunity to make it controversial. Several issues, where resolution was confidently expected but which were capable of raising public anxiety were thus dealt with as privately as possible. The outcome was then announced in the conference and duly reported in a factual and harmless manner. O'Neill suggested that by these means the potential disruptive effect of the Press was contained. Provision of more than ample information on numerous highly technical subjects and an inability to monitor the real progress bored many of the correspondents. This, in turn led them to be satisfied, particularly towards the end, with questionable or fairly superficial information.

The characteristic openness also influenced domestic activity. Parties likely to be affected by the decisions would soon know about any proposals being discussed, and were ready to complain loudly and publicly about any detriment they could foresee, particularly if it represented an unexpected development. Therefore the British undertook widespread and regular consultations with Commonwealth governments, EFTA members, and representatives of all sectors of the economy. They were informed about the likely outcome, as well as the present position and the negotiating steps being taken. The interests of all affected parties were therefore taken into account and the opportunities for opposition successfully contained.

On the positive side, the open character of the proceedings discouraged all parties from employing excessively devious, dishonest or diversionary tactics. All involved had to behave sensibly and reasonably. Nevertheless, the need to maintain a positive public image imposed several unwelcome restraints. For example, looking back at the numerous interested parties, it was important not to make any excessive demands in the early stages since any subsequent concession would be interpreted as a failure. On some occasions, eg. budgetary contributions, unrealistic opening bids were made, but these were always as a deliberate and well considered tactical response to particular circumstances, and this general rule held. Similarly, looking at British negotiating opponents, it was important not to make proposals which went too far beyond what was anticipated as an eventual outcome. On the other hand having made a reasonable proposal it was just as important to stick to it as long as possible and avoid becoming engaged in a progression of descending compromises.

O'Neill also makes the thoughtful comment that, in contrast to the previous negotiations luck frequently favoured the British application this time. One example he quotes is the unexpected turn around of the British economy, and in particular an unusual strength in the balance of payments. This, combined with a dramatic reduction in the country's indebtedness dispelled any doubts the Community used to harbour regarding Britain's ability to contribute sufficiently, and to avoid becoming either a Community burden or a drag on its future development. Similarly, the disappearance of the Community butter mountain, and the unusual appearance of a world butter shortage greatly facilitated an agreement over New Zealand. Finally he mentions that stability in the governments of the Six resulted in few interruptions to the general progress, and that those changes which did occur were almost invariably favourable.

This time the result seemed destined to be different.

Chapter 15: Negotiations – Results.

The ultimate conclusion after all the meetings, thoughts of tactics etc., was actually very close to the initial Community doctrine that everything be accepted unless a compelling case for mitigation was presented. Many such mitigations, modifications and adaptations, usually of secondary importance, were eventually agreed by means of exceptional measures almost always valid just for transitional periods only, though in a small number of cases open to possible prolongation or further modification by later agreement after entry. The most important areas of contention defined by George Brown and repeated by Anthony Barber produced the following results.

1. Tariffs & Trade.
Central to the whole concept of the "Common Market" was the elimination of tariff barriers throughout the Community. This should not be confused with the more general concept of "free trade" as traditionally favoured by the British. Although the Community maintains a single, tariff free market, it introduced a Common Tariff Barrier applying to imports from outside the Community. The single market is therefore inherently protectionist. This is most noticeable in the agricultural field where producers are paid prices well above world levels, as a means of obtaining permanent security of food supply. This amounts to the "Community Preference" condition, which involves manipulation of the market by a complex arrangement of intervention prices, threshold prices, quotas, and levies. The mechanism is different and variable for each product group.

This is one area where Britain's interests did not coincide with the other candidates for entry. Denmark was an important agricultural supplier and favoured more rapid introduction of the Common Agricultural Policy. Ireland was in a similar position. The Irish though were highly dependant on access to the British market in general, and for many years there had been a free trade agreement between the two countries. Their Ministers had admitted that the whole justification for Ireland's joining was that they could continue to supply the British market, but now at the much higher Community prices.

The British aim in the negotiations was to minimise disruption at home and provide some temporary protection to its traditional suppliers by means of a transition period. The principles involved had been accepted. Separate transition periods for industrial and agricultural goods (five or six years) were agreed. Stepped changes leading to the dismantling of tariffs on industrial goods, the immediate introduction of "Community Preference" with phased out tariffs and a phased in adjustment to Community price levels were the features of a complex and tightly defined agreement.

2. Commonwealth Sugar

The basic problem in this area was that Britain had committed itself to the import of sugar from various Commonwealth producers until 1974. At the same time the actual amount of sugar to be imported (approximately 1.8M tons), was similar to the current level of overproduction in the Community. The issues to be resolved concerned the transition period, but more seriously the effects on British balance of payments, and the fact that several of the sugar producing countries concerned were economically very dependant on sugar and needed protection beyond the formal expiry date. This issue became one of the most complex to negotiate because of the large number of Commonwealth countries and other interested parties involved, as well as their differing interests.

Britain was allowed to honour its commitments under the agreement, and also for the following year, when the whole subject of sugar, (and a few other commodities) would be considered when the Community's existing arrangements under the Yaounde Convention were due to be reviewed. The Commission had said it was prepared to suggest guaranteed quotas for the period after 1975, but because of the uncertainties in the market, these could only be low. They regarded such an exercise as "inopportune". Therefore, Britain had the task of selling the deal to the producers on the basis of trust in the Community of Ten. Grudging acceptance was eventually obtained, and in the event the Community did indeed agree under the subsequent Lome Convention, preferential access amounting to 1.2M tons at prices close to the Community level, and well above the prevailing world level.

3. New Zealand Trade

Con O'Neill expresses the opinion that the most successful figure in all of the complex accession negotiations was Mr. Marshall, the Deputy Prime Minister of New Zealand, and its Minister for Overseas Trade. His report is unstinting in his admiration for his professionalism, his persistence, and his determination. He is full of praise for the gentlemanly, but ruthless New Zealand tactics employed and for their brilliant organisation, even though this caused the British considerable difficulty and anguish. Then while recording that the result was unduly generous and extravagantly favourable to New Zealand he regrets that the final cost to British was higher than the benefit the New Zealanders obtained.

The fundamental problem was the extent of New Zealand dairy (and to a lesser extent lamb) industry on the British market. This amounted to 34% of total New Zealand exports, although this proportion had been falling over the recent years. It was much higher than the comparable figures for Australia and Canada. In consequence New Zealand accounted for 40% of Britain's butter requirement, and 56% of cheddar cheese imports. There was also an excess of supply within the Community, and the close interest of Irish and Danish producers in the overall market to be considered.

The situation was comparable to the Commonwealth sugar issue but differed in two important respects. Firstly, protection by price adjustments to maintain values of trade rather than volumes was not acceptable to New Zealand in view of the costs and social consequences of scaling down their dairy industry. Secondly, was the highly effective lobbying by New Zealand throughout Europe, right across the political spectrum in Britain, and in the media. Some of the tone of New Zealand pleading can be summarised by Marshall's statement that having been faced with "sudden death", discussions regarding transition periods now concern "slow strangulation".

The New Zealanders had long prepared for this eventuality and had already made considerable progress in diversifying their exports. In addition the Community practice of dumping butter from their famous mountain into other New Zealand markets was beginning to abate, and as world dairy production was becoming more balanced prices were beginning to rise. Nevertheless their politicians worked very effectively to secure their position in Britain. Thus O'Neill reports that the British, although occasionally briefing the Press, discreetly, on some of the realities of the New Zealand case, the British team could never credibly suggest that the New Zealanders did not deserve the fullest possible support. Duncan Sandys himself told the French Prime Minister in May 1971 that, although he believed passionately in European unity, he would find it impossible to support an agreement which betrayed New Zealand's trust in Britain. He continued by making a point which was to become a real fear amongst the British negotiating team, "Without a generous arrangement for New Zealand ... no settlement, however satisfactory on other points, would stand a chance of being approved by Parliament." According to O'Neill this was probably true. The team realised that expert manoeuvring by New Zealand had positioned Britain nicely over a political barrel.

The final agreement contained none of the bland assurances applied to the sugar producers. It included detailed volumes for each year, methods of calculating the prices, and institutional arrangements for making of decisions after the five year transition period. One important figure from the final tightly specific agreement demonstrates their success. The British had originally believed that a transition period leading to a future guarantee of 45% of current volumes would be just acceptable. Later, the embassy reported that 60% would be required politically since the government's electoral position had to be considered. The final result amounted to 71% (measured by milk equivalent) of current volumes by 1977, with an added bonus of especially small reductions at the beginning of the transition period.

4. Community Finance

Discussions involving hard cash have a unique capacity for arousing intense feelings. These negotiations were no different. Certainly the scale of the issue made arguments worthwhile. The Community budget for 1973 was £1,400M, and projected to rise. Clearly each 1% contribution was worth £14M. In addition, the method of financing agreed after 1969 was that most of the proceeds of customs duties and agricultural levies automatically became the property of the Community. An additional element amounting to 1% of VAT receipts, was never controversial because of its equitable nature.

From the British viewpoint there was inherent detriment in this financing system, although it was clear from the beginning that it would have to be accepted. Firstly, not only would Britain have to pay higher prices for its food whatever its source, but if produce was from outside the Community it would have to impose a levy and then pay 90% of this extra to the Community. Proceeds from duties were also payable to the Community budget. Thus Britain, as a major importer generally would have correspondingly greater duties and levies compared with other Members, and hence its contributions would be disproportionately high.

Secondly it was known that 90% of Community expenditure was absorbed by the Common Agricultural Policy. This was designed to favour the major producing Members, particularly France, and so the receipts to be expected by Britain were correspondingly low.

Because of this profound bias, although never accepted as such by the Community, the negotiations instead centred on specific figures to define the British nett contribution. This was a process of pure but extended haggling described in each intricate step by O'Neill. Britain argued that the financial questions should not be treated differently from other highly important matters. Thus, the fair share should be calculated, and then subject to factors determining the transition period. Thus Britain's opening bid was that a contribution of 13-15% should be paid after a five year transition period. Negotiators had not expected the logic of their suggestion to be accepted but they had underestimated the serious negative impact of proposing a first year contribution of less than 3%. Shortly afterwards President Pompidou was one of the most calm of the critics across Europe. "One must admit that the British have three qualities amongst others: humour, tenacity and realism. I have the feeling that we are still slightly in the humorous stage." The French proposed a flat contribution of 21.5%; and this impasse lasted for many months while discussions continued behind the scene.

The eventual outcome, explicitly tied to the New Zealand result, was for contributions of 8.64% in year one, rising to 18.92% in 1977.

5. Fisheries Policy

The Common Fisheries Policy was agreed in outline only on the first day of the accession negotiations. Nevertheless it established the principles that there would two parallel aspects – a common market for fish, and common access to fishing grounds, including national waters, "up to the beach". This issue became the most highly charges political issue due more to the emotional appeal of the industry and its occurrence right around the coast, rather than its economic importance. It also led to the most serious disputes among the candidate countries, and particularly with Norway who held out till the very last day for a better deal. It was also notable that in both Britain and Norway initial assessments had concluded that the policy would be marginally beneficial from a economical standpoint. This was because of the access to the wider market. For Norway and Denmark especially, as major fish exporters, free access to the Community market was of the highest importance; and if this were coupled with marketing rules which would help to maintain the price of fish it would be a major benefit. For Norway in particular this industry had social and employment significance which was very real indeed. Immense stretches of the Norwegian coastline, especially the northern half, were peopled almost entirely by small and isolated communities which depended almost entirely on fishing. This dependence was even greater than in the closest British equivalent of the Shetland Islands.

However, in all fishing countries rational consideration had been washed away by the political reaction to access provisions. At the same time requests for consultation during the continuing formation of policy details between the Six were brusquely rejected. The Community strategy was to finalise a policy in its own interests and then offer very limited concessions to Britain and Ireland with further measures to meet special problems of Norway, and of Denmark with respect to its Faroe Islands and Greenland. In this area the British did not enjoy the high level of preparation which had generally served so well, and negotiators were slow to realise how sensitive the issue would become. Not only did the candidate countries become divided but in Britain there was an important split between the trawler and the inshore fishing sectors; the latter having most to fear. Access to Norwegian coastal waters would benefit trawlermen, but access to British areas would damage the inshore industry.

The final result was that exclusive national fishing limits would stretch for six miles from the coast and last for ten years. Twelve mile limits would be allowed in areas with particular problems which included the Orkney and Shetland Islands, some areas of the Scottish Coast and the North-East Coast, Cornwall and Devon. The negotiators were pleased with their results and described their achievement, as amounting to `no change at all in the protection now afforded in areas from which about 95 per cent by value of the total inshore catch is taken'. This did not prevent protests being received from numerous quarters, which were so vocal that the whole settlement remained controversial.

Summary

It is important to remember two crucial aspects to these negotiations. Firstly they did not concern any of the larger political questions. Subjects such as future integration and governance, development of Community institutions, international relationships, were well beyond the remit of the conference. However, the conference only took place at all because leaders of the Six, and in particular President Pompidou, were finally convinced that Britain was ready to bring a constructive European attitude to all such questions in the future. This meant that all of these negotiations were really nothing more than a complex commercial deal, and a prelude to the more fundamental issues on the horizon. This chapter, as the negotiations themselves, followed the Wilson strategy of discussing details in order to divert attention from the questions of principle.

In some cases larger issues were deliberately played down. Towards the close of the negotiations, several sections of the Community wanted Britain to acknowledge unambiguously in the formal agreement the supremacy of Community law over our own national law. O'Neill commented that this was superfluous since this was an implicit and underlying condition of membership, and it would be expedient to leave the issue obscured by the detail. Any specific statement would have *"drawn public attention in an unwelcome manner to a delicate issue."*

Secondly, the results show how firmly the Community succeeded in sticking to existing policies, and how Britain was obliged to accept many which it regarded as unpalatable. The transition periods were precisely that, and therefore looked at in a longer term context, the negotiations, hard fought thought they certainly were, amounted to nothing more than a complete and diverting irrelevance. Perhaps not now, but certainly within ten years Britain would indeed have "swallowed the lot".

Thus, the job was done. The Treaty of Accession was prepared. It listed and defined in complete detail the extent of all the instances when the Acquis Communitaire would be adapted, modified or eased, almost invariably on a temporary basis, allowing the candidate countries to join. Last minute delays meant that it was not signed until 22 January, 1972. Three days later the European Communities Bill was introduced and had its first reading in the House of Commons.

Chapter G: The Law and the Treaty of Rome

Treaty-Making Powers

The legal effect of the government signing an international treaty differs between Britain and much of Europe. In France and Italy, for example, any obligations under international law once assumed by the executive branch of the government enter immediately into their legal systems, without any domestic legislation. Such obligations will even take precedence over national law. In Britain such a conclusion has never been accepted since it would breach the concept of the sovereignty of Parliament. In fact, treaty making powers had long been part of the royal prerogative, and so had been modified by the Acts of 1688. Consequently in 1876 when Queen Victoria signed a treaty with the emperor of China and the issue was raised in the courts (in *Rustomjee v Reginam)*, the court replied,

> "She [ie the Queen] acted throughout the making of the treaty and in relation to each and every of its stipulations in her sovereign character, and by her own inherent authority; and, as in making the treaty, so in performing the treaty, she is beyond the control of municipal law, and her acts are not to be examined in her own Courts."

Thus the courts had no authority to question this prerogative power. On the other hand they were also under no obligation to take notice of any provisions of the treaty, since their only duty was to uphold law as enacted by Parliament.

This means that there is instead a dual existence of separate, independent systems for international and domestic legislation. The Government may be bound by the terms of its treaty, but bodies within the country would not be affected. This is a principle which Britain had exported to those countries which had gained their independence from its Empire, as an essential constraint to executive power. Consequently it was in the Empire that the doctrine was most carefully examined.

Accordingly the definitive statement of this dualist principle actually derives from a case of 1937 (*Attorney General for Canada v Attorney General Ontario*) when the highest court of the Empire, the Privy Council in London, was called upon to resolve a constitutional dispute between the central Dominion Government and the Provinces. The provinces were challenging legislation resulting from Canada's joining of the International Labour Organisation. The Lord Atkin speaking for the Privy Council held,

> *"There is a well established rule that the making of a Treaty is an executive act, while the performance of its obligations, if they entail alteration of the existing domestic law, requires legislative action.*
>
> *Unlike some other countries, the stipulations of a treaty duly ratified do not within the Empire, by virtue of the treaty alone, have the force of law. If the national executive, the government of the day, decide to incur the obligations of a treaty which involve alteration of law they have to run the risk of obtaining the assent of Parliament to the necessary statute or statutes. To make themselves as secure as possible they will often in such cases before final ratification seek to obtain from Parliament an expression of approval. But it has never been suggested, and it is not the law, that such an expression of approval operates as law, or that in law it precludes the assenting Parliament, or any subsequent Parliament, from refusing to give its sanction to any legislative proposals that may subsequently be brought before it. Parliament, no doubt, as the Chief Justice points out, has a constitutional control over the executive: but it cannot be disputed that the creation of the obligations undertaken in treaties and the assent to their form and quality are the function of the executive alone. Once they are created, while they bind the State as against the other contracting parties, Parliament may refuse to perform them and so leave the State in default."*

The same limitation extends to the courts. In a judgement of 1990 (*Tin Council* case) Lord Templeman confirmed that courts have no power "To invent laws or to misconstrue legislation in order to enforce a treaty." The application of this principle was actually seen in relation to proposed membership of the Common Market. In a case of 1969 (*R v Home Secretary ex parte McWhirter*), Mr. McWhirter sought a declaration from the courts that joining the EC would be contrary to the Bill of Rights of 1689. He argued that all powers of the government are vested in the Crown and Parliament and could not be transferred by means of a treaty. The then Master of the Rolls, the colourful character Lord Denning, appeared to agree but stated that, "Even though the Treaty of Rome has been signed, it has no effect as far as the courts are concerned until implemented by Act of Parliament. Until that day, we take no notice of it."

This comment did not address the question of whether an Act of Parliament could indeed effect such a permanent transfer. The point is that there is ultimately a contradiction between the two basic tenets. A Parliament cannot logically have unlimited legal power, while also being prevented from binding its successors. There are two aspects to remember here. Firstly, in practical and political terms Parliamentary sovereignty is in fact limited since valid law is of no real value and effect if it could not be enforced. This was shown to be the case in constitutional disputes which followed from the transfer of sovereignty from Westminster to Dominion Parliaments in Australia, Canada, Eire, New Zealand and South Africa. Secondly, tt would appear that the duty of the courts is to uphold any Statute properly passed by Parliament in any case before it, and without considering a hypothetical aspect such as the Act's future applicability. A new Statute will therefore be enforced over an older contradictory one, without considering Parliament's previous intention. The present intention takes precedence.

The Treaty of Rome

It was in 1971 when Mr. Albert Blackburn opened a legal challenge to the government's plan to join the common market. He was seeking a declaration from the courts to the effect that, by signing the Treaty of Rome, Her Majesty's government would be surrendering in part the sovereignty of the Crown in Parliament and would surrender it for ever. He says that in so doing the government will be acting in breach of the law.

The leading judgement was again that of Lord Denning. He opened with a description of the case against signing the Treaty of Rome.

> *"Much of what Mr Blackburn says is quite correct. It does appear that if this country should go into the Common Market and sign the Treaty of Rome, it means that we will have taken a step which is irreversible. The sovereignty of these islands will thenceforward be limited. It will not be ours alone but will be shared with others. Mr Blackburn referred us to a decision by the European Court of Justice, Costa v ENEL in February 1964, in which the court in its judgment said: '... the member-States, albeit within limited*

> *spheres, have restricted their sovereign rights and created a body of law applicable both to their nationals and to themselves.'*
>
> *Mr Blackburn points out that many regulations made by the European Economic Community will become automatically binding on the people of this country; and that all the courts of this country, including the House of Lords, will have to follow the decisions of the European Court in certain defined respects, such as the construction of the treaty.*

Lord Denning next appears to reflect the British courts' traditional or even stubborn refusal to pronounce on "hypothetical" issues.

> *"Negotiations are still in progress for us to join the Common Market. No agreement has been reached. No treaty has been signed. Even if a treaty is signed, it is elementary that these courts take no notice of treaties as such. We take no notice of treaties until they are embodied in laws enacted by Parliament, and then only to the extent that Parliament tells us."*

Next he comments on treaty making prerogatives.

> *"Mr Blackburn acknowledged the general principle, but he urged that this proposed treaty is in a category by itself, in that it diminishes the sovereignty of Parliament over the people of this country. I cannot accept the distinction. The general principle applies to this treaty as to any other. The treaty-making power of this country rests not in the courts, but in the Crown; that is, Her Majesty acting on the advice of her Ministers. When her Ministers negotiate and sign a treaty, even a treaty of such paramount importance as this proposed one, they act on behalf of the country as a whole. They exercise the prerogative of the Crown. Their action in so doing cannot be challenged or questioned in these courts."*

Finally, the question of Parliamentary sovereignty is addressed.

> *"Mr Blackburn takes a second point. He says that, if Parliament should implement the treaty by passing an Act of Parliament for this purpose, it will seek to do the impossible. It will seek to bind its successors. According to the treaty, once it is signed, we are committed to it*

> *irrevocably. Once in the Common Market, we cannot withdraw from it. No Parliament can commit us, says Mr Blackburn, to that extent. He prays in aid the principle that no Parliament can bind its successors, and that any Parliament can reverse any previous enactment.*
>
> *We have all been brought up to believe that, in legal theory, one Parliament cannot bind another and that no Act is irreversible. But legal theory does not always march alongside political reality. Take the Statute of Westminster 1931, which takes away the power of Parliament to legislate for the dominions. Can anyone imagine that Parliament could or would reverse that statute? Take the Acts which have granted independence to the dominions and territories overseas. Can anyone imagine that Parliament could or would reverse those laws and take away their independence? Most clearly not. Freedom once given cannot be taken away. Legal theory must give way to practical politics."*

In closing Lord Denning concludes that it is not the business of the courts to attempt to bind or restrict Parliament.

> *"What are the realities here? If Her Majesty's Ministers sign this treaty and Parliament enacts provisions to implement it, I do not envisage that Parliament would afterwards go back on it and try to withdraw from it. But, if Parliament should do so, then I say we will consider that event when it happens. We will then say whether Parliament can lawfully do it or not*
>
> *So, whilst in theory Mr Blackburn is quite right in saying that no Parliament can bind another, and that any Parliament can reverse what a previous Parliament has done, nevertheless so far as this court is concerned, I think we will wait until that day comes. We will not pronounce on it today."*

The other two Law Lords, while accepting the conclusions of Lord Denning were more emphatic regarding the lack of role of the courts in the decision making process. Lord Justice Salmon stated,

> *"Whilst I recognise the undoubted sincerity of Mr Blackburn's views, I deprecate litigation the purpose of which is to influence political decisions. Such decisions*

> *have nothing to do with these courts. These courts are concerned only with the effect of such decisions if and when they have been implemented by legislation. Nor have the courts any power to interfere with the treaty-making power of the Sovereign. As to Parliament, in the present state of the law, it can enact, amend and repeal any legislation it pleases. The sole power of the courts is to decide and enforce what is the law and not what it should be—now, or in the future."*

Similarly Lord Justice Stamp was more concerned with the separation of state powers and again of the limited power of the courts regarding hypothetical concepts.

> *"I agree that the appeal should be dismissed; but I would express no view whatsoever on the legal implications of this country becoming a party to the Treaty of Rome. In the way Mr Blackburn put it I think he confused the division of the powers of the Crown, Parliament and the courts. The Crown enters into treaties; Parliament enacts laws; and it is the duty of this court in proper cases to interpret those laws when made; but it is no part of this court's function or duty to make declarations in general terms regarding the powers of Parliament, more particularly where the circumstances in which the court is asked to intervene are purely hypothetical. Nor ought this court at the suit of one of Her Majesty's subjects to make declarations regarding the undoubted prerogative power of the Crown to enter into treaties."*

Chapter 16: The First Battle

Battle Tactics of Edward Heath

For British membership of the EEC to begin on 1st January 1973, the European Communities Act had to become law in 1972. The Government had published its White Paper in 1971 and political positions had begun to solidify. The central figure was undoubtedly Edward Heath, with his unwavering belief in the benefits of the EEC, and his life's ambition to obtain British entry. Such determination was not to be impeded by inconvenient facts or traditional sentiments. Heath may have appeared a quiet and uninspiring gentleman but he remained a highly accomplished politician who pursued his aim with a ruthless, single minded concentration.

The controversial issues surrounding the question of membership were undoubtedly the political ones, and these had to be avoided as much as possible. Debate therefore concentrated on the effect on jobs and trade, and on Britain's new opportunities. These would be the government's chosen battlegrounds.

From a viewpoint more objective than politicians were able to adopt at the time, (or since), there is considerable justification for such omissions. Britain was being forced by the political and economic realities of the world to re-align its foreign policies generally. A greater emphasis on Europe was unavoidable, and actual membership would activate a more effective platform. There was also a real possibility that Britain's fading economic power would be shored up in a collective Europe, at a time when the political nature of the EEC, still with "Economic" in its very title, was distinctly uncertain. This was a view of the politics in Europe which seemed tenable but was probably designed to be misleading. Progress towards integration was often faltering as members struggled to protect or maximise the interests of their own economies, but all the Six governments broadly supported European integration and more importantly, so did their people. European opinion polls in 1970 showed majority support with just 9% opposition to concepts including a United States of Europe, a directly elected parliament, and common foreign, defence and economic policies. Two quotations typified the contrary view presented in Britain. "The more one studies the way in which Europe is working out, the less likely it is that there will be a close-knit federation". "There is no political unity among the Six and the likelihood is that there will not be for a generation"

This convenient image of future political development did not represent the honest view of Edward Heath. Speaking later, in 1992, he contemptuously derided those who were suggesting that the political developments then appearing were new and unwelcome developments. "From the first, the Community was political. It is still political. It will always be political." However, his stated position in 1972 was slightly different. He never adopted the strategy of denial explained above, but instead and at most suggested that the politics of integration was benign. The paper for future development was described as blank and thus open to British ideas and contributions. This was so even though these ideas were obviously quite contrary to the stated long term intentions of the Community, and the opinions of its people. Even specific developments like the recent commitment of the Six to "economic and monetary union" by 1980 were overlooked, and even though all of these policies were in fact being accepted by the Treaty of Accession. "What we shall have is an opportunity which we do not possess and will not possess unless we join, of working out schemes for the future of the major part of Europe".

The issue of sovereignty, which had haunted the minds of previous politicians was also handled in a manner which amounts to the deceptive. Heath's White Paper of 1971 says "There is no question of any erosion of essential national sovereignty. What is proposed is a sharing and an enlargement of individual national sovereignties in the general interest." The verbal obfuscation was clearly deliberate. Whether the supremacy of European Law would be regarded as a breach of "essential" or of some lesser variety of sovereignty was not explained. Similarly, whether in logic something could be shared and enlarged while retaining its individuality was pedantic. "No erosion" was the operative phrase, the critical "sound bite" of the day; whether accurate or not.

Subsequently, Ministers were never be drawn to admit that EEC law would take precedence over national statutes and judgments. Of course the Minister responsible for the drafting of the Act, Geoffrey Howe, himself a respected lawyer knew the consequences perfectly well. He simply had to play down the issue suggesting that whenever conflict might appear the courts would just have to do their best to reconcile the "inescapable and enduring sovereignty of Parliament" with the need to give effect to Treaty obligations. He failed to mention that actually the solution would be to over-rule Parliament. Later, he was able to admit that, "Less of our thinking than was appropriate was explicitly exposed to the House of Commons".

Such thinking was also kept well away from the electorate. In the academic world, where such legal "technicalities" were bound to be noticed, ministers and officials continued to emphasise the inviolate continuity of the common law and the unfettered independence of English courts and judges, even though in fact and well known to all concerned, the latter in particular was about to be fatally compromised.

Those civil servants responsible for drafting the legislation also knew very well what was involved. They were simply instructed to tread carefully knowing that any open admission of what was being done to parliamentary sovereignty would be "so astounding" as to put the whole Bill in danger. Never would it be admitted that in practice membership was expected to be irrevocable, and thus contrary to the fundamental constitutional premise that one Parliament cannot bind a subsequent one. Never was it explained that Parliament was surrendering some of its independence to the clauses of a written constitution, and subject to a distant but binding judiciary.

Firm and inspiring leadership might have encouraged Heath to say that the outdated views of the past were to be discarded and replaced with the new European philosophy which was already creating peace and prosperity and in which Britain needed to join. This might have been honest, but the House of Commons and the country was judged not ready to accept such revolutionary change. The attainment of the ultimate objective could not be risked by disclosure of any unpalatable facts. Stealth was a preferred strategy; debating in the words of the journalist and author Hugh Young, "The cost of living rather than the cost to the nation state".

Defeating Parliamentary Opposition

Heath's leadership, while lacking in charisma, remained firm within the Conservative party. On Europe, opposition was looming but it remained gentlemanly if severe. Most voices were expressing little more than concern regarding the old issues such as the Commonwealth and some were casting doubt on the economic arguments on which the whole purpose of entry was ostensibly based. Then one strident voice rose from the mists of Conservative opposition with the clarity of a lone bell and the intensity of an Old Testament prophet.

Enoch Powell ⁻🕆 remained a highly controversial figure for much of his life. He rarely invoked a neutral response. He was a former professor of classics and brought to politics a compelling oratory, and a rigorous and detached intellectualism. People, for one reason or another either hated him, or admired him. He was an unapproachable individual but it was always difficult not to respect his argument, when heard first hand. He had earlier been sacked from Edward Heath's Cabinet for an anti-immigration speech which was widely interpreted, many would say mis-interpreted, as racially inflammatory. Now, in one of the many examples of conversion among British politicians he had forgotten his previous pro-European credentials he returned to haunt Heath for many years. "The people" he explained," would not tolerate sovereignty being abolished or transformed".

Thus, with this notable exception the opposition on the Conservative benches of the House of Commons was although principled, neither vocal nor powerful. Nevertheless, with the government enjoying a theoretical majority of only 30 it seemed sufficient to prevent Heath from getting the European Communities Bill passed.

On the opposite benches Harold Wilson was never so secure. In fact, leadership of the labour party involved a constant battle of balances and compromises with the left or the right wing of the party. Wilson was an acknowledged master in such a situation, but under these unrelenting pressures of party plotting and constant manoeuvring even he suffered occasional depression and paranoia. The issue of Europe produced another polarising split in the party multiplying the complexity of Wilson's task. This was defined as maintaining a sufficient appearance of unity, to keep the party electable, and then to win the next General Election.

One factor which helped Wilson was that, despite its pro-worker background and principles, the Labour party generally did not consider any individual issue as worth defining as matter of incontrovertible principle. This enabled Wilson to hide his intentions in an ambiguity frequently approaching duplicity, and to engineer shifts in policy without open controversy. While the party believed Wilson was the man to beat Heath, they would follow him.

Having lost the 1970 election Wilson also lost one of the important levers of his party power. As Prime Minister he had the power of appointment of Ministers in his Cabinet, and Wilson used this ruthlessly to maintain balances in support of his objectives, although he still needed to look over his shoulder to ensure that the different factions in the party were represented. The principle of collective Cabinet responsibility also silenced internal critics. Neither of these restraints applied out on the opposition benches.

In 1970, Europe was by no means a priority issue for the Labour party. Therefore it felt no contradiction in opposing entry to the Common Market, and at the same time electing one of the most ardent supporters of European integration as deputy leader. Roy Jenkins, contrasting with the working class, north country roots of Wilson, was a cosmopolitan figure with a European background. He had been a Labour delegate to the Council of Europe and had campaigned for the Common Market. He was a frequent traveller, and knew personally most of the important continental politicians, and particularly those in socialist parties. Unusually in the party he was a principled supported of Europe who never changed his mind. In other fields Jenkins was seen on the right wing of the party but he became the unofficial leader of the pro-European faction which included such figures as William Rogers and Roy Hattersley as well as left wing idealists led by Michael Foot.

Thus a hard core of Labour pro-Europeans formed which was not to be ignored. Indeed it frequently became unexpectedly vocal. Certainly, they didn't always follow the urbane quietness of Jenkins or even the gentle but forceful persistence of Heath. For example, in 1971 a previously quiet supporter, John Mackintosh, produced an eloquent and unusually rousing speech attacking those "fainthearts" fearing loss of sovereignty. Wilson began to grumble about a party within a party, while Jenkins would try to persuade him not to follow a reputation as "devious, tricky, and opportunistic", but to stick with European cause and present himself as a man of principle.

On the opposite side of the argument sat figures such as Dennis Healey who had also enjoyed a long background among European socialists. He however, formed from similar inputs a distinctly different opinion from Jenkins. He believed in a north-south divide in Europe separating entirely different attitudes to authority, corruption and work. Thus a federation, which had worked well only on previously empty continents could not work on regions comprised of individual nations and would require forcible sanctions against future secession. He, in line with Gaitskell could not contemplate the end of a thousand years of history. So, after some spectacular wavering, Healey came out fighting in 1971, with savage criticism of Heath's terms, and its speculative economic promises.

Similarly, James Callaghan had also gradually emerged as an anti-European. He feared a "complete rupture in our identity," and "French linguistic hegemony," as a threat to British culture. He also complained about European protectionism as "an aroma of continental claustrophobia," concluding that entry was unacceptable on Heath's terms – in line with party policy.

Wilson was struggling with increasing desperation to maintain a semblance of party unity. He who had almost desperately sought Common Market entry in 1967 was now opposed to it, but solely because the terms were "unacceptable." At the same time he had exerted every pressure he could on the party to ensure that no organ voted to withdraw. The door was to remain open. Labour would do no more than oppose the terms. Labour MP's were generally following this policy, for example passing a Commons Motion in early 1971 that "Entry into the EEC on the terms so far envisaged would be against the interests of this country", despite the fact that the terms were at that time hardly known.

Another nuance had gradually become incorporated into Labour policy. In September 1971 Callaghan had warned Heath that success in the Commons would only be temporary. A new Labour Government would renegotiate "those terms which had been found objectionable and harmful to the interests of the British people." Wilson picked up this suggestion and re-negotiation became a commitment, as a means of allowing a future reversal of Labour policy. Meanwhile, he was still struggling to hold back the tide of anti-European feeling. For example, in 1972 the National Executive passed a motion specifying those terms to be re-negotiated for withdrawal to be avoided. They included:- the Common Agricultural Policy; restrictions on economic planning and social legislation; stopping of payments to the Community budget, retention of Parliamentary sovereignty.

Matters came to a head in October 1971. The government's Commons Motion supporting in principle entry to the Common Market under the terms negotiated was passed, by a majority of 112. Thanks to sixty-nine Labour MP's who supported the government, the thirty Conservative "rebels" who didn't were defeated. This however is a bald statement, not reflecting the acrimonious exchanges of these debates. At this time of close political balance "betrayal" of party loyalty and duty for questionable principles and, particularly in Labour, the unprecedented scale of the "rebellion" created bitterness and resentment which was to consume the minds of the Westminster participants for months to come.

Of course a Commons Motion, no more than a decision of a Cabinet, has no legal effect, and during 1972 the European Communities Bill had to pass through the legislative process. MP's suffered considerable pressure throughout the debates and the subsequent 104 divisions:- from the party whips; sometimes from constituencies; from trade union sponsors of labour MP's who disliked seeing them support a Tory government on anything; and from the party leaders. All of these divisions were won but some of them very narrowly and sometimes dramatically as parliamentarians exerted their tactical skills with whatever cunning they could muster. Cross party co-operation in the heart of the decision making process and contrary to the wishes of the leaderships was firmly established as a feature of European issues. Despite all the spirited opposition from all its sources the Bill completed its tempestuous passage through Parliament and received royal assent. The Bill became the European Communities Act of 1972, and with its coming into force on 1st January 1973 Britain was a full member of the European Community.

Chapter H: European Communities Act 1972

So, the culmination of the dreams of many and the efforts of many more came into fruition when Parliament passed, and when royal assent was given to the European Communities Act. It opens with the introduction of the Act's long title, the standard wording of a Statute and the short title followed by a number of definitions.

> *An Act to make provision in connection with the enlargement of the European Communities to include the United Kingdom, together with (for certain purposes) the Channel Islands, the Isle of Man and Gibraltar.* [17th October 1972]
>
> BE IT ENACTED by the Queen's most Excellent Majesty, by and with the advice and consent of the Lords Spiritual and Temporal, and Commons, in this present Parliament assembled, and by the authority of the same, as follows
>
> ***1 Short title and interpretation***
> *(1) This Act may be cited as the European Communities Act 1972.*

Next follows a short paragraph whose brevity disguises the broadest power of legislative delegation known to British history.

> ***2 General implementation of Treaties***
> *(1) All such rights, powers, liabilities, obligations and restrictions from time to time created or arising by or under the Treaties, and all such remedies and procedures from time to time provided for by or under the Treaties, as in accordance with the Treaties are without further enactment to be given legal effect or used in the United Kingdom shall be recognised and available in law, and be enforced, allowed and followed accordingly; and the expression "enforceable Community right" and similar expressions shall be read as referring to one to which this subsection applies.*

This is followed by a general power of secondary legislation relating to any measures enacted in Europe which need to implementation in UK law:

> *(2) Subject to Schedule 2 to this Act, at any time after its passing Her Majesty may by Order in Council, and any designated Minister or department may by regulations, make provision—*
> *(a) for the purpose of implementing any Community obligation of the United Kingdom, or enabling any such obligation to be implemented, or of enabling any rights enjoyed or to be enjoyed by the United Kingdom under or by virtue of the Treaties to be exercised; or*
> *(b) for the purpose of dealing with matters arising out of or related to any such obligation or rights or the coming into force, or the operation from time to time, of subsection (1) above;*
> *and in the exercise of any statutory power or duty, including any power to give directions or to legislate by means of orders, rules, regulations or other subordinate instrument, the person entrusted with the power or duty may have regard to the objects of the Communities and to any such obligation or rights as aforesaid.*

Next having determined that law enacted in Europe would be applied in the UK either automatically or by the simple means of secondary legislation, the question of its enforcement was considered.

> ***3 Decisions on, and proof of, Treaties and Community instruments, etc***
> *(1) For the purposes of all legal proceedings any question as to the meaning or effect of any of the Treaties, or as to the validity, meaning or effect of any Community instrument, shall be treated as a question of law (and, if not referred to the European Court, be for determination as such in accordance with the principles laid down by and any relevant decision of the European Court or any court attached thereto).*

(2) Judicial notice shall be taken of the Treaties, of the Official Journal of the Communities and of any decision of, or expression of opinion by, the European Court [or any court attached thereto] on any such question as aforesaid; and the Official Journal shall be admissible as evidence of any instrument or other act thereby communicated of any of the Communities or of any Community institution.

Therefore, on all matters relating to the Treaty all British courts are obliged to follow the judgements and even any opinions expressed by the European Court of Justice.

Chapter 17: Let The People Decide

Referendum?
The victory for Edward Heath in Europe was not matched by success on the domestic front. Continuing economic pressures were leading to increasing industrial unrest leading to the 1973 "winter of discontent". Even earlier during the passage through Parliament of the European Communities Bill, Labour MP's were sensing that Heath was becoming vulnerable. They were reminded of their political imperative of beating Edward Heath and of engineering a Parliamentary defeat on any issue. The smell of blood or of renewed power began to concentrate the leadership's minds on avoiding the damage to the party being caused by its most divisive issue.

The first labour figure to suggest referendum was actually Douglas Jay writing in the Times. He considered that "It would be a constitutional outrage if Parliament abrogated both Britain's sovereignty and its independence without consulting the people." Tony Benn made a more famous reference to the same idea when he suggested that what the Party couldn't agree, "Let the people settle."

This was greeted by all party leaders as an outrage, for several different reasons. Firstly it was a constitutional innovation without British precedent. All matters, of whatever constitutional significance were to be decided by Parliamentary vote. People calmly going about their daily lives, neither interested nor capable of understanding complex issues of policy, delegate all such decisions to their elected representatives. The voice of the people was only consulted by means of a general election, which provided the ultimate recourse against unpopular measures. Although many realised that this was a very blunt weapon, few people advocated referenda in general, and few spoke of its advantages in principle. On the contrary, political leaders saw nothing but a serious threat to their own power and were adamantly opposed. One commentator explained that, "only a more threatening source of prospective impotence could induce him to revise his opinion".

Tony Benn however saw things differently. He saw that Harold Wilson was consistently refusing to join any "Out of Europe" campaign, leaving Labour anti-marketeers with few options. Without Wilson and his supporters adding electoral credibility to the whole party there was no benefit in imposing on him an unacceptable anti-European policy by means of the party machine. To Benn, a referendum provided the appealing prospect that the political leadership could be overruled by a sceptical public. So, his manoeuvring continued as, in Wilson's absence, he persuaded Labour's National Executive to pass a mild and polite motion asking the Cabinet to reconsider the idea. He also supported an amendment to the Bill proposed by Enoch Powell, which would have required public approval by referendum before accession. Both moves failed, the latter only because of abstentions by Labour MP's.

On the other side of the argument Roy Jenkins saw a proposed referendum quite differently. Of course, it was really the only practical route for the anti-marketeers to progress and so it was the biggest risk to the pro-market success in getting Britain in. It was therefore nothing less than a "betrayal of parliamentary democracy". He explained that Ministers were, and should be responsible to their conscience, to the House of Commons and to their electorate. A referendum could force politicians either to adopt policies which they didn't believe in or were contrary to their view of the national interest, or instead to sacrifice their political careers. Politicians would become time servers, running errands for the electorate, constantly passing back the buck of ultimate decisions.

The effect of this dispute was unusual. Whereas the issues as to whether Britain should remain in Europe and whether referenda should become a legitimate political tool would logically appear quite separate and independent questions, there was in this case an almost complete correlation. The status quo was obviously "in". The proposed referendum was most likely to be the last line of resistance for a generation at least. Therefore anyone supporting withdrawal from Europe had to be in favour of a referendum, and vice versa.

In all probability Harold Wilson was honestly afraid of the possibility of withdrawal, and there is little doubt that he found the idea of government by referendum repugnant. He therefore remained firmly against a referendum for as long as the political balance allowed. He was also undoubtedly amused that Edward Heath had left a door open in this argument. To Heath's embarrassment and no doubt inadvertently, Heath had stated during the negotiations that expansion of the Common Market would not be appropriate "except with the full hearted consent of the parliaments and the peoples of the new member countries". This could now be, and certainly was used to blunt his personal opposition to the idea.

It was known that referenda on membership were being held in the other applicant countries of Ireland, Norway and Denmark, although in these countries this was an established constitutional device. But then President Pompidou announced that the French would also be asked to approve enlargement. One can imagine the glee of Tony Benn shouting how outrageous it was that the French people are allowed to decide whether they want Britain in, while the British people are not. A referendum became a necessity from the principled point of view of political legitimacy. The fact that throughout 1972 and 1973 opinion polls were consistently opposed to Europe was a mere coincidence.

Theoretically Wilson also had the option of consulting the people by means of a General Election. However, having spent such energy in winning General Elections with such marginal results, there was little reason to call another General Election on the issue, and risk losing office. Besides, single issue elections had not been effective as Edward Heath had discovered in his "Who runs Britain" campaign. In any event he was aware that if he couldn't bring himself to take Britain out, he would inevitably have to keep Britain in. There was no way of achieving this without disintegration of the Labour party, unless there could be a referendum.

The Shadow Cabinet reversed its position and committed the party to a referendum. Roy Jenkins resigned, naturally as being opposed to a referendum in principle, and because of its potential use against progressive causes dear to the hearts of Labour such as the extension of public ownership, or even in furtherance of the repatriation of immigrants. His resignation proved popular in the press but was roundly criticised within the party. Shirley Williams and Roy Hattersley didn't resign but they wrote to Wilson saying that they would if party moved even further against Europe. Nevertheless a short period of functional tranquillity reigned within the party, while it was still possible to hide its divisions behind a commitment to a new version of popular democracy.

Opposition to Edward Heath was the other imperative of the Labour party, and this was readily achieved by attacking the "disastrous and humiliating" terms of entry he had negotiated. Wilson however had always prevented the party from supporting outright withdrawal in principle. Thus Labour published in its 1973 "Programme for Britain" and in its Manifesto for February 1974, a commitment to consult the people, (possibly by means of a General Election), following a "fundamental" re-negotiation of the terms of entry to the European Community. The objectives of renegotiations were defined in very stern wording as removing the imposition of food taxes on top of rising world prices; the crippling fresh burdens on our balance of payments and the draconian curtailment of power of Parliament.

In March 1974, Harold Wilson returned to Downing Street with another novelty in British but not continental politics – a minority government. Edward Heath had been unable to take control of a hung Parliament, and the Queen had asked Wilson to form the next government. With four more seats than the Conservatives, but 17 short of an overall majority his position was precarious, and depended on minority parties unwillingness to precipitate a new election. This meant that while his commitment to re-negotiation and consultation continued, the survival of his government was constantly at risk and domestic priorities demanded more urgent attention. Even in the autumn, when Wilson called another election and obtained a barely workable overall majority of just three seats, survival had to remain top priority. Europe was important but would have to wait.

Public opinion itself had determined these priorities. When asked what were the most important problems facing the country, issues such as cost of living, unemployment, strikes were always raised. These were the more concrete and even personal issues, likely to have one way or another a bearing on an individual's life or that of his family or friends. In contrast, Europe was a complex, difficult subject to understand especially in the light of conflicting "expert" opinion; it was abstract; it was remote from everyday life; and later on it had essentially been settled by Edward Heath. It was irrelevant. Thus from 1970 to spring 1972 Europe was only mentioned as important by 4-8% of respondents to surveys, reaching 10% only on two occasions up until autumn 1974 despite the raging public battles regarding Europe. This was hardly surprising. During this year Wilson was confronting a miners' strike and a three day week in consequence; there was an oil crisis, 25% inflation, stubbornly high unemployment and renewed Irish terrorism. Europe was irrelevant.

Such opinions regarding Europe which did exist were likely to be relatively unformed and volatile and they were also often largely uninformed. For example in 1971, only 13% in one survey could name the member states of the Community while 24% could not identify a single member. Even so, from joining in 1973 until February 1975 there was according to Gallup, a consistent majority of opinion believing that joining the Common Market had been a mistake (on average by 48% to 35% with a sizeable 17% don't know), and this was usually reflected in a parallel opinion that Britain should leave.

The American, Anthony King in his academic study of the management of public opinion during the referendum campaign reflects on the significance of the nature of opinion as reported by opinion polls. He explains how a reported opinion can at one extreme represent a well considered and fully informed view formed after having evaluated the alternatives, or at the opposite pole, little more than a random response induced by a reluctance to admit to an absence of any informed opinion. A simple survey like those frequently publicised cannot discriminate between the two. More importantly, between the two extremes are views formed on the basis of some thought, but not held with any conviction. These are all fundamentally different from "don't knows" who may simply not have considered the subject or may be well informed but still unable to decide.

King's main point was that people with half-formed opinions were likely to be influenced disproportionately by any new information which might enable them to make sense of the issue. In addition people were encouraged to consider again because of a definite need to decide, as precipitated in this case by an invitation to vote in a referendum. Thus a present focus on something newly presented can dispel previous uncertainty and provide people with a new understanding explaining the unknown and unfamiliar in terms of something relevant. The information itself may be unimportant or it may be misleading; but it is still likely to have significant or even disproportionate effect. The electorate was therefore vulnerable to well presented mis-information, and this was not a commodity in short supply. From the detached viewpoint of a political scientist or for either a principled or cynical politician there was a clear conclusion – Governments could go their own way on Europe, without concerning themselves with the electorate.

New Terms?

In the real world of Government, Wilson and Callaghan, as Foreign Secretary, opened their re-negotiations within the Community. They were working closely together with neither man having much patience with the extremists on either side of the European dispute. They were practical and pragmatic politicians. James Callaghan though had some weaknesses at that time. He was known as a shrewd and sensitive politician in familiar surroundings when he knew the people and the rules of conduct. However in less familiar circumstances and in the company of strangers he lost his relaxed and effective style and appeared arrogant or even surly. This unfortunate manner set off discussions with his new European colleagues with an unpleasant and confrontational start. He rapidly succeeded in offending all other members of the Community.

This hostility gradually abated as he got to know his fellow politicians and found he could actually deal with them. His approach gradually shifted from his adversarial opening, "The image of the Community in the United Kingdom is not good." to the mildly co-operative two months later, "Let us together put these matters right and *when* we do....."

Wilson had quickly announced to Britain's partners that they would not seek to re-negotiate Treaty of Rome or Treaty of Accession. This was fortunate since the alternative would have been impossible. Instead he remained confident that the required adjustments could be attained within the existing framework. This immediately posed the question as to how "fundamental" these renegotiations were to become. They were quickly and widely regarded throughout Europe as cosmetic and referred to disparagingly as "so-called" renegotiations.

Of course Britain had already been a full member for 18 months, and fortunately for Wilson many of the issues on his agenda were overtaken by normal course of Community business. As examples;- there was no current intention to harmonise VAT due to the opposition of other member states; the Common Agricultural Policy was then having limited effect because of rapid increases in world prices; the feared interferences with regional, industrial and fiscal policies were limited and Britain was an unexpected beneficiary of regional aid schemes; the new Lomé convention provided beneficial terms to African and Caribbean Commonwealth countries. Only on the question of contributions to the Community budget did serious controversy persist. Britain was arguing that it was paying more than its fair share. To its credit the Commission agreed, producing figures comparing its 22% contribution with its 15.9% of GDP.

Britain had also been helped by changes of leadership within the Community members. Valeri Giscard d'Estaing replaced Pompidou, and was both more amenable to the British position and less committed to the terms negotiated by Pompidou. Helmut Schmidt, the new German Chancellor was also more sympathetic to Britain and soon developed a trusting relationship with Harold Wilson. It was said to be after private meetings between the two at Chequers that Schmidt had been most influential and that afterwards Wilson knew where he wanted to go, and set about his machinations in that direction.

Meanwhile frustration continued within the Community, often increased by the presence of British anti-market Ministers who were less than co-operative. Even so the key figures in Europe were all themselves professional politicians and understood that symbolic results were sometimes necessary for domestic purposes. Consequently there was widespread understanding of British predicament, leading to a practical tolerance and patience. Only where it was likely to cost them hard cash, was there serious resistance. The problem of budget contributions therefore threatened an amicable settlement.

The British side quoted the Community's reassurances during the Heath negotiations, "Should unacceptable situations arise within the present Community or an enlarged Community the very survival of the Community would demand that the institutions find equitable solutions." However the other members were unwilling to re-open the Pandora's box of real re-negotiations. Attention therefore shifted to creating an improved "correcting mechanism". It was not until the March 1975 Community summit meeting in Dublin that the details of a very complicated mechanism which would in effect reduce the nett cost to Britain were agreed. At the same time New Zealand's privileged access for dairy products was extended from 1978 to at least 1980. These were the "real" achievements which could be proclaimed back in Britain. Wilson had the new terms her required for credibility, and the new information he needed to influence public opinion.

Two decisions had already followed that of the referendum. Firstly the government would pronounce its verdict on the success, or otherwise, of the negotiations. There would be an official recommendation to the people, one way or the other, on which way they should vote. Secondly Ministers would be freed from the doctrine of traditional collective responsibility and would be able to campaign for the dissenting view. Of course, there was never a realistic possibility that the government's recommendation would change the minds of committed pro- or anti-factions. Therefore, once again the choice was not freedom v collective responsibility but freedom v collapse of the government. Wilson, with little choice announced this decision but soon afterwards fearful of the consequences of this novel situation attempted to apply restrictions to Ministers preventing them from arguing publicly against each other. The strategem worked successfully, although Wilson hated the very principle and was often infuriated with pro-European colleagues, particularly Jenkins for his scheming contacts with the opposition benches.

This had all been settled before the government's policy was actually decided, and preceding the heated Cabinet debate. In public Wilson had prevaricated for so long, even though his reluctance to bring Britain out of the Common Market had determined his pragmatic opinion. Now he was finally forced to fall to one side or the other, and to obtain the agreement of his Cabinet colleagues. This did not prove easy. Previous positions of each minister would have produced a majority of 12-11 against staying in. However according to Hugo Young a combination of wheedling and enforcement mostly by Callaghan changed the minds, or at least the votes of five dissenters. Thus Wilson had guided the machinery of government against all the opinions of his cabinet colleagues, as well as his personal friends and his political advisers.

The party itself was more resistant to Wilson's persuasive skills. While negotiations were proceeding, Labour party was consistently hardening its opposition, demanding among other things "The right of Parliament to reject any Community legislation, directive or order". Then, shortly after the government's recommendation for continued membership was announced 137 Labour MP' voted in support of the government, but 147 against. Only support from the other parties kept this policy afloat. Thus Wilson had created the remarkable and unprecedented situation of a Labour government promoting a major policy opposed by the majority of Unions, its own party and National Executive, and even its own MP's. Undoubtedly this was an extraordinary reversal of political normality.

The Referendum Bill, authorising this unprecedented procedure now had to pass though Parliament and the Conservative opposition could not be ignored. However although their rejection of the referendum in principle remained, their opposition was moderated since by then they expected to win. They remained highly critical, but were eventually resigned to the outcome and appeared content to describe it as an "unwelcome dodge and device adapted by Wilson in a moment of [party] difficulty."

Some real obstacles to the legislation remained. For example, would a threshold turnout be required before the government could be mandated to withdraw? Would a very low turnout be regarded as a valid endorsement? Fortunately this question was easily avoided. Since there was no constitutional precedent to the contrary the legal position remained that

Parliament could not be bound. The government actually pledged itself to accept any simple majority, but legally the referendum was of consultative authority only.

The actual counting was also controversial. The normal constituency basis was thought to be dangerous because of the reprisals an individual MP might suffer if his opinion proved contrary to his constituents. Therefore in England and Wales results were to be announced by county. Politicians were also fearful that Scotland might vote differently from England, causing a fillip to separatism. Results there were to be announced regionally. One single result was to be announced for the whole of Northern Ireland.

The wording of any referendum is always controversial, as slight nuances in meaning may influence the result. For example the term "Common Market" was viewed as much less appealing than "European Community", and were used accordingly by both sides. However it was concluded that after an intensive, high profile, three month campaign voters would be unlikely to be swayed by such nuances, and pro-marketeers even agreed to the inclusion of the words, "Common Market".

The opinion of the public was now the key to the final resolution of twenty years of national prevarication, and the rescue of the Labour party from imminent collapse. Despite an indifference to Europe amounting to a general ignorance they were to make the decision which their politicians couldn't.

Campaign and Result

Most analysts looking back at the campaign of 1975 were amazed at what happened. Opinion polls had recorded the public's consistent view that joining the Common Market had been a mistake, with a majority 41% to 33% in favour of withdrawal in January 1975. There had been support for re-negotiation, amounting to 48%, which would appear logical on the basis that nothing can be lost by it. But then, when the "fundamental re-negotiation" had been completed and the government announced its support for "new" terms reported opinion immediately reversed. The "out" responses dropped to 37% and the "in" rose to 45%.

The new terms in themselves were not at all important. Questioned by Harris about the new terms only 20% were aware that Britain's contribution to the EEC budget had been reduced and over 56% could not reply. Moreover, those who switched sides in the preceding weeks were less knowledgeable rather than more about the new terms. It appeared as simply a positive response to new information.

Conservative voters were not influenced greatly since they were generally still supporting a well established policy in favour of European membership. For Labour voters the situation was different. They had followed the anti-European drift in the party as a whole and before the announcement opinions were 45% to 37% in favour of withdrawal. Here was the main shift in opinion changing to 53% to 33% in favour of remaining in afterwards. Voters were therefore following the leadership rather than the party itself which remained hostile to the EEC.

The pro-European campaign was co-ordinated by a new body, Britain in Europe, led by Roy Jenkins and with Edward Heath as deputy. Interestingly, the Conservatives were aware that Labour supporters were likely to determine the final outcome. So, since the issue was to them of such overwhelming importance they were content to give undue prominence to Labour leaders. Many Labour MP's though found difficulty aligning themselves and co-operating with what looked like an establishment and big-business lobby, and carried on their campaign separately.

Pro-marketeers, backed by most of the large industrial concerns also enjoyed much more financial backing than the opponents. The Confederation of British Industry had backed Europe on a vote of 415 to 4, and were making donations accordingly. Aware of this disparity the government made a grant of £125,000 to each side. This however amounted to only 8% of the donations made to Britain in Europe (£996,000), but amounted to 94% of the total funding of their opponents, co-ordinated by the National Referendum Campaign (donations of £8,610). These figures overstate the imbalance. Leaflets for both sides were delivered to every household, (with an additional one to state the government's view!), newspapers reported any major issue raised by the anti-market groups, broadcasters were required to report in their traditional balanced manner and equal free television time was provided.

Contrary to expectations before the government's recommendation was announced, the National Referendum Campaign therefore faced a daunting task. Britain was already a member of the Community, and had not suffered in any obvious way as a result. Food prices had risen, but this process was well advanced and the blame for this did not only lie with the EEC. Sovereignty was of intense interest to only a small number of voters, who were already committed to the anti-European cause. Their spokesmen were less well known, and less well regarded. Against all this were anxieties that undefined but nevertheless serious damage could be caused by pulling out, and that Britain would find it difficult to survive alone as a single country in some small islands. Compelling reasons for accepting the unspecified risks of withdrawal appeared in short supply.

The lack of well-known supporters of the NRC proved more serious than the lack of finance. The group could never muster a comparative weight in the eyes of the electorate. Leaders such as Michael Foot, Peter Shore, Ian Paisley, and even Tony Benn were, according to a similar poll, simply less highly regarded. The only notable exception was Enoch Powell, but he was such a controversial figure that he had as many enemies as supporters both in Parliament and in the public view. So during the campaign this small and disparate group of leaders therefore rapidly became over-exposed in the media Either the same people were to appearing every day discussing every issue, or some obscure union leaders or little known back bench MP's would appear but produce very little public impact. In contrast Britain In Europe was always able to produce a well recognised and popular individual to comment on any issue which arose.

The Britain in Europe campaign was also in itself clever in that despite its grand organisation and comparatively plush facilities it frequently presented itself in more ordinary surroundings such as shopping centres, crowded pubs etc. They were very important people but still in touch with the common man. It was becoming clear that the electorate was content to follow the political leaders which they respected. An individual considering voting for withdrawal was certainly aligning himself with the eccentrics of British politics, and Britain in Europe was successful in amplifying this feeling by insinuating that voting against Europe was a vote in support of cranks, extremists or other undesirable elements. Curiously, therefore, even though people have mostly regarded themselves as cynical when it comes to believing political statements, they still followed the opinions of their leaders in an uncritical manner.

Looked at from the viewpoint of finance and personalities, the campaign which followed turned out to be decidedly one sided. Edward Heath of course never changed his view, and he was replaced by a new pro-market leader, Margaret Thatcher. Other conservative leaders mostly retained the same policy. Similarly the recognised Labour leadership, as well as the Liberals were now committed to the same. Therefore all the most important figures which ordinary people would recognise in both parties tended to be supporters of membership.

Another feature on both sides was that there was no balance and little reasoned debate. The issue was totally black or totally white, and there would be no dilution of the message to be conveyed by balance, or concessions even to established facts. There were in any case few such facts. Campaigners either found many ways of saying but none of proving that membership would provide economic prosperity or would spread fear and unsupported speculation regarding price rises. Any campaigner would present only one side of every issue. Whether concerned with prices, jobs, inflation, investment, sterling, the balance of payments, social issues, sovereignty, etc., probably even the weather; the conclusion was to be the same. Gone were the more balanced positions like Wilson's in 1967, that prices would rise but it would be worth the pain. There would be no pain whatsoever, unless you reached the other conclusion on any issue at all, in which case there would be nothing else but pain.

Thus the leaflet for the "Yes" campaign avoided any discussion of sovereignty issues. "English Common Law is not affected", remained the position in deceptive reassurance. Meanwhile the "No" propoganda leaflet explained that the Common Market, "sets out by stages to merge Britain with France, Germany and Italy and other nations into a single nation....our right to change policies and laws in Britain will steadily dwindle", a position loudly derided by its opponents.

This polarisation however, while leading to bitter dispute particularly within the established parties rarely led to extremist, fear inducing arguments. One exception was from Tony Benn. "Mass unemployment and increasing emigration of our workforce and their families to the Continent...will be the painful consequence.... Mr. Heath, who has come back from retirement has given no hint that he understands the horrifying possibility that for the British people EEC membership will mean inhabiting a group of offshore islands whose industry is permanently unable to provide the jobs and national income to support them."

Dennis Healey made a telling remark, "When war breaks out, truth is the first casualty". With a highly emotive issue, passionate feelings and a shortage of hard, indisputable facts, there were undoubtedly many such casualties on both sides. Callaghan had an ingenious reply. He said that there were three sides to the argument – the pro-market, the anti-market, and "the truth" which was represented by himself.

Regrettably this was also an exaggeration. The leaflet produced to explain the government's recommendation and describing its wide ranging successes in the renegotiations was not characterised by its total accuracy, even though it was possible to justify all its points. For example: "There was a threat to employment in Britain from the movement in the Common Market towards an Economic and Monetary Union. This could have forced us to accept fixed exchange rates for the pound, restricting industrial growth and putting jobs as risk. This threat has been removed". Although Wilson himself had signed up for economic and monetary union he did not believe it was a realistic possibility at that time. Similarly, "No important new policy can be decided in Brussels without the consent of a British Minister answerable to a British Government and British Parliament", depended on continued acceptance and real use of the unofficial veto power, and it also avoided defining which policies were actually covered by some of the Treaty of Rome's more open ended objectives. "Membership of the Common Market also imposes new rights and duties on Britain, but does not deprive us of our national identity", which was true only providing identity was defined in a narrow manner and did not include independence.

Of course this was nothing new in politics. Politicians have always presented their arguments and policies in the most favourable light and sought to minimise the significance of any potentially unpopular measure. But since the 1970's this has been a permanent feature of Britain v Europe, often designed to mask the real significance of what was actually being agreed or decided. Wilson's concentration on commercial and temporary terms diverted discussion from the principles involved and their permanent effects, while Heath was never willing to expose his personal convictions as an honest disclosure of the implications he well understood and approved.

The referendum provided a powerful demonstration that despite the cynicism with which the public regarded politicians even then, the people do ultimately trust their leaders to take decisions of national importance. It is the author's view that politicians betrayed this trust, taking advantage of public indifference, to subject them to deliberately misleading and often blatantly false statements. There is no doubt that the public were never aware of the far reaching implications of the decision they were being to take.

Thus, whether the people had anything to say or not, their voice was now to be heard. On Thursday, 5th June 1975 voters entered their polling booths to be faced with the following:

> The Government have announced the results of the renegotiation of the United Kingdom's terms of membership of the European Community.
> DO YOU THINK THAT THE UNITED KINGDOM SHOULD STAY IN THE EUROPEAN COMMUNITY (THE COMMON MARKET)?

The turnout was 64.5%. This was regarded as high considering the people's continuing lack of interest in the subject as whole and the predictability of the final result, but it was low in comparison to the turnouts in other European referenda - Ireland saw 71%, Norway 79% and Denmark 90%.

The result was remarkably uniform throughout the country in terms of regions, and ages. Political affiliations had some influence with 82% of Conservatives but only 52% of Labour supporters intending to vote for continuing. It was only the relatively small communities in Shetland and the Western Isles voted in favour of withdrawal. Overall, continuing membership was approved by 67.2% to 32.8%.

Opponents of Europe now had little choice but to accept the democratic verdict with as much grace as they could find, in the hope that they would succeed in limiting the damage to their political careers. Enoch Powell was rare in refusing to accept the result. "If I were young, I should despair, but I do not. I am convinced that in this referendum the vast majority of those voting had no notion that they were saying Yes or No to Britain continuing as a nation at all. The fault did not lie with many of the advocates of British membership who declared candidly that the nation state was obsolete and that Britain therefore must become a province in a new European state and cease to be a self-governing nation. So incredible was this, however, to most people that their words simply bounced off them; they had no meaning in their ears. Now what will happen is that gradually, and perhaps not so gradually, it will come home to them that their Yes vote to Europe was No to Britain as a nation."

Chapter I: European Law Arrives in Britain

Entry of European Law

We have seen how the opinions of the ECJ developed regarding the status of European law and the story continues as the European Communities Act was passed and introduced its concepts to Britain.

One of the early cases where European law was considered was *Bulmer v Bollinger* where the French producers of champagne had argued that Bulmers should not be allowed to use the word "champagne" since under EC Regulations this was reserved to wine produced in that particular region. Their case actually succeeded when an injunction was granted by a lower court. This was sufficient to remove the phrases "genuine champagne perry" and "champagne cider" from British advertising, even though this decision was later reversed by the Court of Appeal. However the historical importance of the case arises from a subsidiary issue as to whether or when English courts would be obliged to refer a particular issue to the ECJ. In this case it was decided by a literal interpretation of Article 234, (then 177), that the court was not so obliged, and that a referral was essentially discretionary for all courts but the House of Lords. Nevertheless the case remains important as a first recognition at Court of Appeal level, of the effects of European law. Coincidentally, the main judgement is again that of Lord Denning who said,

> "The first and fundamental point is that the Treaty concerns only those matters which have a European element, that is to say, matters which affect people or property in the nine countries of the common market besides ourselves. The Treaty does not touch any of the matters which concern solely England and the people in it. These are still governed by English law. They are not affected by the Treaty. But when we come to matters with a European element, **the Treaty is like an incoming tide. It flows into the estuaries and up the rivers. It cannot be held back,** Parliament has decreed that the Treaty is henceforward to be part of our law. It is equal in force to any statute."

Lord Denning is at pains to emphasise that this is simply a result stemming from the European Communities Act 1972, as enacted by the British Parliament, even though it has far reaching effects.

> "The statute is expressed in forthright terms which are absolute and all-embracing. Any rights or obligations created by the Treaty are to be given legal effect in England without more ado. Any remedies or procedures provided by the Treaty are to be made available here without being open to question. In future, in transactions which cross the frontiers, we must no longer speak or think of English law as something on its own. We must speak and think of community law, of community rights and obligations, and we must give effect to them. This means a great effort for the lawyers. We have to learn a new system. The Treaty, with the regulations and directives, covers many volumes. The case law is contained in hundreds of reported cases both in the European Court of Justice and in the national courts of the nine. Many must be studied before the right result can be reached. We must get down to it."

He explains that the role of British judges has not actually changed in terms of giving judgements and enforcing the law of the land, even though the necessary guidance in their interpretation would henceforth come from a different source.

> "It is important to distinguish between the task of interpreting the Treaty - to see what it means - and the task of applying it - to apply its provisions to the case in hand. Let me put on one side the task of applying the Treaty. On this matter in our courts, the English judges have the final word. They are the only judges who are empowered to decide the case itself. They have to find the facts, to state the issues, to give judgment for one side or the other, and to see that the judgment is enforced.
>
> Before the English judges can apply the Treaty, they have to see what it means and what is its effect. In the task of interpreting the Treaty, the English judges are no longer the final authority. They no longer carry the law in their breasts. They are no longer in a position to give rulings which are of binding force. The supreme tribunal for interpreting the Treaty is the European Court of Justice, at Luxembourg. Our Parliament has so decreed."

Lord Denning proceeds to explain that for issues covered by European law the traditional rules of statutory interpretation will no longer apply.

> *"In view of these considerations, it is apparent that in very many cases the English courts will interpret the Treaty themselves. They will not refer the question to the European court at Luxembourg. What then are the principles of interpretation to be applied? Beyond doubt the English courts must follow the same principles as the European court. Otherwise there would be differences between the countries of the nine. That would never do. All the courts of all nine countries should interpret the Treaty in the same way. They should all apply the same principles. It is enjoined on the English courts by section 3 of the European Community Act 1972, which I have read.*
> *What a task is thus set before us! The Treaty is quite unlike any of the enactments to which we have become accustomed. The draftsmen of our statutes have striven to express themselves with the utmost exactness. They have tried to foresee all possible circumstances that may arise and to provide for them. They have sacrificed style and simplicity. They have forgone brevity. They have become long and involved. In consequence, the judges have followed suit. They interpret a statute as applying only to the circumstances covered by the very words. They give them a literal interpretation. If the words of the statute do not cover a new situation - which was not foreseen - the judges hold that they have no power to fill the gap. To do so would be a "naked usurpation of the legislative function": see Magor and St. Mellons Rural District Council v. Newport Corporation The gap must remain open until Parliament finds time to fill it.*
> *How different is this Treaty! It lays down general principles. It expresses its aims and purposes. All in sentences of moderate length and commendable style. But it lacks precision. It uses words and phrases without defining what they mean. An English lawyer would look for an interpretation clause, but he would look in vain. There is none. All the way through the Treaty there are gaps and*

lacunae. These have to be filled in by the judges, or by Regulations or directives. It is the European way. That appears from the decision of the Hamburg court in In re Tax on Imported Lemons"

Finally, he describes in his own, typical style, how the same principles apply to secondary legislation of the EC which again differs considerably from the British tradition.

"Likewise the Regulations and directives. They are enacted by the Council sitting in Brussels for everyone to obey. They are quite unlike our statutory instruments. They have to give the reasons on which they are based: article 190. So they start off with pages of preambles, "whereas" and "whereas" and "whereas." These show the purpose and intent of the Regulations and directives. Then follow the provisions which are to be obeyed. Here again words and phrases are used without defining their import. Such as "personal conduct" in the Directive 64/221, article 3 (E.E.C.) which was considered by Pennycuick V.-C. in Van Duyn v. Home Office [1974]. In case of difficulty, recourse is had to the preambles. These are useful to show the purpose and intent behind it all. But much is left to the judges. The enactments give only an outline plan. The details are to be filled in by the judges.
Seeing these differences, what are the English courts to do when they are faced with a problem of interpretation? They must follow the European pattern. No longer must they examine the words in meticulous detail. No longer must they argue about the precise grammatical sense. They must look to the purpose or intent. To quote the words of the European court in the Da Costa case [1963], they must deduce "from the wording and the spirit of the Treaty the meaning of the community rules." They must not confine themselves to the English text. They must consider, if need be, all the authentic texts, of which there are now six: see Sociale Verzekeringsbank v. Van der Vecht [1968]. They must divine the spirit of the Treaty and gain inspiration from it. If they find a gap, they must fill it as best they can. They must do what the framers of the instrument would have done if they

had thought about it. So we must do the same. Those are the principles, as I understand it, on which the European court acts."

Thus, in this introductory case the new principles applicable throughout the judiciary in Britain and the new duty of British judges clearly explained. However what is also significant is the limitations in the jurisdiction of European law and in this respect Denning's famous image of the legal tide flowing up the rivers turned out to be truly prophetic.

Establishing the ECJ

From the point of view of judicial precedent in England, the case of *Bulmer v Bollinger* remained authority for the proposition that referral of a case to the ECJ was discretionary, unless it was "necessary" to judge the case. A referral was not necessary where the interpretation of a European provision had already been made by the ECJ and so was clear. This precedent was used followed by lower courts as well as the Court of Appeal until a case of 1981 when two gentlemen were convicted of importing pornography contrary to the Obscene Publications Act of 1959. The defendants raised a defence that the statute itself was contrary to Article 28 (the 30) of the EC Treaty since it obstructed the Free Movement of Goods. They demanded a reference to the ECJ to resolve the issue. At both levels the judges read the articles concerned. They found that the Article prohibited any "Quantitative Restriction" or quota on imports, but that a total prohibition did not amount to such a restriction. Even if it were it would then be justified under Article 30, (then 36) which allows restrictions for protection of public morality. They judged that "Since the issues in the case arising out of arts 30 and 36 were too clear to be argued the court would exercise its discretion not to refer them to the European Court."

Eventually the case proceeded to the House of Lords as *Henn and Darby v Director of Publications* and because a national court from which there is no appeal *shall* refer European issues to the ECJ under Article 234 (177), the case was duly referred to Luxembourg.

In its judgement the ECJ was very respectful, bearing in mind that this was the first case to be referred to it by the House of Lords. It was interesting that the British government exercised it right to present its observations to the ECJ regarding the case, as many governments frequently do. Here though, they dissociated themselves from the view of the Court of Appeal stating, "It is clear that a total prohibition represents a greater invasion of the fundamental principle of free movement of goods than a partial restraint on imports." No doubt the ECJ regarded this as a commendable view on the purposive interpretation of European law.

The Advocate General was polite but emphatic on the same point. "A total prohibition is a quantitative restriction, the quantity being zero." The contrary view expressed in the Court of Appeal was "irreconcilable with the use in article 36 of the phrase 'prohibitions or restrictions,' but it is irreconcilable also with the very purpose of Title 1 of Part II of the Treaty which makes the free movement of goods one of the 'foundations of the Community'." The ECJ went on to rule that although it was a prohibited restriction this could nevertheless be justified on grounds of public morality and no doubt Parliament in Westminster would be relieved that the ECJ was not intending to overturn one of its criminal statutes for the sake of market regulations. This was indeed the result but it should be remembered, using a hypothetical deduction so hated by courts, that this case nevertheless established that the direct effect of Article 30 *could* be raised as a defence in a criminal trial.

Following correct procedure the case now returned to the House of Lords, and the appropriate judgment issued following the "preliminary" ruling of the ECJ. The appeal was dismissed. However it also contained a warning to the lower courts. Lord Diplock stated,

> *"It appeared to me to be so free from any doubt that an absolute prohibition of importation of goods of a particular description from other member states fell within article 30 that I should not have been disposed to regard the instant case as involving any matter of interpretation of that article that was open to question. But the strong inclination expressed by the Court of Appeal to adopt the contrary view shows that there is involved a question of interpretation on which judicial minds can differ. It serves as a timely warning to English judges not to be too ready to hold that because the meaning of the English text (which is one of six of equal authority) seems plain to them no question of interpretation can be involved."*

It was a warning that discretion in referring matters to the ECJ should not be used as an excuse for avoiding the changes implicit in European doctrines. In this case the House of Lords formally acknowledges its duty under the European Communities Act to give full effect to provisions of European law, as determined by the ECJ. All lesser courts in Britain are consequently obliged to follow.

It took a few more small steps before the preliminary reference procedure finally reached its maturity. For example in *CILFIT v Ministro della Sanita* [1982] the ECJ decided that national courts could decline to refer matters to the ECJ if they were clear, only providing they were also convinced that the matter would be equally obvious to the courts of all other Member States and the ECJ. Even so necessary precedents for involving the ECJ had now been set. Actually it would be several more years before the mechanism became routine in Britain and in other member states. Nevertheless, the highly inventive "trojan horse" strategy of enforcing the provisions of the Treaty through local courts, had finally been completed, and was firmly established in Britain.

Chapter 18: Margaret Thatcher – The European

Thatcher - Battling With but For Europe

New actors are constantly replacing the older ones on the political stage. Within a year of the referendum Harold Wilson had surprised everyone by announcing his retirement from politics and was replaced by James Callaghan. Roy Jenkins however, was not for retiring even though he had become marginalised in British politics. Instead he left Britain to become President of the European Commission, and from Brussels was to exert almost un-noticed, a continuing influence on Britain.

The European Commission had a sole responsibility for initiating policy recommendations but Jenkins had become frustrated by its lack of any authority to implement anything at all without Council approval. His own ambitions for progressing towards integration were limited by national governments' pre-occupation with domestic issues in particular relating to the oil crises and the consequent recession. However in this climate of economic instability he did obtain support for European Monetary System. He was the prime instigator of the European Exchange Rate Mechanism (ERM) within this system. This was similar to the earlier "Currency Snake" which allowed only small variations of currency exchange rates against the dollar, supported by co-ordinated intervention from the Central Banks of the Community. Britain had joined but only briefly as the pound was soon forced to float ie. sink. Denmark, Italy and even France suffered the same indignity, leaving the snake as little more than a Deutschmark zone, from which a single currency could not grow for many years.

Europeans were attracted by the idea of a zone of stability created by fixed exchange rates following the collapse of the international Bretton-Woods agreement which had provided precisely that between 1944 and 1973. French President Giscard d'Estaing and German Chancellor Schmidt agreed to tie the system into the institutions of the EC, allowing France to compensate for its relatively weak economy with its institutional political influence, and the EMS began as early as March 1979. However the British Treasury, with its memories of traumatic devaluations remained committed to floating exchange rates. Prime Minister Callaghan accepted Treasury advice and opposed ERM, to the extent of keeping Britain outside the scheme. For his pains he was roundly derided by the pro-European Margaret Thatcher who suggested that it was a "Sad day for Europe" with the Labour party "content to have Britain openly classified among the poorest and least influential members" of the Community.

Thatcher's credentials regarding Europe were well known. She had followed the reasoning that Europe needed to co-operate to maintain peace, and believed in the force for democracy that the Community could become. She argued that even "a cultured, developed, Christian country like Germany had fallen under Hitler's sway" showing that civilisation, in the hands of weak people, could never be taken for granted. She regretted that Britain "missed the boat at Messina" and did not believe that EFTA, the Commonwealth, or even the USA were adequate to meet Britain's trading needs. She also described De Gaulle's veto statement when he was offering association, "The best European bus that ever came along". She was well established as a supporter of the European ideal, even though subsequently the contradiction between its actual meaning and her understanding of the ideal was to cause her downfall.

In her first speech as leader of the Opposition Thatcher spoke critically against the Referendum Bill, in principle. Such a device she said, could only be appropriate for "cases of constitutional change", which therefore did not appear applicable to Europe in 1975! Indeed she had welcomed Geoffrey Howe's assurance regarding the continuing independence of British courts even though he himself was later to admit that the phrase "essential sovereignty" was an "extraordinary example of artful confusion to conceal fundamental issues." Then, having made clear her opposition to the referendum she took little part in it, despite her professed faith in Europe. More comfortable in the world of two party, verbal warfare she despised the customary European politics learned from backgrounds of continuous coalitions involving lifelong haggling and dealing, compromise and consensus. So, while supporting Europe in principle she was not enthusiastic about closer involvement. Christopher Soames described her as an "agnostic who continues to go to church."

On becoming Britain's first woman Prime Minister she was to enter the European political arena with the subtlety of a hurricane, as soon as discussions moved from esoteric theory to hard cash. The complex formula Wilson had negotiated eventually produce no savings at all to the British budgetary contributions. These calculations had been based on GNP but although Britain was in these terms already less rich than France Netherlands, Denmark, it had the benefit of North Sea oil.

Simply raising the subject of contributions had proved difficult. Of course there was the thought that for one member to pay less others had to pay more; so there appeared to be a general consensus that it was simply bad form to raise the matter. Discussion of net contributions almost amounted to heretical, and certainly contrary to the high minded European spirit which should not to be sullied by pure commercialism. Countries with net gains were even very much opposed to publishing figures. The Danes especially seemed almost passionate in principled opposition, although possibly fearing that any publicity given to net gains might lead to their erosion. The Community had established a general commitment to the pooling of resources followed by its distribution according to a carefully negotiated, neutral formula. It took graphic descriptions by Mr. Thatcher of British taxpayers' money being routed into pockets of German farmers to explain why the issue had to be discussed.

One unexpected obstacle in these discussions had been described by the former Foreign Secretary David Owen. He described, in remarkable contrast to the previous generation of civil servants, a culture of federalism in the Foreign Office. He described how many officials had grown into EEC zealots, and had converted to campaigners rather than diplomats. This led to a serious institutional reluctance to oppose the Community on any issue, or "to spill a little blood on the diplomatic carpet". They were also not easily submitting to political control. He compared the Foreign Office very unfavourably with French officials who always talk Europe, but always think France, and fight at every level for France. They show a consistent, well mannered ruthlessness contrasting with a lack of similar tenacity from British officials. The Foreign Office felt it was their imperative to make Europe work, without regard to constitutional theory, or of the possible cussed reaction of the mob. Politicians at home were viewed as more serious obstacles than the European diplomats and were people to be resisted.

Foreign Office exposure to the new regime opened in Dublin after Thatcher had been in office for six months. To her the subject of contributions was a gloriously black v white issue of quantifiable money, tinged with blatant injustice. To her, there was to be shown no patience with the established subtleties of Euro diplomacy. Instead her dealings at the Summit were characterised by "hideously plain speaking, a triumphant lack of sensitivity to other people's problems." She made little more than a very aggressive demand for balance. There was a shocked reaction from the leaders, as well as horror from the Foreign Office, followed by a rude, derisive, uncompromising rejection.

Background negotiations continued in the more diplomatic circles and eventually Ministers Carrington and Gilmour in a meeting when she was sizzling "like a firework whose fuse had been lit" succeeded in persuading her to accept a rebate of two-thirds of the deficit for three years. This she agreed, through "gritted teeth".

Of course a three year deal was bound to lead to a repeat of the same issue, but in this interval a number of factors had changed. Mrs. Thatcher's power rose with her victory in the Falklands War, and with a landslide election victory in 1983. At the same time two quite different characters moved in as her new opponents in the European arena. Helmut Kohl replaced Schmidt, and François Mitterrand replaced Giscard d'Estaing.

Kohl actually worked hard to establish cordial relations with Mrs. Thatcher whose fundamental dislike of Germans appeared to stem from right back to her childhood in Grantham. Kohl though was at all times courteous, and tried hard to convince her that he was "not German but European". Thatcher however remained more comfortable and understood better the more direct confrontations characterised by Schmidt. It became clear to Mrs. Thatcher that "Gasbag" Kohl was interested in conferring on Europe a steadily larger grandeur, continuing movement gradually towards the dismantling of the nation state. Typical of the time was the Declaration of Stuttgart which was an expansive document describing measures to enhance the identity of Europe. This was to lead to such measures as a European passport, and to adoption of the EU Flag, unveiled to the sound of the anthem "Ode to Joy" in front of the Commission building at Berlaymont in May, 1986.

François Mitterrand in contrast to Kohl, often appeared to Thatcher as an intellectual, or almost a philosopher, rather than a down-to-earth practical politician. The French government had been following socialist policies with little interest in Europe. This had caused some friction with Germany, particularly as in economic field they had caused devaluations of the franc, in turn threatening the European Monetary System itself. Now though, Mitterrand was turning the French more towards the Thatcherite path.

One thing that didn't change was the use of aggressive tactics. For example in 1982 Thatcher attempted to use a veto under the Luxembourg Accord to prevent the adoption of an agricultural price package; as a means of putting pressure on the Community to agree to changes to the budget. This was one of the few occasions where interestingly, the Council rejected the veto and proceeded to outvote Britain. The use of a "veto" was only to be used for measures which constituted a direct threat to national interest. A tactical manoeuvre did not qualify.

A head of steam was now building up. Mitterrand had attempted to sway Thatcher towards his vision of Europe but she remained resistant to his grandiose reflections. But Mitterrand was determined to start his term as President of the Council with a new level of vigorous activity. This was an early model of the future role of the alternating six-monthly Presidency as a highly effective tool in promoting and accelerating the competence of the Community. In times to come every forthcoming Presidency would routinely prepare its special plans and specific objectives for advancing the Community during its tenure, in accordance with its pet projects or domestic priorities or its current vision for the future. For six months it would manage and drive these projects as rapidly as it could, and would finally would be judged (by the Commission) in a review of its performance. National pride, and the reputation of the individual leaders would depend on the quality of its integrationist measures.

As Mitterrand was due to become President he had complained that the Europe was "beginning to look like an abandoned building site". His solution was a major construction programme including such structures as agricultural reform, the accession of Spain and Portugal, liberalising the internal market, and an increase in Community funds. Mitterrand's ambitions appeared to be heading towards a serious obstacle from Britain both in the form of contributions once again, but also in a more general lack of enthusiasm for his plans.

Britain had thus given ample notice of escalation as the expiry of the 1980 budget deal approached, and required a permanent solution. The issue was being brought to a head in the 1984 summit in Fontainebleau, at the same time as decisions required for Mitterrand's major push forward. Germany had by then been saying that necessary compromises could be agreed, but France had been showing less patience. Thus, debates across Europe included for the first time the possibility of a two speed Europe, of "in" and "out" countries, of the "core" members and the "periphery". There was even the suggestion of an enforced "empty chair" policy where members not agreeing to particular new objectives would be excluded from the meetings discussing and deciding the details. It became clear that obstruction of renewed development was not going to be permitted. Achievements to be started during Mitterrand's presidency were not be stopped.

Thus despite the background threat of exclusion from community developments Thatcher had the leverage required to make the deal she needed. Before the crucial summit her target had been a rebate of 66% of deficit, at that time worth £1bn. The negotiating positions stood at 55% v 70%. At the meeting Thatcher continued her forceful style. Kohl moved to an offer of 60%, then Mitterand tentatively suggested 65%. Finally Thatcher persuaded to Mitterand to move the extra one percent, with a link to a new level of the Community take from VAT receipts, which the Community badly needed to finance its new plans. The Council also conceded on proposals regarding liberalisation of the internal market, the abolition of customs control, and on some more radical measures for institutional reform. It was a famous victory for Thatcher where she obtained in the words of a French official, "more than was reasonable".

Thatcher's success now produced in her what seems today a remarkable and unprecedented outbreak of euro-enthusiasm. She saw a new vision of Europe, with the advantages of a single market united in a purpose of tacking unemployment and improving living standards. Even the building of a Channel Tunnel had a symbolic attraction, although not quite sufficiently strong to justify public funds. Thatcher was to become a driving force in removing the obstacles which remained in the single market following the removal of the tariff barriers. Contradictory technical, health and safety standards, and remaining barriers to the free movement of labour, services and capital should be removed. The "level playing field" would extend to all commercial activity. Thatcher had a vision of a real free and dynamic market, shorn of elements of protectionism, curiously in line with the Commission's specific objectives, although as will be seen with one critical and philosophical difference. Whereas Thatcher was beginning to battle for a free market by elimination of obstacles, the level field could also be achieved by equalisation and harmonisation by centralised regulation. By fighting for one Thatcher ultimately achieved the other, causing in her mind the confusion of purpose that led to her downfall.

Towards a Single Market

Thatcher's new conversion to the European cause, no less strident than her previous obstruction attracted a new ally in the person of the new Commission president, Jacques Delors. Delors had been the French Finance Minister responsible for reversal of socialism within France and with a reputation for financial discipline which appealed to the Thatcher government. He was also a strong advocate of the single market measures Thatcher supported, so he became Britain's preferred candidate. Politically though, Delor's background was quite different and a future conflict regarding de-regulation or otherwise was predictable. Delors also foresaw that the economic growth anticipated in European economies provided a new opportunity for further Community development. However Thatcher, saw the Commission in a limited role analogous to that of her own Civil Service and was confident in her influence at the higher Council level. She therefore believed that extreme political views or ambitions even at the head of the Commission could be safely neglected. However as a safeguard it seemed prudent to appoint a special commissioner, Arthur Cockfield, a successful businessman who had become Secretary of State for Trade, to assist Delors in building the single market. This, she would soon realise, was to become a serious mistake.

Cockfield had a reputation for a "tenacious commitment" to any task given to him, with a strong sense of logic not constrained by any political considerations, nor by any factors such as national sovereignty, sentiment, or individual freedom. Thatcher was later to write that this attitude made him "the prisoner as well as the master of his subject." So, to Cockfield it was merely logical to suggest that the removal of barriers should obviously extend to all conceivable barriers, including for example the harmonisation of national taxation systems. The white paper he produced listed 297 imperfections in the single market and included proposals for removing all of them by 1992.

Certainly many of these proposals were anathema to Thatcher's thinking. However her support for the principle of the single market continued unabated, no doubt with confidence that the more eccentric proposals could be safely ignored. Thatcher, produced her own paper in mid 1985; "Europe: The Future" which included her proposals for completing the internal market, including suggestions for streamlining decision making. Remarkably she also called for a stronger European role on foreign policy, speculating on how useful it would be if Community support could be relied on in incidents like the Falklands conflict. In France the newspaper Le Matin described this as a "Spectacular evolution of the British position", likely to "confuse those critics sceptical of Britain's euro-enthusiasm."

Having a large measure of agreement as to what was to be achieved there was now an important question as to how the Cockfield-Delors model could be implemented. The "streamlining" of the decision making process was regarded by Delors as essential to maintain the rapid progress required. Clearly it would not be sensible if an individual country could block a particular and possibly minor measure which it found to its disadvantage. They therefore proposed an extension of qualified majority voting in matters relating to the single market, with weighting of votes according to each country's size. Thatcher and Howe responded with a peculiarly English suggestion of a gentleman's agreement to waive unanimity for single market measures. This was essentially an informal approach, which would produce no binding legal changes. This was clearly inadequate from the European perspective and the Community leaned towards the Delors proposal for an Inter-Governmental Conference (IGC), to amend the Treaty of Rome, and provide effective enforcement procedures to the European Court of Justice.

Thatcher tried very hard to avoid the avoid IGC. She saw it as the start of potentially dangerous, uncontrollable constitutional ventures, likely to be federalist, and certain to be legalistic. Then, the Irish politician James Dooge charged with suggesting improvements to European co-operation produced a document confirming Thatcher's worst fears. He extended the proposals for development of the single market, by adding closer political co-operation; achievement of a European social area; institutional reform; the promotion of common cultural values; and rebranding as a European Union!

Careful lobbying of the Germans and especially the Italians preceded the summit in Milan in 1985, but this time the limits to the Thatcher confrontational method became clear. European leaders' backgrounds in coalition politics made then more familiar with civilised compromise, a virtue traditional praised but not practices in Europe by the British. In Europe the concept of an individual victory seemed less prized than achieving group co-operation. Goodwill among leaders was an important currency which could not be increased by intransigence and shouting. Such bad manners caused personal irritation to leaders of national standing with their own deeply held views and their own voters to consider. Thus the new Italian leader obtained a majority Council vote in favour of the IGC – the first time a member state had been outvoted despite an attempted veto.

Thatcher now felt betrayed, bulldozed and even humiliated, particularly by Craxi, and must have realised that the European beast was not as tame as she had anticipated. Officials, still enthusiastic about the European project, now again exerted an important role in persuading Thatcher not to boycott the IGC. After all they argued, unanimity was still required to amend the Treaty and Britain's interest would be best served by participating in the decision making process from the inside. This is another familiar theme, reflecting once again a reluctant acquiescence to forces beyond control, moving in an undesirable direction. The lesser of evils is regarded as participation in a project not itself accepted, with an objective no more than to minimize the inevitable losses. The result though is always the same. Even though the effects of the forces may be minimised in the present, they nevertheless strengthen every time, making the next advances even more difficult to resist. Any concessions obtained can be later removed taking advantage of the new boundary and a renewed application of these strengthened forces. Even in 1986 Margaret Thatcher was unwilling to countenance the alternative, which could easily escalate to total opposition, and at least diplomatic warfare, with real national interests at stake or a very public climb-down. As a result officials were sent to participate, with the brief of obtaining an acceptable fusion of the two visions of Europe.

In fact there was never any chance of such a compromise because the contrast between the alternative cultures was simply unbridgeable. Instead, the concept of free trading nation states was to give way to the common European models of state social protection and privileged state enterprise. Therefore, swept by the European flow, Thatcher found herself speaking in favour of surrendering of powers to the Assembly to be renamed the European Parliament; the first Treaty reference to Economic and Monetary Union; and majority rule on all single market measures, and unimpeded movement of goods subject to harmonised standards etc. Only relatively minor concessions were obtained. Evolution of the European Monetary System would still require unanimous consent; Community taxation was rejected, and national control of immigration was retained.

Thus the Single European Act was produced, and agreed. Ratification by all Member States was required and Thatcher's task was now to deliver the approval of the House of Commons. To this end she could show no sign of the fundamental contradictions involved, and which she undoubtedly felt. Supporters were talking about the new free market, and Thatcherism on a European scale although the real proposals were in reality quite different. Majority rule might seem "federalist" but it was actually just practical; a way of imposing a free market, and a defeat for national protectionism. Asked about the Preamble to the new Treaty, "To contribute to making concrete progress towards European Unity", Thatcher replied. "I am constantly saying that I wish they would talk less about European and political Union. The terms are not understood in this country. In so far as they are understood over there, they mean a good deal less than some people over here think they mean". Thus the argument that Europeans did not mean what they said persisted. The precedent of pretence or deception followed that of the original arguments over the Treaty of Rome. "Euro-twaddle" should not be taken seriously, even though the use made by the Commission and the ECJ of all of these statements should have been perfectly well known.

In fact all these contrived arguments met broad acceptance and passage of the Amendment Bill 1986 was a low key and uncontroversial affair. MP's mostly believed in the "economies of scale in a united European market." The events of this time were however re-forming the career of an important figure in European matters who remains influential today.

From the mid 1970's William Cash had been a pro-European, and had become an MP after considerable difficulty in 1984. As a new MP he quickly used his training as a lawyer and sat on the Select Committee on European Legislation. He was keenly in favour of Europe, writing to people explaining from a positive viewpoint the need to take European legislation into account. But, it was on this committee that he began to notice the some of the deeper implications. He began to feel disturbed that the political trends in Europe, supported by the growing but insidious power of European law were at odds with the streams of political thought in Britain. He suggested mildly that, "The European Community was in danger of rapidly becoming a political federation." Similarly after a visit to Brussels he commented, "I was disturbed by the number of officials I met from the European Commission whose federalism was beyond doubt."

Nevertheless Cash, as a loyal Thatcherite, supported passage of the Single European Act, speaking against leading opponents such as Enoch

Powell and Teddy Taylor whose own admitted obsession with European opposition had prevented him obtaining government office from the early seventies. A few words of anxiety, appeared from Cash during the third reading of the Bill when he said, "It is essential to maintain the democracy of this House and its sovereignty and to ensure that the legislation done in our name is known to be done on behalf of the people of this country." Not achieving the impact he had expected from such an important comment he tried to emphasise it further, now positively fearful of the effects of European law and its untamed evolution. (See Chapters E and F). He tabled an amendment to the Bill saying, "Nothing in this Act shall derogate from the sovereignty of the United Kingdom Parliament." To his surprise this amendment which suggested a matter of overwhelming importance was totally ignored leaving a bemused Cash simply to toe the line and vote for the Bill. Afterwards he remained somewhat in obscurity, although actively engaging with politicians across Europe pursuing his parliamentary role, and fighting rearguard actions against the tide of European law as he continues to this day.

There was of course some real opposition from Conservatives like Teddy Taylor, and Nicholas Budgen who strongly objected to the increased powers of the ECJ, and the naming of a European Parliament. However, it was only Enoch Powell who voted against the guillotine motion which restricted debate and smoothed passage of the Bill. The final vote, 149 to 43 demonstrated remarkable indifference to a Bill of disguised but nevertheless fundamental constitutional effect.

Chapter J: The Single European Act

Signed in February 1986, and coming into force on 1st July, 1987 the Single European Act represented the next major political step introducing intergovernmental co-operation in the sphere of foreign policy, a new procedure enhancing the role of the European Parliament in the legislative process, and a recognition of the role of human rights.

HIS MAJESTY THE KING OF THE BELGIANS, HER MAJESTY THE QUEEN OF DENMARK, THE PRESIDENT OF THE FEDERAL REPUBLIC OF GERMANY, THE PRESIDENT OF THE HELLENIC REPUBLIC, HIS MAJESTY THE KING OF SPAIN, THE PRESIDENT OF THE FRENCH REPUBLIC, THE PRESIDENT OF IRELAND, THE PRESIDENT OF THE ITALIAN REPUBLIC, HIS ROYAL HIGHNESS THE GRAND DUKE OF LUXEMBOURG, HER MAJESTY THE QUEEN OF THE NETHERLANDS, THE PRESIDENT OF THE PORTUGUESE REPUBLIC, HER MAJESTY THE QUEEN OF THE UNITED KINGDOM OF GREAT BRITAIN AND NORTHERN IRELAND,

MOVED by the will to continue the work undertaken on the basis of the Treaties establishing the European Communities and to transform relations as a whole among their States into a European Union, in accordance with the Solemn Declaration of Stuttgart of 19 June 1983,

RESOLVED to implement this European Union on the basis, firstly, of the Communities operating in accordance with their own rules and, secondly, of European cooperation among the signatory States in the sphere of foreign policy and to invest this Union with the necessary means of action,

DETERMINED to work together to promote democracy on the basis of the fundamental rights recognized in the constitutions and laws of the Member States, in the Convention for the Protection of Human Rights and Fundamental Freedoms and the European Social Charter, notably freedom, equality and social justice,

CONVINCED that the European idea, the results achieved in the fields of economic integration and political cooperation, and the need for new developments correspond to the wishes of the democratic peoples of Europe, for whom the European Parliament, elected by universal suffrage, is an indispensable means of expression,

AWARE of the responsibility incumbent upon Europe to aim at speaking ever increasingly with one voice and to act with consistency and solidarity in order more effectively to protect its common interests and independence, in particular to display the principles of democracy and compliance with the law and with human rights to which they are attached, so that together they may make their own contribution to the preservation of international peace and security in accordance with the undertaking entered into by them within the framework of the United Nations Charter,

DETERMINED to improve the economic and social situation by extending common policies and pursuing new objectives, and to ensure a smoother functioning of the Communities by enabling the institutions to exercise their powers under conditions most in keeping with Community interests,

WHEREAS at their Conference in Paris from 19 to 21 October 1972 the Heads of State or Government approved the objective of the progressive realization of economic and monetary union,

HAVING REGARD to the Annex to the conclusions of the Presidency of the European Council in Bremen on 6 and 7 July 1978 and the resolution of the European Council in Brussels on 5 December 1978 on the introduction of the European Monetary System (EMS) and related questions, and noting that in accordance with that resolution, the Community and the central banks of the Member States have taken a number of measures intended to implement monetary cooperation,

HAVE DECIDED to adopt this Act

One of the original important aims of this treaty was to complete the formation of the single market and to set a deadline of 1992 for all the actions required to achieve this. As an integral part of this process there was a strengthening of the mechanisms for ensuring harmonisation. In fact these had already been strong. The original Treaty of Rome included in Article 101 (now 96) an important power for the European Commission to investigate any provisions laid down by law, regulation or administrative action in Member States, likely to create "distortion" in the establishment or functioning of the single market. This could be enforced by the issuing of Directives passed by Qualified Majority Voting. The SEA introduced a new Article 100a (now 95) which extended these areas of Commission concern to include the "harmonisation" of national measures.

Thus in 1986 the political impetus towards completing the Single Market resulted in a strengthening of the legal bases on which EC regulations and legislation would be introduced and enforced. Interestingly, and particularly for the British, these political measures were taken before all the effects of earlier legislation had worked their way through the judicial systems of Europe. Even in Britain a change in the law, while having some effects immediately is never fully realised until the courts have established the range of precedents which determine the balance with other related measures, the boundaries of its application and the detailed interpretation of its terms and concepts. In Europe the same process was much more complex since it concerned essentially an entirely new legal system which was still simultaneously evolving, and expanding its spheres of influence. From its foundation the ECJ gained immediate power over the institutions of the Communities since its supervisory role within the Community was expected from the start and was respected by all concerned. However the projection of its power through the network of national courts was slow to develop. The principle itself caused consternation in some countries, such as Britain, and the scope of its decisions had not been finally determined. But, in just a few more years, governments were to realise just how extensive were the effects of the Treaty of Rome. let alone the Single European Act.

Chapter 19: The Lady WAS for Turning.

Accelerating Europe

The Single European Act led to a new dynamism in Europe with multiple agendas for integration and co-ordination, and the beginning of a relentless acceleration in the production of detailed plans and proposals and a new level of real purposeful activity. Thatcher had seen the SEA as some form of ultimate achievement, about which she felt increasingly ambivalent. She did not see that it was part of a continuing process rather than an event from which she could now move on. Nor, with her preference for a set and ferocious battle had she understood the Community ethos of perpetual negotiation and compromise, bound within the context of an overriding sense of direction. She had become trapped by the powers she had helped create, powerless in a new era of incremental progress which now had a life of its own.

Jacques Delors was making it clear that the SEA was a mere stepping stone. "In ten years 80% of laws affecting the economy and social policy will be passed at a European and not national level. We are not going to manage the decisions needed between now and 1995, unless we see the beginnings of a European Government." He was clearly inviting national parliaments and politicians to consider the actual realities which were already flowing from the SEA, and their relationship with a new "federalist centre". Thatcher though, described his comments as "over the top", "extremist", "airy-fairy", apparently oblivious to what was really happening, but certainly unable to admit at least publicly the truth of what she had done.

The Commission had an ethos quite contrary to that of the civil service and under Delors it had become a prolific initiator of policy. Gradually it was extending its competence into culture, education, health, and social security. It was active in forming special "advisory committees" independent of national governments, which were being used to circumvent national structures. It was using the most casual of vacuous quotations from Council decisions to justify new proposals which conformed with its expansive agenda and had found a special budget procedure "Actions ponctuelles" to finance exploratory projects without any established legal basis. Critics were beginning to explain that treaty articles were being regularly and deliberately misinterpreted in order to pass directives under Qualified Majority Voting (QMV) procedures, avoiding the need for unanimity. For example, Health and Safety measures could be passed by

QMV, whereas measures of general social policy required unanimity. Therefore supporters need only find a health or safety benefit to workers to in order to defeat opposition. Interpretation of the SEA referring to the fundamental purposes defined in its preamble allowed a gradual shifting of the boundary. Critics were accusing even the ECJ of collusion by twisting the words and intentions of the Council to favour integrationist and expansionist interpretations.

Politically the Commission was also gaining ground by the introduction of popular measures. Environmental and health regulations were difficult for established politicians to oppose, and were cunningly being introduced and publicised by the Commission with this in mind. Commissioners were also presenting themselves as true friends of British workers, by advocating extensive social legislation, and the protection of workers rights. This enabled the TUC to support "frère Jacques" as a very welcome weapon against Thatcher and her market forces, naturally to her considerable irritation.

At the same time the next battleground was appearing, and Thatcher attempted to define a new line in the inexorably shifting sands. It was in 1985 that the Exchange Rate Mechanism (ERM) had been established as a zone of monetary stability and as the next progressive step in the realisation of Economic and Monetary Union (EMU) already agreed in principle in the SEA. It could be seen as an obvious and merely logical extension to the concept of the single market. However its prospect germinated in Thatcher a renewed scepticism which gradually grew to a persistent and aggressive opposition. It was a subject which grew to dominate her political life and ultimately destroyed any semblance of Cabinet unity.

Foreign Secretary Geoffrey Howe, and Chancellor Nigel Lawson supported by their pro-European civil service teams wanted to join the ERM for valid economic reasons. They favoured an anti-inflation strategy based on exchange rate restraint rather than on Thatcher's monetarist policy which was becoming discredited. Lawson had supported a tie of Sterling to the Deutschmark since 1981 as junior minister, and had become convinced in 1983 when he started responsibility for the Treasury, in the face of officials' scepticism. Thatcher objected to the loss of economic freedom the ERM would entail. Economically she viewed it as an entrapment of exchange rates. Gradually though she was being talked round. Lawson was biding his time, increasing his influence, selling his idea that joining was actually inevitable, waiting just until the time was right.

Eventually Thatcher began thinking in terms of when rather than if. Lawson stressed economic advantages which ERM members were beginning to obtain over Britain, and explained that the risks of belonging were lower than those of staying alone outside. He had enlisted support from the Treasury, the Bank of England, and nearly all the Cabinet. There was however one background un-elected voice of influence on Thatcher – the economist and her personal "guru", Alan Walters. His comment, "If you join EMS, you will have to do so without me", proved to be decisive and Thatcher dismissed the suggestion and simply swept aside all the Cabinet support for joining. Lawson was outraged, and in later, calmer days regarded this as the greatest missed opportunity during his tenure as Chancellor. The amazing consequence was that Lawson then decided to follow his own, unauthorised exchange rate policy and proceeded to manage the value of sterling to shadow the DM, holding it down to 3.00. This he continued until Thatcher abruptly forced him to stop in March 1988, not many months before the policy once again appeared on the agenda.

Halting at Bruges

In the meantime Thatcher had delivered one of her most important speeches, in Bruges, at the College of Europe, in September 1988. This provided her with a defining moment or possibly a last stand for her true beliefs as applied to the European situation. Hugo Young records how, during preparation of this speech, furious exchanges between Downing Street staff and the Foreign Office, coupled with "Yes Minister" type consultations, resulted in a considerable toning down of the original strident and insolent text. Even the resulting text was viewed by the Foreign Office as so provocative that they immediately implemented "damage limitation" measures such as warning Brussels, who were able to ensure that Delors himself would not be present to suffer any embarrassment.

The vision of Europe which Thatcher presented was entirely consistent with her well known support of free enterprise, and with her domestic policies. "The lesson of the economic history of Europe in the 1970s and 1980s is that central planning and detailed control don't work, and that personal endeavour and initiative do". "A state-controlled economy is a recipe for low growth; and free enterprise within a framework of law brings better results." This meant that practical measures in the single market should be the Community's priority. "That means action to free markets, action to widen choice, action to reduce government intervention." "Our aim should not be more and more detailed regulation from the centre: it should be to deregulate and to remove the constraints on trade." "We certainly do not need new regulations which raise the cost of employment and make Europe's labour market less flexible and less competitive with overseas suppliers."

She also broached an issue highly emotive to several Members ie the Common Agricultural Policy, remarking that substantial reform was required urgently to release resources for regional development, and job training schemes which were really needed. Regarding monetary matters she suggested that speculation on a European Central Bank was less important than practical measure such as improving the free movement of capital, and obtaining a genuinely free market in all financial services.

However her speech is best remembered for its anti-federalist flavour, viewing the Community as a family of nations. "Willing and active co-operation between independent sovereign states was the way to build a successful European Community." Finally the most famous and even ominous quotation, "We have not successfully rolled back the frontiers of the state in Britain only to see them re-imposed at a European level, with a European super-state exercising a new dominance from Brussels."

Thatcher herself described the reaction to her speech with satisfaction as one of "stunned outrage", and was pleased at the generally favourable response in the media back home. Geoffrey Howe, though, believed the speech to represent a real tuning point, indicating that Thatcher was now allowing her heart to overrule her head, and that reasoning could no longer be used to produce a sensible and pragmatic policy. This was the time of a final philosophical rupture between them, even though Howe was not yet prepared to leave the Government.

The message from Bruges was clear and in its own way very positive about the future of Europe. However, the description it contained was so different from the prevailing and long held views of all the other European leaders that none of them could take its proposals seriously. Nothing short of a fundamental change in direction could have accommodated Thatcher's vision, and as Tony Blair was to discover in later years European leaders cannot and will not change their lifetime habits and thought processes. For practical purposes, and in ultimate effect the rest of Europe was simply deaf to her message, however strident and insistent it may have sounded, and however sensible and logical it may have been. The stunned outrage from Bruges, immediately and mechanically gave way to the next item of business, without any review or even thought about the Thatcher principles. Her alternative vision was ignored. ERM returned to the agenda.

The Battle for ERM

Jacques Delors had already secured a second term as Commission President, ironically with Thatcher seconding his nomination when her preferred candidate refused to stand against him. Then with the support of most of the other European leaders he had taken charge of the committee of central bankers given the task of deciding on the next steps towards EMU. The governor of the Bank of England, Robin Leigh-Pemberton was Britain's representative with the remit of reporting progress to Ministers, and of obstructing any moves towards a European Central Bank, which Thatcher adamantly opposed. However, one single member could dictate neither the agenda nor the decision to the others and eventually a three stage programme leading to full monetary union was agreed. Leigh-Pemberton also signed up to this, telling Lawson that he was not prepared to remain in a minority of one.

The question to be posed for decision at the June 1989 summit in Madrid, was whether Britain would formally sign up for Stage One of the EMU process and join the ERM. It was by no means a simple, technical decision. It had taken on the critical dimensions of a test of loyalty to the European ideal. A negative answer would be taken to imply a negative attitude to European participation in principle and to question any future participation as a serious player. Although not appreciated at the time it was a telling parallel with Macmillan's talks whereby obtaining any consideration of Britain's position depended on initial acceptance "in principle" of committed membership. Thatcher may have thought that this attitude was perverse, or even absurd, but it was definitely real. Continuing active membership depended practically if not legally, on accepting the next step.

Geoffrey Howe's position was clear. He supported EMU. Nigel Lawson was not quite so clear in that he opposed full EMU but nevertheless wanted to join the ERM, to benefit from currency stability. Delors however, was making his position clear, that Stage One should inevitably lead to

Stage Three. Thus Howe and Lawson joined forces to ensure a positive answer at Madrid.

Treasury and Foreign Office officials now united to produce a memorandum for an audience of one. It argued deviously that although the British objective was to derail EMU, this would be best achieved by joining, or at least committing Britain to join the ERM, and thus remaining within the EMU machinery. It should have been a familiar argument – we must join something we oppose in principle but cannot stop, so that we can continue working from the inside to minimise its detrimental effects. Thatcher however, influenced by her "kitchen" cabinet of her private staff, including Alan Walters and her influential press secretary, Bernard Ingham, thought differently. She proposed to submit a list of single market measures to be implemented before ERM was accepted, and avoided discussing the issue with her Ministers as long as possible. It was therefore only on the day before the Madrid summit that both Howe and Lawson told her that neither would feel able to remain in the government if she failed to move forward on ERM.

A shocked Thatcher regarded this as an ultimate betrayal by her most senior colleagues, and as a premeditated ambush, without realising that her own tactics had forced them into this action. Relations were so bad that at the opening of the summit meeting Howe still had no idea what Thatcher would say. In fact she accepted that the UK intended to join the ERM, subject to some conditions and without any specific date, although reminding her partners that the ultimate adoption of a single currency would not be acceptable to the House of Commons. Thus with Thatcher making the actual commitment demanded by Howe and Lawson, and with the Prime Minister emphasising the conditions proposed both sides at the head of government were able to enjoy a victorious if precarious compromise.

In Thatcher's memoirs she remarks that only someone with a "particularly naïve view of the world" could have believed that the Madrid conditions would even slow the pace of EMU. That however was what she was telling the Commons, presenting her conditions as a victory for common sense over the surreal dreams of Jacques Delors, and inexplicably, just as at the time of the Single European Act, the media agreed. Thus Thatcher felt sufficiently confident as soon as the storm had settled, to re-shuffle her Cabinet, offering to Geoffrey Howe the insignificant job of Leader of the House of Commons. Soon, he resigned, presenting to the Commons a dramatic personal statement politely but pointedly critical of

Thatcher and her style. However, this was not before repeatedly reminding her in the Commons of the need to stick to the ERM terms agreed in good faith in Madrid. By October, Lawson had also left the Government, frustrated at the continuing intervention of Alan Walters from Downing Street. More malleable successors were soon in position – John Major in the Treasury and Douglas Hurd in the Foreign Office.

Despite the shuffle, Government division continued with both Major and Hurd receiving emphatically pro-ERM advice from their officials. A compromise proposal involving ultimate circulation of ecu's (European Currency Units) in parallel with and in competition with national currencies was widely promoted by Major, but never considered seriously in Europe. Hurd started warning that Britain should not appear defensive or negative, lest we "isolate ourselves by shutting ourselves off, raising the drawbridge of argument, acting as if we were a beleaguered island."

The Thatcherite belief in floating exchange rates with its opposition to European measures judged as federal grew increasingly out of step with all opinions that mattered. Thatcher's excessive hostility produced a counterbalancing zeal in favour of ERM entry which failed to consider factors such as the timing and the sustainable exchange rate which were essential to determine the ultimate success or failure of the venture. It was now the principle which mattered. Thatcher was being forced to yield to the pressure from her colleagues but didn't do so without insisting on a higher rate than advised. So, at the Conservative Party conference in October 1990, John Major was free to announce to almost universal acclaim that Britain was to join the ERM at a rate of DM2.95 to the pound.

The question appeared settled. But this was not sufficient. Europe had not been waiting idly by while Britain prevaricated yet again. Europe was still moving forward. Therefore three weeks later, at a new summit meeting called by the Italians, the next stage of EMU was on the agenda. The purpose of the meeting was to agree the date for implementation of Stage Two. The communiqué produced confirmed this would be delayed by a year from original proposals to January 1994. It included many phrases designed to placate Mrs. Thatcher and made no specific commitment to a future single currency. She nevertheless attacked its "grand but vague words", making a vigorous criticism of the discussion concerning non-urgent and distant items. At a press conference she judged that, "People who get on a train like that deserve to be taken for a ride." The vehicle was on its way to "cloud-cuckoo land". Then when Jacques

Delors predicted that there would indeed be a single currency by 2000 she retorted that Britain would never agree and would stop it in its tracks. Approval of her stance in the tabloid press is illustrated by the famous headline in the Sun, "UP YOURS DELORS."

Back in the Commons her prepared text of assured reason and calm gave way to her personal feelings during the questions which followed, with a rapidly rising level of rage and vehemence. She would never stand idly by while a federal Europe was created by the back door. The European Commission was trying to extinguish democracy as well as the nation state. Then came her climax as a blunt answer to all the Delors federalising schemes, famous for its startling fury as much as its uniquely definitive and uncompromising stance, "No…No….NO!."

Cheers rained from much of Britain in response but now she had gone too far for the Conservative party. Geoffrey Howe's powerful resignation speech which now followed, and the considerable pro-European forces in the party precipitated a "routine" leadership election among Conservative MP's, many of whom feared losing their seats as a result of Thatcher's fervent language and her recent poll tax humiliation. The colourful and committed European, Michael Heseltine, who had resigned from Thatcher's cabinet over the Westland helicopter deal five years earlier, saw a chance for revenge and stood against her. She won the vote by 204 to 152, but this was four votes short of the majority required to avoid a second round. It was regarded as a defeat. Therefore, after receiving private advice from a succession of her closest colleagues Thatcher herself resigned, tearfully leaving Downing Street. Then, what a mystery it was, that the almost obscure John Major should go on to win the leadership election with even fewer votes than Thatcher had won.

Thatcher's legacy had proved entirely contradictory. While almost sacredly upholding the concept of the nation state she had acted to increase the collective powers of the community at the expense of national governments. Even as she appeared to be taking Britain further in, she was talking of a direction entirely different from Europe's. On her departure opinion was much divided between those supported her final stance and those who welcomed a new era of reasonable discussion, in contrast to an almost dictatorial, quasi-presidential leadership. John Major now presented the new voice of Britain which now was determined to be "At the very heart of Europe".

Chapter K: European Law Takes Effect.

Commission Enforcement
　　In Britain's first ten years of membership of the EEC the introduction of European law created little difficulty for Britain. The twin theoretical prongs involving enforcement from domestic courts and from intervention of the European Commission had very little impact on the legal system. However the ending of the transitional arrangements negotiated prior to entry did finally mean that Britain was now being forced to implement fully all the measures it had agreed to by the very fact of joining the Community. In fact Britain was much better behaved in this respect than many of its partners who were more regular infringers of Treaty provisions. Until the mid-1980's there were only around two cases a year where Britain was brought before the European Court by the European Commission. This right was granted by Article to the Commission in its role of "Guardian of the Treaties," by Articles 226/7 and includes a duty of the Member State to take all necessary measures to comply with the judgement (article 228). In fact this article was later to be strengthened by the Maastricht Treaty with a power to exact fines for non-compliance.
　　So, cases involving Britain as defendant were rare, but even these few cases gradually made it very clear, that Britain really would be compelled to honour the obligations it accepted. It is notable though that Britain's obligations now had to be met by a changed government. The real, legal consequences of signing the Treaty of Rome were never felt by Edward Heath or Harold Wilson. Instead it was their successors who found a new restriction of their powers. Whereas any government had always been entitled to change any legislation it inherited, no longer was such an option available where European law was concerned. Traditional Parliamentary sovereignty had been curtailed, and the rights of British courts had begun a fundamental transformation of the institutional balance in the British constitution. This effect is even more serious because, as will be seen, such consequences of joining the Communities in 1973, were not even apparent by the time Margaret Thatcher was approving the Single European Act in 1986.
　　The cases where the EEC Commission brought proceedings against Britain were of very little interest outside the groups directly concerned, particularly since many of these concerned agricultural subjects. Thus, the first such case decided that the UK must stop giving financial aid to pig

producers. Others included an insistence that Britain should remove a ban on potato imports, and reduce its duty on imported alcohol which discriminated against wine producers by unfairly protecting domestic beer producers. There was however an early controversy in the late 1970's when the EEC issued a Directive which required lorry drivers to fit tachographs in their vehicles. This was hotly resisted by British drivers with a considerable number of vociferous demonstrations and numerous references to "Big Brother" intrusion. The British government was reluctant to force the measure through in the face of such popular opposition and was taken to the ECJ by the Commission. The Court was totally unsympathetic to the political difficulties being experienced in Britain.

> *"It cannot be accepted that a member state should apply in an incomplete or selective manner provisions of a community regulation so as to render abortive certain aspects of community legislation which it has opposed or which it considers contrary to its national interests. Practical difficulties which appear at the stage when a community measure is put into effect cannot permit a member state unilaterally to opt out of fulfilling its obligations.*
>
> *For a state unilaterally to break, according to its own conception of national interest, the equilibrium between the advantages and obligations flowing from its adherence to the community brings into question the equality of member states before community law and creates discrimination at the expense of their nationals. This failure in the duty of solidarity accepted by member states by the fact of their adherence to the community strikes at the very root of the community legal order."*

The government must have been surprised that its duty was no longer to its electorate but to solidarity with its partners in the Community legal order.

Bearing in mind the history of the Common Fisheries Policy it is perhaps not surprising that fishing rights concerned several of the important cases raised. A series of disputes started in October 1977 when a French trawler, fishing within United Kingdom fishery limits, was boarded by British fishery protection officers. The master of the trawler was summoned before a magistrates' court and convicted for having used nets of a mesh smaller than the minimum size authorized by a British order. Following the French complaint the Commission soon delivered a reasoned opinion that by bringing the disputed order into force the United Kingdom was in breach of its obligations under the Treaty and its Common Fisheries Policy. The ECJ agreed.

Also in 1977 the European Council had failed to reach agreement on the renewal of conservation measures applicable to several formerly British waters. Consequently Britain decided to introduce its own. This caused excitement in Europe partly because British fleets were then fishing more than previously, and partly because the Community machinery of consultation was being ignored. In due course the court was highly critical.

> *"The effect of the Council's inability to reach a decision to extend the fishery conservation measures which it had previously adopted has not been to deprive the Community of its powers in this respect and thus to restore to the Member States freedom to act at will in the field in question. In such a situation, it is for the member states, as regards the maritime zones coming within their jurisdiction, to take the necessary conservation measures in the common interest and in accordance with both the substantive and the procedural rules arising from community law."* They must continue to operate, *"without prejudice to the obligation to cooperate imposed upon them by the treaty."*

A similar, but slightly more emphatic judgement followed a year later relating to further measures which Britain had introduced, (Case 804/79).

> *"Since the expiration of the transitional period laid down by the act of accession, power to adopt, as part of the common fisheries policy, measures relating to the conservation of the resources of the sea has belonged fully and definitively to the community. Member states are therefore no longer entitled to exercise **any** power of their own in the matter of conservation measures in the waters under their jurisdiction. The adoption of such measures, with the restrictions which they imply as regards fishing activities, is a matter, as from that date, of community law.*

> *The transfer to the community of powers in this matter being total and definitive, the fact that the council has not adopted, within the required period, the conservation measures referred to could not in any case restore to the member states the power and freedom to act unilaterally in this field."*

The ECJ had decided. Britain was definitely not to regain any control over its fishing waters.

New Rules of Interpretation

The second prong of enforcement directly involved British courts which were required to follow ECJ judgements, and any rules which were laid down in the process. There were two aspects to these developments. Firstly the substantive features of the law emanating from Europe needed to be incorporated into the national schemes for enforcement. However, of greater significance was the fact that new methods of reasoning and decision making, and new underlying assumptions had to be integrated within the daily workings of the courts. Now, all of the principles of enforcing EU law are entrenched in the procedures and precedents of British law, and are applied as a matter of routine and without further thought. However it took several years before all the component steps had been taken, and considerable analysis and reflection was involved at each stage in the process. Law students will quote the following cases as illustrating how this transformation was achieved in Britain.

Apart from all the rules and regulations which related to the common agricultural policy and the common market itself, EC law began to exert a significant influence on social policy, largely through the medium of ECJ judgements. The legislation most affected was the Equal Pay Act of 1970, and the Sex Discrimination Act of 1975. In Britain there had been little difficulty with these provisions which were generally accepted. In contrast, the concept of equal pay had been opposed by many countries in Europe and although it had been incorporated as an important principle by Article 141 of the Treaty this inconvenient fact had been ignored. An agreed deadline to eliminate discrimination in pay by 1964 also passed without action. Commission pressure and threats to institute proceedings were ignored. It was not until 1972 that Heads of Government agreed to give greater prominence to social issues, leading to the first Directive on Equal Pay in 1975. Now, with sex discrimination couched in much broader terms, the ECJ was to use its powers of definition to considerable effect. Member States, Britain included, were to have difficulty keeping up.

In 1981 Mrs. Wendy Smith, employed as a stockroom manageress for a pharmaceutical wholesaler, found out that the man previously employed to do the same job had been paid £60 per week whereas she was paid only £50 per week. Her problem was that the Act concentrated on present pay differentials and did not say that comparison could be made with a previous employer. The employment tribunal therefore decided that use of only the present tense in the statute meant that previous practice was of no relevance. The case of *Macarthys Ltd. v Smith* arrived before the Court of Appeal, who decided that since resolution of this dispute involved the interpretation of Article 141, the question should be referred to the ECJ.

The point regarding the grammatical construction was not disputed at the hearing. However the Commission pointed out that if an undertaking could replace male employees with female employees and by that fact alone pay lower wages, this would amount to unjust discrimination against women, manifestly contrary to the social objectives of the legislation in question. The ECJ accepted this argument and concluded that the effect of the article was not restricted to contemporaneous employment. Back at the Court of Appeal the Equal Pay Act interpreted accordingly and judgement pronounced for Mrs. Smith, disregarding the grammatical inconvenience. Interestingly it was again Lord Denning who made the constitutional observation.

> *"We should, I think, look to see what those [EC] provisions require about equal pay for men and women. Then we should look at our own legislation on the point...assuming that it does fully comply with the obligations under the Treaty. In construing our statute, we are entitled to look at the Treaty as an aid in its construction: and even more, not only as an aid, but as an overriding force. If on close examination it should appear that our legislation is deficient, or is inconsistent with Community law – by some oversight of our draftsmen – then it is our bounden duty to give priority to Community law. Such is the result of section 2 of the European Communities Act 1972.*
>
> *Thus far, I have assumed that our Parliament, whenever it passes legislation, intends to fulfil its obligations under the Treaty. If the time should come when our Parliament deliberately passes an Act with the intention*

> *of repudiating the Treaty or any provision in it – or intentionally of acting inconsistently with it – and says so in express terms - then I should have thought that it would be the duty of our courts to follow the statute of our Parliament."*

Over subsequent years the concept of sex discrimination was incrementally extended by the ECJ, and by the British courts interpreting the Statute with the increasing flexibility in consequence. For example, in *Garland v British Rail Engineering* in 1983 the issue concerned words of the statute excluding from prohibition of discrimination "any provision relating to retirement." The benefit involved was a non-contractual travel concession only granted to former male employees. The ECJ insisted that the Article allowed no such exception and the House of Lords held that exception would not apply to benefits which resulted from employment even if they continued beyond retirement. In later years the issue of retirement and pensions was to be further changed with equalisation of pensionable ages and rights, also at the instigation of the ECJ. This was particularly controversial because no amount of EC legislation, nor interpretation from the ECJ was able to eliminate the actuarial fact that the lifetimes of men and women are not equal.

The important point of legal philosophy is that since Parliament intended to comply with its obligations under the Treaty, the traditional restrictions on the rules of statutory interpretation must be modified if necessary to meet this objective. Sometime though this principle went beyond the bounds of interpretation. Thus in the 1990 case of Litster v Forth Dry Dock Ltd., an insolvent company found a loophole in regulations designed to provide workers with protection after a company takeover. Implementing a Directive, the regulations applied to person employed "immediately before the transfer." So, the company unfairly dismissed twelve employees and forty eight hours later transferred the business. Obviously, the employees were not employed "immediately before the transfer." Equally clearly though, this would have removed all the protection required by the Directive. Consequently the House of Lords agreed to insert, *by necessary implication*, the words, "or would have been so employed if he had not been unfairly dismissed." It cannot be over emphasised that insertion of such words could not have been contemplated without an obligation to interpret a provision of Community law purposively. Interference with the wording of an ordinary statute was a blatant infringement of the rights of Parliament, forbidden since 1688.

As a result of ECJ judgements it had occasionally been necessary for Parliament to amend the law, (albeit by statutory instrument). For example the government introduced regulations to implement the principle of non-discrimination not just for equal work, but for work of "equal value". Even its amendments failed to comply completely with the purpose as defined by the ECJ, so in *Pickstone v Freeman* the House of Lords introduced the necessary result by a process of "strained" interpretation. Similarly, the government amended the 1975 Act to comply with the Equal Treatment Directive of 1976, as interpreted by the ECJ. There was a narrow escape from controversy in 1988, in *Duke v GEC Reliance*, when the House of Lords declined to give retrospective effect to such an amendment. This followed the traditional judicial abhorrence of and resistance to retrospective statutes as a matter of principle. They held that Parliament, having had the opportunity to do so, had not intended to make the amendment retrospective, and consequently neither would they. The ECJ subsequently held in 1992, (the *Marleasing* case), that Community provisions should be upheld irrespective of the timing of national measures, preventing this argument being used in future.

As a final example of the consequences of expansive interpretation emanating from Luxembourg it is interesting to recount the story of the pregnancy of Ms. Carole Webb. In 1987 Ms Webb accepted temporary employment to cover the temporary absence of another employee who was due to go on maternity leave. She agreed to start immediately in order to undertake the necessary training, so that she would be fully prepared when the absence began. After two weeks she announced that she herself was pregnant and the employer, taking the view that she would not be capable of undertaking the duties for which she was employed, immediately dismissed her. The case of *Webb v EMO Air Cargo* started its seven year journey.

At first instance Ms. Webb's complaint to an industrial tribunal that she had been discriminated against by virtue of her sex was dismissed. Any man who had also proved similarly unable to complete the task for which he had been recruited would have been similarly dismissed. Later, the Court of Appeal agreed but listened to the contrary arguments patiently. The dismissal of Ms. Webb resulted directly from her pregnancy; pregnancy is sex related, therefore the dismissal was discriminatory. Lord Justice

Balcombe remarked, "It would indeed be remarkable if the law compelled us to reach so unjust a result. I am clear that it does not." Lord Justice Glidewell commented, "To postulate a pregnant man is an absurdity, but I see no difficulty in comparing a pregnant woman with a man who has a medical condition which will require him to be absent for the same period of time and at the same time as does the woman's pregnancy." Nevertheless aware of the importance of the argument leave to appeal to the House of Lords was granted.

The House of Lords, well aware of the ECJ as the source of the definitions regarding discrimination, reviewed recent judgements carefully. They concluded that this was essentially a question of interpretation, so, as court of last resort in Britain the Lords were obliged to refer the question to the ECJ. This did not mean that they had no view of their own on the matter. For example, Lord Keith commented, "If ...an employer who fails to engage a woman who, due to pregnancy, will not be available for any part of the period of the proposed engagement is to be made liable for wrongful discrimination, the result would be likely to be perceived as unfair to employers and as tending to bring the law on sex discrimination into disrepute."

The ECJ took a contrary view and it is instructive to examine the legal reasoning which enabled to court to reach their conclusion. The main principle behind ECJ judgements is usually to comply with the stated purpose of the legislation. So first, the ECJ explained that the Equal Treatment Directive 76/207 was intended to implement in member states the principle of equal treatment for men and women in employment matters as regards access, training, promotion and working conditions. However this example illustrates a serious weakness of purposive interpretation in that whenever you take the purpose of a statute as an overriding principle, there is no necessity to consider any balancing with competing issues. Thus the concept of "fairness to employers" mentioned by Lord Keith is irrelevant, and was not even mentioned in the ECJ judgment.

Secondly in Article 2 of the 1976 Directive there is a phrase that this Directive shall be "without prejudice to provisions concerning the protection of women, particularly as regards pregnancy and maternity." This would normally be read as exempting measures regarding protection of pregnant women from the concept of equal treatment. The Court took the opportunity to turn this exemption into a positive obligation under the equal treatment concept itself. It "acknowledged the principle of protecting a woman's biological condition during and after pregnancy and the special relationship between a woman and her child over the period following pregnancy and childbirth." Of course many people would support this conclusion, without too much concern as to the logic behind it. Indeed, even in British law, dismissal "on grounds of pregnancy" was automatically unfair.

So, the attitude of the ECJ can be summarised in the following extracts from its judgement.

> *There can be no question of comparing the situation of a woman who finds herself incapable, by reason of pregnancy ...of performing the task for which she was recruited, with that of a man similarly incapable for medical or other reasons."*
>
> *"A sick woman is to be treated in the same way as a sick man, whatever the cause of her illness... but pregnancy is not in any way comparable with a pathological condition, and even less so with unavailability for work on non-medical grounds, both of which are situations that may justify the dismissal of a woman without discriminating on grounds of sex."*
>
> *"Furthermore, contrary to the submission of the United Kingdom, dismissal of a pregnant woman ...cannot be justified on grounds relating to her inability to fulfil a fundamental condition of her employment contract. The availability of an employee is necessarily, for the employer, a precondition for the proper performance of the employment contract. However, the protection afforded by Community law to a woman during pregnancy and after childbirth cannot be dependent on whether her presence at work during maternity is essential to the proper functioning of the undertaking in which she is employed."*

Thus, an employer was to become responsible for employing a pregnant woman, even if she was unable to perform her work. On receipt of the opinion of the ECJ, the House of Lords dutifully re-interpreted British law, and with no obligation to consider fairness to an employer, EMO Air Cargo lost their argument. The case was remitted to the original tribunal to assess the compensation they should pay.

It should be remembered that this brief account only touches the surface of the extensive effects which European interpretation of sex discrimination legislation has produced. One particularly wide ranging result was the principle that discrimination need not only be direct. A measure which is apparently neutral but which happens to affect a greater proportion of women than men is also discriminatory. For example, regulations applying to part time workers were discriminatory since most part timers are female. Secondly it is important to note that all the above examples, result only from EC legislation of 1976, taking up to twenty years before the ECJ has established their real scope. In the meantime many new legislative measures and extensions of the original concepts have been introduced. Furthermore, and recently, a whole new range of grounds for discrimination were introduced and regulations implemented dealing with equal treatment in respect of racial or ethnic origin; religion or belief; disability; age or sexual orientation. Most people would agree with the principles concerned, but few would be prepared to predict their ultimate effects.

British Courts v UK Government

The procedure for domestic courts to make a preliminary reference to the ECJ, at first appeared to have limited significance. In a very early case of 1974, the Home Office refused entry to a Dutch national Yvonne van Duyn, because of her membership of the cult organisation, the Church of Scientology which the Government regarded as objectionable, socially harmful and damaging to the health of its practitioners. In *Van Duyn v Home Office,* Miss Duyn alleged violation of her rights of Free Movement as guaranteed by Treaty and further defined by Directive. The grounds for refusal related to the "personal conduct" of the individual, and the High Court referred this concept to the ECJ for clarification. The ECJ approved the reasoning of the Home Office, even though British nationals were not prevented from such employment, apparently allowing national discretion (subject to control by institutions of the Community), and was not concerned with discrimination against non-British nationals.

European law did not rest in such a sympathetic mode for long. While in this particular case the Home Office was vindicated subsequent cases in Europe soon developed a much harder line. Just one year later in *Rutili v French Minister of the Interior*, an Italian was banned from entry into France due to alleged subversive activities. The ECJ discovered the concept of "proportionality". Such a restriction, being contrary to a fundamental Treaty right is not purely discretionary. It must be justified as being "a genuine and sufficiently serious threat to public policy." Next, in

R v Bouchereau (1982), this public policy must reflect "one of the fundamental interests of society." Finally appeared the case of the French "waitresses" of *Adoui and Cornuaille*. Since their proposed employment would not have been prohibited to Dutch nationals, it was not permissible to discriminate against nationals of other Member States. The permissive precedent from Van Duyn was soon eroded as the ECJ hardened its attitudes towards enforcement of Community rights against the national governments, and these developing precedents were immediately of binding force in courts throughout the Community.

Despite these gradual developments, in Britain the most significant change was again related to fishing. From the 1970's the common fisheries policy had operated mainly on the basis of open access to all Community waters. But in 1983 fears about over-fishing caused the Council to approve conservation measures involving allocation of quotas based on ships registered in the Member State concerned. The accession of Spain to the EC in 1986 created resentment in the fishing industry since Spanish vessels owned by Spanish owned companies registered in England, were taking a significant proportion of Britain's quota. There was considerable anger at "quota hopping" and "plundering" of British fish. Thus in 1988, Britain decided it would enforce the quota system established by the Fisheries Policy, by requiring new registration of vessels which would be denied to non-British ships. The Spanish owned company Factortame, began a case which ground through the British and European legal system for many years, destroying on its way many of the cherished precedents of British constitutionalists.

In the High Court the essential question was whether discrimination against nationals of other Member States, clearly contrary to the EC Treaty could be justified by enforcing a policy which required allocation of resources on the basis of individual nation states. Respecting the European aspect of the case the court referred the matter to the ECJ. However the Divisional judge also made an interim order "disapplying" the operation of the regulations and forbidding the Secretary of State from enforcing de-registration on the parties to the case, pending resolution of the basic question.

The progress of the case now split as the Secretary of State appealed against this interim relief order. His argument was upheld by the Court of Appeal. They held that the Courts had no jurisdiction to grant interim relief disapplying an Act of Parliament. The trawler owners appealed further to the House of Lords. The main concern of the House of Lords concerned nothing less than the supremacy of Parliament. Judicial review of Acts of Parliament was entirely contrary to the British tradition. Similarly in accordance with common law there was no mechanism of applying injunctive relief to the Crown. Lord Bridge described the problem as one of conflict of presumptions.

> *"The difficulty which confronts the applicants is that the presumption that an Act of Parliament is compatible with Community law unless and until declared to be incompatible must be at least as strong as the presumption that delegated legislation is valid unless and until declared invalid."*

He was also concerned that if such relief was to be "invented" on the strength of Community law, and applied pending an ECJ opinion, even a weak case referring to European law could then be used to obstruct the clearly expressed intention of Parliament. Applying such reasoning to the case before them he commented,

> *"Any such order, unlike any form of order for interim relief known to the law, would irreversibly determine in the applicants' favour for a period of some two years rights which are necessarily uncertain until the preliminary ruling of the European Court has been given. If the applicants fail to establish the rights they claim before the European Court, the effect of the interim relief granted would be to have conferred on them rights directly contrary to Parliament's sovereign will and correspondingly to have deprived British fishing vessels, as defined by Parliament, of the enjoyment of a substantial proportion of the United Kingdom quota of stocks of fish protected by the common fisheries policy. I am clearly of the opinion that, as a matter of English law, the court has no power to make an order which has these consequences."*

Thus the Lords were of the opinion that whereas they might well protect rights established by European law against the Crown, they could not do so for merely alleged rights. Nevertheless they were persuaded to submit this question to the ECJ.

On this point the ECJ was adamant and uncompromising. It quoted from the case of Simmenthal described earlier.

> *"In accordance with the principle of the precedence of Community law, the relationship between provisions of the Treaty and directly applicable measures of the institutions*

> *on the one hand and the national law of the Member States on the other is such that those provisions and measures ... by their entry into force render automatically inapplicable any conflicting provision of ... national law."*

So far the House of Lords would have been willing if not obliged to agree.

> *"The Court has also held that any provision of a national legal system and any legislative, administrative or judicial practice which might impair the effectiveness of Community law by withholding from the national court having jurisdiction to apply such law the power to do everything necessary at the moment of its application to set aside national legislative provisions which might prevent, even temporarily, Community rules from having full force and effect are incompatible with those requirements, which are the very essence of Community law."*

The operative phrase is "even temporarily" which means without waiting for the point to be proven.

> *"It must be added that the full effectiveness of Community law would be just as much impaired if a rule of national law could prevent a court seised of a dispute governed by Community law from granting interim relief in order to ensure the full effectiveness of the judgment to be given on the existence of the rights claimed under Community law. It follows that a court which in those circumstances would grant interim relief, if it were not for a rule of national law, is obliged to set aside that rule."*

Thus, if the issue at stake involves Community law, the court must be empowered to override <u>any</u> rule which might impede its application. The European Communities Act had apparently provided the courts with the power to override the will of Parliament. Parliament had no longer any power to protect Britain from any detrimental effect of European law. In addition a new presumption was to forced into English law. Community law was not only presumed to take precedence over national law but was to be assumed valid until proven otherwise.

On receiving this ruling back from the European Court, the House of Lords granted an order restraining the Secretary of State "from withholding or withdrawing registration in the register of British fishing vessels maintained by him pursuant to the Merchant Shipping (Registration of Fishing Vessels) Regulations 1988."

Judges and Politicians in Proportion

British judges thus acquired a duty to ensure that national legislation conformed to the requirements of European law as defined by the ECJ, and judicial review of national legislation was instituted. The interpretive obligation was to be purposive whereby courts were to be "precluded from adopting any interpretation of national implementing legislation which does not accord with the specific result to be achieved by the directive." But, if this was not possible conflicting measures were to be simply set aside. British judges were therefore to assess the validity of national law in accordance with overriding European principles such as the four freedoms of movement (goods, workers, services, capital), equality of treatment (by sex and nationality), respect for legal certainty, protection of fundamental rights, completion and operation of the single market, and a concept new to British law, proportionality.

The principle of proportionality is defined as preventing excessive means from being used to attain permissible objectives, or in the words of Lord Diplock, "A steam hammer should not be used to crack a nut." It has its origins from Germany where it developed from a concept of administrative law to a constitutional constraint on the Rule of Law, applied in the protection of fundamental rights. Use in European law stems from the case of *Fedechar* under the High Authority of the European Coal and Steel Community, and since then its assessment has been by means of three tests. Firstly the means must be appropriate and effective as a method of achieving the stated objective. Secondly the means extend no further than is necessary to achieve the objective, and thirdly, that there are no less restrictive measures which could be used to achieve the same result. Clearly each of these tests calls for a careful exercise of judgement, criticised as being essentially subjective. Traditionally, British judges had no particular difficulty in making such balancing judgements using the presumptions of common law and earlier precedence as guidance. However, the closest this ever came to a challenge to the executive had was in using the concept of "Wednesbury" unreasonableness. A measure could be annulled if it was so unreasonable that no reasonable body to reach that particular conclusion. Even this test, designed to prevent judges merely from substituting their own judgments about the issue in question had no application at all to legislation itself.

Judicial review of legislation incorporating the much broader tests of proportionality was only later incorporated into British law and with great difficulty.

Although it was not seen in such a light at the time of its introduction there appear to be real benefits to the public in allowing judicial restraint on legislation. For example in the case of *Internationale Handelsgesellschaft* of 1970 the ECJ stated, "the individual should not have his freedom of action limited beyond the degree necessary for the public interest." However the fundamental difficulty lies with the setting of the rules to be applied. Judges could not set the rules to be used to control Parliament if their duty was to follow the will of Parliament, and a rule set by Parliament unable to bind its successors would prove ineffective. As Lord Devlin once summarised the dilemma, "The British have no more wish to be governed by judges than they have to be judged by administrators." Consequently the conclusion adopted in Britain was to rely on the democratic accountability of Members of Parliament. Some attempt at external, rational restraint has been made with incorporation of the Human Rights Act of 1998 into British law but even this prevents courts from overriding conflicting legislation. As will be described the European Communities Act was much more effective, essentially because the ECJ was not prepared to accept the traditional and ultimately democratic constraints on judicial power found throughout the Community.

Two further quotations illustrate the unease which senior judges felt about using judicial power against democratically elected representatives. The first arises from a case where EEC fishing regulations, once again, were claimed to be beyond the power of the UK Parliament because they were contrary to the Acts of union between England and Scotland. It was suggested that such laws could only be valid if they were, as stated as a condition of union, "for the evident utility of the subjects within Scotland." Lord Keith stated,

> "The making of decisions upon what must essentially be a political matter is no part of the function of this court, and it is highly undesirable that it should be. The function of this court is to adjudicate upon the particular rights and obligations of individual persons, natural or corporate, in relation to other persons or, in certain circumstances, to the State. A general inquiry into the utility of certain legislative matters as regards the population generally is quite outside its competence."

Later, in an early case involving the legality of Sunday trading laws Lord Hoffman agreed that such questions were of constitutional rather than practical importance,

> "In my judgment it is not my function to carry out a balancing exercise or to form my own view as to whether the legislative objects could be achieved by other means. These questions involve compromises between competing interests which in a democratic society must be resolved by the Legislature. The function of this court is to review the acts of the legislature but not to substitute its own policies or values. This is not an abdication of judicial responsibility. The primacy of the democratic process is far more important than the question of whether our Sunday trading laws could or could not be improved."

Lord Hoffman was not correct. The "error" of his ways was to be established as a pervasive principle of British law as the final but unlikely result of a series of cases involving restrictions on Sunday trading. These cases made an important contribution to the development of European law relating to the free movement of goods, but they also left in their wake another transformation in the power of British courts.

In 1987 several large retailers decided to challenge the rules preventing shops in England and Wales from opening on Sundays which were imposed by the Shops Act of 1950. Politically they based their arguments on the almost undeniable fact that the restrictions appeared arbitrary, inconsistent and in particular archaic. However, since arguments of this type were irrelevant as far as any consideration of the law could be concerned, a different approach had to be found.

In the test case of *Torfaen Borough Council v B & Q plc*, the well known D-I-Y retailer had defied the restrictions and was being prosecuted by the local Council. In its defence it argued that the regulations were invalid as being contrary to Article 28 (then 30), guaranteeing the free movement of goods. They produced statistical evidence to show that imports of EC goods were reduced by the loss of sales caused by retailers being forced to close on Sundays. In 1988 the case was remitted to the ECJ as a preliminary reference who replied that a restriction on trade which applied without distinction of origin within one Member State was a justifiable derogation from the principle of the free movement of goods if the trade restriction was intended to achieve some objective acceptable in law and that the means chosen were proportionate to that end. It considered that the restrictions were in principle "a legitimate part of economic and social policy," but they would only be only be compatible with Community law if their adverse effect on the free movement of goods was outweighed by their beneficial effects in reflecting the particular socio-cultural characteristics of the nation or region in which they applied. It concluded that,

> "The question whether the effect of specific national rules do in fact remain within that limit is a question of fact to be determined by the national court."

Thus national courts were being instructed to apply the European doctrine of proportionality to assess the validity of the law.

This instruction provoked unusual hostility from the judiciary. Lord Justice Mustill asked in one of the following cases,

> "How could a desire to keep the Sabbath holy be measured against the free-trade economic premises of the Common Market?"

He was quite happy for a court to establish whether the regulations represented a "quantitative restriction on imports", whether the measure was justifiable in itself under Community law, and whether it went any further than necessary. But the final step of assessing whether the ultimate effect was disproportionate to the objective was in his view, beyond the determination of a court.

Lord Hoffman expressed similar misgivings in the 1990 case of *Stoke on Trent City Council v B & Q plc*. He asked,

> "Is this court to apply its own opinion of the importance of ensuring that shop workers do not have to work on Sundays and weight tha against its opinion of the importance of selling more Dutch bulbs or Italian furniture? If the legislature has declined to adopt any modifications of the existing exceptions, is the court to say that modifications should nevertheless be introduced because in its opinion they would not detract from the legislative object and would mean that the Act was less of a hindrance to trade?"

The ultimate answer from the ECJ would be that this was precisely his duty. But, a few more steps were necessary to establish this result.

At some lower levels courts had been somewhat more flexible on the issue. In a case appearing for appeal before a Crown Court, (B & Q Ltd v

Shrewsbury and Atcham Borough Council), the Judge Northcote, reading about the principles of proportionality identified possible alternative means of protecting employees with less hindrance to international trade. On the basis that such alternatives were available he simply disapplied the offending provisions from the Shops Act. However this was not strictly a resolution of the proportionality issue, and it was Lord Hoffman's case which was appealed to the House of Lords, and thence to the ECJ.

The opinions in the ECJ had meanwhile been developed in similar cases relating to French and Belgian regulations and mostly clearly expressed by Advocate General van Gerven. The first point in his argument was to remind all concerned that "the principle objective of the preliminary ruling procedure which is to ensure the uniform application throughout the Community of the provisions of law so as to avoid that their effect vary according to the interpretation given them in different Member States." Therefore the ECJ's previous opinion from *Torfaen* that such matters could be delegated to a national court was no longer tenable. National courts could decide on appropriateness and the "necessity" of a measure but the decision on real "proportionality" had to be done only by the ECJ so that compatibility with Community Law was assessed in a "uniform manner", which could "not be allowed to vary according to the findings of fact made by individual courts in particular cases." The court decided that it had to follow the conclusions of its recent cases. It therefore replied to a request to clarify the method of decision making with just the conclusion.

> "It must therefore be stated in reply to the first question that Article 30 of the Treaty is to be interpreted as meaning that the prohibition which it lays down does not apply to national legislation prohibiting retailers from opening their premises on Sundays."

The effect of this judgement was two fold. Firstly it confirmed that national judges were indeed required to employ the ECJ's conception of proportionality. Nevertheless, recognising the difficulty of applying these principles consistently across national boundaries, the final decision in such cases would rest with the ECJ. This was to be the case even though its effect is to give the ECJ the power to rule directly on the validity of national legislation. In this particular case the ECJ confirmed that the UK legislation was consistent with the Treaty. However, it follows necessarily that the ECJ reserves the right to declare any national legislation incompatible with EC measures on grounds of proportionality. There is no appeal against such a decision, and only a theoretical and cumbersome procedure of amending legislation by Council unanimity. Moreover national courts are again obliged to uphold the ruling irrespective of any concerns or even actions of the national government.

Despite the impact of the Sunday trading saga, judges remained reluctant to challenge primary legislation and it was not until a House of Lords judgement in 1994 (*R v Secretary of State for Employment, ex parte the Equal Opportunities Commission*) that the issue was finally resolved. This case involved the consideration of the supremacy of Community law, applied to a case of indirect sex discrimination, and judged on grounds of proportionality. Considering what he regarded as a rather novel form of discrimination Lord Justice Nolan commented,

> *"Although it may appear somewhat strange that legislation which is not intended or worded to create discrimination on the grounds of sex should be liable to be treated as discriminatory simply on the basis that a large proportion of those affected by it happen, as a result of particular social considerations, to belong to one sex rather than the other, it has been held [by the European Court] that an arrangement which has a disproportionate effect on employees of one sex rather than the other is indirectly discriminatory."*

The case proceeded with an exhaustive examination of all the issues until finally the Lords made their pronouncement. Formal declarations that parts of the Employment Protection Act of 1978 were incompatible with European law were issued, and judicial review of primary legislation was henceforth authorised by virtue of judicial precedent.

Chapter 20: The Battle of Maastricht

A New European Treaty?

The Treaty of the European Union produced Britain's most ferocious political battle of recent times, and right in the centre was Prime Minister John Major. This was before he had obtained the reputation epitomised by his presentation in the cruelly satirical programme "Spitting Image" as the completely grey man, with a vision not extending beyond his breakfast. In November 1990 he had appeared an ideal compromise candidate, offering a gentlemanly and gentle succession to the turbulence of the Thatcher era. The Conservative Party handed to him the task of obtaining the next General Election victory, due in 1992. He was viewed as someone who really could unite the party. He was a healer rather than a warrior; a pragmatist rather than an ideologue; and a person who by appealing both to the Thatcherites and the pro-Europeans could rally the party to face its real priority. His first reported intervention regarding Europe had been in 1979 when he wrote to The Times calling for fundamental financial reform and advocated withdrawal if this was not forthcoming, and since then he had gained support from the 130 Conservative MP's who had organised themselves as the Bruges Group to perpetuate the Thatcher scepticism. But he spoke on his first day as leader, of Britain's need to stop shouting from the terraces and start playing on the field of Europe.

The playing field next due to appear was situated in the small Dutch town few people outside had previously of, namely Maastricht, and the object being played for represented such a decisive step towards integration that it was quickly transformed to a famous political battleground. Britons were already losing their black, hard-backed passports in favour of the red, flimsy European format. Now there was to be a real European Union and people were to become citizens of that Union. The word "Economic" would be dropped from its title and treaty language would refer to its territory, and its borders. Institutions such as a European Central Bank, and increased powers of the European Parliament were proposed. All this was before the more practical matters involving an unprecedented extension of the designated European areas of competence were considered. Describing the dilemma facing the Conservative party in addressing these issues as challenging was clearly a serious understatement.

Managing the party against the background of bitter division over Europe required a skilful combination of facing both ways to satisfy both sides of the argument, the diversion of attention to alternative less contentious issues, and the appeal to party loyalty to preserve a sufficient semblance of unity to maintain electoral credibility. In 1992 he succeeded, admirably.

His address to the 1991 party conference typified the ambiguous stance he was forced to adopt. "We can't go on as we were in terms of Europe: we should be at the centre of Europe if we are going to properly protect our interests". "But being in the centre of Europe doesn't mean we've sold out, doesn't mean we've suddenly become Europhiles and adopt every fetish that emerges from the European Commission. Of course not". "What it does mean is that we are in a better position to influence the way in which Europe goes".

This purported positive attitude was important as negotiations regarding the final form of the Maastricht Treaty were still continuing in Europe. There, confusion regarding Major's true position was detected, but it was still regarded as a considerable improvement on Thatcher's open hostility. Besides, Major had been seen trying to get Britain back on board by means of membership of the ERM well before his eventual success. As a European, he seemed to his partners, as close as the British get

In the Exchange Rate Mechanism

In fact Major had not been completely neutral regarding European issues, and during his tenure as Chancellor he had become a real supporter of ERM. For some considerable time he had been arguing that the recession, which had been the longest and deepest since the 1930s, with actual economic contraction of 2.5% in 1991 and a further 1% in 1992, would be dispelled because of the successful strategy of membership of the ERM. This belief was presented as a central but purely practical panacea of the government's economic policy. Membership of the ERM would be a guarantee of low inflation and impose the monetary discipline which had been the cause of the Deutschmark's envied success. In addition, the resulting stability would improve Britain's ability to compete in a more successful European Single Market, while holding out the appealing prospect of gradual reduction in interest rates without risk of rekindling inflation.

This was not a matter of doctrine to Major, but of simple national interest. Thoughtfully he described his reasoning. " Every day I sat at the

Treasury (as Chancellor) and I saw Sterling being kicked around by rumour. And when Sterling is being kicked around, the economy is being kicked around because it affects monetary policy, and monetary policy ripples through and affects everything else. The more I realised, day after day, was that the most priceless gift you could offer British business over the medium term was a stable exchange rate and a stable inflation rate. And what was the best mechanism to achieve this, or the best and most proven mechanism to achieve it over the years would be an Exchange Rate Mechanism. The soft option, the devaluer's option, the inflationary option would be a betrayal of our future; and it is not the Government's policy...All too often in the past the solution was the same - to let the exchange rate go. And every time - sooner or later - the result was the same: rising import prices, rising wages, rising inflation, and a long-term deterioration in Britain's competitiveness which offset any short-term gain." Nevertheless Major had to avoid any hint of adherence to a dogmatic pro-European policy. He therefore emphasised "ERM entry does not mean that we are now on a road leading inexorably to a single currency" even though the Delors Report which served as the blueprint for the Maastricht Treaty did imply exactly that.

and Negotiating Maastricht

Thus negotiations in Europe regarding the final Treaty were dominated by Major's need to preserve another delicate balance between opposing forces. Two Inter Governmental Conferences dealing separately with EMU and with political union had converged into the Maastrict Treaty, ready for approval by the member states. Dutch proposals from the political wing had included incorporating all foreign-ministry and interior-ministry matters under the Brussels umbrella. The proposers provided the image of a tree with many branches springing from common roots as their explanation. However both the British and the French rejected the federalist implications and produced the rival model of a Greek temple. One pillar represented the single market and the existing Commission+ECJ structure, while the other two pillars supporting the Council of Ministers were to be the foreign-and-security policy, and the justice-and-home-affairs policy outside the legally binding machinery of the first. These were two pillars facing both ways with a European dimension of co-operation but separated from intervention from the artefacts of Europe.

In Britain the preference would probably have been for there to be no treaty at all. But, there was again no option or means of overcoming the integrationist momentum. Britain, once again, was simply doing its best to minimise its effects and soon it had to decide once again. Of course, many influential figures such as Edward Heath, Michael Heseltine, Douglas Hurd, and Geoffrey Howe would have been perfectly happy with the Treaty even as originally drafted by Delors. They had no ideological objections, to the extent of supporting a "Social Chapter" which provided a fast-track procedure for passing binding European legislation across a whole range of employment and social fields. Major though, pointed to the huge costs it would impose on industry and the potential loss of jobs. Mrs. Thatcher had characterised the social chapter memorably but extravagantly as "Marxist", and many anti-Europeans were pushing Major not only to refuse to sign up but to veto the whole project.

The final result served as a tribute to Major's quiet and undemonstrative negotiating skills as he crafted a supportable but nevertheless fragile compromise between the two irreconcilable positions within the party. He signed up to the Treaty, including the commitments to the first stages monetary union, in which he believed. This committed Britain to join the narrow bands within the ERM, and to participation in the "European Monetary Institute", the precursor of the European Central Bank. The decision in relation to the final stage of monetary union was, by way of concession, deferred for approval by the British parliament until Stage III commenced. Two other important concessions were achieved. Firstly, the provocative word "federal" was deleted from the Treaty, even though, to the continentals, this was a purely semantic change which also failed to prevent opponents recognising the integrationist trap. Secondly Britain was to be completely exempted from the whole of the Social Chapter. The main author, the Dutch Prime Minister Ruud Lubbers, had tried hard by including the appropriate degree of non-oppressive subsidiarity but Major had remained adamant. As with the EMU obstacle to agreement, Major had simply sat at Maastricht, quietly, pleasantly and patiently but firmly refusing to accept alternative routes to the same end. He had appeared unconcerned that he was sitting as one against eleven. After all it was they who wanted a treaty. The final summary from his spokesman, "Game, Set and Match," to the British, was a serious exaggeration bearing in mind the myriad of other measures Britain was accepting. However, although the comment offended the other participants Major had been pleased with his negotiating performance, and certainly succeeded in avoiding the most serious consequences of remaining in the very heart of Europe.

Major's reception back home, viewed in terms of the controversy which later surrounded Maastricht was remarkable. The Euro-sceptic factions of his party praised him for standing firm and for resisting European pressure. Journalists described him as "the man of consensual instinct with a touch of steel", reporting "A Houdini-like escape from the toils of the Eurocrats", "An emphatic success", "A copybook triumph". How soon, all of these voices changed to scathing and scornful criticism of the Treaty and the man to be held responsible.

There had clearly been some element of delaying tactic in the EMU part of the settlement, and it was this aspect which was repeated as the General Election campaign of 1992 interrupted arrangements to ratify the Treaty. Because of the potentially destructive power of the dissenting voices, Major had quietly persuaded most of his party to adopt a vow of collective silence on the issue of Europe. Internal disagreement was to be suspended, and its resolution postponed. Fortunately for Major, the Labour Party opposition, now led by Neil Kinnock, remained similarly divided over Europe and had an identical interest in avoiding public debate about Maastricht. It was therefore in the narrow interests of both parties to ensure that Maastricht, although concerning the most fundamental constitutional change in Britain for generations, never became an election issue. The importance of the issue was denied or disguised, with attention diverted to the mundane domestic issues and personalities. This time the motto regarding Europe was, "Do NOT let the people decide".

Back from Re-Election

To general amazement within the country John Major was returned to power with a small but workable majority of twenty-one from the April 1992 election. Now he found that his personal commitment to the Maastricht Treaty, since he had been the one to negotiate and sign it in February, now demanded that he obtain Parliamentary approval. Real decisions regarding Maasticht could no longer be deferred and Major could no longer remain balanced on the tightrope. Thus, his definite and purposeful shift to the pro-integration side of the party released all the restraint of the dissenting voices. For the second time, and probably the last time John Major was to fight for something to which he really felt committed. Ratification seemed a matter of personal honour as much as politics and Major, despite his later image of weakness and indecision was now ready to use every weapon and device, and every ounce of political capital available to him in order to achieve this result. He was to need it all.

There had always been a nucleus of anti-European zealots within the Conservative Party, with principled objections to the creation of a United States of Europe, always ready to speak against if not vote against European measures. The strident though defeated views of Margaret Thatcher had undoubtedly lent a new air of respectability to those forces of European opposition. Moreover, her rousing speeches with their distinctly nationalist flavour also wakened the public interest from its boredom with the complex, and perpetual and irrelevant European debate, lending a mild sense of patriotic support. Euro-scepticism had become an acceptable and powerful doctrine. The arguments deflected in 1975 and neglected in 1986 now came to the forefront of British politics. Major though, was now prepared to wage a major war against these Eurosceptics within his own party, and was not deterred by the prospect of being sustained in office only by votes from the Labour party, which took a relaxed, bipartisan view of the Treaty, by votes from the Liberal Democrats, or by votes from the Ulster Unionists. These were all preferable to the making of concessions to the Eurosceptics on his own benches.

In many ways Major's position before his election had been similar to that of Harold Wilson prior to the referendum. Party unity had been the driving imperative. Now though, comfortably back in office, Major's new characteristic of determination provided a stark contrast. In fact, had peace and harmony been the real objective the battles could readily been avoided as several events could have provided a relatively uncontroversial escape route from Maastricht.

Ratification was proceeding across Europe when voters in France surprised Europe with a bare 51% voting in support of the Treaty. Surprise though moved to shock when in June 1992 Denmark voted against the Treaty in their referendum by 50.7 to 49.3%. Since national unanimity was an essential condition of ratification Major could easily have argued that the "No" vote technically invalidated the Treaty and that it would therefore not proceed in the British parliament. Instead of this he quickly took the view, favoured on the continent and advocated by the federalist minded Danish government, that the Danes should be forced to vote again. From a historical viewpoint this co-ordinated disrespect for the voice of the people of a nation state meant that Major was providing critical support to the federalist cause. But he felt that even this was not sufficient. So with the support of Douglas Hurd he immediately decided to force through the Maastricht Bill even faster, in order to demonstrate British resolve and thus encourage the Danes to correct their opinion. Commentators critical of Europe's effective rejection of the Danish people's decision created stronger anti-Maastricht feelings, sensing the blood of the Treaty. Major's determination though was never to waver.

ERM Ejection

It cannot be a coincidence that in July 1992, Britain was to assume the EC Presidency for six months, and many believed that Major wanted to use this opportunity to attach some sense of reality to his vision of Britain in the "Heart of Europe" The smug sounding foreword Major wrote in the Foreign Offices propaganda booklet produced to celebrate this event was in curious contrast to the rising political turmoil. "For us, in Britain, Europe is part of our lives. As an island some of our traditions differ. But our history and culture are linked closely to those of other European nations". The economy was also linked, but this time artificially with the ERM, and this had begun to prove problematic. Given the state of the British economy markets had begun to doubt the permanence of the exchange rate. The conventional response would have been a rise in interest rates but this was exactly contrary to the needs of the real and stumbling economy. Arguments began for indeed raising interest rates, or for "re-aligning" sterling within the ERM, or for lowering interest rates and leaving the ERM. Instead the Chancellor Lamont repeatedly refused to budge. It was the lynchpin of the government's anti-inflation policy and could never be changed. The world should have "no scintilla of doubt", that "we will do whatever is necessary" to maintain sterling's parity.

It is ironic that shortly after attaining the EC Presidency, John Major would find that his previous achievement and victory, that of joining the ERM, should come under such inexorable pressure. During September 1992, Major and Lamont issued numerous statements confirming their determination to maintain the value of Sterling within the 6% ERM band around the DM 2.95 value. A meeting of EC finance ministers held out the prospect now appearing unavoidable, for a negotiated "realignment", but suggestions from the Germans that sterling should be treated like the peseta and the lira caused such acrimony that chances of agreement were buried behind Lamont's rage. So, on Wednesday 16th, Major and Lamont were sitting in Canute-like resistance to the waves from the currency markets which sensed only one possible direction for Sterling's value. Short-term interest rates were raised from 10% to 12%, to no avail and finally to 15% before defeat had to be admitted. More than £10 billion had been spent to no effect other than the enrichment of the speculators.

"On 16 September 1992, "Black Wednesday", the Major government ignominiously suspended sterling from membership of the ERM after swearing on a stack of bibles that it would not devalue, let alone creep away from the ERM itself with its tail between its legs. Major's great act of policy as Chancellor had collapsed. On Black Wednesday, it was not merely the credibility of sterling that was undermined but that of the Major government as well... Major is unique in that he was already Prime Minister when his credibility as Chancellor was so unmercifully drained. No one seriously expected him to resign as Prime Minister for what he had done as Chancellor. A sacrificial lamb was, after all, available in the form of his friend and successor as Chancellor, Norman Lamont, though he was allowed a short stay of execution before being despatched eight months later."

Major could also have used this as an opportunity to argue that the exit of the Pound from the ERM invalidated the Treaty because ERM membership was an essential pre-requisite to the entire process of monetary union. In reality he already had every reason to argue that it would be inconceivable to contemplate the abolition of the Pound and it was not a large step to reject the acceptance of the single currency without the Pound being inside the ERM. Moreover, the Treaty presupposed that countries such as Britain, who were at the time in the wide 6% band, would move to the $2^1/4\%$ narrow band, and Britain was clearly in no position to achieve this.

Despite this failure of his first achievement Major refused to allow it to affect his second objective. He spoke of mere "fault lines" within the ERM as compared with the impression of system implosion, hinted at Bundesbank betrayal of promises to support Sterling within the ERM, all the time suffering unfounded and hurtful tabloid questions regarding his mental health and suitability as the country's leader.

Pressure on Major was raised yet again during the October party conference. In speech after speech the Euro-sceptic voices such as Norman Tebbit were celebrating freedom and escape from the ERM shackles, to cheers from the rafters. It was certain that any priority of uniting the party would now have required a complete reversal of the

Maastricht direction and that the resistance from the pro-Europeans would have been overcome by these rising storms. Major, though was not to be forced off course by either markets or strength of feeling in the party. His resolve did not waver.

Battle for Maastricht

It seems amazing that Major's determination did not falter even when collapse of the entire project could have been almost effortlessly, though probably noisily engineered. On the contrary, at the routine, end-of-Presidency summit in Edinburgh, Major again acted as the prime rescuer of the Maastricht Treaty. Shortly after ERM ejection, Major had called a preliminary summit in Birmingham proposing measures such as an increase in subsidiarity, to offset the rising public discontent within Europe. The prime target was Denmark which needed to justify a second appeal to its people, but the French were also vulnerable having just won their referendum by the narrowest of margins. Delors was naturally opposed, and relations with Germany still strained so it was not until the December summit in Edinburgh that the necessary decisions were taken. Major pushed through measures which, he argued, had to be agreed if the Maastricht Treaty was not to be simply abandoned. Danish opt-outs for EMU, EU Citizenship, and co-operation in justice, home affairs and defence; modest budget increases particularly favouring Britain, promotion of subsidiarity, modifications regarding the European Parliament, and several principles of future enlargement were all agreed, as a result of Major's skilful Chairmanship of the meeting.

So, having secured a European future for the treaty Major was now able to return to the unfolding domestic battle to ensure British participation. Earlier history had shown how the disputes regarding Europe had firstly been limited to the governing classes, later spreading more widely through the political parties. The issue even reached the people during the referendum campaign although it is clear that practical issues were used to disguise the constitutional significance of integration. This battle was different for two reasons. Firstly, The forces of opposition had grown, encouraged and amplified by the disastrous failure of the ERM, by European manoeuvring in response to public disquiet across the Channel, and with for the first time a widespread realisation of the actual implications of Maastricht for Britain as an independent nation. And secondly, although the Britain's governing executive had declined to halt a disintegrating treaty, Parliamentary approval was still essential, and therefore Parliament itself was to become the battleground.

Real Parliamentary battles are a rarity in modern politics. The governing party depends on the support of its MP's, but in turn provides a large proportion of them with ministerial and lesser roles within the government, at the same time holding out the prospect of personal advancement within the government machinery. MP's quickly become reluctant to jeopardise their political careers over matters of either policy or principle. In addition the individuals do have a loyalty to their party, reinforced by practical considerations, involving as a last resort their possible de-selection as the party candidate if they were to lose support of their constituency organisations. Of course they would also prefer not to defeat a government and precipitate a General Election, especially if they were at risk in a more marginal seat. The issue of Europe though, is unique in its ability not only to cross the traditional party lines but also undermine otherwise resolute party allegiance. The behaviour of MP's during the passage of the Maastricht Bill provides the best example of individual and co-ordinated rebellion in recent years.

The Conservative opponents of Maastricht possessed neither a coherent membership nor a consistent philosophy. One of the unofficial leaders of the committed anti-Europeans was the Conservative MP, Bill Cash whose parliamentary career became a thorn in the side of the government. Other followers included some people believing in free trade and some in protectionism; monetarists and fixed exchange rate supporters; figures on the right and figures on the left. They included old-guard figures like Teddy Taylor who had always opposed transfer of sovereignty, or supporters of the Commonwealth and global free trade, or people like John Biffen who passionately believed in the nation state as the only legal entity capable of enjoying public legitimacy. There were also many who over the years had converted, some during passage of the Single European Act and more afterwards admitting to "the error of their ways". It was only during the later Parliamentary bitterness that Major introduced an unusual and all encompassing category which could include all such opponents within his party, "the bastards".

Eurosceptics also experienced a considerable difficulty in offering the country an alternative direction. Outright withdrawal seemed and still seems such a truly awesome decision that few would dare to suggest it. While there was a consensus that Britain should enjoy the benefits of the single market, there was never an explanation of how other members could allow Britain to achieve its benefits without accepting the political consequences. No half-way house could be found. It is an indication of how powerful Europe had become that opponents of integration could hope to achieve little more a temporary halt.

All of these people, no less than ordinary many members of the public, bemused by the bewildering complexity and academic confusion of the subject had now heard Helmut Kohl describe what was really happening in 1992. "In Maastricht we laid the foundation stone for the completion of the European Union. The European Union Treaty introduces a new and decisive stage in the process of European Union which within a few years will lead to the creation of what the founding fathers of modern Europe dreamed of after the last war: the United States of Europe." The fundamental nature of the argument was laid bare, and its implied permanence united the opposition, and galvanised them into activity.

Conservative dissenters, committed though they were numbered no more than 22 in May. However in June after the result from Denmark this immediately grew to 69. The government was forced to concede that the Bill's passage would only be completed after the second Danish referendum, and the vote approving this was almost lost with a result of 319 to 313.

For almost a year the Bill passed through unprecedented legislative contortions. Bill Cash for example personally tabled 240 amendments to the three clause Bill and many of them came close to sabotaging it. He boasted that he had voted against 47 three line whips, creatively exploiting his procedural knowledge.

The Labour opposition, still in an extreme anti-European mode, but ably led by the more pro-European John Smith, adopted the principle of putting party interest first and continued in incessant opposition, willingly encouraging Conservative rebels. Even so, heated and bitter though the Parliamentary manoeuvres were, rebels were on the final vote obliged to give way in the face of a Prime Minister's ultimate Parliamentary weapon, a motion of confidence in the Government. Major had been forced into putting the very survival of the government directly on the line. So, in July 1993, Parliament approved the ratification of the Maastricht Treaty.

Chapter L: A New Vision of Justice

A New Role for the ECJ

While the concepts of Community Law were gradually being received into the legal systems of the Member States, the ECJ was itself continuing with several significant extensions of the legal power of the Treaty. Its strategy in doing so was frequently based on its duty to uphold the law but extended with the necessity it gave itself by deduction, that this must be achieved in a completely uniform manner across the Community. It made the logic of this argument immensely powerful by using it to support the effective overriding of any national provision which conflicted with an EC measure. Moreover in doing so it was acting with an entirely new and essentially political motivation, designed to ensure its complete authority in pursuing the objective of "an ever closer union." It was actually acting in a way contrary to legal traditions all across Europe. In Britain for example, courts had never had authority to question the will of Parliament and had severely limited powers of discretion in interpreting the legislative texts. Similarly, in France, the wording of the Constitution was sacrosanct. So, although in 1971 the Constitutional Court essentially gave itself the power to review French statutes, the judgements always resulted from comparison with the actual words of the Constitution.

In contrast, having divined the purposes of the Treaty of Rome, the ECJ was not to be constrained by its wording, even though and again in contrast to national systems, there was no practical legislative mechanism for overturning their judgements. Traditionally the role of judges was to serve the law. In contrast, the judges of the ECJ were becoming by their own appointment, the undisputed masters of the legislative texts.

An interesting historical comparison can be made with the situation during the formation of the USA after their Constitutional Convention of 1787. Thomas Jefferson in his Kentucky Resolutions argued that the new US Constitution should be freely adopted by the individual States. He needed to persuade their people that the new federal state would not become a centralised dictatorship, destroying the rights and powers of state governments. One important condition he declared was that "the government created by this compact could not be made the exclusive or final judge of the extent of the powers delegated to itself." The Europe of two hundred years later was not to be so constrained.

Adding a Few Words

In 1982 representatives of the European Parliament voted in committee to distribute funds to political parties established within the Parliament who were standing at the next European election. Unfortunately for Green Party had recently reorganised itself, changing its name slightly. Therefore the Parliamentary committee concluded that the newly constituted party, being new, was not entitled to a share in the elections funds. The Greens instituted proceedings against Parliament for annulment of this decision before the ECJ.

The Court found a small obstacle in the Treaty Article defining their jurisdiction to review and annul acts of the Community institutions. It stated,

> *"The Court of Justice shall review the legality of acts of the Council and the Commission other than recommendations or opinions. It shall for this purpose have jurisdiction in actions brought by a Member State, the Council or the Commission."*

Clearly the European Parliament was not included, implying that it could not be reviewed, and neither did it have standing to bring proceedings. To many this was not surprising. Was it really intended that Parliament should be directly subject to judicial review?

Of course the role of the European Parliament is quite different from the sovereign, national Parliaments and has only a limited role in the legislative function. Nevertheless the Court argued that the Parliament's decisions can produce legally binding effects. The Court stated,

> *"It must first be emphasized in this regard that the European Economic Community is a Community based on the rule of law, inasmuch as neither its Member States nor its institutions can avoid a review of the question whether the measures adopted by them are in conformity with the basic constitutional charter, the Treaty. In particular, the Treaty established a complete system of legal remedies and procedures designed to permit the Court of Justice to review the legality of measures adopted by the institutions."*

It should be notice that the Treaty has become a "constitutional charter".

> *"It is true that, unlike Article 177 of the Treaty, which refers to acts of the institutions without further qualification,*

> *Article 173 refers only to acts of the Council and the Commission. However, the general scheme of the Treaty is to make a direct action available against ' all measures adopted by the institutions. . . Which are intended to have legal effects ' , as the court has already had occasion to emphasize in its judgment of 31 March 1971 (Commission v Council [1971])."*

Therefore the Court was using its <u>own</u> decision of 1971 to broaden the scope of a treaty article to cover "all measures intended to have legal effect." In fact it became a regular strategy of the court to introduce an important principle as a matter of passing interest during a judgement, and then to use it to decisive effect in a subsequent case.

> *"An interpretation of Article 173 of the Treaty which excluded measures adopted by the European Parliament from those which could be contested would lead to a result contrary both to the spirit of the Treaty ...and to its system. Measures adopted by the European Parliament in the context of the EEC Treaty could encroach on the powers of the Member States or of the other institutions, or exceed the limits which have been set to the Parliament ' s powers, without its being possible to refer them for review by the court. It must therefore be concluded that an action for annulment may lie against measures adopted by the European Parliament intended to have legal effects vis-a-vis third parties."*

There was also a political aspect to the case. The Parliament itself declared that,

> *"In its opinion, the list of potential defendants in Article 173 of the Treaty is not exhaustive. The European Parliament does not dispute that in areas such as the budget and questions relating to the organization of direct elections, where increased powers have been conferred upon it by amendment of the treaties and where it may itself adopt legal measures, it is subject to judicial review by the court. However, it considers that, if Article 173 of the Treaty is to be interpreted broadly so as to render the measures adopted by it challengeable by way of an action for annulment, it should in turn have the capacity to bring such*

an action against measures adopted by the Council and the Commission."

Thus the Parliament was quite happy to be subject to judicial review, especially in the limited areas it mentioned, providing it had the right to bring cases against the other institutions. The ECJ therefore decided that The European Parliament would henceforth be regarded as included within the list of institutions defined in Article 173.

Whatever one's opinion regarding the justice of this decision, the remarkable result is that the ECJ regarded itself as empowered to read words into the Treaty itself, clearly changing its meaning in order to comply with its, underlying purposes, as divined by the ECJ. In fact the actual decision was not particularly controversial, and subsequent amendments of the Treaty formally added the Parliament, the Court of Auditors and later the European Central Bank to the jurisdiction of the Court.

Changing a Few Words

Article 234 of the EC Treaty had always been the essential tool for enforcement of EC law, defining the relationship between the ECJ and national courts. We previously encountered some of the difficulty this produced in Britain. The clause's important feature was that courts against which there was higher appeal, MAY request a ruling from the ECJ on questions involving the "validity and interpretation of acts of the institutions." It is interesting but logical to note that in its reference to the Treaty, the question of validity is excluded. The terms of the Treaty, while occasionally needing interpretation are always valid.

In 1983 a German company purchased some binoculars of East German origin from a company in Denmark. German customs mistakenly allowed the import free of duty. This mistake was discovered after clearance of the goods, but the higher customs authorities decided, partly because it was a customs error, that they would not seek recovery of the duty. Under Commission regulations such matters were within their competence and the Ministry referred the matter to Brussels. The Commission issued a legally binding "Decision" requiring the customs authorities to recover the unpaid duty. The customs authorities continued to decline and challenged the validity of the Commission's Decision in the national courts.

The case was remitted to the ECJ which produced the following judgement.

> *"National courts against whose decisions there is a judicial remedy under national law may consider the validity of a community act and, if they consider that the grounds put forward before them by the parties in support of invalidity are unfounded, they may reject them, concluding that the measure is completely valid. In contrast, national courts, whether or not a judicial remedy exists against their decisions under national law, themselves have no jurisdiction to declare that acts of community institutions are invalid."*

This second point would appear to be entirely contrary to the wording of Article 234. The ECJ explains,

> *"That conclusion is dictated, in the first place, by the requirement for community law to be applied uniformly. Divergences between courts in the member states as to the validity of community acts would be liable to place in jeopardy the very unity of the community legal order and detract from the fundamental requirement of legal certainty."*

Thus the ECJ asserts that the principle of uniformity, which the court itself invented, takes precedence over the wording of the Treaty, and soon transmitted through European legal systems was the binding precedent that only the ECJ had the power to invalidate even the most minor measure of legal effect from any Community institution. Nowadays this is taken for granted across Europe.

Adjusting an Old Concept

It was in 1969 that Regulations added substance to the Treaty's up till then theoretical competence in the field of Transport policy. However at the same time national governments of the Member States had together been re-negotiating under a United Nations programme, adjustments to an earlier European Road Transport Agreement. There was some question as to whether the Member States were acting in an inter-governmental capacity or on behalf of the Community, however eventually, acting as the Council they concluded the agreement on behalf of the Community. The European Commission brought before the ECJ an action for annulment of the agreement which they argued usurped a role which was reserved for the Commission.

Two important issues appeared for resolution before the ECJ. Firstly, since this was an international treaty made by Member States, was a review of the decision within the jurisdiction of the ECJ? Of course, the reply to this point was predictable. As a preliminary point they decided that Transport was an area of Community competence. Moreover, after reviewing the actions of the Member States acting in the Council that," in carrying on the negotiations and concluding the agreement simultaneously in the manner decided on by the Council, the Member States acted, and continue to act, in the interest and on behalf of the Community in accordance with their obligations under Article 5." Presumably, had they not been doing so the action of the Council would indeed have been annulled, overruling the objections of "sovereign" governments which had agreed the necessary undertakings. Secondly, although powers of review extended to those legally binding acts by the institutions defined in Article 249 (then 189), the obligations resulting from an international agreement are quite different. The ECJ was not at all convinced, and was not to be limited by definitions within the Treaty.

> *"The objective of this review is to ensure... observance of the law in the interpretation and application of the Treaty. It would be inconsistent with this objective to interpret the conditions under which the action is admissible so restrictively as to limit the availability of this procedure merely to the categories of measures referred to by Article 189.*
>
> *An action for annulment must therefore be available in the case of all measures adopted by the institutions, whatever their nature or form, which are intended to have legal effects."*

Finally, the judgement was to add a highly important precedent to be used extensively by the Commission in years to come. The starting point in this reasoning was Article 282 which states,

> *"In each of the Member States, the Community shall enjoy the most extensive legal capacity accorded to legal persons under their laws; it may, in particular acquire or dispose of moveable and immovable property and may be a party to legal proceedings."*

This seems entirely reasonable, otherwise Community institutions would be prevented from buying property or from forming and enforcing any contract in a Member State. In a truly audacious jump from this innocuous statement the ECJ concludes,

> "The Community enjoys the capacity to establish contractual links with third countries over the whole field of objectives defined by the Treaty."

This represents a remarkable expansion of the concept of the Community's legal identity and capacity. Suddenly it provides the Community with international legal competence in any field covered, one way or another, by the Treaty.

The significance of this conclusion was not immediately apparent. It had little relevance to the case in hand, and served instead as a powerful and unnoticed precedent, ready and established for use by the Court on a later occasion. National leaders would also not have been too concerned. After all, the Member States were frequently deciding that their interests were likely to be best served in international negotiations by pooling their resources and strengthening their positions with joint or co-ordinated action. Politically the Member States were therefore pleased that the ECJ was approving of their Transport Agreement. However, if they had read further they would have seen that the judgment was not approving politically expedient international co-operation but was actually imposing legally binding restrictions on such negotiations in future. Thus, the judgement continued,

> "In particular, each time the Community, with a view to implementing a common policy envisaged by the Treaty, adopts provisions laying down common rules, <u>whatever form they may take</u>, the Member States no longer have the right, acting individually or even collectively, to undertake obligations with third countries which affect those rules or alter their scope."

Thus, using a flimsy interpretation of the concept of legal capacity the ECJ officially abolished the rights of Member States to interfere in Community matters internationally. Moreover the rules of supremacy ensured that it was this interpretation of the law rather than the original words agreed by the authors of the Treaty which was transmitted across Europe for enforcement. Further, and just to emphasise this point, such international dealings were not to be treated any differently from internal Community matters.

> *"With regard to the implementation of the provisions of the Treaty, the system of internal Community measures may not be separated from that of external relations."*

Therefore, in the longer term it was the European Commission which was celebrating this particular intervention of the ECJ, even though the Council thought they won the case.

There is one further constitutional effect which results from this decision of the *ERTA* case which refers back to the words of Lord Denning described in Chapter G,

> *"Even if a treaty is signed, it is elementary that these courts take no notice of treaties as such. We take no notice of treaties until they are embodied in laws enacted by Parliament, and then only to the extent that Parliament tells us."*

This constraint which British courts had traditionally imposed on the executive branch of government by insisting on Parliamentary implementation of Treaties had also been abolished. A British Minister, sitting in the European Council could agree to an international treaty, and this would take legal effect in Britain again through the doctrine of supremacy. The Minister could in theory use this as a back door for agreements likely to prove controversial at home. Moreover, in many policy areas where qualified majority voting is authorised this Minister may even have opposed the treaty. Under the correct interpretation of the European Communities Act, considerations of whether British Ministers agreed, whether Parliament had a view, or whether the measures concerned the single market, harmonisation of the law or international obligations were all entirely irrelevant. The treaty would be the law.

Stopping a Few Changes

In 1991 the political leaders of Europe were in a move to broaden the benefits of free trade to non-EC countries by creation of a European Economic Area. This was to encompass the countries of the separate European Free Trade Area (EFTA) and the EC in a complete trade area covering the entire continent. In order to meet the politically based objections of the EFTA states the leaders negotiated a treaty ensuring common rules of free movement, and competition but without transfer of any legislative power to a supra-national body. Enforcement of the pan-European rules was to be accomplished with a separate EEA court, comprising ECJ judges and representative judges from the EFTA states.

The European Commission referred the proposed treaty to the ECJ so it could express its opinion on the scheme.

The "Opinion" (no.1 of 1991) started with an extraordinary statement, dealing with the point that the proposed wording of the provisions dealing with legal supervision were identical to those of the EC Treaty.

> *"The fact that the provisions of the agreement relating to the creation of the European Economic Area and the corresponding Community provisions are identically worded does not mean that they must necessarily be interpreted identically. An international treaty is to be interpreted not only on the basis of its wording, but also in the light of its objectives."*

Clearly this deserved a little explanation.

> *"With regard to the comparison of the objectives of the provisions of the agreement and those of Community law, it must be observed that the agreement is concerned with the application of rules on free trade and competition in economic and commercial relations between the Contracting Parties. In contrast, as far as the Community is concerned, the rules on free trade and competition have developed and form part of the Community legal order, the objectives of which go beyond that of the agreement. Indeed, the EEC Treaty aims to achieve economic integration leading to the establishment of an internal market and economic and monetary union and the objective of all the Community treaties is to contribute together to making concrete progress towards European unity."*

Because of this fundamental difference co-operation between two judicial bodies was unlikely to lead to homogeneity in interpretation. The requirement that the ECJ would have to co-operate therefore represented a serious encroachment on the exclusive jurisdiction of the Court of Justice under the Treaty of Rome and would thus undermine the ability of the Community to pursue its own particular objectives. Consequently the proposed system of judicial supervision in the EEA was found to be contrary to Article 220 (then 164) of the Treaty of Rome. The Member States obediently returned to the negotiations, and removed any risk of EC law being affected by the co-operation. A year later the agreement was approved by the Court.

Before then, in the original proceedings it had been suggested that the proposal could nevertheless be implemented by specific amendment to the Treaty based on Article 310 (then 238) which allows the establishment of reciprocal rights and obligations internationally. With this question the Court was essentially asked whether its opinion could be circumvented. Of course, every court in Europe would have replied that its duty was to uphold democratically created legislation, or a legally modified constitution. The ECJ however, examined this possibility in the light of the expansive view it had taken if its duty under Article 220 (164) to ensure "the law is observed" and concluded,

> *"Article 238 of the EEC Treaty does not provide any basis for setting up under an international agreement a system of courts which conflicts with Article 164 of the EEC Treaty and, more generally, with the very foundations of the Community. For the same reasons, an amendment of Article 238 could not cure the incompatibility with Community law of the system of courts to be set up by the agreement."*

The opinion of the court appears to be that the political leaders acting even unanimously to amend the Treaty correctly in accordance with its procedures cannot thereby compromise the duty of the Court to enforce "the law" (as defined by itself), nor introduce any amendment which the Court would regard as conflicting with "the very foundations of the Community." This is in turn quite a remarkable proposition. It was certainly a serious matter to determine that European law to be enforced as stated definitively by the ECJ throughout Europe and without recourse or appeal. But with this judgement Member States even collectively, would be denied any right to amend the Treaty as a means of countering or overruling any consequences of this law. Moreover, in view of the duty of national courts to uphold and enforce ECJ judgements, these courts could even prevent their national politicians from taking the steps necessary to do so. If true this would certainly represent a judicial power unparalleled in the history of democratic states.

This is a conclusion which seems so contrary to the democratic principles of all Member States that it is interesting to speculate on its source. The Court indeed looks carefully at the aims of the Treaty as described in its preamble, but it gives greater weight to its own understanding of the purposes of the Union. Of central importance was the idea that the Treaty was intended as a new European constitution but for political reasons could not be presented as such. Hence the description later appeared from the ECJ itself that the treaties represented a constitutional charter. Support for this idea came from a former President of the Court, Robert LeCourt writing in 1970,

> "*Once the idea of a court of arbitration was abandoned and a judge was charged with ensuring the respect for the law which the Treaties were instituting, that judge could not ignore the very aims of that law. ... Thus, within the Community, the judge is the repository of the will of the Treaties authors who disappeared on the day the Treaties were signed, only reappearing on the rare occasions when new agreements are concluded. They have made the judge the guardian of their joint work, which is to say of its objectives, its institutions and of its law.*"

These founders of the Community left considerable vagueness and have since departed. Should their original intentions be sought, even though they have long departed? Should their intentions be given precedence over those of present leaders? In 1991 the ECJ was appearing to answer affirmatively, giving supremacy not to a written document but to presumed intentions of the departed. But this raises further questions as summarised by Professor Weiler,

> "*How do we determine their intention in relation to issues which they did not contemplate, or which they deliberately left vague or over which they compromised or disagreed? What do we do in the case of conflict between text and intention? Should we interpret the text with the purpose of elucidating the intention, or should we seek the intention in order to elucidate the text?*"

Whatever the answer to such philosophical points, the fact remains that judgments of the ECJ limit the powers of Member States and Community Institutions while leaving the ECJ itself illimitable and unassailable, and accountable, possibly, only to the ghosts of the past.

Chapter 21: Major Trials

Battling Eurosceptics

At the time of his desperate victory over the Maastricht Treaty John Major undoubtedly breathed more than just a sigh of relief. But although at the climax of his pro-European career, politics just as life goes on, and Major now found himself with the same objectives which he had had two years previously. He was leader of an almost fatally divided party, and even though he had been largely responsible for the recent fractures, he now needed to repair the damage and move on towards an election with at least a semblance of party unity. Such was the hostility felt towards him by many of his own MP's, caused by both principled opposition and disgust at his heavy handed parliamentary tactics, that Major could only respond with compensatory leanings towards the Euro-sceptic cause.

This former enemy camp had been swelled by several influential converts. Kenneth Baker, a former Home Secretary who had been an important supporting figure in the Maastricht negotiations was a new Eurosceptic. Norman Lamont, sacked by Major in 1993 had left behind his memorable description of the government as "being in office but not in power." Freed from Cabinet collective responsibility, Lamont realised that he was a euro-sceptic who had never really agreed with the ERM policy. Opposition was not limited to the back benches. In Cabinet were Peter Lilley, the usually quiet Social Security Secretary; Michael Portillo, the Chief Secretary to the Treasury previously silently but nevertheless fiercely opposed to the single currency. Major even added to their strength when he brought into the Cabinet John Redwood, a man to be likened to Star Trek's Mr. Spock as he became more familiar.

Major now began to make remarks regarding Europe which, while sounding cautious rather than sceptical, sought to allay fears about the consequences of his Maastricht enterprise. Unfortunately, from someone with such an intimate experience of the workings of the Union they showed a definite naivety which impaired credibility. In the aftermath of ratification he published in the *Economist* magazine, an article praising Britain's reluctance to accept new Commission proposals and commented that the structures and strategies of the Treaty of Rome were outdated. He returned to an argument that most Europeans thought had indeed been resolved in the 50's, with Britain's belated agreement in the 70's. "The new mood in Europe demands a new approach....It is for the nations to build Europe, not for Europe to attempt to supercede nations. I want to see the Community become a wide nation, embracing the whole of democratic Europe, in a single market and with common security arrangements firmly linked to NATO." Then, regarding EMU he expressed the hope that his fellow leaders would not recite the mantra of economic and monetary union as though nothing had changed. If they did recite such things they would find they had the quaintness and the potency of a rain dance.

This theme continued with an interview with the German magazine, Der Spiegel. "My scepticism is about the economic impact of it. Let us presuppose we moved to a single currency in the sort of date specified before 1997, 1998, 1999. If we were to move to a single currency and it was to be successful, you would need proper convergence of the economies across Europe. They would all need to be operating at the same sort of efficiency. I know of no one who believes that is remotely likely, it simply is not going to happen.

Major showed a similarly optimistic view on the decentralisation stemming from the doctrine of subsidiarity, describing a Europe the business community certainly could not recognise. Having been told to expect Thatcherite de-regulation, and reduced impediments to trade they saw nothing but harmonisation and interference from a flood of directives and regulations. At a speech in July 1994 Major explained. "We did not manage to stem the tide of European regulation during the 1980s. Now we have put up breakwaters: the principle of "minimum interference" we secured at Maastricht; and, of course, our opt-out from the Social Chapter, enshrined in a legally binding protocol. With the German government, we are working to reduce regulations across Europe. The tide is turning. The number of proposals for new directives tabled by the European Commission has fallen."

It appeared that Major and his close Foreign Secretary of the time, Douglas Hurd really believed that Europe was moving in Britain's direction. Hurd in particular frequently reported that Europe was "moving our way", that the "climate was changing", that British ideas were prevailing. The essential message was that Britain should be quite satisfied about the direction of Europe, and that being at the very heart was now working to Britain's benefit because of de-regulation, decentralisation and practical thinking regarding EMU. What a pity none of this was true.

With his new view of European activities Major felt quite justified in demanding a vote of confidence once again, when Parliamentary approval was needed for a deal Major had made requiring an increase in budgetary contributions. This time eight MP's who nevertheless voted against the measure were severely punished by the equivalent of expulsion, the withdrawal of the party whip. This was widely seen by grassroots Conservatives as a draconian measure such that a ninth Member withdrew his support in protest. The group, touring the country and revealing a campaign of dirty tricks being conducted against them by the party hierarchy, attracted so much sympathy and admiration they risked becoming martyrs. They were forgiven six months later, but had left their mark of division and dissent on the entire party and its leadership. With an election on the horizon, Major was in urgent need of a review of his party management strategy.

His cosy and reassuring description of Europe was increasingly seen as flying in the face of the facts. The issue of Europe, unlike any other, has a continuing and growing life of its own, with the next hurdle approaching just as soon as the last is negotiated. Despite the narrowly avoided collapse of its previous project the European Union was now discussing the next steps in its greater project, with scarcely a pause for breath. Quickly on the agenda were issues of enlargement and the next stage of EMU.

One decision, regarded as obscure and arcane by outsiders, appeared as unexpected another source of confrontation. Enlargement of the Union with the joining of Austria, Finland, Sweden and Norway, (who eventually declined), had always been strongly supported by Britain. However, it would clearly call for revision of rules regarding Qualified Majority Voting, QMV whereby Member States held votes in Council loosely related to their country's population. Before the SEA many European supporters were sustained by the belief that the national veto could serve as the ultimate protection of national interests. Subsequent extension of QMV had removed this protection and the only remaining safeguard was the "blocking minority" which would be number of votes sufficient to prevent a new measure being adopted. Two small countries and one large one were sufficient for blocking any new measure, but under new proposals small countries would be capable of stopping the three larger ones. In any event the proposal to raise the threshold from twenty-three to twenty-seven represented a further dilution of veto power. Douglas Hurd was sent to the summit in Ioannina to resolve the issue by sticking at twenty-three.

Hurd, in a minority of one, and his with hands tied by Cabinet instructions had a difficult meeting to say the least. He was accused of scuppering the entire process of enlargement, and only succeeded in a compromise obtained by stealth, ie. constructing some of the communiqué while the French delegate was out of the room. This "preserved the substance" of the proposal but committed the relevant Council to do "all in its power", "within a reasonable time" to reach a consensual solution if ever the potential blocking minority fell within the range of 23 to 26 votes. Major knew immediately that this looked like a climbdown. The Cabinet was divided, and MP's understanding that the issue could have been resolved quietly began to question his leadership. Personal disappointment must have followed when one of his closest friends and long-standing supporters Tony Marlow told him in Parliament, "to make way for somebody else who can provide the party and the country with direction and leadership."

Gradually Major's public statements were shifting to a more definite opposition to some of Europe's policies, and he began to sound like the disruptive Thatcher he had replaced. For example he attacked the Social Chapter. "Europe is not winning. 18½ million people are unemployed - the size of Denmark, Finland and Sweden put together. We are not creating enough new jobs. ....Over the last 20 years America has created 36 million new jobs of which 31 million were in the private sector. In that time, the EU as a whole only created five million new jobs, of which only one million were in the private sector. ....I believe the answer lies in the policies Europe has followed. ....The European Social Model is fundamentally flawed. It deprives today's companies of the chance to compete, and drives away tomorrow's investment and new jobs. Over-regulation does not work. And, as a result, nor do millions of Europeans. The figures say it all. For every £100 paid in wages in Germany non-wage costs add on an extra £31, in France £41 and in Italy £44. In Britain, it is only £15."

Then in a speech in Leiden in Holland he attacked again the concept of federalism. "The vision of the Founding Fathers of the European Community was proved right for its age. But it will not do now....Popular enthusiasm for the Union has waned....The Maastricht Treaty strained the limits of acceptability to Europe's electors. Europe's peoples in general retain their favour and confidence in the nation state. I believe that the nation state will remain the basic political unit for Europe." This vision, returning to a lost battleground was clearly incompatible with Maastricht, and was scathingly rejected by Helmut Kohl and Francois Mitterrand. Kohl replied that the Europe of nation states had failed, that it had led to the world wars, and that such an outdated model of sovereign nations was incompatible with Germany's vision for the future.

Major's aim of pleasing his audiences occasionally caused undisputable contradiction. For example in May 1994 during the European election campaign, and trying to accommodate the divergent aspirations across Europe he described a new vision of Europe as, multi-track, multi-speed, multi-layered." Less than four months later in the Leiden speech he declared, "I see real danger, in talk of a "hard core", inner and outer circles, a two-tier Europe. I recoil from ideas for a Union in which some would be more equal than others. There is not, and should never be, an exclusive hard core of countries or of policies."

Then to demonstrate to his domestic audience that Britain retained influence in Europe he blocked, with his single vote, the proposed successor to Delors as president of the Commission. The Belgian Prime Minister Jean-Luc Dehaene had been approved by all other members but Major rejected him as being a "federalist". The eventual candidate, unanimously approved was the former Prime Minister of Luxembourg Jacques Santer. Major had succeeded in making his point, even though other Member States were unable to detect a significant difference between the two and regarded this as a futile gesture. However there is little doubt that Britain had felt that the Commission under Delors had become too powerful, and that Delors personally had become too forceful and vocal, as well as uncompromising in his integrationist zeal. Santer, seen as a weaker President was seen as desirable. The disastrous consequences which were to result from such weakening four years later were not predictable.

At home, party management was becoming more and more difficult for John Major. Concessions to the passionate Euro-sceptic activists served only to increase their aggression and their appetite for further anti-European statements and actions, threatening even that core of pro-European attitude that daily government dealings with Brussels demanded. Major was trying hard to hold the line against the sceptic flood, for example addressing one of their groupings in 1995, the Way Forward. "We cannot accept that sterling should be part of a Single Currency in 1996 or 1997. We don't believe anyone could sensibly want to go ahead then, but, if they do, we wouldn't be with them. ....What we will aim for is a more flexible European Union. That is the only way forward which makes sense as

Europe enlarges. ....Nor will we agree to a more prescriptive, centralist Europe, or removal of the nation states' veto. The Cabinet are clear about that and our European partners know our views. Moreover, although they may only mutter it sotto voce, a number of our partners agree with us on these points. ....We need to re-examine and review the institutions of the European Union."

Even this was not enough as more anti-European action was demanded. So Major, exhausted by relentless anti-European pressure decided on a terminal confrontation with his vociferous critics. He would issue a direct challenge to his opponents by resigning as party leader and offering himself for re-election. The party was becoming increasingly unmanageable at a time when discipline was becoming more important as bye-elections were whittling away at Major's majority. It was time for his enemies, he stated, "To put up or shut up." The sceptics tried to rise to the occasion but had some deciding who should stand. Norman Lamont was first to emerge but he was viewed as tainted by the ERM fiasco. Michael Portillo raised his head suggesting a complete rejection of the next pending European proposals. He appeared happy to end the futile attempts to straddle competing party views even at the risk of formally splitting the party. The party appeared afraid to admit that Conservative beliefs in their core values could not overcome differences over Europe. Finally, it was John Redwood who stood, on a platform of complete rejection just of the single currency. Redwood's brief campaign appeared definite about Europe, but was otherwise lacking in substance, and the man himself appeared eccentric rather than charismatic. Major, of course could not claim charisma either, but figures like Douglas Hurd and particularly Kenneth Clarke rallied to his defence, pointing out that his ability to unite the opposing forces, tattered though it was, would be crucial in a forthcoming election. Major won the ballot by 218 to 89, and immediately claimed a decisive victory.

It was predictable that the result, although appearing conclusive would fail to dispose of any of the European policy questions, and Euro-sceptics were always unlikely to stop arguing. Neither Major's optimistic and even imaginative views of the Union, nor the possibility of futile gestures could mask the fact that a potentially explosive question was returning to the agenda, looming in the form of another Inter Governmental Conference. Would Britain sign up to the single currency or not? The IGC was approaching inexorably, and Britain appeared so paralysed by uncertainty, that other Member States were simply proceeding with their own plans without regard to Britain's views. To them, Major's situation at home made him simply incapable of making a decision and therefore unable to be taken seriously at all.

BSE

Just as John Major must have felt at a low ebb, another disaster forced him to suffer another blow. The Government had disclosed evidence that BSE, popularly known as "Mad cow disease", might be linked to the human brain disease Creutzfelt-Jacob disease, CJD. Although not scientifically proven, the possible link was sufficient to produce a panic at home and in Europe where the Commission, responsible for both trade and public health imposed a ban on British beef not only in Europe but worldwide. Only in Britain was the public free to eat their own beef, and even this was limited by banning the most suspect cuts, eg. beef on the bone. Delay in informing Brussels had produced suspicion on their part and they immediately adopted an uncompromising stance, which Major impotently attacked as "hysterical".

In Britain the government found itself facing in two directions. Firstly it had to deal effectively with the crisis and was doing its level best to contain the BSE epedemic. At the same time the government appeared truly incensed by the attitude of the Commission. The veterinary committee convened to advise Brussels appeared to be deciding in accordance with national instructions, producing real suspicion that European beef farmers were happy to take advantage of removing British competition. This was dubious because European consumers were themselves suspicious of beef in general and slumping sales did not recover for years. Even so the committee was widely regarded as unscientific and tainted with national politics as they rejected Britain's safety measures.

This precipitated a new "war" with the powers of Brussels. John Major announced to the Commons that Britain was implementing a policy of non co-operation with Europe. A legal challenge was launched, but not expected to rule within a practical timescale. A counter ban on European meat had been considered and rejected, and another empty chair policy had also been rejected as it would no longer have an obstructive effect. Instead all decision making that required unanimity was blocked and within a month seventy measures, many of which Britain actually supported had been stopped. Major also considered escalation by refusing to attend the next summit, in Florence, but had relented due to the prospect of negotiating a BSE settlement.

The media regarded the issue as a European attack on English roast beef and of exposing Brussels' agenda of interference and to farmers it really was a potent attack on the Conservative Party's traditional countryside supporters. At the same time the incident was demolishing Major's earlier emphasis on the success of subsidiarity, and Hurd's insistence that things had been "moving our way". Half going into battle over the unfairness of the ban, Major was making no progress, and soon felt forced to settle in Florence. The European ban would begin to be lifted as a cattle slaughter programme, supervised by European vets was implemented. Major, trying hard to present this as a victory was undermined by the total lack of European commitment or timescale. He had simply inflamed passions further by provoking a confrontation and then apparently conceded while pretending to win. He was left looking ineffective and impotent. This has one lesson to future leaders, to the unfortunate detriment of the people in all Member States. It suggests that in any dispute, whatever its merits from a national viewpoint, a national leader can no longer hope to overcome Brussels power. A public battle is likely to be not only futile but damaging to the leader instigating it. Therefore a strategy of immediate and quiet concessions will best serve that leader's individual position. An alternative, and public admission that the matter was now under European competence and therefore beyond national controls would have the merit of honesty, but which politician could admit such real impotence to his electorate?

Economic and Monetary Union

In the event Major was further damaged at home and in Europe with other leaders seeing him as petulant and not in control, and privately ridiculing him as in a "half-empty chair". They were quietly proceeding with the arrangements for a single currency simply ignoring Major's prevarication. Major had already decided that Britain was not in a position economically to join the single currency immediately, but he was also unable to rule out the possibility as a future option. He would not even rule it out for the relatively short period of the next Parliament. He was obstinate in refusal to see the single currency in the constitutional terms explained by the Euro-sceptics. He even refused to see that there were profound political implications involved. He stuck to the view that there might be circumstances in which introducing the single currency to Britain might in future be in the country's own interest. He could not therefore rule it out as a matter of permanent principle. Consequently he became increasingly firmly attached to a policy of neither accepting nor rejecting the single currency. This wasn't indecision he explained. It was merely a sensible response to uncertainty. This in turn was not "wait and see", it was "negotiate and decide".

He occasionally admitted some of the implications. For example in 1997 when he suggested in the Commons that, "I wouldn't like to be the Chancellor of the Exchequer who went to the despatch box and said 'Well, I no longer have any control over interest rates, I am sorry they have gone up 3%, but it's nothing to do with me, Guv'". Then reminded that this was precisely what he had agreed under Maastricht, he retreated to his "negotiate and decide" bunker and in this captive vein he was forced to approach the 1997 General Election.

One final disaster was inflicted on the Conservative Party by themselves. As a means of extinguishing the conflicts regarding the single currency Major had considered, following Wilson, the use of a referendum. Of course this immediately raised the temperature of Cabinet opposition, particularly from the pro-European camp which saw the growing public opposition to Europe. This time the lines of opposition to the idea were not so clearly correlated with a European leaning. Michael Portillo for example, feared the democratic consequences since a wrong decision would endorse the loss of Parliament's sovereignty for the indefinite future. The risk was too high. On the other side of the argument Kenneth Clarke and Michael Heseltine believed that abrogating the decision would reduce even further their room for continuing negotiations in Brussels. Nevertheless, and hoping that the issue would be effectively sidelined, the Conservative Party pledged that a new Conservative government would hold a referendum if it were to contemplate entry into EMU. The Labour Party immediately matched the commitment.

There was one further factor in making this decision which was of some significance, in the shape of Sir James Goldsmith. This curious, but fabulously wealthy businessman, had in recent years grown an obsessive and fundamentalist opposition to Europe and proposed to use some of his wealth to promote his political conviction. He formed his own party, the Referendum Party. This was a novel idea in Britain, in contrast to the USA where wealth is a prerequisite of a political career. Never before had an organisation funded by a private individual been formed to promote a single issue. His argument and the policy for which he sought electoral endorsement was deceptively simple. There should be a referendum on Europe.

With £20 million available for a campaign Goldsmith was able to promise to field a Referendum candidate in any constituency where the established party candidates did not pledge themselves to support a referendum. With several prominent Tory MP's especially at risk in marginal seats, this was a potent threat. His campaign included televised party political broadcasts showing him appearing peculiar and obsessive. Voters saw an outspoken criticism of Britain's loss of sovereignty and a great deal of reasonable explanation of the issues involved, but again they showed little interest in the case his supporters were presenting. His eventual result was defeat in 550 seats with an average of 3.1% of the vote, leading most commentators to judge his intervention as an expensive and ineffective failure which he richly deserved. But there seems little doubt the Major's decision regarding the EMU referendum was influenced as a pre-emptive and defensive measure against Goldsmith.

One minor irritant may have been removed, but the issue of Europe survived Major's attempt to sweep it to the sidelines. During the last weeks of his premiership he actually made some thoughtful, sensible sounding points regarding Europe. For example he expressed the view, "That it is nonsense, copper-plated nonsense that Britain could leave the European Union and form an Atlantic alliance." At the same time, "Europe was going in the wrong direction, and should be thinking of enlarging to the East rather than deepening relations with the Western European countries." He appreciated that Helmut Kohl, "had the luxury of driving the motor of integration," and understood that Italy needed a strong Union to compensate for its traditional instability, and Spain and Portugal had only recently emerged from being "Run by men in epaulets and dark glasses." Britain was quite different. Yes, but Major could not take the argument further to admit that this divergence in values and interests were so profound that Britain would never be capable of changing the Union's values from within – a view which would have appealed to many of the ordinary party members.

Several commentators revealed later the scale of Conservative scepticism. "So great was the frustration and bitterness felt by many of the normally loyal membership that this created a sense of grassroots alienation from the leadership quite without precedent in the Party's history. Formerly diehard party workers departed in droves. Donations and subscriptions collapsed. Only the most ferocious efforts by Party managers to suppress public evidence of what was going on succeeded in obscuring the full scale of the Tory Party's internal disaster from general view." Similarly Sir Charles Powell summarised the feeling of euro-scepticism within the party which Major still struggled to contain.

"Six years ago the Conservative Party dispensed with Lady Thatcher as Prime Minister for saying No, No, No to a more federal Europe. John Major's Government embarked instead on a "charm offensive" designed to put Britain "at the heart of Europe". That reflected a touching belief that being nice to our partners in Europe, after years of handbagging them over Britain's budget contribution, would incline them to lower their sights and moderate their treasured goal of a single currency. It also reflected the deep-seated delusion of British diplomacy that the gulf between Britain and the rest of Europe on the future shape and direction of the European Union is capable of being bridged....Now the same Conservative Party which sacked Lady Thatcher is falling over itself to say No, No, No to Europe as vigorously as she once did."

Thus Major entered the 1997 election campaign with the issue of Europe hanging around his neck as a potent symbol of indecision and division. More than half the party's candidates, primarily concerned with their own seats were speaking against the official "wait and see" policy. The Labour Party swept to power with an overall majority of 179 – unimaginable by any post-war government.

Chapter M: The Cows Come Home

Defenceless Britain

As the nations of Europe settled after the internal turmoil of the Maastricht Treaty it is interesting to speculate how many government departments across the European Union were really aware of the limitations which had been applied to their traditional administrative powers as the result of the transfer of competences to Europe. Certainly at lower levels it was quite possible that civil servants really believed they were implementing decisions taken in the traditional manner by their government departments. It probably would not even have mattered to them, since their job of implementing political decisions was not affected by adjustments to the decision making process even if this involved its relocation to Brussels. Moreover it was rarely in the interests of Ministers to explain that their areas of responsibility had in reality been transferred well away from their departments, and that they were in fact responsible merely for administering European policy. It was easier for all concerned if they maintained the position that they enjoyed undiminished responsibility even attitude was close to being fictitious.

The change in government procedure was certainly not appreciated by the public at large. In Britain, Ministers continued to act as though they were fully responsible, of course to Parliament, even in the field of agriculture which had been the first area of policy to be "delegated" to the EC. It is unlikely that these Ministers were actually operating under a delusion of this type, and in any case this view would have become untenable and unsupportable by the late 1990's. Of course, acceptance of this fact would not necessarily change the Ministers' public stance, but they personally could not fail to have recognised the reality. In a few instances major divergences in policy emerged between Britain and Europe and Ministers were made keenly aware of their limitations. Gradually they were failing to protect Britain from policies with which they fundamentally disagreed. Instead, they were being forced to adopt and implement European policy, behind a saving face of placid acceptance.

Britain's traditionally sovereign Parliament was faring no better. The judgements relating to Factortame had already established that Parliament was powerless to protect British fisherman in any way which discriminated against those of other Member States. Shortly, a new step was to mean that the executive branch of the British government would also fail to protect

Britain from social regulations which it had opposed. Firmly committed to resisting a flow of socialist regulation in the interest of maintaining a more dynamic labour market for Britain, this had been the purpose of Britain's hard won and controversial "opt-out" from Social Chapter of the Maastricht Treaty. To the surprise of the British government this opt-out was to be tested very soon when the Commission proposed the Working Time Directive of 1993, prohibiting any workers from working more than 48 hours per week. Recognising that Britain had an opt-out and could therefore avoid adopting such a measure the Commission changed the legal basis for the Directive so it could be approved by Qualified Majority. Of course, many people supported this principle, but here the method of the Directive's introduction is more important than its merit.

The elected British government was furious that despite its opposition at every stage the measure was implemented as a health and safety measure. They immediately challenged the Directive before the ECJ. Firstly they argued that this was in reality a harmonisation measure, with a purpose related to the functioning of the internal market. (This would have required unanimity in the Council for its adoption). The ECJ replied that the Community gained legislative competence in social matters from Article 137, (then 118). Britain then argued that "that provision permits the adoption only of directives which have a genuine and objective link to the "health and safety" of workers. That does not apply to measures concerning, in particular, weekly working time, paid annual leave and rest periods, whose connection with the health and safety of workers is too tenuous." Britain supported this interpretation by referring to the words of the Article. The provision relating to health and safety refers directly to the 'working environment' and Britain argued that this implies "that directives based on that provision must be concerned only with physical conditions and risks at the workplace." Wrong. The ECJ replied,

> "There is nothing in the wording of Article 118a to indicate that the concepts of 'working environment', 'safety' and 'health' as used in that provision should, in the absence of other indications, be interpreted restrictively, and not as embracing all factors, physical or otherwise, capable of affecting the health and safety of the worker in his working environment, including in particular certain aspects of the organization of working

> *time. On the contrary, the words 'especially in the working environment' militate in favour of a broad interpretation of the powers which Article 118a confers upon the Council for the protection of the health and safety of workers."*

Further objections were based on the principle of proportionality, subsidiarity and abuse of power. For example, there was no evidence that the measures were desirable, let alone necessary methods of achieving the stated aims. The pronounced lack of sympathy for all these arguments is expressed by another quotation form the ECJ judgement,

> *"Legislative action by the Community, particularly in the field of social policy, cannot be limited exclusively to circumstances where the justification for such action is scientifically demonstrated."*

Britain had thought that by opting out of the Social Chapter it had avoided the imposition of social legislation of which it disapproved. However this was clearly unjustified optimism, which they later saw as, but never admitted as, their own failure to appreciate the extent of European deviousness. Of course many people rejoiced that further measures to protect workers were being introduced, and were not at all concerned about the mechanism of their becoming law. However the important aspect constitutionally is that the Commission and the Council having decided that the measures were desirable, deliberately selected the particular legal basis which would prevent Britain from opting out. Britain's government was powerless, as the ECJ had confirmed. Negotiation and agreement with other Member States had proved no more effective than unilateral Parliamentary action.

Protection Required?

Right from the taking effect of the European Communities Act of 1972 the principle of supremacy of European Law had been introduced to Britain. It took many years but eventually the House of Lords confirmed their duty under the Act. Britain could not no longer be protected by its Courts. Parliament's limitations had been similarly revealed in the Factortame cases and now the elected government had failed by the same means. It had negotiated, in good faith, a compromise with its European partners, only to find itself outmanoeuvred and forced to implement legislation entirely contrary to its own policies. In each case the European Court of Justice had spoken, and that was the law.

These constitutional failings were noticed with alarm in several quarters, and in April 1996, a figure then unknown to the general public, stood up in Parliament with a simple, and elegant solution. Mr. Ian Duncan-Smith proposed a Bill, "To provide for disapplication of judgements, rules and doctrines propounded by the European Court of Justice." Under this proposal after a motion passed by the House of Parliament, the effect of any such judgement could simply be disapplied by an Order in Council.

Mr. Duncan-Smith provided a concise and impressive justification for his Bill. He referred to Parliament's will being overturned, and its sovereignty undermined. An attempt to protect Britain against Spanish fishermen had resulted in overturning of the Act, followed by a humiliating payment of compensation. He complained that the social chapter opt-out had been circumvented by the ECJ, and that general statements on sex equality or health and safety had been converted to powerful doctrines beyond democratic control. He reminded MP's that national courts enforced Directives but could not question any European measure. Therefore, he concluded that "The ECJ is a political court which sees its role as an architect of European integration." Parliament should now speak in order to preserve its own rights.

It was left to the Liberal Democrat leader, Charles Kennedy, to oppose the Bill. His speech started in a quiet and unassuming manner, praising what he described as a "cogent and fair-minded case." However, remembering his opposition he pointed out, somewhat weakly, that such a measure might provoke retaliation by the EU against British companies, thus damaging Britain's prospects in European trade. Then, forgetting the reasonableness of the previous speech he strongly criticised Duncan-Smith for evading the issue. If he really wanted Britain to leave the EU, he should say so directly and not disguise such an intention behind a mere anti-ECJ statement. The vote on the Bill was taken; Ayes 77 v Noes 83.

Bovine Spongiform Encephalopathy

It was only one month after this decision of Parliament that the British government called on the ECJ to protect it from what it regarded as a grave injustice it was suffering from the hands of the European Commission. "Mad Cow Disease" had been identified in Britain as long ago as in 1986. In 1988, the only possible cause appeared to be the practice of producing cattle feed from infected sheep. Preventative measures were therefore introduced. In accordance with normal procedures the European Commission was informed and they took the opportunity to issue a few legally binding "Decisions" to ensure the effectiveness of these measures.

It was in March 1996 that the governments advisory committee SEAC, (Spongiform Encephalopathy Advisory Committee), that they had identified ten cases of a new variant of the previously known Creutzfeldt-Jakob disease. Their announcement stated, "Although there is no direct evidence of a link, on current data and in the absence of any credible alternative the most likely explanation at present is that these cases are linked to exposure to BSE before the introduction of the [offal] ban in 1989." That day several Member States banned imports of beef from Britain. Two days later the Scientific Veterinary Committee of the European Union concluded that, it was not possible to prove that BSE was transmissible to humans, but in view of such a risk the measures introduced by Britain should be implemented across Europe. The report was widely and immediately publicised and sales of British beef dropped to zero. However, it was not the reaction of consumers which was decisive. Within one week of the SEAC announcement the Commission produced a Decision to ban export of beef from Britain, not only to other Member States, but also to third countries. This was justified as an emergency measure because the risk of transmission to humans cannot be excluded and because of "serious concern among consumers."

Britain, angry that mere concern could be used to justify a legal embargo, raised the case with the ECJ, arguing for an immediate annulment of the ban. An interim decision was requested realising that examination of the legal issues would take time. This was required because of the lasting and irreparable damage which the ban would cause. So, at the first, emergency hearing Britain maintained that its beef did not actually present a danger for human consumption and that the ban was not legally justified. Britain argued that there was no scientific basis for the ban on exports, which had decided to reassure consumers and protect the beef and veal markets, and in terms of consumer confidence it was proving entirely counter-productive. The court reserved its position regarding the legal questions but its reply regarding a lifting on the ban was dismissive. It was reasonable to assume that serious and irreparable damage would be caused to Britain's beef industry but it was not shown that the damage would be caused by the Commission decision. Damage was caused by the UK government announcement, and bans in non-member countries. Given "the media coverage of the issue and increasing health awareness among consumers," it could not be held that the Commission "Decision" significantly magnified the damage being caused by the disease.

Once again, European consumers could have been pleased that they were being protected from even "the possible risk." However, at issue was the legal basis for the ban, and the rational basis of the ECJ in enforcing it. Most people would agree that this first judgement showed a serious deficiency in logic. In fact the case also illustrates the inadequacy of the law in such matters because the issue was not fully resolved for a full two years when the main judgement appeared. By that time, with the disease almost forgotten, the judgement was important only for what it would say about future comparable incidents, and the right of the Commission to respond to any perceived risk, irrespective of the scientific merits of the case, or any reasonable risk assessment.. As with any legal case a large number of arguments were presented, and exhaustively analysed. The result was, as far as Britain was concerned, a total loss. The principle arguments against the Commission and the response of the ECJ were as follows:

The claimed legal basis for the Decision were Directives (90/425) which were concerned with the harmonisation of regulations for veterinary checks. They contained no provision which could be interpreted as authorising an export ban.

> *"The wording of the Directive is in very broad terms allowing the Commission to act 'in all cases' and to 'adopt necessary measures'. A ban on the movement of animals can therefore be appropriate."*

The Directives were worded to cover an "outbreak of disease" which this was not applicable because measures were already being taken. The Decision was not justified by any information suggesting that the measures already taken against BSE were ineffective nor by information pointing to a threat which had not already been considered. The idea that BSE could be transmitted from one animal to another was based solely on conjecture. The risk to human health (if any) did not justify the contested decision since it was negligible, having regard to the measures already adopted.

> *"It would be contrary to the objective of the Directive if the Commission were to be precluded from adopting the necessary measures in response to the publication of new information significantly altering what is known about a disease,*

> *particularly as regards its transmissibility or its consequences, on the ground that the disease had been in existence for a long time."*

The stated aim of the decision – to restore consumer confidence was not an objective authorised by the Directive.

> *"The phrase referring to consumer concern should be read in the context of the preamble to the Directives as a whole."*

The lack of a quantifiable or demonstrable link represented a failure to provide reasons.

> *"The degree of precision of the statement of the reasons for a decision must be weighed against practical realities and the time and technical facilities available for making the decision*
>
> *Reference to the adoption of measures by the Member State with the greatest experience of BSE constituted in itself a sufficient statement of reasons for the decision by the Commission likewise to adopt <u>additional</u> measures."*

A total ban was disproportionate

> *"Where there is uncertainty as to the existence or extent of risks to human health, the institutions may take protective measures without having to wait until the reality and seriousness of those risks become fully apparent.*
>
> *The Community judicature must, when reviewing such measures, restrict itself to examining whether the exercise of such discretion is vitiated by a manifest error or a misuse of powers or whether the Commission did not clearly exceed the bounds of its discretion. In the light of the information from SEAC there was no manifest error in risk assessment."*

The Commission had no power to ban exports to countries outside the Community.

> *"Careful reading of the Directives reveals no provision which precludes it from taking such measures as may be necessary in relation to third countries."*

The Decision is not justified by any of the objectives of the common agricultural policy set out in Article 39.

> *"The Directives form part of a coherent and exhaustive body of law established in order to substitute a set of common rules for unilateral action on the part of each Member State pursuant to Article 36 of the Treaty. As*

> *regards the implementing powers conferred on the Commission, it follows from the context of the EC Treaty and also from practical requirements, that the concept of implementation must be given a wide interpretation, particularly in the context of the common agricultural policy, and a fortiori in urgent cases."*

The ban was contrary to the principle of free movement of goods, and could not be justified as a valid exception since, in the absence of an identified risk they constituted economic measures.

> *"The protection of public health is an integral part of the proper functioning of the internal market. Besides the Directives themselves were adopted with the aim of facilitating the movement of agricultural products."*

This was a total and emphatic rejection of every legal point made by the British. The British had believed that the whole episode had been blown out of proportion by near hysteria in the media, and this indeed did prove to be the case. Even though there was greater uncertainty at the time they had believed that their legal case against the Commission ban had been compelling on the grounds of competence and the legal basis of the Directives. Britain did not get the version of dispassionate evaluation or rational interpretation of the law which it had expected. British lawyers thought that many of the ECJ replies failed to answer the questions posed, but there never has been any means of arguing with an ECJ judgment. That was the law. Others thought that these weaknesses indicated a message from the ECJ perilously close to the political – the ECJ would not restrain the Commission if it was quoting in justification *any* risk to health, irrespective of other opinions.

As an instructive postscript to this unfortunate incident we move to the Decision of 1998 that beef exports were to be resumed by 1st August, 1999. This had been obtained by Britain only after arduous and tortuous negotiations, and in the face of seriously obstructive tactics. The reaction of the French was unequivocal. They refused to lift the ban. The Commission took them before the ECJ and in December 2001 France was held to be "in breach of its obligations." France ignored the judgement. A further case was brought before the Court and in October a fine was imposed against France amounting to 156,000 euros per day. France then refused to pay but also opened discussion with the Commission. Eventually the French ban was lifted, and the Commission announced that

France would now comply with the judgement. Under the circumstances, they added, there was clearly no purpose which could be served by actually imposing any fine.

Foot and Mouth Disease

It was a tragedy to British agriculture that so soon afterwards, in February 2001, an outbreak of Foot and Mouth disease was announced. This time the British government had learned its lesson, and the Ministry of Agriculture and Fisheries, soon to be absorbed into DEFRA (Department for the Environment, Food and Rural Affairs), now understood that the Commission was in control of British agriculture, and took charge of the entire fight against the disease. At the height of the crisis the Commission was addressing instructions to Britain in the form of legally binding Decisions every single week.

Unless you were a farmer whose herds were being slaughtered it was difficult not to feel some sympathy for Nick Brown, the Minister of Agriculture. The situation was not as it seemed to the country. Here was the Minister responsible, touring the country to face angry and abusive rural communities and reporting to a critical House of Commons. But, throughout this period Mr. Brown was never doing anything more than his simple duty – to obey the instructions of the European Commission. Strangely, this is the only point about the crisis that he never mentioned. Hopefully he was able to console himself that he was also able to send the bill for compensation to Brussels. Preliminary estimates in August 2001, approved in Brussels amounted to 355 Million euros, with the final sum still to be determined.

Chapter 22: Labour Revival

Realignment – Kinnock & Smith

During the 1980's the Labour Party had kept the anti-European attitude that had reached its earlier climax during the Wilson era. Several conferences had moved so far as to demand actual withdrawal, supporting the sovereignty of Westminster without regard to the referendum result. Anti-European sentiment, as well as a continuing shift towards the left in other policies caused the separation of a new party, the Social Democratic Party, led by Roy Jenkins, and with Shirley Williams, David Owen and William Rogers. The SDP, attracting the most important of the moderate voices, freed the Labour Party of some of its internal constraint or balance. The anti-European attitude reached its heights in the 1983 General Election when the party was led by the well regarded left wing but eccentric figure of Michael Foot. The Labour manifesto, described by dissenters as "the longest suicide note in history" called for withdrawal from the EEC, as well as widespread re-nationalisation of industry and unilateral nuclear disarmament, a lifelong dream of Foot as an old activist in CND, the Campaign for Nuclear Disarmament It is difficult to find in British political history a party more out of step with the public mood on all its major planks of policy. On Europe, for example, opinion polls showed a 23% lead of the Conservatives over Labour. Only the scale of the defeat giving Labour 188 fewer seats than the Conservatives under Mrs. Thatcher, was a surprise. An urgent review was clearly required to save the Labour Party from its idealism.

The elected saviour was Neil Kinnock, a Welshman, eloquent almost to the point of poetic, providing a comfortable reminder of mining villages and the Welsh valleys. The necessity of abandoning the policies of nuclear disarmament and of supporting the sale of council houses caused a serious personal struggle with his conscience. A similar struggle involved his eventually successful attempt to sideline the more extreme elements inside the party, requiring for example a scathing attack on the group "Militant" at the 1985 Party conference. This was followed by new party imagery, with a red rose replacing the traditional red flag, masterminded by a new Campaigns and Communications Directorate, headed by Peter Mandelson. Reversal of the party's European policy did not produce the same difficulty but Kinnock approached it with considerable caution. "We could only realistically accept enduring membership if, at the very least, we suffer no significant material loss or disadvantage."

Despite the obvious minimalism of Kinnock's opening European statement as leader this did hold a real significance. It indicated a significant move from Labour's adamant rejection of anything European. It brought Labour back into the mainstream of British politicians in two respects. Firstly it implied that Europe was to be judged solely in terms of economic advantage – an approach favoured since the days of Harold Wilson. Secondly it indicated that judgement should be made from a national viewpoint, ignoring the question of whether pooling of sovereignty was desirable or otherwise as a matter of principle. In this final respect Kinnock was now following every political leader except Edward Heath.

The party had opposed the Single European Act, and later almost succeeded in destroying the Treaty of Maastricht but the reasoning was always pragmatic rather than principled, helped by the luxury of opposition. For most Labour MP's the principle was to put party interest above any particular issue, in a perpetual attempt simply to defeat the Conservative government. Thus statements from any Labour MP or aspiring MP from the period around the mid 1980's must be interpreted with this in mind. There is simply no comparison to be made with the principled statements which can be quoted from their Conservative opponents. Until Maastricht, Europe, having been consistently downplayed by Wilson and then Callaghan, was regarded as administrative extension of government. Public interest was negligible and a young politician, for example Tony Blair, would find no opportunity to make an impact and would simply demonstrate loyalty and follow the party line.

As leader Kinnock had begun a new engagement with Europe, forming friendships with many socialist politicians across the continent. Their success had demonstrated that alternatives to Thatcherism could be successful, and gave Labour a renewed hope of power, with a new enthusiasm and optimism. Thatcher had painted Europe as a repository of socialism, but this same resource provided the Labour party with a new sense of direction. A new mood within the party, and a new acceptance within the country had been skilfully created. Unfortunately for them their confidence proved illusory. To the surprise of much of the country, and the dismay of the Labour Party Neil Kinnock lost the 1987 General Election, attributed by many to a premature and almost presumptive celebration, following the style of an extroverted, American party convention, the night before the election. The resurrection of Labour was postponed.

A bitterly disappointed Neil Kinnock immediately resigned the leadership and was replaced duly replaced by John Smith, a highly personable Scottish lawyer who was committed to continuing Labour reform. He tackled union block votes by introducing "One Member, One Vote" in the face of determined opposition. Conducting an effective opposition in Parliament he appeared to be on the well on the way to the success which had eluded Labour for so long. Then, in May 1994, he suffered a sudden and massive heart attack which tragically terminated his brightening political career after only two years as leader.

New Labour

In the leadership contest which followed Europe was not an issue. The party was determined to regain power and continuing the process of reform appeared the best way of its achievement. The Party elected Tony Blair, as its youngest leader in history. He was a known reformer and modernizer, and true to form he immediately entered a battle to change the party's constitution by removing some of the old outdated baggage, such as related to wholesale nationalisation. For the third time a new leader's first priority had been the reform of his party. At the same time, there was a definite evolution in the party's European policy.

As a Labour candidate in the 1980's Blair had advocated withdrawal from the EEC, in obedience to party policy of the time. However, the Kinnock and Smith legacy had been to construct a comfortable acquiescence with Europe, believing in its engine for advancing social democracy, and crafting a unity which the Conservatives could only regard with envy. The Labour leadership by the mid 90's was divided only by degrees of zealousness in their pro-European beliefs. It is true that this gradual conversion had been a matter of expediency rather than conviction; but this was because there was nevertheless a basic accord with many of the policies being introduced by Europe. Questions regarding sovereignty and the constitution were academic, and subservient to the introduction of appropriate policies. As an example, this included a proposal to extend the dreaded QMV to Council decisions in the fields of social, environmental, industrial and regional policy. Conservative Ministers were naturally horrified, but Blair was succeeding in promoting Labour as the party which could do business constructively with Europe, in contrast to the Conservative impotence and indecision.

Preparations for government were completed by production of the manifesto "New Labour, A New Life for Britain", emphasising the widespread realisation that things in general had to change. After a successful build-up in image, the 1997 election campaign proceeded with Labour's tactics noted for stage-managed media presentations, tight co-ordination of everyone's activities, close management of their public exposure, and their use of "focus groups" to ensure the most advantageous selection of issues to be presented on a daily basis. This systematic and sophisticated approach, new to Britain, contrasted with the impressions conveyed by the Conservatives. Increasingly they displayed a combination of division and indecision against a background of sleaze and rising taxation which produced for Labour the most spectacular election win in modern times. John Major had been widely regarded as a "decent chap", but appearing out of his depth and in a policy vacuum he presided over the virtual annihilation of his party in many parts of the country. A Labour victory had been widely predicted but its scale, achieving an overall majority of 179, was simply stunning.

The new government represented a new generation of politicians supported by a new generation of MP's willing to follow gratefully the party leadership. Having removed outdated "baggage" from his party Blair was now ready to do the same for the country, and in particular to Britain's European policy. He had already made several defining statements regarding his new European policy. "The drift towards isolation in Europe must stop and be replaced by a policy of constructive engagement". However this was no slavish adherence to European dogma but solely because of the national interest. To hesitate before our European destiny was "To deny our historical role in the world." Britain's role as a major global player would be forfeit unless "we accepted Europe as our base." His conclusion was that Britain should be "at the centre of Europe" and "should set about building the alliances within Europe that enable our influence to grow".

At the time the similarity between this final statement and the position of John Major in his first, pro-European phase, was not noticed, except by cynics. Certainly the public had forgotten about the earlier John Major. In any case the striking contrast in tone obscured any such comparison. The same could also be said about the great European project of EMU. In his days of opposition Blair showed no objection to British participation in principle, but considerable practical anxiety as to whether it could be made to work, bearing in mind the existing regional disparities. He never seemed convinced that the well debated convergence criteria could really ensure permanent long term stability in such a short time. His resulting policy seemed rather similar to the "Wait and see" it replaced. Labour policy however was not to be confused with Michael Heseltine's summary of the government's new "Prepare and Decide" policy, which he derided as meaning, prepare for a currency that others had invented and then decide to reject it. No. Labour policy was to engage constructively and then "protect and advance", meaning that while protecting the issue by the promise of a referendum, they would advance the case for participation. On the European issues therefore Blair had been able to enter the election campaign showing moderate and cautious euro-enthusiasm; watchful EMU preparedness, and a practical absence of dogmatic principles, all in the national interest.

With his massive victory Toby Blair sat in a position of unique and unrivalled authority, surveying ahead the prospect of many years of government power. He felt armed with a decisive mandate for change and "modernisation" across the whole of British politics.

Chapter 23: New Government

A New Bank for England

With the election emphatically won, people were ready to see decisive change. Action was not long in appearing with Chancellor Gordon Brown first off the mark with a measure with no apparent European dimension. On 6th May he dramatically announced that the Bank of England was to be granted independence from the Treasury. Monetary policy, and specifically the setting of interest rates would become the responsibility of the Bank overseen by a new Monetary Policy Committee. This would be subject to the government's setting of a target rate and range for inflation, but in future Chancellors would indeed appear at the despatch box with no responsibility for setting interest rates. The Bank's supervisory role in the banking and financial services sector generally would be removed. Although this converted the Bank of England to the European model of a Central Bank any such intention was denied. As Brown stated, "The specific reforms I am proposing are British solutions, designed to meet British domestic needs for long term stability. Our monetary reforms provide the platform for stability and are the building block for a new economic policy that will equip us for the challenges of the future."

Some people may have remembered that central bank independence from national government was a pre-requisite of progression to EMU Stage III, noticing that Article 108 of the Treaty Establishing the European Community had required, "Neither the ECB nor a national central bank shall seek or take instructions from Community institutions or bodies, from any government of a Member State or from any other body. Governments of Member States undertake to respect this principle and not seek to influence the members of the decision making bodies." In Europe, Brown's move would be seen as a significant step, keeping the EMU option open, but in Britain the public were told to believe that this was a mere coincidence.

A New Social Chapter

The Foreign Secretary, Robin Cook was also wasting no time. Just four days after victory he announced an impressive signal of Britain's new European co-operation. Britain would sign up for the "Social Chapter" of the Maastricht Treaty. This was a procedure designed to facilitate measures relating to the improvement of the working environment, working conditions, the information and consultation of workers, sexual equality etc. Facilitation was to be by widening of qualified majority voting and thus removing any nation's right of veto over the proposals. The Conservatives had been fiercely opposed to many of the individual proposals because of the increased regulation and cost to be imposed on industry, but also in principle to the harmonisation of labour regulation. As John Major had put it in 1994, "The 'Social Chapter' would create jobs, but in Japan, not here. A maximum working week would create jobs, but in the Pacific basin, not here. A minimum wage would create jobs, but in the United States, not here". This stance had also created friction with European partners. For example in 1993 the American company Hoover, moved production from France to Scotland because of lower wage levels. The British government was promptly accused of attracting investment from other EC countries by maintaining low pay and conditions, described by many as 'social dumping'. John Major, however, was unrepentant but also provocative stating, "They can have the 'Social Chapter'. We'll have the jobs." Finally in 1996 Major submitted the British response to IGC proposals under the Social Chapter. "The need to create more jobs is one of the highest priorities in Europe. No-one should pretend that jobs can be wished into being simply by legislating for them in the Treaty. The key to creating new employment in Europe is to improve competitiveness and productivity. It is no secret that other Member States wish to see the UK's Social Chapter "opt-out" removed at the IGC. The UK will not give up its opt-out and cannot be forced to do so." It was this submission that persuaded the Irish presidency that IGC decisions on social legislation should be delayed - awaiting the outcome of the UK election.

The Labour party had traditionally been more amenable to social legislation and the simple view of the new government was that it was unacceptable for workers in the UK to enjoy fewer rights and privileges than their European counterparts. The decision did prove to be a little more complicated than expected because of the need to catch up on previously passed measures. It was of course possible for Britain to pass domestic legislation to accord with the directives in question, but this would have been inadequate because mere domestic legislation would not be subject to the same discipline and binding force as a Community instrument. A mini-directive was therefore passed and addressed to the UK for this purpose. This had the legal effect that future proposals could again be approved on the basis of the Maastricht Treaty itself instead of the Agreement of Social Policy which was only binding on fourteen Member States. A second effect was that Britain would be no longer excluded from the Social Affairs Committee, a matter which had threatened a novel political embarrassment. Britain was shortly to hold the presidency, and would have chaired all committee meetings except this one from which she was excluded. Now, the British government had committed itself to support and implement European social policy irrespective of its views on any particular aspect, so the political will necessary to resolve such technical issues appeared in the Council.

One other early casualty in establishing a new mood of co-operation was the removal at the September ECOFIN meeting of the earlier British veto on measures to curb "unfair tax competition" which had become important to Germany, desperate to maintain high taxation to pay for unification difficulties. Britain quickly restricted this to business taxation but had nevertheless given away an important precedent which it soon had to fight hard to retrieve.

Meeting Minds at Amsterdam

The New Prime Minister first formally met his colleagues in Council in Noordwijk and received the warm welcome of a celebrity. He was determined to establish a new British tone in Europe and spoke of collaboration rather than confrontation and of emphasising positive results rather than negative triumphs. There had indeed been an instant change of atmosphere from the first meeting held by the Minister for Europe, Douglas Henderson, who was surprised to find that in IGC meetings Britain was not the only obstacle to progress in integration. Small countries were fiercely resisting Council and other reforms being pressed by France and Spain; Denmark and France were resisting proposals to move the pillar of justice and home affairs back into the main stream Community structure, and proposals to allow flexible use of institutions in policy areas restricted to Members opting-in were being hotly disputed. There were indeed many controversial issues to be settled for the next step. At the Noorwijk meeting the new constructive attitude enabled Blair to establish even a negative position on some issues without appearing more obstructive than anyone else. Moreover the new absence of controversy and its imminent replacement by a quiet, routine diplomacy with incremental and unspectacular progress removed much of the interest of the press and with the spotlight elsewhere, European business could proceed quietly and undisturbed.

The actual summit amicably agreed the Amsterdam Treaty three weeks later, but the price for this agreement was that its integrationist scope had been severely curtailed. The relentless forces of integration were contained by leaders who had become wary of moving faster than their own public opinion, and of provoking domestic opposition. Members were not ready to surrender sovereignty on foreign policy so proposals to introduce QMV to the Common Foreign Policy and Security pillar were diluted to closer co-operation. In the third Maastricht Pillar, of Justice and Home Affairs, border controls were to be abolished under the Schengen agreement from which Britain insisted on an opt-out, but the Community was to be given a role in the other areas. Thus measures relating to visas, asylum and immigration were transferred to the First Pillar as relating to free movement of persons, and the remaining Pillar was re-titled Police and Judicial Co-operation in Criminal Matters. Again Member States were not willing to transfer their sovereignty but they were willing to accept the discipline of formal co-operation and common action in areas relating to immigration and international fraud, judicial and police co-operation especially concerning terrorism and drugs. The Commission would be involved in these areas, the European Parliament would have a right of consultation and QMV would apply to implementation decisions. Progress on institutional reform had been regarded as an important prerequisite in the preparations for the major enlargement contemplated, but the logical conclusion that this would reduce the voting rights of the smaller nations had been resisted, so agreement on changes to voting rights and the appointment of Commissioners was postponed.

One other extension to Treaty of Rome was sparsely reported at the time, but could have been foreseen as becoming very significant. The EC had always outlawed discrimination of nationals from other Member States and prohibited sex discrimination in employment. The ECJ had regarded the relevant Articles as providing fundamental rights to citizens of the union and by interpreting the definitions so broadly as to surprise all governments and national courts it had developed a remarkably powerful and pervasive body of law. (The example of Ms. Webb was described in Chapter F). The Treaty of Amsterdam was to extend the principle of prohibited discrimination, and provide a new legal basis for measures countering discrimination on grounds not only of sex, but of racial or ethnic origin; religion or belief; disability; age or sexual orientation.

One other important advance concerned the legal position fundamental human rights. Since the 1970's the ECJ had recognised that "respect for fundamental rights forms an integral part of the general principles of law protected by the Court of Justice." However this was determined by the constitutional traditions common to the legal systems of the Member States. This principle had been endorsed by the Parliament, the Council and the Commission in a joint declaration of 1977, but the actual treaty all Members had signed, the European Convention on Human Rights, was not mentioned in EU treaties until Maastricht and was not then recognised as legally binding. The Treaty of Amsterdam extended the jurisdiction of the ECJ to apply the provisions of ECHR directly to EU institutions. Another highly significant aspect of this decision was that Member States' permanent observance of ECHR was to become more than just a matter for their own domestic law. It was to become a condition for continued participation as a member. Any Member State held to be in breach could be subject to sanctions from the EU, including suspension of their voting rights.

These legal development did not command much attention from Britain's new Prime Minister, with a greater interest in practical issues relating to economic development. He was hoping to harness the potential power of joint European action to counter what he saw as the most serious social threat, continuing and rising unemployment.

So, within a month of his victory Blair was touring Europe improving his personal contacts but also promoting his view on liberalising the economy, and the benefits of flexible labour markets. Other than as a prior and overriding act of faith in Europe itself, it was not easy to see how this was consistent with removing Britain's opt out from the Social Chapter and the transfer of competence for such issues to the European Union. Few though, were in any mood to remember John Major's negative comments on the Social Chapter. However, under the new method of thinking Blair was happy to transfer responsibility to Europe knowing it might well introduce some policies with which his government disagreed as part of the purchase price for increased influence. He didn't worry that the problem with such a contract is that the concession is permanent, while the purchased commodity is temporary.

In many ways Blair's tour was comparable to the disastrous European preaching undertaken by Major's last Foreign Secretary, Malcolm Rifkind not very many months earlier. Both were attempting to convince Europeans of the error of their ways, but Blair's apparent starting point made the exercise much more palatable. He was making good use of his temporary superstar status in the European press, which had made him the man to meet all across Europe. Only in France, where Prime Minister Lionel Jospin could be justifiably be regarded as "Old Labour" were his views unwelcome, dampening the enthusiasm which reverberated from his address to the National Assembly in French. It remained a sign that Blair was trying to develop an influence across Europe as well as within the institutions of Europe, but also showed that behind the cordiality a wide philosophical gap remained across the Channel.

In fact British politicians for many years had been forced to deal with the reality of Europe, simply as a fact of everyday government. Now Britain's "New Labour" government exhibited a positive attitude towards Europe from top to bottom, with none of the background fear characterising previous generations of politicians. The reception of a new delegation in Brussels was regarded as a breath of fresh air. Gone was the hostility, the pessimism and the obstructive agenda of the British. Gone also was the impotence of a government incapable of guaranteeing the implementation by cabinet and parliament of measures actually agreed during a summit. How refreshing it was to all concerned to be dealing with a government that was constructive and supportive.

But, No Further on EMU

Unfortunately it was not quite so easy to be really European. Although the traditional fear of loss of sovereignty appeared to be part of the jettisoned baggage, there were limits to Blair's Europeanism. While certainly in favour of Europe in general, Blair's Britain still hesitated to follow completely the European agenda and this was no more apparent than in the project closest to European hearts, EMU. Blair had never been confident that EMU could be made to work, and was reluctant to support abolition of the pound. So, just as Britain originally decided to wait and see if the Common Market would be successful before wanting to join, Blair decided not to join the monetary union scheduled to start in 1999. He was in favour of joining the euro, but not yet. Chancellor, Gordon Brown announced that Britain and Europe were at different stages in the economic cycle and that more time was required for convergence. Of course he meant economic convergence but it seems clear that the lack of convergence of public opinion also served as an important factor in the decision. Even with his large majority and the absence of an effective opposition there were still powerful voices in the media virulently opposed to the single currency, and no obvious benefit in rocking a boat of unprecedented stability.

Opposition was unashamedly political in nature. The pound was a proud symbol of national independence, not to be given up for any convenience, and possibly not even for a marginal economic benefit. In Europe there was no doubt that EMU was primarily a political objective, and the single currency just a final step in the process already agreed. In any case the necessary co-ordination of economic policy between member states had already become binding. Other than in Denmark, the political aspect was too obviously beneficial to merit public debate, so attention focussed on the convergence criteria determining whether the Euro could be safely introduced in each state without risk to that economy or the new currency itself. Euro supporters in Britain also avoided the description of a currency as an essential attribute of an independent nation which would henceforth be European. Although no British voices were raised in support of this as a worthy objective, there was a prominent idea that a single currency is of little significance; simply a logical completion of a single market which itself is unquestioningly accepted as beneficial. Gordon Brown and his supporters similarly argue that economics should be the determining factor and that purely dogmatic factors were irrelevant. Ministers would also argue that the old concept of sovereignty was outdated in a world where governments were routinely committed to accepting intrusion of supranational bodies as well as subject to international forces and markets beyond their control. Domestic control is really determined by the effectiveness of reaching international agreement. There was also one other important school of thought arguing simply, but for many complex reasons, that the Euro would not work.

Facing all this Blair concluded that there was no real need for, nor a discernible benefit in provoking another fierce and divisive battle across the country. A referendum had been promised, and this would certainly provoke the extreme xenophobic hatred of Brussels applicable to a final last ditch battle to save Britain. The dictates of a probably honest scepticism in the traditional sense of the word, coincided with the path of least resistance and confrontation.

The consequences of Blair's decision not to follow European EMU became apparent during the British Presidency in the first half of 1998. The

Presidency saw competent but unspectacular progress across the whole range of European issues with Blair succeeding in incorporating a much greater emphasis on unemployment matters. Blair was indeed laying claim to his government's promise of leadership of Europe by pressing for deregulation and increased flexibility in labour markets. Indeed some of the statements from Europe were beginning to sound less interventionist under the Commission President Jacques Santer. For example, one of the current slogans was, "Legislate less to act better" which was interpreted by the Commission to mean concentrating on policy priorities, with strict application of the subsidiarity and proportionality principles ('legislate less'), and with improved consultation procedures and clearer, simpler and more accessible legislation ('act better'), with a view to enhancing Europe's image in the eyes of the public, improving the operation of the single market, strengthening the competitiveness of firms and managing the European Union on a sounder basis. Comments such as this enabled the Foreign Secretary, Robin Cook to explain that, "The high tide of integration has passed", although Brussels immediately dismissed the comment as "absurd, wishful thinking." However the most ironic event at the Cardiff Summit was when Tony Blair, although presiding over the meeting was relegated to the sidelines as an observer of the eleven members signing their final agreement for introducing the single currency.

It is interesting to note that even among the eleven members there remained some fear of the consequences of EMU. The Germans had been satisfied that the location of the European Central Bank in Frankfurt, would make the institution acceptable as well as maintain influence for the Bundesbank with its impressive record managing the Deutschmark to become the envy certainly of Europe. However there was a serious battle with the French who were demanding, in their unique version of European co-operation that the President be a Frenchman. Other members favoured Wim Duisenburg, a man of impeccable credentials having been a successful governor of the Dutch Central Bank for fifteen years. The resulting compromise, crafted by President Blair as official arbitrator, that Duisenburg would voluntarily resign after four years, half the period specified by the Maastricht Treaty was received with unrestrained derision by the media. Duisenberg, robust looking and at 62, ten years younger than his famous counterpart across the Atlantic announced that his health made him too frail to last the eight year course. Despite having vowed that he would not accept the job for a shorter period he asked his audience to believe that he had reached this decision, "Entirely of my own free will and not under pressure from anyone." The independence of the ECB had been enshrined in the Treaties, but this was clearly not a convincing way to demonstrate its power to resist political interference.

Although Harold Wilson was famous for his comment that a week is along time in politics, a six month Presidency is a negligible period in the continuing history of the European Union. The system nevertheless functions as an important engine for integration. Each approaching Presidency is accompanied by a set of objectives and each terminating Presidency publishes a report on its performance and in praise of its extensive achievements. Such reports are invariably long and vague rather than substantive, but they do reflect the continuing pressure under which the European Council, and in particular its temporary President are forced to operate. Of course there are numerous official and informal meetings across the Union during the six months. But the Council itself, during its minimum of two annual sessions, usually lasting just two days, has to pass numerous legislative measures implementing its earlier decisions, has to steer the all current proposals in the direction to be negotiated, and has to maintain a consensus regarding the strategic direction of the Union, all considering the "guidance" of the Commission, the opinion of the European Parliament, and also with an electoral eye on the domestic situation. Opportunities for changing the direction of the European steam-roller are minimal. It is therefore hardly surprising that the ambitions of each Presidency rarely bear much relation to its conclusions and certainly judicious selection of initial objectives, giving priority to those coinciding with the general European flow has become very important in maximising the opportunity for obtaining European approbation, domestic kudos and personal standing.

Tony Blair was certainly not the first to encounter this reality, but with British battles still fresh in the public mind he had particular reason for demonstrating how Europe was moving in the correct direction. Even so, issues proudly trumpeted initially, such as reforms of agricultural policy, progress regarding expansion, common environmental action following the Kyoto agreements on global warming, all made at best modest progress. Blair's aims of de-regulation and flexible labour markets had failed to percolate through the institutions and co-operation on international issues foundered for example on a showdown with Saddam Hussein when the French accused Blair of being President Clinton's poodle. Even so, intangible factors such as the overall sense of constructive co-operation and lack of heated controversy were reducing public dissatisfaction and dampening the still prevalent hostility.

Regarding the Euro Blair continued to make positive sounding statements, frequently suggesting that Britain wanted to join, although always hedged by the proviso of Gordon Brown's five economic tests and the promised referendum. Options were comfortably being kept open, although frequently to the discomfort of the opposition. The Conservatives under William Hague remained divided over Europe. A ballot of the party had overwhelmingly rejected entering the Euro but this did not stop Kenneth Clarke, and Michael Heseltine congratulating the Prime Minister when he introduced his "Changeover plan" designed to prepare Britain for the Euro, in or out. Even so Hague would go no further than rejecting the Euro for the next two Parliaments, at least, arguing that future flexibility might be required, while at the same time accusing Blair of betraying 1,000 years of British history and self determination.

No Further on Tax

An additional issue demonstrated another limitation of any such betrayal. Having mentally completed arrangements for the single currency, integrationists were already making their next move. Crucial to this development was the German finance minister, the colourful, (usually red) Oskar Lafontaine who was promoting tax harmonisation. Of course central taxation would appear as simply another logical step in creating the complete single market. Thus considerable discussion involved the elimination of "harmful tax competition", caused for example by variable rates of corporation tax.

With the support of the Commission and of Dominique Strauss-Kahn, the French finance minister, proposals for the first step were produced for a minimum "Withholding tax" on savings held by individuals in other EU countries. This led to an immediate and surprisingly vehement rejection from Gordon Brown. Fearful of the effects of such a tax on the London bond markets, and aware that these could be easily be relocated to third countries at the speed of electronic transfers, Brown did not hesitate to talk of a British veto on any taxation proposal. He also reacted negatively to Commission proposals to tie in British acceptance of this tax with the financial services reforms for which Britain had pressed for many years. He affirmed, "Tax policy would continue to be made in Britain, not Europe."

The Government was naturally fearful that accepting any taxation proposal would be only the first step towards a European income tax, and that public opposition to that prospect would dwarf any previous European row. The prospects for introducing a Euro which included European taxation would be remote. It was also a threat to the policy during the Government's first term of cutting rather than raising direct taxation, as a means of encouraging employment. On the other hand a veto would severely damage Blair's claim to be at the centre of Europe, and could risk putting him on a parallel path to John Major, as the Euro-11 proceeded with closer integration without Britain at all.

Opposition to tax harmonisation therefore needed to be conducted more subtly, and Blair hoped to obtain support from Chancellor Gerhard Schröder, who was not known for his personal liking of Lafontaine. Blair appeared to make some headway with his more liberal economic thinking and "third way" initiatives, although this was to cause Schroder some political damage in the European elections.

Even so during 1999, although Lafontaine resigned, the threat of centralised taxation did not recede within the larger questions of reform which were appearing on the agenda. By the end of the year Tony Blair experienced a cold reality at the summit in Helsinki, when he was effectively isolated on the withholding tax issue. Both France and Italy had joined in support of the scheme but Britain was stubbornly opposed. The logical argument that the tax would damage London and produce only a low yield cut no ice. It appeared that protection of City of London markets was not a factor for Europeans to consider. The opposing view was more fundamental, and likely to become of greater significance. It was simply that it would be impossible to have a single market with complete mobility of capital, while allowing some members to act as "tax havens".

With the coming of the single currency it was clear that particular policies would be required, and so the question of the relationship between those members of the Union within the Euro zone, and those outside was destined to grow. In this case, since taxes could not be introduced without unanimous consent, Britain was effectively preventing the euro-11 even starting with a common fiscal policy. Of course, history also shows that such integrationist measures are never defeated, but merely postponed, put back on the agenda for the next meeting, and in this case they were duly referred to another Working Group. The Commission itself remarked that since direct taxation appeared blocked, alternative administrative means would have to be explored. Ultimately, obstruction from a euro outsider was unlikely to be tolerated. As the President's Report of the Helsinki summit stated, "While ensuring coherence between the different formations of the Council, the role of the ECOFIN Council in economic policy coordination should be enhanced. Cooperation related to the shared responsibilities for the single currency should be further developed within Euro 11."

The issue also illustrates another fundamental divergence of opinion on the necessity of harmonisation where Britain had previously been dragged along, originally with the acquis communitaire. National standards and regulations were banned as obstructions to the free movement of goods, and thus an unacceptable obstacle to completion of the single market. This prevented governments from introducing regulations which effectively or conceivably discriminated against imports from other Member States. Since standards of some kind were necessary to protect consumers the choice was made to harmonise them all. The extent of this harmonisation dismayed the likes of Margaret Thatcher who would have preferred a minimalist, free market approach which would maximise the benefits consumers could gain from competition. Thus, in principle the choice had been to increase interventionist state power over the market, rather than allow competitive forces between governments to enhance freedom and choice. To many European politicians harmonisation was an end in itself, to be extended wherever possible. To others it was an acceptable price to pay for separate effective action to reduce unemployment or promote competitiveness. The issue of a withholding tax was merely the first extension of the entire harmonisation principle to a new wider area of taxation in general. Effectively Britain was now advocating that the Community adopt the opposite answer to the question for real practical and pragmatic reasons, but disregarding the established Community principles.

A year later the issue was still alive, and some support for a direct and definite EU tax had appeared from the Commission, but also being considered carefully by Finance Ministers of France and Germany, and Prime Ministers of Belgium and France. Parliament was also keen on the ideas, providing they set the rate. It was argued that with 14% of the €93bn budget obtained from a VAT levy, and the rest from a national contributions according to an intractable formula, a tax on citizens would be transparent. Finance ministers however, meeting at the ECOFIN finance and economic committee did not believe the public was ready for such a step. The Dutch finance minister said that the last foreigner to impose a tax on the Netherlands was a Spanish governor general who started an 80 year war. Gordon Brown, recalled the tax on tea imposed on American colonies with a similar result. The Chairman, the Belgian finance minister said that he would continue with the idea while trying to avoid war in the Netherlands and revolution in the United Kingdom. So, the idea was postponed. Soon though, taxation appeared once again on the European agenda as the Commission investigated tax preference schemes which might be incompatible with the single market, or contrary to rules of free competition. Withholding tax again emerged but this time as a complaint that the existing system allowed for tax evasion, something clearly abhorrent to all finance ministers.

Eventually Gordon Brown was able to hold off this increasing pressure for harmonisation by suggesting as an alternative that national authorities could exchange information regarding nationals of other members. Austria, Belgium and Luxembourg were firmly opposed, fearing transfer of accounts to Switzerland. Therefore Brown, with the assistance of the Commission, had to spent considerable effort pressurising the Swiss to join in the information exchanges. Of course banking secrecy had been a highly sensitive issue for the Swiss, where the distinction between tax fraud and tax evasion is much clearer than it was to EU finance ministers, and only limited exchanges on request were agreed. However this was sufficient for Member States to agree that Members could impose an EU withholding tax, or opt to join an information exchange arrangement. A victory for all sides, according to Mr. Brown, but perhaps not so praiseworthy seen from the side of a taxpayer. Britain has, temporarily at least, held its line in the sand against EU taxation. But individual investors, although admittedly often seeking to evade domestic taxes will be scrutinised by intergovernmental machinery, similar to that designed for counter-terrorism and money laundering, and not even restricted to EU countries. It is possible to sympathise with the Treasury view that evasion is simply dishonest and must be countered, but difficult to reconcile this requirement for honesty with the Chancellor's reputation for "stealth" taxes.

In any event it was early 2003 before Brown succeeded in resolving the issue, but until then it had been a very significant political factor, interpreted as a matter of Anglo-Saxon rejection of harmonisation, which itself was interpreted as Europeanism. It had led to disappointing isolation for Tony's Blair at the Helsinki summit and following the EU tradition of horse trading, Britain now had to pay a price for its obstruction. Progress in any of the directions promoted by Blair was halted, immediately demolishing any of his optimistic suggestions that Europe was moving the British way, and his reassurances that fears of further interventionist economic policies were unwarranted. He had made important concessions to Europe; he had invested time and energy developing his influence; he had spoke loyally and consistently in support of Europe. But for Europe this was not enough as relentless European pressure was again pushing a British leader further than he could go. So, failure to surrender to the latest steps forward led to immediate isolation, and a rejection of any positive suggestions. He was going to be ignored.

Euro Elections

Meanwhile in June 1999 politicians throughout Europe had been involved in the election of the European Parliament about which voters generally knew very little. Britain would be selecting 87 out of the total of 626 MEP's, and for the first time this was to governed by a complex system of proportional representation and regional lists which few members of the public could understand. The Labour Party was anticipating a serious loss of seats since in previous first-past-the-post system when it had secured 75% of the seats with only 45% of the popular vote. The real concern though was the expected low turnout. After all it was difficult to convince voters that real power was at stake.

The public was less than inspired by the prospect of voting, and not only in Britain. Throughout Europe elections were of candidates affiliated to the national political parties, and references to European policies in their manifestos were purely symbolic. In the previous election of 1994 most voters had simply taken the opportunity to issue a mild protest at the incumbent national government. There was no doubt that European voters view their politics in purely national terms, blissfully unaware of the effect that decisions taken in Europe have on their lives. Only when their domestic institutions are overridden do they tend to take notice, and this lack of a European identity devalues in a circular fashion the argument that elections provide a democratic legitimacy or accountability to the Parliament. The campaign in Britain was no different with both the Conservatives and the Liberals explaining their views on European issues rather than on what their MEP's might deliver and both calling for reform and decentralisation. The Labour election leaflets stressed Blair's domestic agenda as much as his European objectives.

Across Europe the average turnout was the lowest ever at 49%, including those countries where voting is compulsory. In Britain the turnout was a mere 24%. And in France perhaps the harshest sign of disaffection was illustrated by the statistic that 6%, or almost one million voters turned out to deliberately leave their ballot papers blank. Voters had clearly not been inspired by the campaigns, nor had they been grateful to the European Parliament for its service in punishing corruption in the Commission. It seems more likely that having suffered exposure to numerous stories of a variety of misconduct in "Europe" voters were not prepared to differentiate between its different institutions.

Tony Blair showed a visible disappointment at the low British turnout but he also suffered the minor embarrassment of winning fewer seats than the Conservatives who had mounted an unashamedly populist "Save the Pound" campaign. So, if anybody was winning any argument it could only be the forces of euro-scepticism – a conclusion which was supported by the gaining of two seats by the UK Independence Party which advocated actual withdrawal. The British public was therefore less than convinced that Blair was making progress in steering Europe to his way of thinking, and certainly he must have been discouraged after the Helsinki summit. Nevertheless, in European tradition he persisted with his arguments for flexibility in labour markets etc., and again in European fashion many of his ideas were to reappear on the next agenda, in Lisbon where the Portuguese Presidency was in support, and anxious to progress in the same direction.

Re-Grouping at Lisbon

In his preparations for the next summit Blair had travelled to Ghent and spoken of Britain now being a good European, in contrast to the Thatcher years. Under his leadership, Mr Blair said, "Britain was no longer repeating its post-war pattern of hesitating on Europe." It had already put itself at the heart of Europe especially in the debate on defence and economic reform. Of course, this was excluding the policy of the new single currency which was at the heart of the Europeans' policy, but he continued to stress the opportunity to turn away form "heavy-handed intervention and regulation" which did not exactly seem remote from the philosophies of Margaret Thatcher. He was promoting a new agenda for "jobs, competitiveness, economic change and dynamism." And warning that attempts to hold back the forces of competition and dynamism and innovation are ultimately damaging.

By Lisbon he had added some specific measures for discussion. He wanted to remove barriers to electronic commerce, integrate capital markets, transplant his domestic initiatives for "life-long learning" into Europe, and "modernise", (a favourite word of the New Government), the European social protections systems to emphasise improving employability rather than preserving outdated jobs. He was telling Europe that it is not labour market regulation that will protect jobs. "What will protect jobs is skills and employability and knowledge." It is noteworthy that at home the British Chambers of Commerce were already complaining about £10billion of new labour regulation being introduced as minimum wage and working time directive, and other social chapter measures but of course the government had been obliged to introduce these measures irrespective of their merit. Blair could also not resist some exaggeration when he claimed in an *Economist* inteview that Britain's labour market was as flexible as in the US, despite studies from the European equivalent of the CBI (UNICE), estimating that Europe's worker protection laws were already 14 times more strict than America's. Nevertheless Blair successfully managed to enjoy a high profile summit at Lisbon with considerable publicity given to his views of a modernised Europe, and how Europe could harness and benefit from the dotcom boom. Moreover the level of his developing influence could reliably be measured by opposition from non-modernisers such as *Le Monde* which began to complain about a British strategy of using its appointees to the Commission to promote British government views. There was certainly a credible argument that thoughts in Europe were moving "our way".

The difficulty with this view was that proposals for concrete measures at Lisbon were carried forward, and the next Presidency was to be held by France. This was to climax with the conclusion of the IGC, concentrating on treaty changes implementing the reforms necessary for enlargement. Despite business view linking over-regulation in Europe with the superiority of US economic performance French politicians were advocating Europe's "social agenda", guaranteeing workers' rights and stressing a need to fight "social exclusion". To the argument that a strong economy produces an inclusive society the French labour minister replied that "economic growth and social cohesion are mutually reinforcing. When society is more inclusive, the economy performs better." Despite the UNICE's complaints that "Smaller companies don't have the bureaucracy to deal with the bureaucracy," the French were pushing for their next proposal regarding mandatory worker consultation. Despite his successes in "winning the argument" it was clear that the French Presidency was unlikely to progress to action on the reforms advocated by Blair.

In fact the liberalisation alliance of Blair and the Spanish Prime Minister Jose Maria Aznar was soon outflanked by the French chairmen with German support. "Liberalisation is not an end in itself, but a tool," commented the French Prime Minister Lionel Jospin a year later when he blocked proposals to liberalise gas and electricity markets. Perhaps he had noticed that similar liberalisation from state control in Britain had led to takeover by French companies of several British utility companies.

By this time though Tony Blair had a greater priority. He had successfully used his first term to reassure voters that there really was a New Labour. Trade unions could expect no special favours; There would be no old-style tax and spend or stop-go economic policies; business would be welcomed as a partner rather than an opponent. He had freed the Bank of England and rewrote much of the British constitution with devolution to Scotland and Wales. He had half-repaired relations with the European Union by signing the "social chapter" promoting a more independent European defence policy, although forging a close relationship with the USA.. He pushed Britain to the forefront of NATO's Kosovo war and negotiated a part-peace in Northern Ireland. He launched a "New Deal" for the young unemployed and imposed a minimum wage. Now he was putting his argument to the voters again, and he was to amply rewarded with another massive Parliamentary majority. No Labour leader had ever been given such an opportunity.

Chapter N: The Sky's the Limit

Ever Expanding Competence

It is interesting to observe how, at the time when Tony Blair was patiently but actively trying to turn by degrees many of the directions of the EU, the momentum from the decisions of earlier years was inexorably working its way through the legal systems of Europe. The institutions responsible for implementing and interpreting earlier decisions were involved in wars of their own, which in several areas had already lasted over many years. With rules of interpretation long established several of the disputes with Member States now concern the boundary between national and Community competence. Since its inception the Commission has acted to increase its authority step by step, ignoring the principles of subsidiarity in favour of centralisation under its own control.

One of many such areas which involved an interesting battle of principles, concerned the legal area of "Intellectual Property." National lawyers had always been sensitive to their own concepts of property law in general. Thus, Article 295 states that "This Treaty shall in no way prejudice the rules in Member States governing the system of property ownership." Clearly this should extend to intangible, (or intellectual) property such as patents, trademarks and copyright but this frequently became contentious because of such property's intimate connection with physical goods.

From the point of view of the EC Treaty the relevant overriding principle is that of the free movement of goods enshrined in Articles 28 and 29. However in Article 30 exceptions to this principle were defined, including the "protection of industrial and commercial property," providing they did not constitute a "disguised restriction on trade." Therefore matters of trademark law, for example were of national concern only, and for many years the combination of these two Articles was sufficient for Member States to resist any Commission incursion.

The ECJ's influence in intellectual property cases dates from the early 1970's when it was concerned to protect the single market. However its effect in the field was limited and even indecisive until the Commission persuaded Member States of the necessity for some limited harmonisation. However, in several judgements dating from 1975, the Court did employ some judicial innovation to remove the apparent restriction on Community competence. Even though it was years later that the precedent was used the Court did establish that,

> "Whilst the Treaty does not affect the existence of rights recognised by the legislation of a Member State in matters of industrial and commercial property, yet the exercise of those rights may nevertheless, depending on the circumstances, be restricted by prohibitions in the Treaty."

Thus a distinction was invented between the existence of a property right and its exercise. Its existence is protected under national law, but its exercise must remain subject to the principle of the free movement of goods, and of course it follows that questions relating to its exercise would be decided by the ECJ. This resulted in identification of further obstacles in the single market, which were in due course, addressed by the Commission.

One of the most interesting cases recently to reach the ECJ involved a recurring question of parallel imports. Jeans manufactured by Levi Strauss were available much more cheaply than in Britain and Tesco Stores purchased real Levi's from Mexico, at these lower prices. Consequently they were able to sell much more cheaply than were Levi's official outlets. Levi Strauss began an action alleging infringement of trademark rights which lasted several years. There were extensive legal arguments about the function of the Trade Mark itself in view of the traditional English opinion expressed in the High Court, that the purpose of such a mark was to identify the goods as originating from a particular manufacturer. Their view was therefore that having legally purchased genuine Levi products Tesco could not be infringing a trademark right. Besides, in the absence of dishonesty it would seem unfair to deny consumers the benefit of honest competition.

The matter was referred to the ECJ by Judge Laddie, who is one of Britain's most experienced judges in the field. Since there was a Community Directive, he was obliged to do so in such matters of interpretation, despite his strong contrary instincts. The Court referred to the Directive "approximating" the laws of trademarks in the Member States and decided that the trademark owner could not be regarded as having consented to the use of the trademark on those particular goods, in the Community. In interpreting the Directive it did not seem concerned about the balance between trademark owners and consumers. As suggested earlier the concept of balance cannot be incorporated into a purposive analysis. Instead it broadened the previously understood function of a trademark, by holding that activities outside the single market were irrelevant. It would however be different if the goods had been placed elsewhere on the (internal) market by the trademark owner. The English court, receiving this guidance regretted that a trademark owner should in effect, obtain a second bite of the trademark cherry but nevertheless was obliged to give effect to the ECJ judgement. Consumers would have to pay the price determined by Levi's.

A second example is, at the time of writing not quite resolved. This concerns Mr. Matthew Reed who for some thirty years has been selling souvenirs and memorabilia to fans of Arsenal Football Club. In recent years such merchandising has become an important source of income for football clubs and Arsenal decided to curtail sales of unofficial and unauthorised souvenirs. They noted that goods sold by Mr. Reed included copies of the club's registered trademark, and they sued him for infringement. Mr. Reed's defence was that he was using the sign as a "symbol" of the club. He actually displayed a sign which made it perfectly clear to his customers that he was not selling officially authorised merchandise. Therefore he was using the mark as a badge of club loyalty and not in "a trademark sense".

Mr. Justice Laddie reviewed the case law and decided again to refer the questions of law to this ECJ. It is interesting that in this case there was no Community or international element. Once it had been true that any dispute involving a company in Europe or cross border trade would automatically mean that Community law was applicable, while internal matters were unaffected. However, with increasing use of Directives to harmonise laws themselves this ceased to be a necessary condition. In the interest, usually of the single market, the law had to be equalised as a matter of principle, and not simply as it applied to inter Community trade. A trademark had become a European concept.

So despite years of British precedent which would have been quite clear, Laddie felt forced to ask whether, under the new regime, the use of a trademark merely as a badge of loyalty was sufficient to amount to infringement. The ECJ replied that "in the circumstances of the present case", use of the sign as a badge is immaterial. There was definitely an infringement of trademark rights. Most observers thought the case settled, and no doubt celebrations had begun at Highbury. However returning before Judge Laddie, Mr. Reed's QC found a novel objection. He quoted several ECJ precedents supporting the accepted understanding that the function of the ECJ was restricted to interpretations on points of EC law. In referring to "the circumstances of the case" the ECJ was making a finding as to the facts of the case and these were a matter for the national court. Therefore the ECJ had exceeded its jurisdiction and in such circumstances the High Court was not bound to follow its conclusion. This was a remarkable suggestion, especially since as the ultimate court there would appear to be little to prevent the ECJ from defining its own jurisdiction, as has been described earlier. This particular learned judge had never been afraid of arguing with the ECJ, but this suggestion moved somewhat further. He appeared to agree with this latest submission somewhat hesitantly, referring to his "invidious" position, and his reluctance to effectively reject an ECJ ruling. Nevertheless he studied the explanation of the law provided by the ECJ, including the purpose of and the actual rights to be protected by a trademark. He applied this reasoning to *his* finding of fact, ie. that Mr. Reed had not been using the symbols in "a trademark sense", and found in favour of Mr. Reed. An appeal seems likely.

Open Skies – for the Commission

As the war on intellectual property is nearing its completion this boundary of competence is likely to be crossed quietly. However, there is another area producing a more heated debate, which has yet to be resolved despite recent firm but also equivocal intervention from the ECJ. This dispute began in 1994 when the USA began to negotiate reciprocal landing rights for airlines with individual Member States. The Commission wrote to Member States warning them that bilateral agreements would have a negative effect on the EU, and consequently such negotiations could only be carried out at Community level. Britain, with the most important share of the transatlantic air travel market resented this interference and ignored the letter. The following year the Commission wrote specifically to the British government seeking an assurance that they would comply with their requirement. Britain signed an agreement with the USA. Eventually the Commission provided a "reasoned opinion" that in allocating landing rights on the basis of the nationality of carrier Britain was discriminating in breach of Article 43 on freedom of establishment. Again Britain refused to comply. Consequently the Commissioner responsible, Neil Kinnock, loyally upholding the principle of Commissioner independence, initiated proceedings against Britain before the ECJ.

First, Britain tried to argue that the agreement with the USA was merely the latest amendment of the 1947 Bermuda agreement, and therefore pre-dated British accession to the EC. This was immediately rejected. The agreement was new, and in any case after accession Britain was bound to reach any agreements in accordance with Community law. Next, Britain argued that an agreement between UK and the USA was not a matter of Community concern. Wrong again. As a basic provision of the EC Treaty, Article 43 concerning rights of establishment, applied to any measure within even national competence. The agreement with the USA was illegal.

What is truly remarkable is that in parallel with this case the Commission brought similar and separate proceedings against Denmark, Sweden, Finland, Belgium, Luxembourg, Austria and Germany, in each case the defendant being supported by the Netherlands. The Commission was therefore battling with no less than nine Member States over the right to reach air transport agreements with the United States. Each of these states clearly believed that they were entitled to do so, and were opposing the Commission's insistence that this should be a matter of Community competence. It should be remembered that the Commission had made several proposals to the Council for a mandate to negotiate rights with regard to airlines, as part of its aim of "liberalising" the industry albeit under Commission control. Several times these proposals were rejected, often because of the Member States, attachment to or their support of their national "flag-carrying" airlines. Nevertheless they had persuaded the Council to approve limited rights for Commission involvement in airline negotiations, for example relating to fares and competition. These cases were therefore an attempt to broaden the scope of Community competence beyond that expected, or probably intended, by the Member States now in the dock.

The principle issue therefore had powerful implications. It was to determine the circumstances under which the Community could acquire competence in a particular policy area, in the face of opposition by even a majority of Member States. Clearly this was possible in those areas explicitly delegated by the Treaty, and specifically "requested" by the Council. However, the Commission was seeking a much broader power. Firstly it caused lawyers to search out a forgotten 1976 case relating to navigation along the river Rhine. Although never previously noticed, this created a precedent which established that wherever EC law had created powers for an institution to attain a specific objective, the EC had authority to enter any <u>international</u> commitments necessary for its attainment, even in the absence of an express provision. Next, referring to the *ERTA* judgement described earlier, it contended that this implied power can result not only from Treaty provisions, but from "any measures adopted within the framework of these provision." The Court concluded that in general where such measures exist, any such measures,

> "Member States may not enter into international commitments outside the framework of the Community institutions, even if there is no contradiction between those commitments and the common rules."

In the present case there were clearly some regulations in force, and the Court identified those areas where an overlap between the negotiated agreements and the Community regulations had "indirectly but definitely" occurred. Using the above precedents the Court found the agreements illegal, commenting that

> "The failure of that Member State to fulfil its obligations lies in the fact that it was not authorised to enter into such a commitment on its own, even if the substance of that commitment does not conflict with Community law."

It is important to note that these judgements do not confirm exclusive competence of the Commission in all areas of air transport regulation as the Commission had hoped. However, they do effectively prevent individual Member States from making any agreements which may "affect" the limited areas of competence previously agreed. The Commission does not have exclusive competence, but Member States may not make separate agreements, which were in any event illegal on the same grounds of discrimination as in the British case. Now, faced with an impasse, the political leaders will be seeking a way forward. The path of least resistance would clearly be for the Council to provide the Commission with a mandate to negotiate a comprehensive air transport agreement with the USA, just as the Commission has been proposing for ten years. It remains to be seen whether the political leaders will be prepared to disregard the previous conduct of the Commission, submit to what could be described as blackmail, and concede control over their national airlines and airports. It also remains to be heard what an excellent forward-looking idea the Council will produce for liberalising and modernising air transport regulations.

The Single Street Market

The reach of European law not only extended to the skies, and to commercial relations on an international scale, but also down to the smallest transaction in the local market. An ordinary greengrocer in Sunderland illustrated the point powerfully. He was using a weighing machine calibrated in forbidden pounds and ounces, contrary to the instructions of his local inspector. Similarly the Trading Standards Office in Hackney purchased potatoes and sweet potatoes from Colin Hunt's fruit and vegetable stall, and he was charged with six offences of failing to display prices in kilograms. In a third case from Cornwall Julian Harman had been charged with selling Brussels sprouts and Grannie Smith apples with prices marked by references to pounds, a unit of measurement not listed in the Units of Measurement regulations. They also prosecuted Mr. John Dove with selling mackerel in the same units, and also with wilfully obstructing of an officer of the weights and measures authority in preventing her from taking price tickets which she required as evidence. Finally Peter Collins was challenging the condition of supply being only in metric units which was being imposed by the London Borough of Sutton for renewal of his street trading licence. He had argued that this was an infringement of his Human Rights.

These were the famous "metric martyrs" who had all lost their cases locally in a rousing chorus of highly emotive and anti-European publicity. The case represented "an attack on the British way of life", "an assault on ordinary people's rights to use units they understood," "unjustified interference from the mandarins of Brussels." Now and more soberly the case was to appear in the Royal Courts of Justice in the Strand of London, by way of appeal. The aptly named, Mr. Justice Laws presented the judgement.

The European Council had adopted a revision of the Metrication Directive in November 1989, which removed the authorisation of selling in pounds and ounces, with a date to be decided by each Member State but not later than 31st December 1999. Here is another example of a government quietly accepting a controversial measure but delaying its effect for ten years. By the time it is discovered in the High Street, nobody is responsible. Accordingly the 1985 Weights and Measures Act was amended by a 1994 Order which abolished sales by reference to all imperial units, preserving only pints reserved for serving draught beer, and milk in returnable bottles, although "supplementary indictors" were authorised until 2010. The other relevant legislation was the Price

Marking Order of 1999, which amended the Prices Act of 1974 with a similar effect.

The relevant legislation was secondary, in that it was prepared by the Minister and "laid before Parliament." Providing there was no opposing resolution in Parliament, the measure would be deemed to have been approved. It was so approved. The defence made much of the description of such measures as "Henry VIII" clauses,

"in disrespectful commemoration of that monarch's tendency to absolution". However the legal authority for making these orders had been the European Communities Act s.2(2), allowing Ministers to implement European obligations. The defence of the martyrs was essentially that since the relevant primary legislation (of 1985) had been approved <u>after</u> the European Communities Act, the ECA could not be used as a basis for amending a later Act of Parliament. This would be contrary to the sovereignty of Parliament, since no Parliament can bind a later one. In accordance with common law, if a statute was found to be inconsistent with an earlier one the earlier one would be regarded as repealed by necessary implication. Thus, to the extent of the measures concerned, the European Communities Act had been subject to implied repeal, and were therefore illegal.

Clearly a simple case of selling greengroceries had escalated into a matter of constitutional significance. The very principle of the supremacy of European Law, dating from *Costa v ENEL* was being challenged. Resolution of these clashing principles without a subsequent crisis required some ingenuity which indeed Lord Justice Laws was able to produce. The first step in his reasoning was powerful enough. He confirmed the legal sovereignty of the British Parliament, irrespective of decisions of the ECJ.

> *"There is nothing in the ECA which allows the Court of Justice, or any other institutions of the EU, to touch or qualify the conditions of Parliament's legislative supremacy in the United Kingdom. Not because the legislature chose not to allow it; because by our law it could not allow it. That being so, the legislative and judicial institutions of the EU cannot intrude upon those conditions. The British Parliament has not the authority to authorise any such thing. Being sovereign, it cannot abandon its sovereignty."*

Secondly, reading carefully the judgements such as that in *Factortame*, Mr. Justice Laws deduced that the common law of England differentiates between two types of statute. Apart from ordinary statutes there are "constitutional" statutes which he defines;

> *"Examples are the Magna Carta, the Bill of Rights 1689, the Act of Union, the Reform Acts which distributed and enlarged the franchise, the Human Rights Act, the Scotland Act 1998 and the Government of Wales Act 1998. The ECA clearly belongs in this family. It incorporated the whole corpus of substantive Community rights and obligations, and gave overriding domestic effect to the judicial and administrative machinery of Community law. It may be there has never been a statute having such profound effects on so many dimensions of our daily lives. The ECA is, by force of the common law, a constitutional statute."*

He suggests that these Acts are of such importance that ordinary rules of implied repeal could not be applicable.

> *"For the repeal of a constitutional Act or the abrogation of a fundamental right to be effected by statute, the court would apply this test: is it shown that the legislature's actual – not imputed, constructive or presumed – intention was to effect the repeal or abrogation? I think the test could only be met by express words in the later statute, or by words so specific that the inference of an actual determination to effect the result contended for was irresistible. The ordinary rule of implied repeal does not satisfy this test. Accordingly, it has no application to constitutional statutes."*

The case therefore had two important conclusions. Firstly, the regulations were valid, the appeal was dismissed and all the defendants were guilty as charged. But, of wider significance, this was the result of applying the law of England, and you cannot beat the law of the land. However, it was not European interference, but traditional Common Law which upheld the sovereignty of Parliament, and upheld the European Communities Act as a constitutional statute immune from implied repeal. The law of England had been spoken, with a European voice.

Chapter 24: European Stumbles.

Sacking the Commission

For many years general criticism of some of the trivial measures introduced by the Commission had been commonplace, particularly in Britain, and had significant influence on public opinion. Was there any limit to their interference? In addition, reports about fairly insignificant schemes of fraud had frequently provoked outrage in the euro-sceptic press each adding another drip to those feeling a vague or even passionate dissatisfaction with Europe. There was also occasionally some principled opposition emerging from within the machinery of Brussels.

A recent example had occurred when an official employed in a unit responsible for monetary affairs, published in 1995 a book highly critical of EMU and of the dishonest and devious ways it was being introduced, entitled "The Rotten Heart of Europe". It was certainly extremist and highly offensive to many individuals and its author, Bernard Connolly was duly sacked. Unfortunately for the Commission he challenged this in the ECJ on the grounds of his right of free expression under Article 10 of the European Convention on Human Rights had been infringed. The Advocate General produced an official opinion which he must have regretted rather quickly. In his judgement he referred to the case of *Wingrove v UK* in the ECHR, which Connolly had used as precedent for the thesis that criticism of government bodies could not be restricted by the use of the derogation allowing them to protect their reputation. This was also supported by English law following the case of *Derbyshire County Council v The Times*, which stated that 'it is of the highest public importance that any democratically elected governmental body, or indeed any governmental body, should be open to uninhibited public criticism'.

After due consideration the advocate general rejected the House of Lords case as having "no foundation or relevance" in European law; and then inverted the ECHR's *Wingrove* judgement to illustrate that government censorship was indeed permissible. This gave Euro-sceptic press, notably in this case of The Spectator, a marvellous opportunity since *Wingrove* was a rare blasphemy case. The advocate general was enthusiastically pilloried for believing that criticism of the European Commission amounted to blasphemy.

The actual ECJ judgement three months later, was more sober and measured, and omitted any mention of controversial cases. Nevertheless, and contrary to ECHR jurisprudence it did support the thesis that protection of the reputation of the Commission justifies a limitation on freedom of expression. In principle this contrasts with the position under British law where the Human Rights Act 1998 while also falling short of making ECHR judgements binding, does require a court to take account of them. Rules of interpretation would compel a British court to follow them as persuasive while in this instance at least, the ECJ showed no such constraint. Even more seriously a judgement of the ECJ concerning Human Rights brings that subject within the scope of European law. In this case a British court would be compelled to follow an ECJ ruling, even if blatantly contrary to the ECHR.

At the same time as this case was maturing, a pivotal confrontation was growing between the European Parliament and the Commission which began to make headlines throughout Europe. This time it was to prove impossible to hide allegations under the proverbial carpet and the resulting scandal would disrupt the continuing evolution of the European Union and eventually lead to a decisive shift in the internal balance of power.

Natural rivalry among Europe's institutions had been amplified by the unusual physical separation of the Council, the Commission and the European Parliament. The struggle for influence and power was certainly not new but although Parliament had been granted greater powers under Maastricht and Amsterdam, and despite its relatively new legitimacy supposedly deriving from its direct election it had remained in the shadow of the Commission. No doubt MEP's were stung by suggestions that they acted as mere rubber stamps, providing a veneer of democratic accountability to the Union as a whole and the Commission in particular. This view soon became due for modification after Parliament rejected the annual accounts following an especially critical report from the European Court of Auditors in December 1998. In fact this was nothing unusual since accounts since 1994 there had always been outstanding queries from the Court of Auditors. Parliament had approved the accounts despite these discrepancies. However this time the Court of Auditors listed more than 100 apparent irregularities in one single $200m scientific development programme, administered by a private company; and plenty more besides. Parliament immediately found themselves obliged to respond, but they were still in a quandary because their sanction was ultimately limited to the sacking of the entire commission, after a two-thirds vote in favour. Under the scheme of the treaties there were no lesser measures which could be enforced. With no other option Parliament did indeed debate a motion to this effect, but in view of its drastic nature felt the need to back down by voting for a compromise enquiry into "fraud, mismanagement and nepotism".

The incident revealed how Europe as a whole was able to react to almost cultural differences between its various nations. During the 1980's François Mitterrand was known to be generous in finding employment for friends and relations including his son. The practice was actually common throughout the French state machinery and anyone employed by the government who was not an official civil servant was provided with fake employment in Air France, Air Inter, the RATP, the postal service, the railways, or the government owned banks or insurance companies. At the same time there were said to be 300 people paid for non existent jobs in Paris city hall when Jacques Chirac was mayor. Thus when the former Prime Minister Edith Cresson was appointed commissioner for science and education she was only continuing in the French tradition. Cresson had never been popular in the Commission. She had been a vocal and abrasive politician who had never proved amenable to European "interference" even when she was Minister for European Affairs. Even *Le Monde* suggested politely that, "Her integration within the college is perhaps not an unqualified success." However her real downfall was caused by her employment of a scientific advise on a high salary, who turned out to be her dentist.

The new Nordic members of the EU were far less inclined than the Mediterraneans to see high political office as a chance to provide benefits and patronage. One Dutch Euro MP summarised the feeling, "There is no common European administrative culture, but there are French and Italian habits, and then there are Dutch and Scandinavian habits." At the same time the Germans were beginning to grow more critical of Commission spending, and increasingly irritated by reports of fraud or wastage largely under domestic pressure relating to their excessive contributions. Santer defended himself insisting that he had inherited irregularities and had either corrected them or was busy doing so. It was true that he had introduced stricter controls since the days when Italian farmers were paid for cultivating olive groves that did not exist, but there were still frequent reports revealing matters such as "export subsidies" for frozen meat smuggled into the EU in the first place, or "production grants" for fields of fictitious cotton. The Court of Auditors regularly reported that 5% of EU spending was lost in a fog of fraud or misspending. So, sensing weakness in support of Santer's Commission, and certainly not forgetting that

Parliamentary elections were approaching, Euro MP's felt more confident and able to become more assertive than in it had previous years.

In response to the rising tide of criticism and opposition Mrs. Cresson decided to follow Mitterrand's precept of, "Never admit anything. Never resign," and began justifying her activities. Though not denying that she had employed her friends, she insisted that she had done nothing wrong. She asked, "Should we only work with people we have never seen before?" Then directly challenged in Parliament, "Do you accept responsibility for creating the atmosphere of illegality and cronyism which seems to have served to profit the family and friends of your circle?" She did not.

Mrs. Cresson was enjoying very little support, and even that was from her colleagues among the French Socialist group. Nevertheless she was well able to exploit the fact that individual Commissioners are actually very secure in their positions. The ECJ does possess the power to dismiss a commissioner but only after an exhaustive legal process but neither the President of the Commission nor Parliament has such a right. The only alternative is for a Member State which can effectively dismiss one of its own commissioners by withdrawing its own nomination. In this case the French government refused to do so, even when the alternative of losing the entire Commission by Parliamentary action loomed as a real possibility. In addition Jacques Santer was also speaking in support, if not of Cresson herself, of a collective responsibility of his entire Commission. One significant response to the fraud allegations was to dismiss Paul van Buitenen, the internal auditor within the commission who provided a comprehensive dossier that was difficult to ignore. Perhaps Santer had merely underestimated the defiant mood which was developing in Strasbourg. He would have been better advised to sacrifice Mrs. Cresson, for the sake of saving his administration but he had no authority and showed no inclination to even attempt to do so. Thus, while Parliament would have been placated if Cresson had voluntarily resigned both Santer and the French government appeared determined to resist Parliament's assertiveness.

Parliament's enquiry began and Mrs Cresson and seven other commissioners appeared before a special committee of independent investigators. After only five weeks they produced their first report. This concentrated on six well-known and well-documented cases of fraud, mismanagement or nepotism and they confirmed misconduct in each case. However, just as damaging was their conclusions that the commission's proud doctrine of collective responsibility amounted in practice to a refusal to accept personal responsibility. They claimed that "it is becoming difficult to find anybody who has even the slightest sense of responsibility."

Santer reportedly pleaded with Cresson to resign, feeling a real sense of injustice since the most serious accusations had concerned actions from his predecessor's era. He again tried to convince both the Jacques Chirac and his Prime Minister, Lionel Jospin, to urge to her to do the same, but he was rebuffed by all three. The college of Commissioners met all night and prevaricated. Eventually, Neil Kinnock (Commissioner for Transport) and Karel Van Miert (Commissioner for Competition), presented letters of resignation to their colleagues, urging each of them to fall on their swords too. This could have isolated Cresson, who if persisting would have been solely exposed to the EP's pending motion. Santer, sensing the drift, then urged that they should resign as a united collegiate body. The following morning the resignation of the entire Commission was announced, and Santer, somewhat like Gorbachev, was to be swept away by the reforms which he had instigated.

Putting a brave face on an apparent disaster national politicians stressed the opportunities that now arose. Tony Blair immediately told the House of Commons that this was no setback but a golden opportunity to push through "root and branch" reform of a commission whose failings had been tolerated for far too long. William Hague was also scathing of Santer's Commission, until reminded that it was the Conservative John Major who had insisted on his appointment. Reform appeared to be on the agenda.

Bearing in mind that appointing a whole new Commission could really represent a real opportunity, what sort of reforms could really be contemplated or achieved? It was accepted that Santer had been the wrong man, but could grasping this opportunity mean that events had forced structural reform of the Commission at the right time? There was in any case little doubt that the existing system of twenty Commissioners appointed by the fifteen members could not survive the expansion to well over twenty members. It was also clear that there were more Commissioners than jobs. Portfolios covering the single market, trading policy, competition, enlargement and farming were clearly necessary and effective but Santer had been obliged to devise twenty roles. The quality of some of the Commissioners themselves was also questionable because appointments had frequently been made to national politicians who had either failed or who could not be suitably employed at home. At least under the Amsterdam Treaty the Commission President would be able to reject proposed candidates from national governments. However, despite professing loyalty to the Union as a whole Commissioners are still considered as national representatives, and their prestige determines that they must be given large budgets, staff and responsibilities even if fictitious. Reform therefore starts at a higher level than the Commission itself and involves the strategic direction of the whole Union. It was unlikely that this could be resolved with the urgency then required.

Under the EU's constitutional rules commissioners who resign go on serving in a "caretaker" capacity until their replacements are appointed. Thus the agenda shifted rapidly to the European Council to arrange replacements, at the same time encouraging national leaders to think again about the correct role for the Commission. The British earlier desire for a weakened Commission had not taken account of the fact that the organisation discharges many practical duties of relevance to national interests and so needs to be efficiently run and with sufficiently strong leadership to maintain order and stability. In addition smaller countries frequently saw the Commission as a powerful check on the powers of the larger countries and so supported the extension of its power into other areas, for example foreign policy, defence etc. Leaders were all aware of the importance of selecting the correct man as President. Once having been appointed by national leaders, and approved by Parliament the President is thereafter regulated only by the EU's founding treaties and so immediately becomes independently powerful.

The Arrival of Prodi

Most observers were surprised that after only three hours of the summit meeting in Berlin in March Members had unanimously invited the former Italian Prime Minister, Romano Prodi, to become the next President. He was to assume office as soon as possible, with none of the disgraced Commissioners remaining, and to discuss as a matter of priority necessary reforms and management of the institution. However expectation before the meeting that progress could be made on budgetary and structural reforms as preparation for enlargement, was to be disappointed. With fifty percent of the budget consumed by the Common Agricultural Policy there can be no budget discipline without this reform. This however is always fiercely resisted by those countries which benefit. Other countries react to this self interest by seeking to maximise their benefits in other areas. Thus as far as European expenditure is concerned ministers show instead of a serious consideration of the larger policy issues, a self interest amounting to a collective irresponsibility limited only by willingness of donor nations to foot the total bill. Paradoxically the Berlin budget discussions also showed the disadvantage of avoiding majority voting. Although regarded as a safeguard to protect an individual nation, the giving of even one state the ability to block agreement, paradoxically allows that state to suggest concessions in some other area by way of compensation to what actually might have been a sensible and equitable proposal. While Europe as a whole suffers through impeded progress, everyone wins a prize they can take back home to present to their voters as a victory. Unanimity or even consensus thus has two edges, and can be employed either to protect or to exploit.

So, by early summer of 1999 all the really important decisions had been postponed to the next IGC scheduled for the year 2000, and the was European Union operating with Parliamentarians occupied with their elections and a "caretaker" Commission. The arrival of Prodi was heralded as the beginning of a new era for Europe but nobody could comment on its direction. In preparation for seeking Parliamentary approval of his appointment he quickly listed his priorities as follows: to strengthen the powers of the Commission and its president; to rid the commission of sleaze; to reform the Commission in preparation for the arrival of the EU's proposed new members; to forge an alliance with the European Parliament as a political counterweight to the European Council and the national governments; to reassure markets that his commission supports business, trade and free enterprise; and to secure some role for the commission in creating a common European foreign policy. He wanted to overcome the apathy and wariness of the European people with an ambitious acceleration towards centralisation.

Prodi's point regarding foreign policy illustrated the realisation by Prodi that the Commission had in recent years been sidelined from the central role in European integration it had earned under Jacques Delors. When national governments had designed the institutions for the single currency they had seen the project as vital, and too important for delegation to a bureaucratic, unaccountable and discredited Commission. The European Central Bank became absolutely independent of any Commission involvement, and governments themselves retained control of policy through a separate intergovernmental body. Similarly the other pillars of the Maastricht structure defence, security and particularly foreign policy had been regarded as the province of governments' national interests and although governments were prepared to surrender some freedom of action in the European interest this did not equate to involvement of European Commission. Even on expansion national leaders were insisting that the Council's political judgements regarding new members should override the Commission's academic approach to the issues of legal, and economic convergence. Prodi's task was, for him at least, the recovery of the drive and authority of the Commission's earlier days.

The Tackling of Corruption

In building a new team to revitalise the Commission and put it back onto the path of an embryonic government, Britain's Neil Kinnock was given a key role. As one of the four survivors from the Santer Commission where he had been in control of transport policy, he was to return with the authority of a vice-President to be responsible for a wide-ranging cultural reform of the organisation, and in particular to prescribe remedies for its perceived organisational an ethical deficiencies. He was responsible for a major "clean-up". His task was likely to involve a serious confrontation with the strong and strike-inclined staff unions of the EU executive, representing its 16,000 staff and fiercely protective of their interests and privileges. Nevertheless Kinnock spoke of his determination that the Commission had to be "efficiently and transparently managed" and had to give "value for taxpayers' money". Above all, this would meant "zero tolerance of fraud".

Within a few months Kinnock had produced his blueprint for "Reforming the Commission". He was to introduce "A Code Of Conduct For Good Administrative Behaviour". There would be "More Efficient Use Of Internal And External Resources" and proposals would be considered on a "Draft Inter-Institutional Agreement on Whistleblowers" and "Transparency of Personnel Policy". Kinnock's love of language was also found in his proposals to improve management of the Commission's activities with philosophy of "Activity Based Management", in a "Policy-driven SPP Framework". A new "Integrated Resource Management System" would include an "Activity Based Budget methodology", which would contribute to strengthening of financial management using "quasi-abolition of central ex-ante visa controls". Everyone was in agreement.

After six months considerable progress had been made in some areas. Kinnock had tightened up many of the auditing procedures, commissioners have been made to declare their financial interests, and an office dedicated to fighting fraud, OLAF was to be created. However serious resistance was appearing against other reforms. Commissioners were not encouraging a new "Standards on Public Life" commission based on the British model. Reform of personnel policies, introducing concepts such as promotion and pay on merit in a less hierarchical structure were opposed by staff unions to the point of angry demonstrations and threat of strikes. This was even without attacking the high salaries and privileged tax status of officials, which they would most vigorously defend.

By 2002 when improvements should have been clear there were still remnants of mismanagement. In May Kinnock suspended his chief accountant, Marta Andreasen, after she refused to sign off the Commission's 2001 accounts and publicly described them as "out of control." She was definitely disciplined and claimed she was systematically smeared by a well co-ordinated whispering campaign against her. There were even claims of harassment. "Every time I left the building, they followed me," she said. "There were usually two of them, one just in front and one behind, and they made it so obvious that I assumed it was meant to be intimidation. Maybe they wanted to stop me meeting anybody." Similar claims had once been made by Bernard Connolly. He had said that his house had been staked out whenever he was away in an attempt to intimidate his wife. Meanwhile Kinnock was claiming that Mrs. Andreasen's accusations were unsubstantiated and that she had been subject only to fair procedures. She had been disciplined for violating staff rules by defaming her superiors, bringing disrepute on the Commission, and violating hierarchy lines. As late as December she received an official Commission warning not to give evidence to a Parliamentary enquiry, threatening her with "consequences for her personal status."

There were other instances of scandal which called the effectiveness of Kinnock's root and branch reform into question. In March 2002 a Danish civil servant working for Eurostat, the EU's statistical office, said she was removed from her post after complaining about fraudulent contracts being awarded to outside consulting companies. She had written to Kinnock personally complaining of victimisation and harassment. Kinnock replied that her allegations were "unfounded", but her dossier was sent to the public prosecutor in Luxembourg. In the summer the director-general in charge of fisheries, Steffen Smidt, was allegedly fired on orders of the Spanish government as a "punishment" for trying to save Europe's declining stocks from catastrophic over-fishing, much of it by Spanish vessels and in a deal between the Spanish presidency and Prodi involving location of the Food Safety Agency. Spain admitted that it had instructed its commissioner, and this itself was a breach of EU law. However Smidt's departure was presented by the commission hierarchy, to the irritation of MEP's, as part of long-term reshuffle. This was described as an "orchestrated lie" for which Kinnock was held responsible. Kinnock later "regretted" the failure in communication but denied the substance of the allegations.

The whistleblower responsible for the Santer Commission resignation, Paul van Buitenen, had also not gone away. Although many would regard his contribution as a public service it was never a service to the Commission. He managed to keep a position but at a much demoted level. But, in August 2001 he reappeared from the depths and presented a massive dossier of continuing fraud involving 234 cases to the fraud office, OLAF. A year later he claimed that investigated cases had been swept under the carpet while officials known to be corrupt stayed in their posts, and disheartened and defeated, he resigned from the Commission. He did however receive a knighthood from the Queen.

Buitenen undoubtedly had a point. After three years of reform and investigations the only officials to suffer were those who had exposed wrongdoing within the Commission. Kinnock himself admitted in an interview in October 2002, that not one official had been dismissed in connection with any of the scandals. Moreover, even in August 2002 the Court of Auditors was still complaining about the lack of accepted accounting standards in the Commission, and the Commission's failure to take remedial action. "Failures abound and are a waste of public funds". Despite this it is quite possible that Kinnock had adopted a policy amounting to amnesty, in return for correct operation of new procedures. Later he was to compare his task with that of reforming the Labour Party before 1997, rescuing it from unelectable left-wing forces. He argued that although the same qualities of argument, extensive patience and total commitment are required administrative reform of the Commission was being accomplished with much less acrimony. There is, he said, "No blood on the carpet this time." Indeed, allegations of real fraud are no longer prevalent and even the Court of Auditors suggests that cases of fraud are found in areas where Member States themselves are responsible. If so this could be regarded as a cultural victory, and certainly an important factor in any future revival of the Commission's public reputation.

Chapter O: Driving the Forces of Integration

Power and Politics

In Chapter N we saw two very typical results of Community activity. It was only long after the politicians had agreed the measures concerned that their final effects were fully revealed to a startled public. There was often a real sense in which politicians lit the blue touch paper and retired. It is important to examine how this happens. Firstly, a policy initiative usually starts from the Commission. It is moderated in some way by national politicians in Council or by politicians in the European Parliament or by one of the consultative bodies, but eventually it emerges as a legally binding measure. Then possibly several years later the European Court has its say, and it is this which determines the real extent of the proposal. These final results may be unexpected to some, and may bear no relation to the intentions of others previously involved in the decision. But, none of this matters. The law is decided.

Ultimate control has always remained the prerogative of national politicians, but only in one limited sense. No separate area of policy can be transferred to the Community without their agreement. But, what freedom of action have politicians really enjoyed in these circumstances? After all, individual politicians have always been from a transient species, appearing on a moving stage managed by forces with a total but patient commitment to ever closer union. This necessitates a perpetually increasing European competence at the expense of those divisive and disruptive national interests. These are the two forces which at the beginning, control the scope of the initial agendas, and at the end determine the ultimate effects. This statement is not to imply collusion, but merely the result of a shared set of values and objectives expressed in the preamble of the Treaty of Rome. Neither does it suggest any motive other than an honest belief in the welfare of the peoples of Europe. It merely observes the historical results of all the combined forces.

Individual politicians operate on their own timescales and with their own agendas. They have no memory of mistakes, successes or the compromises of the past and historical trends are not within their vision. Their role is to react to the snapshot of the moment, and to maximise a benefit they perceive from that moment's controlled agenda of horse trading. Not only that, but they all have to remember the source of their power back home. Each has to remain credible in proclaiming his achievements from a national perspective, while avoiding too much conflict.

This is not to suggest that the politicians do not have their own objectives, or even principles. Consider Margaret Thatcher' enthusiasm for (her vision of) a single market; consider John Major's destination of the "centre of Europe", consider Tony Blair's determination to transform Britain's negative reputation in European affairs. But then, consider the results, the disappointment of each, and how a need to re-define the relationship with Europe emerged in each case. The European Union is not a creature to be tamed by a single national leader whether a visionary integrationist or a disruptive nationalist. Each one qualifies for just one temporary place at a top table soon to seat twenty five representatives. Progress can only ever be made by consensus. Therefore every subject on the agenda involved compromise and concession, remembering that traffic was only ever in one direction. Individual leaders simply join the flow and to some variable extent are carried along by it.

The effects of these interactions are best seen at the level of routine decision making. These are the perpetual negotiations regarding the legislative programmes implementing earlier policy decisions. The Commission supplies the meat on the bones of the Council agreed initiative. Each leader will formulate an opinion in response to his national situation and his government's overall policy. Inevitable some members will want to maximise the scope of any particular measure while others will seek minimise it, and most will want to adjust it in one way or another. Sometimes a Member state will oppose a particular proposal entirely, and attempt to block any progress. This more extreme obstruction can be overcome in a civilised manner by persuasion, or by trading over some quite unrelated proposal. It can also be overcome by use of QMV, if necessary first shifting the legal basis accordingly. Usually however, negotiations will proceed smoothly and eventually some measure will be approved. It may be open to a disgruntled Member State to challenge the measure before the ECJ, but such challenges have rarely succeeded. However, whatever the extent of the final measure one certain result is that some degree of Community competence will be agreed. The boundary will have shifted, irreversibly.

Finally, as in the case of all legislation it is left for the courts to determine its real scope, interpreted in accordance with the underlying political objectives, often of the entire Treaty. This is a process which, as we have seen, may take many years, the final flavour of the measure only becoming apparent to a later generation of politicians. The original authors, responding to the pressures of their time may have long since moved on. Meanwhile, and whether or not this judicial process identifies a missed area, it is quite certain that the Commission will already have been working on the next step, ready to plug any gap which may appear.

The Council can also be viewed historically as a collective leadership despite its constantly changing membership. Clearly, and seen collectively, the role of the Council remains crucial as this body remains responsible for final decision making, in both a legislative and policy making capacity. Looking at the latter, it is apparent that since the inception of the EC this political leadership in the Council has a varied history in setting the pace of integration even thought the general direction remained firm. In the early days, and having started the entire process national leaders had little involvement as construction of the common market progressed through largely technical measures. Later, in the 1970's the leadership certainly wanted to promote faster progress but pre-occupation with the domestic economic crises of the time prevented consensus and halted progress. Momentum increased sharply when, under the leadership of Delors the Commission took over the lead role in driving Europe together. Final decisions remained with the Council but as we saw with Mrs. Thatcher the Delors strategy with his personal persistence prevailed intact.

After Delors the credibility of the Commission waned somewhat and the regularity of the Council meetings transferred much of the initiative back to the Council. Today the Council remains the centre of attention, with national leaders taking their places on this central stage. It is here that they can project their image of importance as they maintain their appearance of control. The six-monthly president of the Council has been under particular pressure. With suitable and active encouragement from the Commission, he could rarely do more than choose on which of the policies helpfully suggested by the Commission he should concentrate. Each presidency, particularly in one of the smaller nations is seen as an opportunity to make a lasting and even historic impact on the EU. The President himself will prepare for six months in the spotlight, anxious to maximise his benefit from his increased international profile. Consequently every presidency has adopted such a mini-agenda setting priorities for moving particular boundaries.

Secondly, the Council is regularly concerned with the much larger questions associated with underlying direction of the EU. Many such issues are resolved informally, often during passage of ordinary legislative measures. Sometimes though, larger scale negotiations aim at agreeing substantial amendments to the Treaties themselves. Here the role and the response of the Council appears little different. Politicians have always been subject to perpetual persuasion, usually from the Commission, to extend the boundaries of European competence. Leaders are often divided among themselves, suffering from conflicting national pressures, and trying to balance between their individual appearance of co-operation or of toughness for particular audiences. Their decisions have therefore always tended to be pragmatic rather than principled if only to remain within the bounds of consensus. Often leaders are pressured into approving policies which they completely opposed and then struggle to present their decisions as evidence of their true European credentials, stressing the greater benefit to all of the spirit of co-operation. More often though, these conflicts are resolved by compromises adding counterbalancing exceptions to the new policies. These inevitably result in added complexity, as well as eventually, further necessity for judicial interpretation. As we will see below, the Maastricht Treaty is the best example.

The Council has by no means always been driven by the institutions towards integration and has never been beyond use of flexible interpretation itself in order to attain its objectives. It can rival the extended example we saw above where the Commission developed the doctrine of implied powers to wrest control of international negotiations from the Member States. Starting from transport policy (*ERTA*) this was, over the years extended area by area into almost the whole international arena. In international aid bodies, in discussions with the International Labour Organisation, World Trade Organisation, GATT, in areas concerning competition, it is the Commission which represents all Member States who following the ERTA doctrine have no longer have right to interfere, or present any independent view or policy. Even in the foreign policy forum, the Commission is already calling for the permanent seats in the UN Security Council held by Britain and France to be transferred to the EU.

The Council in its role as legislator was believed to possess its own version of the Commission's implied powers doctrine, but this time it is written into the Treaty as Article 308, (formerly 235) of the TEC. This states,

> "If action by the Community should prove necessary to attain, in the course of the operation of the common market, one of the objectives of the Community and this Treaty has not provided the necessary powers, the Council shall, acting unanimously on a proposal from the Commission and after consulting the European Parliament, take the appropriate measures."

Originally this article was regarded as a mechanism held in reserve to correct any oversight of the drafters which appeared in unforeseen circumstances. It was to be used to compensate for a discovered absence of legal basis only within an area of activity explicitly stated by the Treaty. This limitation still applied in 1994 the Court decided when considering whether the EC was competent to accede to the European Convention on Human Rights declared

> "No Treaty provision confers on Community institutions any general power to enact rules on human rights or to include international conventions in this field. Moreover, Article 308 cannot serve as a basis for widening the scope of Community powers beyond the framework created by the Treaty as a whole."

Of course, whether or not a particular measure went beyond the framework of the Treaty was a question which could be answered only by the ECJ, and the Court's history on this point had occasionally been more flexible.

Political leaders had never been afraid of adopting a broad interpretation of Treaty articles when these suited their current aims. The Common Fisheries Policy, for example was approved under the legal base covering agriculture. However in the early 1970's the politicians were attempting to revitalise the Community, by expansion into new areas. They wanted to achieve this by use of Article 308, contrary to its accepted meaning by a process of creative interpretation regarding Community objectives. In 1973 this possibility was realised by the ECJ who in a case considering whether it was *necessary* to introduce a scheme of customs valuation by means of Article 235 allowed the term to be replaced by *justified* in this particular case. This much broader interpretation encouraged much greater use of the Article, right up until the Single European Act, successfully extending Community operations, for example into supply of emergency food aid to third countries. Thus the political leaders of the time, wishing to launch the Community into new fields were supported by the ECJ, and so avoided the major inconvenience of Treaty revision. The active collusion of all institutions in this flexible approach meant that there was no longer any core activity of state function which could be confidently excluded from Community action. At the time though, this was not important because the Member States were not sufficiently united on several key issues. Legal obstacles to expanding Community competence had been removed, but political restraint usually resulting from a requirement for unanimity remained.

Power Behind Politics

Now, consider, that all along while the politicians were making the headlines, and from the focus of media interest usually controlling the information supplied to a scarcely interested, or completely confused public, the real forces of integration remained quietly active in the background, achieving their own progress day by day, in studied and deliberate increments.

This process started to work effectively with the merger treaty of 1965. The separate Communities responsible for the Coal and Steel Industries, for the Atomic Energy, were combined with the assumed Common Market of the Economic Community, under political control of the Member States in a single Council, and under the supervision of a combined Commission. The institutions quietly and consistently set about building the basic structures of the common market based on the principles of free movement. The steps were generally small and uncontroversial despite regular opposition from Members resisting the detailed, individual effects of regulations they had in principle approved. In fact, though it was hardly noticed at the time, the most important moves were those taken by the European Court of Justice. The principles of direct effect, and of the supremacy of Community law became established but the proviso, "albeit in limited fields," diluted and disguised the true constitutional force which was later to emerge. After all, the rate of duty applied to a particular chemical was hardly likely to excite national politicians or outrage the public. In addition the effectiveness of the preliminary reference procedure became established well before it could become controversial.

These judicial innovations could be seen as a logical development of the principles behind a supra-national common market, or they could be seen as the beginning of a truly federal governing system. In either case they represented a sensible way of countering the admitted tendency of each member state to agree matters in principle but then to avoid by omission or commission individual measures of which they disapproved. As a result of Court judgements, projected through national courts, such obstruction to the general European interest suddenly became more difficult.

These same principles also determined the "permanent limitation of sovereign rights," which, combined with the unpredicted effectiveness of the preliminary reference procedure, removed the very mechanisms of legal enforcement away from the control of national governments. This was such a truly momentous step, that many national politicians were unable to recognise or unwilling to admit to their public what exactly had happened. Even today, many, especially in Britain have not progressed beyond the phase of denial. Nevertheless these principles commanded a general if occasionally resigned acceptance on two grounds. Firstly, a fair method of resolving disputes benefits all parties, especially those like Britain which see themselves as honest implementers of obligations they have freely accepted. Secondly, in the eyes of most of those that recognise them, the constitutional implications are on balance tolerable, simply because of the limitation in scope to merely commercial matters.

The problem with this view was described as long as ten years ago, even before the Maastricht treaty, when Professor Weiler observed that "the fields do not seem any more to be limited," and Professor Leanarts expressed it somewhat more strongly, "There simply is no nucleus of sovereignty that the Member States can invoke, as such, against the Community."

In explaining how this occurred it is not sufficient to confine attention to national politicians. Collectively these politicians may have created the EC, but certainly they gradually ceased to be the masters of the treaties and in many cases acted as little more than servants of the institutions they created. Just as many national ministries began to function merely as local representatives of the European Commission, similarly national politicians were trapped into following the European agenda. The ECJ was the critical factor in achieving this transformation. Politicians brought up to respect the rule of law, frequently found themselves tied by it, in a way they would not have tolerated in their national governments. European law, though, with its established supremacy was an entirely different matter, and as was discovered in the case of the European Economic Area, it was not even certain that a treaty amendment would be able to contain it.

Naturally it is possible to see this result in two ways. Euro-sceptic critics would always see the process as purely political, and an expression of the insatiable ambition of the European Commission. National sovereignty was being eroded, and negotiated away by irresponsible national politicians disregarding the long term independence of their own countries. On the other hand supporters would praise its every step towards the greater vision of European unity, peace, security and harmony. Whatever one's opinion about its merits it can hardly be disputed that the result has been a year by year increase in those areas designated as within European rather than national competence. (The details recounting this gradual transfer of sovereignty would require a work the size of an encyclopaedia, but the result can be illustrated with the present range of functions within the Commission which are listed in Appendix I).

Of course major expansion of areas of competence have been initiated and justified by using new legal bases following amendments to the Treaty, duly ratified by Member States. Thus regional, environmental and international development policies, and recent extensions in the grounds of prohibited discrimination all result from negotiated additions. However, it is possible to identify a variety of strategies and arguments which have been used to achieve this ever converging union, by expanding the scope of already existing legal bases.

The most commonly used strategy was an expansion of the detailed requirements encompassed by already accepted policies. Thus the need to ensure effective operation of the single market was continually increased. Gradual drift into new areas, for example intellectual property became "necessary" as previous "obstacles" had been removed. Similar shifting boundaries were encountered by each need to respect the fundamental principles of the Treaty. The requirements necessary to ensure completely the four freedoms of movement, and the elimination of discrimination between sexes, or between nationalities continually became more extensive. New measures were constantly being introduced by the Commission to expand existing boundaries while in due course the European Court would independently support the same objectives by interpreting the concepts employed in a wide and expansive manner.

Over the longer term these two institutions effectively combined to form a true engine of integration. Many arguments, based on the above principles and objectives were used by the Commission to direct the evolution of Community legislation and to support a growing requirement of harmonisation in more and more fields despite frequent reluctance from Member States. Then, subsequently, the Court would exert its power in preliminary reference procedures to promote the doctrine of uniform application of the law to extraordinary heights, prohibiting *any* variations, and ensuring central control.

Power Without Politics

The Commission never restricted its contribution simply to negotiating harmonised regulation. Even in those areas where harmonisation could not be agreed, alternative routes could be identified. For example, the Commission tried for many years to reach agreements regarding company law. The problem was that many of the basic principles relating to companies were so different from country to country that harmonisation at any more than a superficial level repeatedly proved impractical. The solution was to construct a totally independent, pan European system for the formation, registration and regulation of companies. The Commission explains:

> *"The completion of the internal market and the improvement it brings about in the economic and social situation throughout the Community mean not only that barriers to trade must be removed, but also that the structures of production must be adapted to the Community dimension. For that purpose it is essential that companies the business of which is not limited to satisfying purely local needs should be able to plan and carry out the reorganisation of their business on a Community scale."*

Therefore after October 2004 limited companies will appear designated as SE (Societas Europaea). Existing Ltd., SA., or GMBH companies will not be affected and national structures will remain valid and respected. The Commission says that these European laws will not circumvent national structures but will complement them with a new legal basis more suited to intercommunity business.

It is important to realise that the court also, in contributing its own powers, did not restrict itself to mere interpretation of the legal provisions. The concept of divining the true meaning of a provision by reference to its underlying objectives, allowed it a much greater flexibility. Therefore, in some cases the ECJ, finding no suitable provisions within the Treaty Articles, simply used its "common sense" and <u>extended</u> what could have been strictly observed limits to its jurisdiction. One example was the Court granting the European Parliament rights to challenge other institutions before the court, despite there being no mention of them having such a right. A more significant example was the incorporation of the values relating to human rights. Nowhere were fundamental rights mentioned in the Treaty, and no intention that the European Charter of Human Rights should have any bearing on ECJ decisions could be detected in its provisions. Nevertheless as early as in 1969 when Eric Stauder (in *Stauder v City of Ulm*) complained about having to give his name and address as a condition of receiving subsidised butter the Court re-interpreted the Commission Decision to remove the element of compulsion. Almost casually, and in passing the judges commented that,

> *"Interpreted in this way the provision at issue contains nothing capable of prejudicing the fundamental human rights enshrined in the general principles of Community Law and protected by the court."*

This was the first time that anyone had suggested that respect for human rights was an integral principle of Community Law. From a legal point of view this conclusion was untenable, and without possible justification. However real opposition to the ECJ could only come from politicians, and they would find it impossible to argue against protecting human rights. The point quietly passed into law, together with the precedent for extension.

The then established fact that human rights were an essential component of the law was actually used to great effect a year later when authorities failed to refund an import deposit after changing the applicable rules. In *Internationale Handelsgesellschaft* the Court started from its earlier assertion and said,

> *"Respect for fundamental rights forms an integral part of the general principles of law protected by the Court of Justice. The protection of such rights, whilst inspired by the constitutional traditions common to the Member States, must be ensured within the framework of the structure and objectives of the Community."*

In fact this initiative by the court which was subsequently extended to become a powerful constraint on Community action, proved a crucial factor in German acceptance of the principle of supremacy. The German Constitutional Court said that since, and so long as the EC observed the same principles of fundamental rights as were traditional under the German constitution, there was no obstacle to acceptance of the ECJ doctrines. Although this is quoted as an extension of Community power contrived by the Court it should be added that in both cases there was widespread political support for the decisions. Both were later to be incorporated in Treaty amendments.

A second ECJ strategy is illustrated by the case of Donato Casagrande (*v Landeshauptstadt Munchen*) who was an Italian national at school in Bavaria where his parents were working. Using educational regulations the city of Munich declined to offer him an educational grant, since these were restricted to German nationals. On a reference to the ECJ the city argued that whereas the Regulations concerning free movement of workers required equal access to education there was nothing in this regulation which could be used to force a local authority to provide a grant contrary to its own educational policy. On the contrary Treaty Article 149 explicitly prevents Community action in the education field. The Court studied the Regulation and replied that it had failed to find any such limitation in its scope. On the question of whether this represented an incursion into a separate policy area, the Court concluded,

> "*Although educational and training policy is not <u>as such</u> included in the spheres which the treaty has entrusted to the community institutions, it does not follow that the exercise of powers transferred to the community is in some way limited if it is of such a nature as to affect the measures taken in the execution of a policy such as that of education and training.*"

It was not that Community law was encroaching on national education policy, it was just that this policy was interfering with the Community principle of free movement. Therefore it had to give way. Education policy was to that extent <u>absorbed</u> by an overriding requirement to respect the free movement of persons. Once, again this initiative was soon to be followed by legislators who introduced specific measures relating to educational access, just in case there was to be any doubt about the matter in future. Again the strategy of absorption was also established.

Rescue by Subsidiarity?

Politicians of the Council therefore found themselves working with or sometimes against, an administrative and a judicial branch of the Union each with a common long term strategy. For leaders of countries such as the Netherlands with firm public support for European integration there was no conflict of values. But, for a country where European interest is secondary eg. France, and for countries where integration is treated with dread or suspicion, the problem is clear and fundamental. Such leaders were inclined to read again Article 5 of the EC Treaty.

> *"The Community shall act within the limits of the powers conferred on it by this Treaty and of the objectives to it therein."*

Several must have wondered if this was still true.

This divergence was most pronounced during negotiations for the Maastricht Treaty. In itself this resulted from numerous compromises between those states wishing to dive headlong into a complete federal Europe and their more reluctant partners which would actually have preferred to reverse many of the integrationist measures already taken. Disregarding this latter option as heretical, the resulting Treaty reveals many remnants of these conflicting views. Firstly there was a completely new expansion into policy areas such as justice or foreign affairs. However here, the desire for closer integration was tempered with hesitancy. The resulting compromise was for a mechanism for close co-operation but constructed outside the supra-national machinery of compulsion developed in the Community. These separate pillars of the EU were to remain intergovernmental in nature. Of course the Commission soon obtained a "co-ordinating" role which it used to erode this distinction gradually, and again the principle of creeping competence applies. Nevertheless the underlying intergovernmental principle does remain intact.

At the same time there was a considerable expansion in market related activities, measures for social development etc., even extending to economic and monetary union. However there was again a clear ambivalence by Europe's political leadership. This expansion of legal competence was also to be tempered by an almost contradictory attempt to shift the balance back towards Member State competence. To Article 5 was therefore added the description of a new moderating principle,

> *"In areas which do not fall within its exclusive competence, the Community shall take action, in accordance with the principle of subsidiarity, only if and insofar as the objectives of the proposed action cannot be sufficiently achieved by the Member States and can therefore, by reason of the scale or*

effects of the proposed action, be better achieved by the Community."

The principle had actually emerged well before Maastricht, and in 1990 Giscard d' Estaing produced in a report to the European Parliament a proposal "Making the principle of subsidiarity more explicit," and attempted to define the sharing of competencies between the Community and Member States. This was an honest attempt to remove the uncertainty surrounding this fundamental issue, but it failed because there was no common political will to push it forward. On the contrary, it contained so many issues contentious to all concerned, and better concealed from public debate. Many Member States were simply unwilling to admit publicly and in black and white, the extent of government competence which had already been transferred. This reluctance was increased by the fact that so much power had actually been transferred without specific authorisation from national parliaments. Then, for exactly the opposite reason the Commission was perfectly happy with the uncertainties of the existing system, which they had operated to their benefit for many years. Public statements would not only draw unwanted attention but more seriously would also serve as defined limits to their future freedom of action. Giscard d'Estaing would have to wait.

In the absence of decisive political intervention the future of the concept would be left to the judiciary. Unfortunately, with wording such as this subsidiarity was clearly a concept wide open to interpretation. It had been hailed in Britain as a real restraint on the feared unbridled European expansionism and used to counter the objections of the anti-Europe camps. It was "a triumph for the nation states." In future only *appropriate* measures would be introduced so there was nothing more to fear. The Commission had been tamed. Elsewhere reaction was rather different. From some quarters there was a grudging approval, but more generally there was a belief that it was entirely irrelevant. After all the Commission only ever proposed measures which were *necessary*. Moreover if it was really to be applied it was sufficiently vaguely worded for it to be safely ignored, given then appropriate will.

The ECJ took some years to determine the extent of the principle, and has now established such a narrow view as to the applicability of subsidiarity as to render it almost irrelevant. The first and critical limitation in the principle of subsidiarity is explicitly stated at the outset. It has no applicability in areas of "exclusive community competence." In fact, there are many areas where competence is essentially shared between Community and Member States. For example, in regulating business and professional activities Member States must conform to the requirements of freedom of establishment (Article 47) but otherwise remain free to introduce their own regulation. In one case when Community competence was challenged in this field (*Germany v European Parliament and Council*), the Court replied that the Treaty itself implied that co-ordination of policies was better achieved at Community level. Thus, the Community was indeed "exclusively competent," not in producing general regulations but in "co-ordination" of national policies. In other words the expression "exclusive competence" was to be very broadly interpreted. Consequently there was no requirement to apply the principle of subsidiarity at all.

In 1997 the Advocate General Léger, largely responsible for the decision on exclusive competence was very positive about measures which legislators should take to ensure compliance with the principle of subsidiarity, and the tests they should employ. However in the full judgement which followed the full court rejected his suggestions, and fell back on the principle defined in the case of *United Kingdom v Council* concerning the Working Time Directive. This had been thought, by Britain, to be a powerful case for enforcing the principle of subsidiarity since the relevant Treaty Article (136) calls for both community and Member States to implement measures. It was therefore a critical test. The Court could indeed have found that hours of working were best left to Member States, since the Commission had failed to demonstrate real benefits from Community regulation. This would have heralded an entirely new relationship between nations and the Community, presumably as had been intended by the original supporters of subsidiarity. Instead though, the Court stated,

> "The Council has found that it is necessary to improve the existing level of protection as regards the health and safety of workers and to harmonise the conditions in this area."

Thus the Court would regard the principle of subsidiarity complied with merely because the Council "found it necessary."

The politicians did not seem perturbed that the invention of subsidiarity had been effectively sidelined and curiously British politicians hadn't even noticed since they continued to quote the principle as a guarantee that Commission power would remain limited. Nevertheless after ten years they all decided that the principle was in need of further explanation. Therefore in a Protocol to the Amsterdam Treaty they emphasised that the principle of subsidiarity would apply wherever,

- the issues under consideration has transnational aspects which cannot be satisfactorily regulated by action by Member States;
- action by Member States alone or lack of Community action would conflict with the requirements of the Treaty (such as the need to correct distortion of competition)
- action at Community level would produce clear benefits by reason of its scale or effect compared with action at the level of Member States.

The politicians pronounced themselves happy with this advance, perhaps without wondering whether this wording would prove a strong enough to influence future judgements of the ECJ.

Chapter 25: Council Control

Austrian Control

The actual demise and the widespread unpopularity of the European Commission left vacant the role of principle driving force for EU progression. The European Council with its high profile and pivotal role, together with its established engine of regular meetings and rapidly advancing objectives was the ideal vehicle. At this time the main direction of attention was undoubtedly eastwards, but even at this highest level the road being built could still be subject to obstructions, diversions and the distractions of routine business.

Early in 2000 Europe was shocked by the result of elections in Austria which had obliged the Austrian President to appoint a government which included the right-wing Freedom Party in its coalition. The real villain was Jörg Haider who although he had toned done his nazi like sympathies still controlled the Freedom Party and represented an unpleasant xenophobic element. Extreme right-wing, nationalist parties were known throughout Europe, and although politicians watched them nervously leaders of mainstream right-wing parties had been able to obtain elected office without dealing with such extremists. In Austria such a party of extremism had achieved a place in government for the first time. European leaders were less than impressed, and began to preach to Austria about its internal affairs, and to threaten sanctions against a government of which they disapproved.

The EU itself was not able to impose any type of sanction since this would require unanimity. Therefore the remaining 14 members decided to co-ordinate separate bilateral sanctions, excluding Austria from political contact. The Commission was not involved in this decision, and legally was not allowed to discriminate against Austria. The Prime Minister of Portugal, Antonio Guterres in the chair summarised the European position that policies of intolerance and zenophobia were unacceptable in the modern Europe, and that the European sanctions, "represents a symbol and a lesson for the world."

Indeed it included an important message for all Europeans. The member states asserted a right to frustrate the will of the people as indicated by the result of a national election, amounting to support from 27% of the population. This continued even when Haider himself resigned from the party, an event which was judged not to herald any change in its basic philosophy. Undoubtedly this represented an unprecedented interference in domestic politics. The question was whether the EU members had any such right, and how they would decide what was acceptable and what was not in future. This was particularly important considering the future enlargement with former communist countries, with their more volatile domestic politics, and their wider range of parties than found in Western Europe.

The justification found in the Treaty on European Union, Article 6, was that the Union is founded on "the principles of liberty, law, democracy, respect for human rights and fundamental freedoms", and the Treaty actually includes a procedure for suspending the voting rights of national governments held to be guilty of "serious and persistent" breaches. However in this procedure defined in TEU Article 7, there are substantial safeguards requiring initial unanimity, excluding the accused, and approval of both Parliament and the Commission. In this case the 14 were introducing sanctions without any actual policies of the Austrian government being in breach of anything, and completely outside the European system of justice. Thus, this was a clear demonstration that in some circumstances leaders will hold that political imperatives have superior authority to the rule of law of the EU, and they themselves will decide when a particular situation merits such action. This in itself is constitutionally dangerous because these politicians can implement such measures immediately, with neither a check to their possibly arbitrary act, nor any accountability to an external body, and if they so choose, with little thought as to the consequences. It should never be forgotten that use of arbitrary political power, even if initially for benevolent motives, creates precedent, and the potential for future abuse.

From a more practical viewpoint both sides of the dispute were now in trouble. Austria was unlikely to co-operate in the continuing businesses such as enlargement, and resentment of the EU was rising throughout the country, as Austrians saw their closest friends ostracising them. The Austrian Chancellor, Wolfgang Schüssel maintained a calm, philosophical attitude in the face of this national insult and humiliation. Nevertheless he was complaining. "There have been many attempts to unify Europe," he said, "but always in the past by hegemonic powers. For the first time, we're trying to achieve a union through the co-operation of equal partners. That vision is still intact. But we're beginning to have real doubts about its practical realisation. The sanctions were totally undemocratic, illegal and unfair. Of course, I understand there were fears when I invited Jörg Haider's Freedom Party to form a coalition government with us in January. But that should have led to dialogue, not exclusion. Now we must decide what kind of Europe we want: a hegemonic directorate by a few or a balanced partnership between equals?"

Both sides were becoming embarrassed by the issue, and Schüssel accepted a delegation of European "wise men" to inspect Austria's "commitment to common European values, in particular the rights of minorities, refugees and immigrants", and determine the "the evolution of the political nature" of the Freedom Party. A former president of Finland duly reported that the Austrian government was indeed "committed to common European values". Respect for human rights in Austria was "not inferior to that of other EU member states", and that although The Freedom Party was "a right-wing populist party with radical elements [that] exploited xenophobic sentiments in campaigns, its ministers by and large worked according to the government's commitments", even when this meant acting "in contradiction with past FP behaviour." Austria passed their inspection.

The seven month boycott was therefore lifted, accompanied by congratulations that the sanctions had been responsible for keeping the Austrian government on the straight and narrow. However, all the smaller countries must have been alerted to the possibility of future bullying by the EU, a factor which could well have influenced Denmark's rejection of the Euro later the same month. Finally the incident led to an amendment of the Treaty which enabled the Council to act for the EU in future when there was a four-fifths majority, and agreement from the European Parliament only that a "clear risk of a serious breach of Article 6," had been established. Thus any future misbehaviour by national voters could be dealt with on an institutional basis more easily. Also, and as a way of further emphasising the importance of human rights to the EU the summit in Nice also "proclaimed" a new "Charter of Fundamental Rights". However the meeting was unable to agree on the legal and political status of the declaration so this matter was carried forward onto the next IGC agenda.

Nice Treaty

From February to December 2000, the latest Intergovernmental conference was scheduled to decide new additions to the treaties and the next steps in integration. As always new powers were expected to be ceded to the Union, but the main purpose of this conference was to make the changes necessary for enlargement. It was recognised that requiring unanimity in a Union of 27 members was a recipe for paralysis. On the other hand the increasing possibility of being outvoted in an area of real national concern was likely to act as a brake on extending QMV beyond the most innocuous of policy areas, and it is potentially dangerous to force a decision on a member seriously aggrieved at being outvoted. Rising euroscepticism also was causing caution among several member governments, including Germany, and the Commission had neither recovered its former dynamism, nor developed any imaginative proposals.

So the Union appeared destined to become wider, but for the moment, not much deeper. In particular moves to enlarge the EU's competence in areas such as taxation and social security were to be successfully submerged, largely by the British. This was to suit Tony Blair and Robin Cook, always with their eyes on the next election, as they continued a crusade to present the EU as benign, as no longer integrationist and where all members benefit from pooling of national sovereignty. In an address in Warsaw Blair found a new soundbite to summarise the new mood - that Europe was intending to become a "superpower", not a "superstate". Similarly Robin Cook was calling the danger of Britain being absorbed in a superstate "the biggest Euromyth of all", because the people of Europe would never allow it. However at exactly the same time Germany's foreign minister, Joschka Fischer, was suggesting that the EU might benefit from a directly elected president.

So, in this IGC progress outside enlargement issues was soon expected to be very limited, and so the final result was a disappointment to the integrationists. Formal power of veto was actually surrendered to QMV in 31 areas, (out of the remaining 73), but these were successfully presented during the subsequent Commons debate as trivial. From summit to summit and from treaty to treaty the EU always strengthens at the expense of nation states but this time William Hague failed to identify any significant damage from the Nice agreements. Romano Prodi, had since been grumbling about the "intransigence" of countries that refused in Nice to settle matters such as taxation and social regulation by majority voting. France's President Chirac also criticised leaders who had defended their short-term national interest "to the detriment of a long-term vision". Blair though would have remained quite happy to hear gentle criticism from his European colleagues and to earn faint praise from the Eurosceptical press.

However, one new concept was being debated, that of "flexibility". The idea was that some member countries could have a policy area integrated into EU law and EU machinery without all members being obliged to join. Monetary union had been the first example, and now some governments were considering that this might be the best way of progressing with a common defence or foreign policy. However flexibility was a controversial concept since it called into question the very nature of the Union, and the new applicants of Eastern Europe were wary lest they could be conveniently excluded. The treaty requirement introduced in Amsterdam therefore contained three conditions:- the proposed activity would have no effect on the single market; its participants must include a majority of the member states; any other member must remain free to join in at a later stage. The reasoning was that a minority of nations should not be allowed to prevent closer co-operation between other consenting members.

One area where closer co-operation was being actively considered was in defence, where the French had wanted to create an independent European military force. Interestingly it had been Britain's refusal to support a sufficiently strong counterweight to US forces which had caused the collapse of a proposed European Defence Community in the 1950's. It appeared that little had changed in the meantime as Britain was still insisting that NATO remain primarily responsible for European defence, and that any European force would remain subservient. Diplomatic manoeuvring was unable to disguise that this was exactly opposite to French intentions. At Nice, any mention of an "army" was removed from the communiqué, and restricted to discussions involving a "rapid reaction force" authorised to act if NATO were to decline. Thus the French efforts in Nice to separate EU defence from NATO were rebuffed and NATO primacy was maintained.

On the subject of enlargement the main question to be decided was the appointment of Commissioners, and the weight of voting in the new European Council. These questions, together with the perennial question of extending areas decided by QMV were known as the Amsterdam Triangle of issues unresolved at the previous IGC, and were carried forward to the next agenda. Fearful of the Commission becoming unwieldy and of fragmenting the responsibilities of Commissioners had led to a proposal to cap the number to 20, but whereas the large states seemed content to lose their second commissioner, the smaller states were afraid of losing their single allocation. It seems clear that nation states appeared reluctant to accept that Commissioners are in no sense national delegates, and are not supposed to be even influenced by their governments. Real life is likely to be different and the Santer crisis did reveal that an aberrant Commissioner, and therefore theoretically a disobedient one could only be sacked if his national nomination was withdrawn. Real politics prevailed as it was accepted that all members would have a Commissioner, but that the size would eventually be reduced to 20 members.

There is a detectable irony due to the fact that these decisions were taken under the Presidency of France which over the years had not been an enthusiastic supporter of enlargement. French critics had pointed out that it would permanently damage the French vision of the EU as "a French jockey on a German horse." A re-united Germany had already become by far the most powerful nation in Europe and expansion into countries traditionally of "German influence" was arousing France's quiescent suspicion of Germany. There was also the realisation that real reform of the Common Agricultural Policy although so long resisted would become essential. Several candidate countries had large agricultural communities and even in Poland, a quarter of the population still earn their living off the land. It would be impossible to treat these communities as generously as the farmers of France, Germany and the Netherlands had become accustomed.

There was also a fear among some members that regional development funds would necessarily be diverted to Eastern Europe, at their expense. Although the Spanish had managed to delay the switching of resources to poorer new members there is no doubt that this was a factor in Ireland's rejection of the Nice Treaty by 54% of votes in their referendum of June 2001. The turnout had been low, and the polls consistently predicting a vote in favour of Nice may have encouraged a certain complacency among supporters. Even so Europe was surprised. Ireland is one country whose economy has clearly benefited from membership of the EU, and 86% of the population admitted as much. Since it joined with Britain in 1973 the average income of its people had risen from 60% of the EU average to 120%. It had received such generous contributions from EU funds (around €30bn, for a population of 4m), that a possible reduction had been bound to provoke fear and resistance. Once again this result produced a purely theoretical crisis, with the Council deciding that enlargement was actually possible without the Nice Treaty. Accession negotiations were to continue and the Irish government was tasked with obtaining a reversal which they duly produced in a repeat referendum in October, a year later.

Philosophical thoughts about enlargement as described later had been part of the debate during the IGC of 2000, but in December the final decisions were of a far more practical nature and the more fundamental questions regarding integration of new members were postponed to a new IGC agreed for the year 2004. Now, President Chirac held a very long, four day summit where he had to charm, persuade, and then bully his colleagues into reaching firm decisions on hard numbers. Disputes were long and heated with each country trying to balance its own interests with the imperative of reaching an agreement. Notable bitterness came with Germany's insistence that with its greater population it should be entitled to a greater number of Council votes. This was fiercely resisted by the French, with Chirac making a revealing comment that, "After three German invasions of France in the space of 70 years, reconciliation between the two countries was possible, he insisted, only on the basis of absolute parity."

Final results were not obtained until 4am on the last night, but they were sufficient to allow all participants to return home to shout about their own national victories. Tony Blair announced that he had obtained a "Stronger Britain in a Wider Europe." This was a reference to the increased number of Council votes he obtained for Britain but an exaggeration bearing in mind that the total number of votes had increased by a greater proportion. The allocation of these votes and also the number of seats in the European Parliament was regarded as the most crucial issue for the future governance of the Union since all governments were concerned about the balance between the fear of being outvoted and the difficulty in reaching any final decision at all. The Table below shows the final results for the Council and Parliament, but excluding the transitional arrangements.

Two features are apparent from the table, with particular reference to the Council as the main legislative authority of the Union. Firstly it is clear that smaller countries are protected with a greater proportion of the votes than would be justified under a strict ratio of populations. Most people would regard this as fair. Secondly the number of votes required for a measure to be passed will change from the present 62 out of 87, to 258 out of 345. The larger countries, including Britain have 29 or 27 votes each. Therefore any three large countries plus one small one would be sufficient for passing a measure. Recognising that this could lead to dangerous domination by the large states there is a second condition. In order to pass a measure emanating from the Council itself, two-thirds of the member states have to vote in favour of it. (Should the measure have been proposed by the Commission only a simple majority is sufficient). This double majority system although complex does ensure that the need for a high degree of consensus is embedded in the voting system. There is also a third safeguard in that a member state may request verification that a measure was passed by countries representing 62% of Europe's population. If it was passed by a lesser percentage, then the measure is not formally adopted. Thus although the system was roundly criticised as complex, it does appear to provide European nations with real protection against European Union dictatorship.

TABLE 1:

Voting Strength after Enlargement under Treaty of Nice

	POP'N Millions	COUNCIL VOTES	Votes /Million	SEATS in PARL	Votes /Million
GERMANY	82.0	29	0.35	99	1.21
FRANCE	60.4	29	0.48	72	1.19
UK	58.6	29	0.49	72	1.23
ITALY	57.6	29	0.50	72	1.25
SPAIN	39.4	27	0.69	50	1.27
POLAND	38.6	27	0.70	50	1.30
ROMANIA	22.4	14	0.63	33	1.47
N'LANDS	15.8	13	0.82	25	1.58
PORTUGAL	10.8	12	1.11	22	2.04
GREECE	10.5	12	1.14	22	2.10
CZECH R	10.3	12	1.17	20	1.94
BELGIUM	10.2	12	1.18	22	2.16
HUNGARY	10.0	12	1.20	20	2.00
SWEDEN	8.9	10	1.12	18	2.02
AUSTRIA	8.1	10	1.23	17	2.10
BULGARIA	8.0	10	1.25	17	2.13
SLOVAKIA	5.4	7	1.30	13	2.41
DENMARK	5.3	7	1.32	13	2.45
FINLAND	5.1	7	1.37	13	2.55
IRELAND	3.7	7	1.89	12	3.24
LITHUANIA	3.7	7	1.89	12	3.24
LATVIA	2.4	4	1.67	8	3.33
SLOVENIA	2.0	4	2.00	7	3.50
ESTONIA	1.4	4	2.86	6	4.29
CYPRUS	0.6	4	6.25	6	9.38
LUXEMB'G	0.4	4	9.30	6	13.95
MALTA	0.4	3	7.69	5	12.82
TOTAL	482.06	345	0.72	732	1.52

Threshold (Commission Proposal)
  Votes for adoption   258
  Majority Member States   14
  62% of population   297.6

Threshold (Council Proposal)
  Voted for Adoption   258
  Two-Thirds Members   18
  62% of population   297.6

With 27 Members Blocking Minority raised to 91, Maximum Threshold 73.4%.

Chapter 26: Surfing the European Waves

Employment & Social Affairs

By the middle of 2001, as Tony Blair was beginning his second term, his government had built a curious reputation for relying on focus groups to guide policies of presentation, for raising the concept of spin to new levels of sophistication, and for saying only what was necessary to achieve support for his objectives. These were not new concepts in British politics, but the precedence Blair appeared to give to media presentation left him open to criticism that the substance of policies was frequently divorced from its presented form, and that Blair was increasingly acting as a "control freak". In fact this conclusion is contradicted by one of his major achievements, the creation of the Scottish Parliament, and the Welsh Assembly. Similarly in Europe powers had been ceded to the Union. However it is interesting to note that Blair having removed formal British objections to the Social Chapter, immediately campaigned throughout Europe against the bureaucratic policies it was inclined to produce.

At home Blair had also cultivated a reputation as a committed "moderniser". Modernisation in any policy area was presented as inherently beneficial. Energetic activity, reorganisation and change was to be applauded as if damage was an impossible result of reform. Britain required a "modern" health service, a "modern" transport system, even a "modern" constitution. This required, first and foremost, some change, and judging from electoral success most people agreed. Unfortunately resistance to this thinking was more entrenched across the Channel.

As Blair prepared for renewed progress in Europe he was acutely aware that the traditional Franco-German alliance was under unusual strain. The disputes at Nice displayed a French mistrust of Germany which had not been so prominent since President Mitterand had opposed, and even tried hard to prevent German re-unification. Of course policy differences had been frequent since then, but the two leaders had always preferred to resolve matters between themselves prior to Council meetings. For many years this alliance had been in effect the driving force of the European Union but from 2001 onwards the rapidly accelerating pace of integration was due to produce real strains. Both sides had occasionally flirted with Tony Blair but usually with specific policy objectives in mind, and of course Blair needed support for the directions he had been advocating. These personal interactions between the leaders were still an important determinant of EU strategy, in a way which can only be diluted when the Union has 25, 27 or 28 members.

It was clear to all concerned that the Treaty of Nice had represented a mere staging point. A vast range of issues remained which needed resolution with an urgency not seen before. Pressure for action was caused primarily by the political necessity for enlargement, amplified by its shortening timetable. Candidate countries had been pressing for real negotiations and timetable for entry, and the Union could not credibly delay further even though its own structures required prior adjustment. The accession process itself was a complex task as all ten new members had different problems requiring detailed analysis, negotiation and decisions. But this was only a small part of the problem facing the Council. Adoption of timescales certainly improves discipline and focuses participants' minds on their necessary priorities, and this determination was successfully driving enlargement negotiations. But now the Union was being driven by these unmissable targets with the knowledge that many reforms and decisions had to be completed before the new members were admitted, in order to prevent them from being able to change the future direction of the Union. In response to the more fundamental dilemmas an intergovernmental conference had been called, and the Convention on the Future of Europe had been initiated as an essential preparation. However the general business of European integration was continuing with a momentum rapidly increasing for the same reason.

The pressure for rapid results across such a wide range has strained previous alliances and highlighted previously disguised or glossed over philosophical differences. The French historical idea of taming Germany, but of still protecting its own national interests appears more transparent, and less tenable as Germany becomes more powerful economically, and more distant from its history. Germany's natural support of multi-layered government based on a mere extension of its own federation of Länder continued to command popular support, except that voices were now objecting to the amount Germany was paying to European coffers. The small nations remained ambivalent in various degrees, both wishing to increase their influence in the world by using the European stage, and at the same time fearing domination by the larger states appears.

Back in March 2000 Blair had experienced a zenith in his relations with Europe as he won praise and support for his far reaching proposals to liberalise transport, energy and communications, and remove much of the bureaucratic regulation impeding the flexibility of European labour markets. This process was ignored by the French who continued with their social agenda, and obstinately obstructed liberalising moves. For example, in Stockholm, Tony Blair supported by Spain's Jose Maria Aznar complained loudly that Electricité de France (EDF) had invaded their markets with unwelcome takeovers while enjoying monopoly protection at home, at the expense of the French consumer. Prime Minister Jospin defiantly argued that energy supply was a vital public service demanding special treatment, and although he realised he would eventually be forced liberalise France continued to delay as long as possible and in the meantime subsidise and strengthen the company to improve its eventual competitive strength.

Instead, whole new areas of social legislation were introduced. One area bitterly fought and lost by the British concerned worker "information and consultation". Companies operating across European borders with more than 1000 employees had to inform and consult their employees before restructuring or redundancy etc. The British Parliament was approving the legislation to implement this Directive, (Transnational Information and Consultation of Employees Regulations). However at the same time debate in Europe was moving on to extend the scope of the Directive to all EU companies of fifty employees regardless of any cross border activity. Employers, even private employers, would be obliged to provide what they would have regarded as confidential financial information following the model of European "works councils".

In a battle typifying the traditional sequence of dealing with European measures Britain, this time supported by Ireland, protested strongly against these proposals. Negotiators then struggled at every stage to reduce their impact, to obtain concessions, to extract derogations, delays in implementation and finally a long transition period. This was one instance where the European Parliament, whose members were quite familiar with works councils and were more than happy to impose them on Britain, resisted concessions which Britain had obtained at Council level and after discussions with the Commission. Eventually, Britain was simply outvoted so that by 2005 even small employers will find their workers demanding to be given sensitive information about their companies and will be surprised to find that they have the backing of British law.

Employment legislation is one area where European legislation has had considerable effect on Britain. Rights of working people have definitely been improved, and this is frequently sited as a benefit obtained from Europe. After all "social cohesion" and improving worker benefits is an important EU aim. Euro-sceptics however, argue that there never has been a necessity to follow European instructions in improving worker rights, since each country is perfectly capable of deciding on its own level. Moreover the existence of different levels of worker benefits would produce an element of competition to cross border employment, which could actually encourage mobility and create a more dynamic economy.

On the contrary, judges the Commission. Provision of improved worker benefits in one country would place an additional burden on employers which would distort the operation of the single market. Since the improvement of working conditions is an aim of the EU such activities must be harmonised. There is actually a broader policy aspect to this subject. Social benefits undoubtedly impose additional costs not only on individual companies but on the economy as a whole. Logically, additional costs always reduce competitiveness and it therefore becomes a judgement as to how much benefits can be afforded before damage becomes unacceptable. The European answer is to introduce the benefits not at an individual company or at a national level but at a pan-European level. While this might make the whole European economy less competitive, the sheer size of the single market may offer sufficient protection against external competition. This market already offers its citizens a higher standard of living, and additional benefits can readily be built on.

Originally the European doctrine of the free movement of workers defined in the Treaty of Rome, was used to dismantle all barriers in terms of unequal treatment of the nationals from other EU countries, and this was used to harmonise regulations regarding entry and residence rights, eligibility and equality of opportunity in employment, rights to social benefits, recognition of qualifications etc. The measures did not actually produce a large population of cross border workers, because of more personal cultural or linguistic barriers but removal of institutional restrictions was seen as a real benefit by all those inclined to take advantage of them.

The Social Chapter of Maastricht provided for an extension of employment measures. Instead of being designed to create a genuinely free and mobile labour market, measures could now be aimed at directly improving employees rights and benefits. Examples recently seen, both as worker benefits and on the other side of the coin as employer impositions include:- Transfer of Undertakings (Protection of Employment Regulations - TUPE); Working Time Regulations; Maternity and Parental Leave Regulations; Part-Time Workers (Prevention of Less Favourable Treatment) Regulations; Fixed Term Employees (Prevention of Less Favourable Treatment) Regulations.

All such matters could have provoked real controversy in Britain, and were consistently opposed by the weakened Opposition. For generations British politicians have minimised the role of legislation in employment matters. Emphasis had always been given to common law concepts of freedom of contract although safety nets had always been included. An employers common law duty to provide a safe system of work justified whole areas of Health and Safety legislation, the Employment Rights Act had imposed minimum rights and prevented unfair dismissal, and discrimination by sex and race had long been illegal, with the courts themselves were concerned to provide fairness in their interpretation of existing law. Successive governments had also sought to minimise government interference with agreements between employers and employees. The proliferation of regulation emanating from Europe therefore represented a real change in the culture of employment. Perhaps it was just another aspect of modernisation if industrial relations issues were to shift from negotiating tables to employment tribunals.

Of course the government was never slow to point to the benefits it was introducing, and being of Labour persuasion would not have anticipated much difficulty in this area. This has however, led to a remarkably cynical system of claiming credit for the proposals. As one example, which applies to all the measures listed above, it should be noted that the Part-Time Worker Directive was passed in Europe in 1997, and as one of the measures affected by Blair's opt-in to the Social Chapter was made legally binding on Britain in 1998 (Directive 98/23/EC), and had to be implemented by April 2000. In January of 2000 the Secretary of State for Trade and Industry in his press statement, "unveiled" proposals to ensure that part-time employees could no longer be treated as second class citizens. As he stated, "We want to establish a minimum standard of fairness for part timers." The measures, naturally coinciding with those in the Directive were published as part of a "consultation document". This consultation lasted till the end of February and was clearly positive since the relevant regulations were introduced and implemented in April.

Since implementation of measures such as "Works Councils" is not due until 2005 we have yet to hear Ministers extolling the virtues and benefits of the measures they opposed at every possible step in Europe. This is an aspect of political reality which would approach entertainment were it not a serious issue to those concerned. It also raises a question as to how a hypothetical Conservative government would have responded to Britain's obligation to implement the measure to which it was even more fiercely opposed than the actual government. The principle of Parliamentary sovereignty would theoretically allow it to refuse, but the government itself would then be exposed to the type of sanctions imposed by British courts, as described earlier. How far would it dare to escalate such a dispute? It also demonstrates clearly that the benefit of allowing Britain to be outvoted on individual measures lies well beyond the importance of the measures themselves. Tony Blair paid this price simply to increase his overall influence in Europe, and then felt free to campaign against all such measures within Europe. The legacy of this decision will take many years to become fully apparent.

The Blair Government's early progress in Europe was limited as some of the items above indicate. Its influence for example on subjects such as "temporary workers" was simply less than that of European unions who wished to damage job agencies "undermining of real jobs", despite clear evidence that they contributed to job creation. Politicians across Europe continued to argue that the purpose of the EU was to protect Europe's social model from the cold winds of globalisation. The declaration from Lisbon in March 2000 that the EU would become the "most competitive and dynamic knowledge-based economy in the world by 2010" was not being supported by action. The economy, which had been growing at a slower rate than America's was continuing to do so, and the introduction of the Euro was not delivering the spurt to growth that its supporters had predicted. On the contrary the biggest part of the economy in Germany was encountering increasing difficulty. Of course flexible labour markets are only one element of economic success, but adverse economic forces were gradually making Blair's voice more difficult to ignore.

So while the British inspired Lisbon, flexible market declaration was soon countered by a declaration in Nice calling for emphasis on countering poverty and social exclusion, Blair persisting in ensuring that Spring Council meetings continued to discuss his liberalising agenda. A strategy, entitled the "Luxembourg process" appeared dedicated to meet the objective of high-level employment. Blair succeeded in incorporating three "pillars" for activity – Improvement of Employability; Development of Entrepreneurship; and Strengthening of Adaptability. Meanwhile his opponents, largely French, had included the fourth – Strengthening measures towards equality. Signs of German impatience with French attitudes led to more friendly relations between Blair and Schröder during 2002, but philosophical differences prevented convergence in most policy areas. So, despite more prominent meetings with both Schröder and Chirac, Blair's agenda made little progress during the year.

The European economy however, was continuing to exert pressure, particularly in Germany and this produced an unexpected, and rare display of unity. Blair, Schröder and Chirac, signed a joint letter to the Greek Presidency in preparation for the spring summit. Referring to the Lisbon initiatives it commented that, "When taking political decisions we have to remember that European industry has to hold its own in global competition. It cannot be used as a laboratory for regulatory experiments which increase costs or burdens on employers." It advocated industry-friendly regulatory conditions which can make a major contribution to increasing employment opportunities. It recommended a review of existing barriers and the acceptance of proposals for simplifying and reducing the burden on business without delay, while in future avoiding new restrictions which might place extra burdens on our companies that would impair their international competitiveness. This indicates a remarkable swing in the pendulum, which if it lasts long enough to produce action, will add considerable credence to British insistence that the tide of excessive regulation is turning.

Enlargement – of the Budget

Other areas have not progressed so smoothly. Bitter personal rows between the leaders have erupted on one of the most sensitive subjects – money. At home Schröder was frequently under pressure because of the high German contributions to the EU budget. One target for German wrath was the British rebate which had survived since the days of the Thatcher handbag. Schröder had argued forcibly that this had become an anachronism that should be eliminated. Blair, not quite ready for such a modernisation brusquely rejected any such suggestion. In fact the rebate is calculated in an unbelievably complex formula separating the value of the rebate, and its distribution among the member states who effectively pay for it by a direct increase in their own share of the costs. In this dispute the Germans followed by the Dutch, the Austrians and the Swedes decided to reduce their contribution to the rebate to 25% of its original level. This did not actually change the rebate itself, so paradoxically the French became the largest contributors to the British rebate, currently worth about €5bn.

Total annual expenditure of the EU amounts to approximately €100bn (2002), and is expected to increase to €110bn in 2006 owing to enlargement. However the largest proportion goes towards agricultural support, (€46bn in 2002). Therefore arguments about costs are immediately associated with agricultural reform. For many years successive British governments have pressed for reform of the Common Agricultural Policy, and not only on grounds of cost. Its original idea was strategic, in that Europe should be entirely self sufficient in food production, but this objective was achieved very quickly. Now the CAP consumes half the budget although farmers account for less than 5% of the workforce, it increases European food prices by 15-20% to levels well above world prices, it produces surplus products which have often been exported (with more subsidies), and it has even failed to protect income of small farmers who have been driven off the land and been replaced by large agricultural businesses even though 35% of their income was by subsidy. It had become hugely political in nature, explaining how the Mediterranean countries of Spain, Greece, Italy and Portugal had managed to increase subsidies just for olive growing to reach 5.5% of the entire agricultural budget. So many olive trees were planted inappropriately that in several areas of Spain the EU had to fund environmental project to repair the damage.

France is usually regarded as the main culprit since their government has been extraordinarily unwilling to confront the volatile and sometimes violent French farming community. Their politicians have always done well in European meetings by competing to sound the most farmer-friendly. However the table below shows that France remains a nett contributor to the total EU budget, and it clearly sees no interest in reducing the contributions it receives. France even justifies the CAP on the grounds that it remains affordable, (European families now spend less than 16% of their own budgets on food), and other advanced countries, particularly USA, also subsidise food production. Besides, farming is an integral part of a nation's culture and cannot be compared directly to industrial production. In any event France has consistently and insistently refused any attempts to reform the policy. As late as 1999 when the budget structure was negotiated at the summit in Berlin, the French conceded willingness to discuss reform, but only after 2006. The only achievement from these talks, trumpeted in advance as reform known as "Agenda 2000" was that the total cost of direct subsidies was capped (at €44bn). Everything else will wait until 2006

It was widely recognised that reform would become a practical necessity as enlargement progressed. Moreover it was important to resolve the issue urgently because with 14% of the population of the next ten members dependent on agriculture, and 20% of Poland's population alone, reform would become much more difficult if new members were involved in the decision, particularly since the majority of them would be seeking to maximise agricultural subsidies rather than reduce them. The Commission itself had realised that the existing scheme would bankrupt the EU if applied under existing rules to the new members, and had campaigned for an alternative. Firstly it proposed that new members would initially get only one quarter of the level of subsidy applicable to existing members, with a transition period. This was dangerous in that it was likely to fuel the opposition forces within the candidate states, but it was clearly a convenient solution for existing members. But more importantly it proposed a gradual "decoupling" of expenditure from production, re-directing it to rural development and environmental projects.

There is also a wider aspect connected with international talks at the World Trade Organisation which is working towards the elimination of all export subsidies in farming. The EU needs to strengthen its position in these talks because although the EU has responded by given free access to the world's 49 poorest countries, its agricultural policy generally denies access to European markets by third world countries. Europe's position is actually more serious because apart from direct agricultural subsidies there are indirect benefits from the artificially maintained price levels, and in some countries favourable taxation regimes. The overall position did not appear sustainable.

The most bitter incident occurred at the summit in October 2002 which was due to resolve the issue. Tony Blair had, as usual been conducting a skilful and patient campaign of lobbying and consultation among all the member states and this time was

TABLE 2:

Budget Contributions by Member State, Year 2000

Member State	Nett Contribution		Gross Contribution
	€ Billions	% of GNP	% of Total
Germany	+ 9.27	+ 0.47	24.4
UK	+ 3.77	+ 0.25	14.3
Netherlands	+ 1.74	+ 0.44	6.50
France	+ 1.42	+ 0.10	16.7
Sweden	+ 1.18	+ 0.50	2.70
Austria	+ 0.54	+ 0.27	2.50
Belgium	+ 0.33	+ 0.13	4.00
Luxembourg	+ 0.06	+ 0.35	0.20
Denmark	- 0.17	- 0.10	2.00
Finland	- 0.22	- 0.17	1.50
Italy	- 0.71	- 0.06	13.0
Ireland	- 1.67	- 1.83	1.40
Portugal	- 2.11	- 1.93	1.50
Greece	- 4.37	- 3.61	1.60
Spain	- 5.06	- 0.86	7.70

expecting real progress. The French had already gained sufficient support in the Council of Agricultural Ministers to block the Commissions decoupling proposals and were proving as resistant as usual. But, to Blair's subsequent fury President Chirac arranged a private meeting with Chancellor Schröder and agreed to withdraw his objection to more rapid enlargement, in exchange for German backing regarding CAP finance. The total agricultural budget would actually rise by 1% per year from 2006 to 2013. Later in the meeting though the German delegation, realising that Schröder had moved too far, backed Britain, the Netherlands, Italy, Sweden, Denmark and even Belgium that the Commission review of decoupling would be implemented after 2004. More serious was the ferocity of Blair's criticism of Chirac. He attacked the deal made as making it impossible for the Council to conduct its business in a rational manner and said that declaring concern for African poverty while refusing to reform the CAP as a barrier to their exports was likely to strike the world as "rank hypocrisy". Chirac was so seriously offended, "never having been spoken to so rudely," that he immediately cancelled the next Anglo-French summit meeting.

Blair had been persistently and consistently working to improve Britain's influence in Europe. He was gradually enjoying some important successes, and often gained important support for many of his ideas. However, politicians are never able to please all of their opponents all of the time and he has never escaped from the necessity of making concessions and compromises. Britain's successes have consistently amounted to minimising its concessions, and Blair for all his skilful and patient diplomacy has not been able to break out of this spiral. Earlier, in common with his predecessors he had spoken of leadership in Europe only to find that leadership is not a viable concept in a culture of consensus. In many ways Blair did succeed in putting Britain at the heart of Europe, and although this has usually led to more harmony, in the opinion of the author, the ultimate result has been the same.

Chapter P: Enlargement

Politics of the Club

Following the collapse of the Berlin Wall in 1989 Germany immediately moved towards re-unification. Despite numerous warnings about its impracticality, or impossibility, the German government with popular support pressed on with principled determination. All the massive differences in industrial and structural organisation simply had to be eliminated at whatever cost. The German people were to be united again. Just ten years later there is little doubt that this scheme proved a remarkably successful exercise in integration although it had been achieved at an enormous cost, much greater than anticipated, and with its own lasting implications. Nevertheless the united Germany has emerged with new strength, new pride and new confidence.

Other countries under Soviet domination were not so lucky. Really, they were on their own. They had achieved their independence but their economies were hardly strong enough to withstand sudden exposure to international market forces. All were involved in amazing industrial reconstruction as inefficient, and artificially maintained state owned enterprises were closed, restructured and privatised. At various rates all achieved a remarkable transformation. Of course, at the same time each one needed to rebuild its political system. In many countries entrenched communists were hard to dislodge, and new democratic forces were slow to coalesce into political parties with a recognisable identity. Nevertheless all moved rapidly in these directions.

The newly established states all needed trade, as well as investment and preferably also assistance and it was quite natural for them to look to their neighbours in Europe for all of these. At the same time they saw a longer term vision of equality with the countries of western Europe and realised that this would mean eventual membership of the EU. The same idea, circulating the capitals of the EU, was far from universally acclaimed. From a principled viewpoint, the idea of a united Europe expanding to embrace all newcomers was difficult to oppose. Many thought that the same determination shown by the Germans in re-unification should be applied, even if perhaps more gradually, to the new neighbours. Others almost gasped at the practical, the political and the economic implications. Did Europe really have such a responsibility? In any event it was an idea of profound importance to both sides of the continent.

This debate began, and was to last many years. European countries were already becoming the most important trading partners for the candidate countries so the effects on equalising tariffs had to be considered. Most economists concluded that Eastern Europe would benefit from the opening markets. However there was also a belief that existing EU members would have little to gain from increased trade, and this would be counterbalanced by increased budgetary costs. The costs of an expanded agricultural policy were potentially enormous, in the absence of reform, and some of the poorer members were wary of a shift in resources for regional aid towards the east. Generally though, it became accepted that the economic aspects were not critical. Overall effects were likely to be limited, and the risks were entirely manageable. The actual price of a stable and prosperous Europe would be small. Therefore on the EU side the subject would be decided largely on grounds much larger than the "counting house."

In some quarters the idea of incorporating the newly independent countries into an emerging superstate encouraged, not least in those countries concerned, a comparison with the former Comecon economic bloc, where all means of production had been subject to an oppressive regime of central planning and control. For newly liberated countries to exchange this system for one of world of shared sovereignties and bureaucratic harmonisation had been compared to jumping, "out of the fire and into the frying pan." It is true that in both cases there was a common objective of protecting the economy from external forces, and there was a definite submission to the regulation of central and supernational authority, enforceable by sanctions. But while critics might argue that less regulation than is found in Europe is required to optimise economic progress, the countries of Eastern Europe needed access to nearby European markets as they found them. They therefore had powerful economic reasons for joining the "Common Market", just as Britain had in its day. But, whereas Britain had judged that the political price was worth paying, to much of Eastern Europe the political adjustment was also a benefit. Political independence in an economically dependent country is an illusion. Joining a collective decision making process is an advantage when for one reason or another you are obliged to conform to its results.

Many of those westerners fearful of the gradual submergence of their own national identities by the growing European superstate wondered from a different angle why countries so recently liberated from oppressive regimes, amid scenes of such emotion and national celebration were suddenly prepared to subject themselves to another empire whatever the financial benefit. Was independence, so longed for over many years really to be given up so readily? What had happened to the national pride that had suddenly become so prominent?

The fact was that EU membership was simply not recognised in such terms at all. The peoples of the former communist bloc were not at all concerned about losing their national identity. In fact many almost craved an *additional* European identity. They did not see this as an alternative or as a threat to their own, but as a symbol of international respectability among countries previously envied for their prosperity and stability. Their peoples had lived for half a century in one of the world's most oppressive political systems and were not afraid of an EU political structure operating by concensus. Their national identities had proudly survived concerted and often ruthless efforts by central authorities to "emphasise" the common culture of their pluralist society, and destroy any remnants of "divisive" nationalist sympathies. These attempts had completely failed to eliminate their people's sense of nationhood. Each country retained its own awareness and characteristics, and had now become free to celebrate its own fascinating history with pride and with a determination to face the future with a new political and economic system. A uniform drabness of surroundings, and a legacy of mismanagement and failure merely disguised the latent dynamism and enthusiasm which freedom and enterprise was releasing. Now, as a climax to national ambitions unimaginable just ten years previously, their countries were to be accepted, not as pitied ex-communist, charitable case neighbours, but as fully participating members of, and partners in a continent-wide and prosperous federation. Democracy would be entrenched and prosperity would be assured, as would a real voice in the future of Europe. This was something the smaller countries especially had never experienced. Countries such as Malta, Estonia, or Slovenia may have been proud sovereign nations but they had never been able to prevent their larger neighbours do anything.

More generally threats to national cultures from the global economy, from internationalised media and from improved communications appear more serious to many observers. In France in particular, the pervasive influence of American society and the use of the English language worldwide have regularly been regarded as assaults on French culture. Despite this most ordinary people would regard such cultural influences as liberating rather than oppressive. However, the important point is that cultural convergence if it really is happening is an international rather than a European phenomenon and this still has a negligible effect on how people see themselves.

This view of the resilience of identity seems eminently reasonable, especially when considering how difficult it would be to argue that the French for example, have lost any of their national identity as a result of their membership of the EU. Similarly it cannot be reasonably argued that Scotland has lost any of its identity following its 300 year union with England and Wales. National identity may well evolve and adapt, but it appears largely resistance to political structures. Thus attempts to create a European identity are unlikely to have much effect, even by teaching of a harmonised European history to the young. People may be influenced into believing in the benefits of the EU, and persuaded to support many of its measures but any attempt to create a European identity will be seen as artificial for the foreseeable future. If accepted, this is an important conclusion, because where there is no identity there is also no loyalty. People will continue to be loyal to their nation states.

Viewed from the EU side, the decision was still one of profound importance. Joschka Fischer, Germany's foreign minister of some years later, explained in an important speech on the future of Europe, "Following the collapse of the Soviet empire, the EU had to open up to the east, otherwise the very idea of European integration would have undermined itself and eventually self-destructed... An EU restricted to Western Europe would forever have had to deal with a divided system in Europe: in Western Europe integration, in Eastern Europe the old system of balance of power with the permanent danger of nationalist ideologies and confrontations... In the long term this would make Europe a continent of uncertainty, and in the medium term these traditional lines of conflict would shift from Eastern Europe into the EU again. If that happened, Germany in particular would be the big loser." Continental stability could only result from unity.

Of course there were opponents to this philosophical conclusion, and most of them were too polite to point out other historical figures who had adopted the same reasoning. It is an insult to the civilised nations of Europe to suggest that they cannot live peacefully together. Submission to a central authority is not the only way of achieving peaceful co-existence. Besides, centralisation can create feelings of remoteness, and even oppression which itself encourages extremist opposition. The USSR itself proved that cohesion cannot be enforced in areas of historical diversity. The democratic structures now in place across Europe, together with a shared interest of continuing prosperity were quite sufficient to ensure continuing development and harmonious co-operation. Finally, a shift in EU borders into the Balkans or even as Iraq if Turkey ever joined, does not remove a necessity to respect neighbours, it merely changes the nations concerned, and moves divisions eastwards.

The issue was soon discussed seriously at the highest levels of the EU. It would seem logical that leaders of such a union would follow the former point of view rather than the latter. Historically they were aware of the success in admitting Spain. Portugal and Greece. This had rapidly succeeded politically in entrenching democracy in countries with a noted tendency towards autocratic government, and economically in rapidly improving the standards of living of the people. This provided a benefit to the whole of Europe. The present issue was on a larger scale, but in principle provided the same opportunity. Consequently at the Copenhagen summit in 1993 EU leaders agreed on the criteria for future membership. A candidate country must have achieved stability of institutions guaranteeing democracy, the rule of law, human rights and respect for and protection of minorities; the existence of a functioning market economy as well as the capacity to cope with the competitive pressures and market forces within the Union; an the ability to take on the obligations of membership including those aims of political, economic and monetary union.

Joining the Club

The European Commission sent analysts to study the economies involved, and discussions proceeded even while the EU was concerned with such matters as economic and monetary union, and the eastern Europeans were pushing forward with their political and structural reforms. At least the EU was providing them with an overall target and a standard model to guide their activities. More practical issues were studied. For example, how this further integration could be achieved without a risk of destabilising the existing union; whether free movement of labour would result in mass emigration from poorer regions of eastern Europe, and how the decision making mechanisms could adapt to larger numbers of Member States without grinding to a halt in acrimonious dispute, and how much would it really cost?

These were all real fears to be considered since this drastic expansion would inevitably transform the EU. The enlarged EU would cover an area some 30% larger, and would have a population some 25% larger. But, the joining economies were so weak that overall GDP would only rise by around 5%, and the average per capita income would actually fall by around 15%. Latvia for example has a per capita GDP only 27% of the EU average. There were also practical concerns about decision making within a group of twenty five, and the anticipated strain on the already struggling translation system. There was clearly a serious task being undertaken.

In an effort to protect the stability of the EU in the face of such challenges, reforms were proposed as an urgent necessity. The first was the reform of the Common Agricultural Policy to maintain some balance as agricultural intensive economies such as Poland were joining. Of course this would need to be coupled with budgetary reform, and as described earlier, it was this aspect which prompted France to delay implementing any such measures until 2006 to the dismay and annoyance of many members. The second issue concerned the fear that the continuing requirement for unanimity would prevent any future measures being approved in an enlarged union. The Union would become paralysed without a thorough reform of the decision making machinery. Euro-sceptics no doubt groaned at this new excuse for expanding European power over nation states, while even supporters of integration were worried that further deepening of the union could not be achieved while the union was concentrating on widening. Nevertheless, most of the issues raised by this fear were addressed by the haggling leading to the Treaty of Amsterdam. The politicians decided that the reforms agreed would enable an enlarged Union to function effectively.

Despite these difficulties the political decision had been taken and the process commenced. By 1997 six nations had opened formal discussions: Poland, the Czech Republic, Hungary, Estonia, Slovenia, and Cyprus; followed two years later by Bulgaria, Romania, Latvia, Lithuania, Malta, and the Slovak Republic. Turkey had also applied but was being kept apart. Negotiations, as with the British experience, involved discussion on the transition periods necessary for full acceptance of the acquis communitaire. By now this represented some 80,000 pages, divided for convenience into 31 chapters. Each chapter had to be "closed" by passing the necessary laws locally.

Following a common strategy of the EU, one early decision was the target date for accession. This would be 1st May, 2004, in time to ensure participation for all the new members in the 2004 elections for the European Parliament. Working backwards, the target for agreement was set at and was indeed met in December 2002, when the doors to the EU opened at the summit meeting, again in Copenhagen. All but Romania, Bulgaria and Turkey were being accepted. "Justice has been done," declared the Latvian President. "History begins again today, after an interruption of 60 years," commented the Hungarians.

Romania and Bulgaria were certainly disappointed, but there seems little doubt that they will be ready in two or three years, and the countries have appeared resigned to this result. The application of Turkey was an altogether different matter. The fact that Turkey is a Moslem country has alarmed many leaders of Europe, despite their insistence internally on the prohibition of religious discrimination. The geographic location has also introduced fundamental doubts. Upsetting a delicate political balance in favour of Turkish membership but not yet, the head of the Convention on the Future of Europe created a diplomatic storm. Giscard d'Estaing, described Turkey as an asiatic nation that should never be allowed to join the European Union. He suggested that allowing in 70 million Turkish Moslems would be "the death of the European Union", and its burgeoning population could make the largest nation in the EU.

Possible Turkish membership is also connected with the situation in Cyprus, which remains divided by military presence of some 30,000 Turkish troops. Recently, powerful efforts have been made to negotiate re-unification of the island, notably by the United Nations. A last minute deal was expected but the Turkish Cypriot leader Rauf Denktash refused to compromise, to the dismay of Turkey which saw its own prospects of joining the EU severely damaged. However, in the absence of trust between the Greek and Turkish communities there seems little prospect of agreement in the foreseeable future. It wasn't diplomatically helpful that during negotiations concerning the accession of Cyprus, Greece had exploited its membership of the EU in support of its close interest. It once exerted pressure by threatening to veto the entire process of expansion if Cyprus was not re-united as well as admitted to the Union, an objective shared by many Member States. This Greek threat was withdrawn after suitable persuasion but there is little doubt that Greece would veto the accession of Turkey before the problem was resolved. The eventual decision to admit a divided Cyprus was controversial to say the least, partly made in the knowledge that the Greek parliament was likely to prevent ratification otherwise.

Although the important decisions had been taken in December 2002, there were several issues outstanding. The details for the individual states had been largely settled in the series of bilateral negotiations resulting in a variety of transition periods lasting up to seven years, but with most chapters of the acquis fully operational by 2007. There was a last minute dispute with the European Parliament which had objected to an unexpected budgetary "adjustment" being added to the whole deal, but Parliament decided not to destroy the whole process. Therefore on 16th April, in Athens the chosen ten nations signed the Treaty of Accession. Celebrations were seriously dampened by the aftermath of the divisions caused by the Iraq war, and Presiden Chirac's rebuke to new members who had supported the coalition were fresh in all minds. The process of enlargement itself though had to continue unaffected.

Preoccupation with the rift between Britain and both France and Germany, meant that a highly significant point made by President Chirac in his allocated three-minute address was hardly noticed. He remarked that it was important that Europe not lose its vitality, and that this could not be achieved "unless a core of highly integrated states was able to press ahead without the laggards." This is an important restatement of the concept of "flexibility" within the Union, ensuring that progress will not be held back either by difficulties of dealing with the widely different economies and fragile institutions of the new members, or by dissenting older members, presumably such as Britain. It also reflects a new confidence in the traditional Franco-German alliance within the EU. This is important because while the architects of European Union may not have know exactly what "ever closer union" meant, they were certain that it should apply to everybody. This is certain to become a critical issue as the IGC of 2004 nears its completion.

Following the signing of the Treaty all candidate countries need to ratify the treaty in accordance with their individual constitutions. This part of the process has already begun. Malta was first in March 2003, but this resulted in just a narrow vote in favour of the EU which was contested by the opposition. The country's final position was not resolved until a general election in April returned the Pro-European government. Two other referenda were more decisive. People in Slovenia voted in favour by a remarkable 89%, while the Hungarians voted by 83%. Turnout may have been lower than expected at 45%, but the decision was indisputable. Then in May, the Lithuanians, the first of the three Baltic States to vote were 90% in favour with a 63% turnout. In Slovakia there was a serious fear that turnout would not reach the 50% turnout required for legality. In the event 52% turned out and of these 92.4% voted in favour of the EU. Poland and the Czech Republic are due in June, Estonia and Latvia in September.

The final step will be joining as full members of the Union in May 2004, and then will begin the agreed but continuous process of transition with regard to the detailed measures. One such measure will be the joining of the single currency. For the new members there is no possibility of an opt-out in British or Danish fashion. However first must be completed the process of convergence, and specifically with the Maastricht requirements to reach a budget deficit below 3% of GDP, and to meet the target of government indebtedness below 60%. Moreover this must be achieved despite the unpredictable costs of meeting the EU social and environmental regulations. In fact the economies of Eastern Europe are already doing well with free trade with the EU already in force, (except in agriculture), and growth is comfortably faster then the EU average. Foreign investment has been pouring in anticipation of membership. Many countries compare favourably with the situation encountered by Italy, Spain or Greece before they committed themselves to join. There remain though important differences, such as stubbornly high unemployment in Poland. But, despite the challenge of restricting monetary policy without damaging prospects for growth most new members are expecting to be within the Euro zone by 2007.

Two uncertainties remain in this respect. The first is whether the condition for a Euro candidate to spend two preparatory years in an Exchange Rate Mechanism will really be imposed. The attendant uncertainty and risk of operating a fixed exchange rate (within 15%) while creating an opportunity for currency speculators is well known. If the final result is to be guaranteed by the EU, there would appear little benefit in taking this chance, and making new members temporarily vulnerable. In any event there are likely to be substantial changes in capital inflows which themselves would create an exchange rate stability. Some commentators suggested a solution of parallel currencies whereby the euro would use would be encouraged without officially becoming a national currency. In addition the guidelines themselves may be under question. These were certainly fudged for political reasons for some of the original members, and now several of these are not observing the conditions of the Growth and

Stability Pact. If these were abandoned, or even quietly ignored, it would be difficult to insist on their observance by new members. Finally there is the question of the decisions the new members will take regarding the management of their own economies. When their positions are secure within the Union they could easily decide that economic growth and increasing living standards are more important than early progress towards adopting the Euro. Closing the gap in standard of living is after all the real incentive for joining the EU.

Thus, in many ways the enlargement process now really beginning is unsatisfactory. The tasks of adapting by the new members remain enormous despite the impressive progress already achieved. Pessimists argue that many of the commitments will prove impossible to fulfil, while the EU itself has delayed the reforms previously regarded as essential to accommodate the internal changes. Problems stemming from the EU's stated rigidity and the determination of the candidates to join at any agreed cost are yet to materialise. However these practical and economic considerations are secondary to a moral and political imperative. A truly historic step in European unity has been taken.

Chapter 27: Rising Tides

Defence and Foreign Policy

Lord Denning's comment about the rising tides of European Law had been a cry to alert the judiciary to its new role. His view of sovereignty however was not affected. The role of the judiciary was simply to uphold and interpret the law as passed by Parliament, and Parliament had delegated legislative authority to the European Community in particular areas. The supremacy of European law and the relentless growth of those areas was a matter for Parliament. Parliamentary control of ministerial actions, or the lack of it, was not a matter for the judiciary. Judges throughout Europe agreed. Increasingly though Ministers must have noticed that after agreeing measures in principle all control was immediately ceded to the supra-national EC machinery, and national governments' influence was permanently removed. All they could do was move onto the next subject, and repeat the process. Ministers from most of the Member States understood and supported this as stepping towards federalism. However government was not only a matter of law and at the time of the Maastricht Treaty politicians throughout Europe, even those dreaming of building a federal state, were reluctant to share their powers in some areas. Consequently the compromise structure of the two intergovernmental pillars was inventive. Foreign affairs, defence, justice and security policies would continue to be decided by national governments and their ministers, acting in a consensus where this was practical.

The separate inter-governmental nature of these pillars did not make co-operation any easier, since the areas concerned are those most jealously guarded attributes of the national governments, who often have entirely different ways of analysing the situations and of viewing their own interests. Sometimes, for example with the German recognition of Croatia, policies seem almost as a national statement proclaiming a nation's individuality. It is not surprising that many of the areas of dispute among the European partners today, arise from many years of divergent thinking, and it is surely significant that few of them can be analysed without discussing the French position. Nevertheless, even British supporters of a common approach maintain that when reaching sufficient maturity such co-operation will allow Britain to magnify and project its power and influence in the world. It is damaging to concentrate public attention on these intergovernmental disputes as this obscures a vital national interest and detracts from efforts aimed at strengthening Britain.

In no area was discrepancy more apparent than with the subject of defence, which was sensitive both to countries with a tendency to support the US such as Britain, to those with a fierce sense of independence such as France, and to those led by Ireland which have a fierce attachment to "neutrality." Original ideas for a European Defence Force failed as long ago as the 1950's when the French couldn't bring themselves to trust German forces. Similar thinking occurred in 1966 when the French pulled out of NATO's military structure, resentful of American hegemony. Recently again, as Europe discussed the formation of a "Rapid Reaction Force," serious dispute arose as to whether the organisation, never to be thought of as a European Army, was within NATO or not. Britain has consistently supported NATO and was horrified by French suggestions that it might operate independently of any USA involvement or consultation. In the French view, it was European, and that was all, and for a long time positions were entirely contradictory. The decision had been taken in 1999 in Cologne, that the EU would develop a means of reacting jointly in international crises. "The Union must have the capacity for autonomous action, backed up by credible military forces, the means to decide to use them, and a readiness to do so, in order to respond to international crises without prejudice to actions by NATO". Activities would include humanitarian and rescue tasks, peacekeeping tasks and combat-force tasks in crisis management, including peacemaking, when NATO itself was not intending any action. It was agreed that a capability of deploying within 60 days, a force of 60,000 personnel for up to one year. It was emphasised that this did not constitute a European army since deployment of national troops would remain a national decision.

This was part of the European Security and Defence Policy (ESDP) which was to have its own permanent political and military structure. However the control of this organisation remained intergovernmental, ie. under the auspices of the European Council. The Secretary-General of the Council was to include the role of High Representative for the Common Foreign and Security Policy (CFSP). The complementary second wing, of the ESDP, agreed in Gothenburg in 2001, is a civilian force to deal with four other areas of crisis management - police, strengthening of the rule of law, strengthening civilian administration and civil protection. Accordingly this was to comprise 5,000 policemen of which 1,000 should be available for deployment after 30 days notice; up to 200 judges, prosecutors etc.; civilian administrators able to supervise elections or manage public services and utilities. Finally, under civil protection the EU provide assistance in humanitarian or emergency actions. The EU will be capable of providing two to three assessment teams within three to seven hours consisting of ten experts, as well as intervention teams consisting of 2,000 people. All these resources are meagre compared with superpower might, but can nevertheless serve as an important contribution to world peace as their proponents intend. The US has also been eager for Europe to accept a greater share of the burdens for defending Europe and as a result the first military force to operate under an EU flag has taken over peacekeeping responsibilities in Macedonia, and it plans to undertake the larger role of peacekeeping in Bosnia by the end of 2003.

Military and civilian forces as described above are clearly important tools of foreign policy, and co-ordination in this area this has proved altogether more problematical. The EU's representative for CFSP, Javier Solana, is certainly a well qualified "personality with a strong political profile" as required by the Treaty. He was former head of NATO, and former Spanish Foreign Minister. He is also the Secretary-General of the Western European Union. His objective was to carve out an EU identity on the world stage, and proceeded to do so with a combination of systematic growth, and targeted activity. On the former aspect he used the dedicated Policy Unit to analyse developments, provide assessments of Union interests, and prepare policy options for decision by Council. Emphasising the national nature of the CFSP, it is important to note that the High Representative effectively reports to the President of the Council, that currently the policy is operated through the embassies of the country currently holding the Presidency and that the policy is determined by solely by the Council. The mechanism is that the Council agrees common strategies on a particular subject which then guide the activities both of Union institutions and Member States.

Of course the EU progresses by the accumulation of its decisions, but it develops by introducing new areas of competence, and achieves this by defining and giving a separate life to independent decision making processes applicable to that new area. These are invariably complex as they deriving from divergent interests and complex interactions of 15 members often insisting on specific safeguards. Foreign Policy, viewed as at the heart of the identity of a sovereign state, was particularly sensitive. It has rarely been of much concern to the man in the boulevard, but it is central to the image a government wishes to project across the world. Thus the first safeguard agreed with little difficulty was that CFSP would remain intergovernmental. The European Council would determine a common strategy by unanimity. Only following could common positions would be decided by QMV at Council of Ministers level. There are two limitations to the QMV requirement. Firstly decisions with a military or defence still require unanimity, and secondly an objecting member, citing a compelling national interest may refer the issue to the European Council for the Heads of Government to resolve on the basis of unanimity, (the "emergency brake" procedure). Options then exist for making this decision easier to achieve.

Next some counterbalancing limitations on the requirement of unanimity were agreed, in order to prevent a single member from blocking a particular action. Firstly a Member State may make a "Constructive abstention". While formally abstaining from the vote it may attach a declaration to the decision which acknowledges that the decision is binding on the Union, but that it is itself exempt from applying it. It should be noted that from the constitutional viewpoint "binding" in this context does not mean legally binding, as EC decisions are, but is equivalent to an international agreement made by the executive arm of the government. Thus the Foreign Secretary would be bound to use the resources of the Foreign Office in furtherance of the agreed policy. The second limitation to unanimity is that the decision to refer the matter to the European Council should be taken by "reinforced" QMV requiring 62 votes in favour cast by at least 10 members. Finally the process of "enhanced co-operation" defined in the Treaty of Nice may be used. Where consensus cannot be achieved, at least eight Member States can join together only to implement a joint CFSP common position.

To date common strategies have been approved on Russia, Ukraine, Mediterranean countries, and the Middle East. These areas, excepting the last, were relatively uncontroversial but the Middle East policy which, in the interests of peace, provided greater support to the Palestinian Authority of Yasser Arafat than previously contemplated at least produced a distinctive EU policy. In fact the EU constitutes the largest source of funding to Arafat's Authority, and this incurred anger from the US, and serious questioning in Britain, not least from Parliamentary committees sensing a significant change in Britain's stated, mildly pro-Israel policy. Certainly it would have surprised Parliament if the British Foreign Secretary had announced financial aid to the Palestinian Authority. Why then, asked MP's, were we doing this indirectly? One predictable result was that Israel was incensed and retaliated by humiliating a subsequent EU mission by refusing to meet them.

This example illustrates a number of important points about the role of the EU in the world. Firstly diplomacy alone is insufficient. Stalin's famous quotation after being told of Vatican disapproval of his policies still applies even in today's supposedly civilized world. "And how many troops does the pope have?" he asked. Foreign policy without military or financial resources to deploy in support remains empty, and this is the main reason for nations wishing to develop a joint EU Policy. No individual members have sufficient power to influence events in most of the world, while the combined force of the EU could in theory rival that of the US. This would increase the influence even of the smallest EU members. However, the national leaders, usually seeing themselves as international statesmen are unlikely to yield any positions of influence which they can achieve, to an EU representative. They all need their world stage and their international prestige. Hence we see the successful adoption of the unglamorous and uncontroversial areas as EU policies. However, we all know that EU policies grow, and gradually the freedom of action of Member States must necessarily decline as areas of common strategy develop, and are never returned to Member States.

Secondly, where military involvement is inappropriate other levers to diplomacy are required and here the European Commission has gained a formal role. The Vice-President of the Commissioner, Chris Patten, the former governor of Hong Kong, has overall responsibility for the Community's External Relations activities. The breadth of this brief is described by the Commissioner's list of the areas it covers: -trade policy; associate countries and overseas territories; relations with other international organisations; research and technical development; environment policy; education; vocational training and youth; culture; public health; trans-European networks; economic and monetary union and, finally, development co-operation. In some areas, notably trade, the Commission negotiates on behalf of the entire EC, which has the legal personality sufficient to bind members under international law. For example in negotiations with the World Trade Organisation the Commissioner Pascal Lamy is the nominated representative and agreements reached are legally binding on all Member States. This is why so many areas of business for example restrictions relating to competition, and international takeovers, or an open-skies policy outlawing agreements with airlines at a national level are now all taken in Brussels.

The extent of this power explains why member states with a high international profile, mainly Britain and France, were not ready to pass responsibility to the Commission. Instead the Commission is required by Article 3 of the EU Treaty to use its policies in respect of trade and development resources to achieve harmony and consistency of purpose. The Commission is obliged to "ensure the consistency of its external activities as a whole in the context of its external relations, security, economic and development policies. The Council and the Commission shall be responsible for ensuring such consistency. They shall assure the implementation of these policies, each in accordance with its respective powers." Similarly the Council is authorised to apply economic sanctions on behalf of the Union by Article 301 of the TEC.

The structure of the CFSP is therefore clear, although subject to a possible fundamental revision at the Convention for the Future of Europe, which could change everything before any successes are achieved. In fact recent events have shown that the Council is incapable of benefiting from the structure it has so thoughtfully constructed. Whereas the idea was that European influence would be magnified by coordinating policy the opposite result has been achieved by recent events. The subject of Iraq has produced the most divisive arguments in Europe for many years, and the mechanism for close consultation has served to intensify the differences between the individual leaders in a highly public manner. A bitter dispute arose regarding Zimbabwe when the French invited President Mugabe to Paris, in defiance of agreed EU sanctions, with a threat of blocking the renewal of these sanctions. Britain was therefore "blackmailed" into agreeing that the visit was an exception. Shortly afterwards, the idea of European solidarity looked ridiculous to the world when France and Germany issued a statement opposing the proposed US led military action against Iraq, and the leaders of Britain, Spain, Italy, Portugal, Hungary, Poland, Denmark and the Czech Republic immediately retaliated by issuing a joint letter in support. Blair had consistently been supporting the US position to the extent of being widely criticised for being George Bush's envoy, but he was undoubtedly improving his influence by doing so. France, even aligning itself with Russia and blocking NATO moves to defend Turkey was appearing more of a threat than an asset to the western alliance. Then as an invasion of Iraq appeared inevitable, and even when it had begun strong French criticism continued. Following its tradition, France was refusing to be ignored, and certainly wouldn't be carried along by a British driver. However, the cost of this dispute was a coherent or plausible European policy, a shift of credibility and relevance back to single nation states, and a seriously heightened level of mistrust particularly between the French and the British. All the more reason, replies the Commission, to accelerate the number of geographical areas permanently incorporated within the CFSP.

Justice & Home Affairs

Thus, although it could be described charitably as "early days" with "teething troubles" in developing a new phase of integration, developments within the second pillar of the Maastricht construction are far from encouraging. A similar lack of impetus and consensus was hindering progress on the third pillar of Justice and Home Affairs. The areas of civil law, and asylum and immigration had been transferred to the first Pillar ie. to EC competence by the Treaty of Amsterdam. The remaining third pillar matters of police and judicial co-operation in criminal matters remained separate but the Treaty did provide for closer co-operation and an ability for a nation to opt under jurisdiction of the European Court of Justice in the event of dispute. The agreed concept was to create the EU as "an area of freedom, justice and security."

Although most British people would have thought they were already living in one, heads of governments meeting in Tampere, Finland in 1999 agreed that European integration had been rooted on common values of freedom based on human rights, democratic institutions and the rule of law. The EU had constructed the major ingredients for shared prosperity and peace: a single market, economic and monetary union, the capacity to undertake global challenges. Now, a genuine area of justice should be constructed allowing criminals no loopholes, protecting the public from threats to their freedom and legal rights posed by crime, and allowing individuals access to justice throughout the Union. The words from Tampere explain,

> *"The ambition is to give citizens a common sense of justice throughout the Union. Justice must be seen as facilitating the day-to-day life of people and bringing to justice those who threaten the freedom and security of individuals and society. This includes both better access to justice and full judicial cooperation among Member States."*

Citizens from whichever country would enjoy a common sense of justice and would not be discouraged from enforcing their rights by variable legal mechanisms and procedures.

> *"A genuine area of justice must ensure that individuals and businesses can approach courts and authorities in any Member State as easily as in their own and not be prevented or discouraged from exercising their rights by the complexity of the legal and administrative systems in the Member States."*

This would clearly require creation of truly compatible, even harmonised systems and therefore convergence of Member States' legal systems must be achieved.

Although the governments were in agreement, the Commissioner appointed to oversee the task, a former deputy prime minister of Portugal, Antonio Vitorino, had frequently lamented that progress was hard to achieve. Issues such as crime and immigration were frequently important in national elections and there appeared little appetite for activities at a European level. That was until the terrorists destroyed New York's twin towers.

British governments do not have a creditable history in introducing legislative measures in response to emergencies. Historically, the most famous examples would be the introduction of income tax, or the Official Secrets Act. However, the Blair government more than most of its predecessors was highly sensitive to media pressure in general and, as in may other fields found that "action!" was essential. Support for the US in its war against terrorism was of course unambiguous and substantial but all parts of government were producing anti-terrorist action. The Home Office produced a new Anti-Terrorism Bill including much supported initiatives strengthening police powers to prevent terrorism and deal with terrorists, or suspected terrorists. At the same time it took this opportunity to add numerous measures which were not at all connected with terrorism but were providing similar extended power to combat crime in general. As a minor example among very many, section 94 of the Anti-terrorism, Crime and Security Act of 2001 gave police power to require the removal of disguises, which could apply to a peaceful individual on an innocent demonstration. Several clauses caused controversy during the passage of the Bill through Parliament, often owing to serious protests from civil liberties groups. Accusations of disproportionate responses and over-reaction were widespread. The Commons Select Committee itself complained bitterly that only two weeks were being given to pass the Bill. But the pressure for action, and a sudden lack of sympathy for suspects' rights determined that it survived largely intact.

It is interesting that one measure did not really survive. The original clause 109 of the Bill was entitled "Implementation of the Third Pillar" of the European Union. This was a remarkable measure authorising a minister to make any regulations which were implementing *any* measure agreed under Title VI of the Amsterdam Treaty. This was to extend even to the creation of new criminal offences, and there was no attempt to limit its scope to terrorist activities. It was a clause likened to the famous Section 2 of the European Communities Act, which provided the door to all the EC legislation. Matters of Justice and Home Affairs were outside the EC pillar, but this measure was clearly intended to provide exactly the same effect, albeit under the control of the minister himself.

It was the House of Lords which objected most strongly to this clause. It was, they said, a blatant attempt "to smuggle through measures on the bandwagon of the emotions of September, 11." The noble lords proposed amendments which were mostly rejected by the government complaining in a somewhat ritual manner about the will of the elected house being frustrated. Opponents of the Bill in general were accused of abetting international terrorism, and the Home Secretary, David Blunkett denied that he was trying to take advantage of the situation with this Bill. He declared that he cared "passionately about the civil society of this country and the need to renew our democracy and communities in the face of apathy about politics." Finally, under pressure to have the Bill approved the government did agree some concessions including a limitation on the duration of the third pillar clause, (section 111 of the Act) to an emergency period of six months.

This was a highly significant incident, revealing a great deal about the motives of the government. Of course Parliament retains some measure of control over secondary legislation, and has scrutiny procedures dealing in advance with legislation even under the third pillar. However, with this measure the government had clearly intended to move the focus of a vast area of judicial, civil and criminal decision making away from the British Parliament and into the jurisdiction of the European Council, advised by the Commission. The extent of this is described below. Certainly, one might understand that closer international *co-operation* is beneficial in fighting both international terrorism and organised crime, but it remains difficult to see how the government's thwarted measures could have been considered either necessary or even of benefit to the British people. Why a British government would choose to transfer away these fundamental powers over its own citizens remains a mystery, and borders on the irresponsible.

The government adopted a different slant. They would not admitted to any opportunism comparable with the case of Jo Moore. This unfortunate junior "spin doctor" had been sacked for suggesting that collapsing twin towers would provide good cover for releasing any bad news that her department might like to issue, even though this might only cover something minor about local council expenditure. It was simply not acceptable, and even tasteless to try to take advantage of such tragedy. New Government action was directed at the new level of threat, and strengthened institutions were a general benefit to society. There was no question of stealth.

A similar view was taken in Brussels where Commissioner Vitorino was suddenly revitalised. European co-operation in the fields of justice was not merely fashionable but had become a new political imperative. Neglected proposals were pulled off the shelf and filled with life and urgency. The EU was not only re-committed to the comfortable principles defined in Tampere. It was now motivated by action! It was to become responsible for policies to deal with: asylum; immigration; organised crime; drug smuggling and addiction; judicial co-operation between national courts, both in civil and criminal matters; co-operation between national customs and police forces; as well as fundamental rights; citizenship in the European Union; measures to combat racism and xenophobia; co-operation with third countries and international organisations; the justice and home affairs "acquis" in the enlargement process; and the external dimension of justice and home affairs.

After years of inactivity progress has been astonishingly fast. Dialogue, mutual assistance, joint effort and cooperation between the police, customs, immigration services and justice departments is established between all fifteen Member States. Efficient information sharing among police forces is now organised through Europol, which many hope might develop into a fully fledged police force akin to the FBI, or the equivalent German Federal Police. Customs authorities are co-operating formally to counter illicit trafficking in drugs, arms, cultural goods, dangerous and toxic waste and nuclear materials. Mutual recognition of judgements made in other Member States has already been formalised in areas of family law such as in divorce settlements or child custody, and expansion of such mutual recognition is an important direction of present activity. All results somehow, from terrorism.

One aspect of co-operation in this area was pushed through by the European Council despite numerous constitutional obstacles. This was the introduction of the "European Arrest Warrant". Individual nations have previously dealt with this problem by extraditing individuals back to the country where they were convicted. This was recognised as a cumbersome process. It was accepted that local execution of a warrant issued in another Member State would be much more convenient and effective. However for years this was resisted because it required a reliance on the justice systems of other countries. Would a British court enforce a judgement made for example by a Greek court, against a British citizen without considering that citizen's common law rights? European politics determined that the answer would be "Yes."

However, most people disliked the opportunist breadth of the decision. Even though the principle was accepted in the fear of terrorism, the European Arrest Warrant was to cover a total of thirty-two criminal offences. These range from terrorism itself, murder and rape; trafficking in drugs, weapons or people; down to racism and xenophobia or environmental crime. Objections that the applicable definitions are those of the convicting court only, are met with the reply that while the warrant is justified because it improves law enforcement in general the system will not really be satisfactory until the definitions of the crimes themselves are harmonised. This statement, criticised as a blatant case of putting the cart before the horse, showed that removal of national rights over their criminal law, were to be the next target. This was the reason that the Daily Mail, again, proclaimed Britain's surrender of 1,000 years of legal sovereignty. The headline was an exaggeration and was certainly premature, but it nevertheless correctly describes the intentions of the European Commission, who had found a powerful excuse, and were using it successfully to breach one of the few remaining preserves of the nation states and another barrier to integration.

Chapter 28: Stemming the Flood

Sovereignty of Parliament

With Parliament's traditional role as supreme British legislator it would be truly amazing if this august body was content merely to sit idly by as floods of European legislation entered by the back door of the European Communities Act. By no means is this the case. It should be remembered that Parliament never did initiate legislation, but merely subjected the proposals from government departments to intense scrutiny and final approval. Each proposal involved Ministers responsible being questioned in the House and legislative drafts were examined word by word in special committees selected for this purpose. Only after successfully surviving this process with resulting amendments accepted or rejected, was the Bill finally approved. This process has changed, with much of the legislation affecting Britain being drafted by the European Commission, amended during a European wide process of consultation and finally approved by the European Council after consulting the European Parliament. Westminster's role would appear to be peripheral at best.

Despite this fundamental change Parliament has adapted by developing its own mechanisms to ensure its place in this new process. Nevertheless a serious doubt does arise as to whether Parliament can actually have any real influence. In some ways this question is not a recent development since Parliament has not for generations been a truly independent branch of government. The party loyalties or ambitions of individual Members of Parliament have ensured that the will of the Parliament closely mirrors the will of the executive. This certainly continues, but because members have been elected, and almost always on a party ticket, the constitutional respect owed to Parliament remains justified. The intention of Parliament, formally expressed as its momentary view still determines the law of the land, to which the courts, upholding the rule of law, will happily defer.

With early statements from Lord Denning among others, and more recently from the metric martyrs case, we have a strong impression, although far from certain, that the European dimension has not altered this fact. It appears that courts in Britain will continue to uphold the principle of the sovereignty of Parliament, in the final analysis, irrespective of the views of the ECJ. The supremacy of European law, authorised by Parliament with the European Communities Act extends only so far as Parliament has not positively, and unequivocally changed its view. This appears to be so even though on European issues Parliament itself declined to provide an express statement to that effect. As usual this can be regarded in two ways. It could suggest that Parliament was simply quite content that British Courts were obliged to give precedence to EU law as defined by ECJ judgements. Alternatively this omission could be regarded as superfluous from a constitutional point of view, not affecting Parliament's ultimate sovereignty. It really reflected the politically reality that there was no necessity for making a statement which our partners would regard as provocative, despite its correctness. It is this argument which lends support to ministerial insistence that the EU remains a "federation of nation states," despite the contradiction inherent in these very words. Accepting this argument returns Parliament to the central if not the most active role in the governance of Britain and encourages further analysis of its behaviour and relationships.

We saw earlier how the flow of individual politicians weakens the influence of even a powerful body such as the European Council, in comparison with an institution, ie. the Commission, when this has an independent and permanent long term political objective. This is quite different from Britain where an impartial Civil Service prides itself on observing a duty to respond positively to democratic changes in government, or ministerial re-shuffles. We saw a case in Britain, where David Owen encountered institutional resistance from the Civil Service but this is clearly quite different from an entrenched obstruction. Therefore policy shifts or entire changes in direction will be accomplished with the Civil Service remaining able to provide the resources of continuity, experience, expertise and the memory of recent events and players, for the benefit of the new decision makers.

The same democratic flow of individuals occurs through Parliament. Each newly elected MP will react to the situation they find and try to leave their influence on topical decisions, with an eye to a future career in the executive. However during most elections it is only a relatively small proportion of MP's who change. There remains a hard core of Members, in safe party seats assured of a Parliamentary career spanning several governments. This represents an important source of continuity which enables Parliament to maintain an independent expertise in a variety of subjects. This is even more true of the House of Lords which enjoys a stability and continuity critics would describe as moribund. But, in its task of scrutinising government proposals and pointing out long term effects or implications unforeseen under the pressures for immediate action, it possesses important key skills which are discarded only at the peril of democratic accountability.

The addition of the European dimension to Parliament's traditional role logically must dilute its power as a final decision maker, but the arguments parallel those for and against participation in the European project as a whole. Does the "pooling" of national sovereignty provide ultimate benefits to Britain, from participation in policy decisions formed and implemented on a European scale? The difficulty is that the traditional concept of sovereignty is not subject to such compromise. An institution, in this case Parliament, is either sovereign or it is not. The concept is not capable of dilution on practical grounds. A decision that a country's best interest will depend on adapting to external views may well be practical, but it detracts from the idea that a country is truly independent and hence sovereign. Consequently many have argued that the very concept is an outdated, and emotional obstacle to true progress in an interdependent world. No country is an island which can remain protected from external economic and social forces, unless it opts for real isolation. Co-operative influence is more important than attempts to impose a national opinion or policy. Sovereignty is actually a myth.

Applied to Parliament is very similar reasoning, and comparable argument. It was always accepted that while Parliament is legally capable of passing any measure, its real power is limited by other factors. Just as legislation concerning the weather would demonstrate legal sovereignty but achieve nothing, legislation neglecting other political and economic forces in the wider world would have the same effect. Parliament must therefore adapt to the real world, and recognise Britain's and its own limitations without being concerned with some abstract irrelevance. Recognition of this principle however does not resolve the problem of Europe, mainly because it cannot be taken too far. It cannot be used to justify spurious reasoning used to support imposition of unnecessary restrictions, nor the perpetual accrual of competences by stealth, nor the creation of a "superstate" with almost dictatorial powers or an uncorrectable judiciary.. While the question regarding benefits resulting from EU membership remains subjective there is in any objective view, a real need for the balancing competences in individual policy areas. Subsidiarity was intended to provide this balance together with accountability and responsiveness to the requirements of local communities. Institutional defeat of this concept gave birth to the Laeken declaration to define the balance, but it seems likely that the subsequent Convention for the Future of Europe will hijack this process, also in favour of centralisation for its own sake.

Scrutiny by Parliament

Whatever the direction for the future, the position of Parliament today remains debatable. One side of this argument is that since EU law takes precedence over any incompatible domestic measure the deliberations of the Westminster Parliament, incapable of affecting European legislation are at best an irrelevance, possibly a pretence, and at worst a deception. People may feel comfortable with this familiar institution but it is in fact powerless and without influence. The other side is that Parliament maintains its role of scrutinising what remains constitutionally, secondary legislation and it still exerts democratic control over ministerial participation in the European legislative process. This argument should be carefully examined.

As far as European legislation is concerned the British Parliament actually does exert its authority by means of an elaborate system of scrutiny operating on several levels. These combine as a systematic review of all documents and proposals emanating from Brussels with an active scrutiny of Ministers and government departments involved in their negotiations and their approval.

In the Commons there are three European Standing Committees each dealing with separate areas of government business. Each has thirteen permanent members and sittings usually involve the inquisition of a government minister on a particular issue, often referring to specific proposals referred from the Scrutiny Committee described below. The Committee will discuss the government's view, its negotiating strategy and will afterwards review the eventual outcome. No minister "invited to give evidence" before one of these committees could leave feeling he could avoid being held to account for his actions. Committees often have considerable relevant expertise, and party loyalties are not so pronounced as to restrain criticism of a deserving minister. Examinations are therefore probing with MP's well trained to resist spin or prevarication. A similar and independent system operates, usually more politely, in the House of Lords. Their committee is organised into six sub-committees based on different policy areas. However they differ in that they tend to deal in fewer issues, conducting full scale enquiries in those subject areas. Once again, ministers or officials appearing before these committees will leave knowing they have been thoroughly grilled. The committees also hear evidence from every incoming EU Presidency, and from the Minister for Europe shortly after each European Council meeting.

Two other aspects are important to this process. Firstly, there is a highly regarded European Scrutiny Select Committee with sixteen members nominated by the House after consultations between the parties. This is a central clearing facility for all documents relating to EU policies and proposals. In 2002 it received and examined 1220 such documents and selected all those with some legal or political importance for more detailed scrutiny. Some 535 documents were included in this category of which 86 which were recommended for Parliamentary debate, either in the relevant Standing Committees or occasionally on the Floor of the House.

This is a highly systematic and organised process. Documents arriving usually from Brussels are deposited in Parliament, but unless exempted by the committee as being trivial, within ten days must be supplemented by an "Explanatory Memorandum" from the relevant government department, and signed by a minister. This document will include among other things, a history of the subject matter, an assessment of the measure's potential impact or implications and a summary of the government's view. Usually in less than a week the committee will make its initial decision on each document. Impressive though this system appears, its ultimate success depends on the support it eventually receives from Parliament itself and on this measure the verdict cannot be so positive. The Committees identify areas of concern, but action depends on either unusual initiative from individual MP's, or on a positive response from the government itself. This of course depends on the relationship between the executive and its party support in the Commons. Consequently, the opinions of the Committees have influence on but little power over government policy, and an even more remote chance of amending any measures coming from Brussels. Years of warnings from committees have failed to persuade successive governments of the need to resist many "routine" regulations. This is a failing which arises as in so many other issues, from the necessity for individual MP's to follow party loyalties or party whips, at the expense of their objective thought.

Parliament does however maintain another important sanction which operates at a more personal level, aimed at all ministers responsible for negotiating European legislation. This is the mechanism of the Scrutiny

Reserve Resolution. This is a standing resolution of the House which restrains Ministers from giving the government's agreement to any proposal which has not been cleared by the European Scrutiny Committee. Thus if a proposal has been referred elsewhere for further information, or if it has been referred for a debate which has not taken place, Parliament does not allow a minister to approve it in Brussels.

This restraint has no legal effect, and has not lasted long enough to become a powerful convention. However it has proved very effective, up to a point. The European Scrutiny Committee is actually scrupulous in demanding that procedures are fully complied with, and in this lies one weakness. For example a proposal recommended for debate in the House, will not actually be debated unless the Government agrees to find time for it. However the proposal will not be regarded as cleared until some resolution specific to the document is actually passed by the House, so there is a real incentive for some action if a minister wants to progress with the measure in Brussels. He does not have an option of simply ignoring the Committee. The Government is at liberty to propose any resolution, for example rejecting the advice of the relevant standing committee. Providing this resolution is passed using the Government's Parliamentary majority the document will be cleared and the minister is authorised to proceed. Committee's concerns can therefore be overridden, but at least positive action is required to do so.

The personal accountability of ministers has always been a powerful weapon of Parliament, as even the Prime Ministers question time may often reveal. Despite its often theatrical aspect, a Prime Minister who fails to become sufficiently prepared risks a ruthless humiliation putting him back in his place. This is actually a more potent factor in the less public Commons Committees and the European Security Committee is no exception. Twice in 2002 ministers were accused of being in breach of the Scrutiny Reserve Resolution, and neither could have found their subsequent appearance before the Committee an experience they would wish to repeat. Nicholas Brown, Minister for Work in the Department of Work and Pensions in negotiating in Europe shortly after he had been appointed attempted to excuse himself for this reason, to explain that the result was beneficial and also to apologise. Several members of the committee were still scathingly critical of him for avoiding the Reserve. Similarly, Michael Meacher Minister of State for the Environment at his hearing, was criticised for agreeing to a common position in Europe without waiting for clearance. He attempted to excuse his action as being justified in the circumstances but mainly as being in the national interest. The Committee responded with an emphatic explanation to him their own view of ministerial responsibility. It can be safely concluded that Parliamentary scrutiny has an important influence on executive actions in Europe despite its lack of legal sanction, and despite the fact that it is essentially a background, low profile activity.

The Parliament of Scotland

The recent devolution of power to Scotland and Wales left EU matters, included under foreign affairs, within the competence of the Westminster Government. Even so the Scottish Executive is responsible for implementing many EU measures using its legislative powers, since these fall in policy areas devolved to Scotland. This inherently unsatisfactory arrangement has actually been made workable by co-operation under the terms of a "Concordat" between the UK government and devolved assemblies whereby close co-operation and co-ordination is arranged. All sides appear to be satisfied with how this system is operating, but nevertheless Scotland in particular wants to increase its influence on EU policies at as earlier a stage as possible. Consequently the Scottish Parliament and Executive have taken many impressive measures to improve its position in Europe.

These measures firstly include the opening of separate representation offices in Brussels and active organisation of lobbying through extensive and well organised networking. There is an increasingly effective "Team Scotland" approach which harnesses and co-ordinates activities of all Scottish members in EU bodies such as the European Parliament, the Committee of Regions and the Economic and Social Committee, as well as influencing the powerful expatriate community in Europe. These all have important roles, supplementing the sources in the UK government, in gathering intelligence and disseminating information to interested parties in Scotland. It is also working in a Conference of Presidents of the European Regional Legislative Parliaments which includes 74 regions (eg German Lander) in eight countries. In addition it has developed closer co-operative contacts with Flanders and Catalonia in the Network of Regional Parliamentary European Committees. These are clearly designed to establish areas of common interest at the level of regional government, and develop a power centre separate from that of national governments.

Governments at regional level have a serious institutional disadvantage within the present EU structure despite the theoretical necessity of subsidiarity. Naturally these bodies would like to redress what they would see as an inbalance, and are actively promoting many such measures at the Convention for the Future of Europe. For example, many would like to see a right of direct access to the ECJ which is presently denied under the Treaty. It remains to be seen how effective these representations will become bearing in mind that it is national leaders who will make the final decisions.

Scotland's problems with the EU machinery are common to that of most smaller countries and regions. Many Scots dislike being dependant on UK government support for many of their initiatives even though they enjoy disproportionate influence. Consequently they frequently and sensibly advocate a distinct and "louder" voice for Scotland, which would certainly be warmly welcomed in Brussels. Unfortunately, such a louder voice is also inevitably smaller, and can be ignored even more readily than a unified British voice, which as we have seen is itself very frequently ignored. However within recent reports prepared by the European Committee of the Scottish Parliament indicate a carefully considered strategy for promoting Scottish interests.

These reports reflect an idealism and optimism about Europe no longer apparent from longer standing Westminster MP's who have experienced and display a certain disillusion or even cynicism even among those who have been and remain fervent supporters of European ideals. It is to be hoped that the generally higher level of support for the EU within Scotland will enable the present Scots strategy to yield more practical results. However, the Parliamentary reports also lament another serious obstacle in the form of a very low level of public awareness and interest in European matters. The Executive and Parliament are therefore working hard to correct this in order to mobilise even more effectively the resources of Scotland in support of their aims.

Constitutional Scrutiny

The other aspect of scrutiny appeared recently in response to the massive flood of consultation documents and position papers related to the Convention for the Future of Europe. Special Committees were quickly formed to deal with these issues, and these are making a respectable contribution to the flow of information, and trying their best to draw the attention of MP's to the wide ranging and fundamental issues being discussed. The regular reports reveal many important details of the process of the negotiations but it is too early to predict any of the results, particularly since the entire British Government is only one player in a very large field. Even so, both of Britain's two Parliamentary representatives at the Convention gave disturbing insights into the negotiating tactics they were finding.

Ms. Gisella Stuart revealed the discrepancy between the opening intentions stated by Giscard d'Estaing that no parts of the acquis would be untouchable and the reality of the negotiations.

> *"The dynamics of the Convention have been such that those who say that there are areas where Europe's action has been quite sufficient, and that we should consider drawing back, are virtually non-existent. The dynamics of the debate stem from organised groups such as those in the European Parliament who, unlike us, have succeeded in overcoming party political divides in order to pursue one agenda, and one only."*

Thus the organisation was wholly biased in favour of further expansion or as a minimum consolidation of EU competencies. Ms. Stuart also described in amazement many of the negotiating tactics being employed. As one example she complained how frequently whole areas of competence were described as being within the European "status quo" when they were clearly not. In addition very tenuous reasons were stated in all seriousness by other delegates. The fact that diseases can travel across borders was being used to justify European control of all matters relating to public health. Her comments could only be treated with alarm, because she has a well establish pro-European pedigree. She has always expresses her intentions as being aimed to ensure that Europe works, but she has been clearly dismayed by the scale of forces she is encountering.

Britain's other Parliamentary representative is Mr. David Heathcote-Amory, a committed Euro-sceptic. In his reports to the Committee even he seems astounded at the direction being taken by the Convention. Reporting as the first draft Articles of the new constitution appeared he reported,

> *"The document before us is an alarming publication. Certainly, if enacted in anything like its present form, it will go well beyond what any British Government have said is acceptable. It will have profound implications for our*

parliamentary democracy, and it will certainly represent the creation of a form of European state."

It would appear that the scope of the constitutional documents being produced is likely to concern all but the most extreme of pro-Europeans. Even apart from direct constitutional "threats" there are numerous fears relating to division of competences. Parliament is fully aware of these developments, but again action depends on the executive branch, and this would appear to be bemused and impotent in its reaction to the flood of proposals. As we have seen it is not clear how an individual government can seriously oppose an unwelcome policy, and particularly one which will inevitably become an integral part of a huge package. Government Ministers have been quick to point out that these documents are no more than proposals and do not indicate the shape of the final treaty. However in view of the forces deployed in the Convention and the inherent antinational bias in the proceedings described by Ms. Stuart, it is difficult to predict any fundamental shift back towards national competences. And looking further forward the intergovernmental conference to come is likely to be subject to the same pressures, and British opposition to entrenched integration, if indeed Britain does oppose it, will still only represent one voice. A battle, likely to dwarf the turmoil of Maastricht would appear to be looming.

Chapter 29. Economics (Trade and Investment)

Trade Performance

It should be recalled that the whole reason for Britain joining Europe in the first place was to participate in the benefits of a common market. Whereas others on the continent may have been building a completely new Europe, British politicians remained adamant that the British could not survive in a wider commercial world without the benefits of an enlarged "domestic" market. The British nation itself was not under threat from joining; the issue was simply one of economic prosperity. In 1975 the people believed this, and by and large have continued to do so. It does after all seem eminently reasonable. Trade with Europe has always been so important to Britain and participation in European moves to regulate the market, with or without Britain, was seen as an essential requirement for continuing commercial success. The case was most eloquently put by Peter Hain, when he was Minister for Europe in May 2002.

> "Britain is a trading nation. We could not afford – literally – to be outside this market. We could not afford to have tariffs imposed on our goods and physical and legal barriers to our trade. Sixty per cent of our trade is with the EU. We export four times as much to the EU as to the US. We export more to France than to the fifty other countries of the Commonwealth. And more to the Netherlands than to South East Asia. Eight of our top ten export destinations are in the EU. British firms engage in virtually every single sphere of economic activity......To send our firms in to bat in Europe while letting our competitors shape the rules is playing a game British business cannot win and a paying a price Britain cannot afford."

This case appears compelling. It explains how even in just the world of business Britain has received great benefits from membership of the EU, which justify all the negative aspects which detractors frequently raise. However because it is so important it requires a closer examination, with the aid of the figures published by the National Statistics Office, in a regular tome entitled "Overseas Trade Statistics of the United Kingdom". Of course, everyone fears that any case can be made by using statistics. It is possible to measure parameters in different ways, to apply mysterious "corrections", to select data for comparison using the most favourable period. However the author promises that no such tricks are used in the analysis below. Those who can remember the days when the adverse "Balance of Payments" and the "Trade Gap" regularly made news headlines will recall the ritual warning from ministers that it was misleading to read too much significance into one month's figures. Thus the period selected has been that from 1992 when a new method of compilation and presentation was adopted. Actual figures from the publication quoted have been included at the expense of readability to enable sceptics to check the accuracy of the facts before considering the remarkable conclusions.

Firstly Mr. Hain says that sixty percent of our trade is with the EU. In 2002 our exports of goods to the EU were actually £109,129M out of a total of £185,848M (58.7%). However imports were £118,276M out of £220,242M (53.7%). So, the argument must be accepted that the EU is Britain's most important trading area. Interestingly though the same volume of the publication includes the figures from 1992. These show that since 1992 exports to the EU have risen from £64,976M, and that UK's total exports have risen from £107,863M. Thus the EU share of UK exports in 1992 was 60.2%, and for imports 57.8%. So, despite the proclaimed advantages of operating in a harmonised single market, the EU share of British trade in recent years has, if anything, been *falling*. These figures also show that during this period exports rose on average every year by 5.32% to the EU, but 5.59% to the rest of the world. A conclusion that Britain's exporters are being slightly more successful outside the EU would appear inescapable. Even so it remains undisputable that the EU is Britain's most important area for trade.

Following on from this reasoning, Mr. Hain's second remark is that Britain exports four times as much to the EU as it does to the USA. The relevant figures are again £109,129M and £28,172M, giving a ratio of 3.87, so this is also essentially correct. But in 1992 US exports were £12,640M and the ratio was then 5.14. The relative importance of exports to the EU has actually been *declining* during this time. The comparable rate of growth for exports to US is 8.34% pa.

It would not be honest to dispute Mr. Hain's points regarding British exports to France, or the Netherlands, nor that eight out of top ten of British export destinations are in the EU. However in 2002 Britain's single biggest export market was USA with exports of £29,172M with Germany second with £21,964M. This compares with 1992 when exports to USA were £12,640M and exports to Germany £15,185M. Until 1998 Germany was

Britain's largest export market, but has been overtaken since then. Exports to Germany rose by an annual 3.76% in this period. Even on a much smaller scale exports to Australia rose on average by 6.41% pa. Also, while it must be admitted that Britain's overall share of world trade has declined, (from 5.5% in 1992 to 4.3% in 2001), this is largely due to the rapid growth in overall world trade which from 1990 to 2001 grew (from US$3,386bn to US$6,178bn) at a rate of 5.6%. Trade within the developed world measured by G7 trade grew (from US$1,788bn to US$2,711bn) at 4.1%, and Britain's share of this held up slightly better reducing from 10.4% to 9.6%.

The above analysis shows that while Mr. Hain's facts as stated should be regarded as essentially correct, they describe only an economic snapshot. There is no way which this picture can support or justify his conclusion, despite its undoubted ring of truth. "To send our firms in to bat... while letting our competitors shape the rules is playing a game British business cannot win and a paying a price Britain cannot afford." British exporters have actually been commendably successful, and in recent years at least, nobody has suggested that Britain's trade would benefit by ceding or "pooling" national sovereignty with the USA. Britain's businesses have been successful without doing so. Despite this fact, which must be widely known throughout the British establishment, more sovereignty is ceded to Europe every year and every month, even though trading performance is consistently superior elsewhere.

Fairness demands the comment that Mr. Hain cogently argues the wider case for Britain's membership of the EU pointing the non-economic benefits to ordinary citizens. However he spoils this case by introducing a fear of tariff barriers which the EU would have applied to British goods. It is true that Europeans would have been unlikely to grant Britain unfettered access to their markets while not accepting the responsibilities of the Union. They actually said we could not expect the gain without the pain. However this argument exaggerates these fears by neglecting other salient points. Firstly, tariffs are generally a small percentage of trade, and technical barriers are not allowed to be imposed selectively to overseas suppliers. Moreover such matters are negotiable between national parties, and regulated by the World Trade Organisation which prevents the EU from imposing external tariffs above around 6% for most goods. In any case despite Britain's compulsory imposition of this tariff on its imports from outside the EU, those imports (from £51,103M in 1992 to £101,966M in 2001) have still risen faster at 7.15% pa than those from the EU (from £69,910M to

£118,276M) growing at 5.40% pa. Besides, any such negotiations would also be helped by the fact that in the period in question at least, Britain has never sold more goods to the EU than it has imported. On overage imports have been 6% greater, giving a consistent trade gap to the benefit of the EU.

Britain's public have consistently been told that anything which might be mischievously interpreted as a political annoyance resulting from EU membership is a small price to pay for the enormous economic advantages derived. However, at least as far as trade is concerned and over the past ten years, this justification does not appear to be supported by the facts. The picture is however slightly different looked at over a longer period. Shortly after joining in 1975 only 34% of Britain's trade (exports plus imports) was with the EEC. Treasury reports at the time showed that even before membership this proportion was rising and after joining it continued to rise steadily till 1985 when it stood at 48%. Over the <u>twenty five</u> years until 2000 UK trade grew on average by 9.33%, while trade with the EU grew at 11.22%. (NB: No corrections have been made for some high figures for inflation for several of these years). Thus there appears to be a very strong argument that trade benefited from at least the first ten or fifteen years of membership. Even over twenty five years though not all indicators are consistent. A comparison between trade with USA and Germany again shows little difference in growth, (11.31% for Germany and 11.23% for USA), throughout this period. The conclusion has to be that the almost universally accepted argument that Britain must be in Europe for the benefit of its overseas trade, is not actually supported by the facts.

Investment

Of course trade, although quoted as the main reason for membership, is only one aspect of economics. One facet of economic activity that has definitely benefited from membership of the EU has been the level of overseas investments made into Britain, and this is important because of the employment it creates. Again, Peter Hain made the point very convincingly.

> *"Being outside the Single Market would also mean missing out on inward investment. The massive Foreign Direct Investment we receive flows directly from our membership of the Single Market. In 1999, we had a massive 400 billion dollars, more than anywhere else in the world, except the US.*

Despite having 17 per cent of the EU's GDP, we receive 23 per cent of all inward investment into the EU."

There is no doubt that British access to the single European market has been a critical factor in these investment decisions. However this cannot be the only factor. For example, Britain's geography as an offshore island makes distribution costs significantly higher than from a centralised European location. Other things being equal investment should be located in the centre. Since Britain actually receives more than its fair share, these other factors cannot be equal. What advantages can Britain really offer?

Industrialists describe many of these factors in terms of the labour force. Compared with continental countries British workers offer lower costs without compromise to the level of skill, and also a reduced level of regulation. Successive governments have so far maintained a highly flexible labour force of the type Tony Blair has been advocating for Europe since the Lisbon summit. However in response to EU regulations the gap between labour forces is closing rapidly. It would seem that continued adherence to the policies being imposed by the social chapter will eliminate any such advantage. British trade unions will certainly praise this advance in working conditions, but the investors of the world will no longer find compelling reasons for not locating in the geographical centre of Europe.

Competitive markets are ultimately unforgiving towards all forms of excesses. So, if the EU really aims to protect its citizens from the cold winds of capitalism, artificial protectionist measures will have to remain, and even strengthen if possible, for as long as possible. Third countries with lower labour costs or with other competitive advantages will continue to encounter obstacles to EU markets, to perpetuate what is really an imbalance, despite the negative effects on the greater world economy and on developing countries in particular. This illustrates the fundamental divide between Thatcher's vision, mostly shared by Blair, for a dynamic, open and competitive economy and the harmonised, protectionist vision of the European Commission.

Most people would agree that governments have a role in managing the economies for which they are held to be responsible, but there is little consensus as to whether they should act as mere facilitators of private commercial decisions as Margaret Thatcher always advocated, or undertake various forms of direct intervention. The extent of any such intervention is also debatable because it can become little more than a habitual interference in free markets for political ends. Actual state management of industries in Britain never achieved a successful track record. The civil service was not able to function as effectively as boards of directors for major industries. Nor did protectionist measures ultimately benefit the economy. Those industries such as car production, which were protected from imports for many years were able to delay or avoid necessary restructuring, and as a result became increasingly uncompetitive in world terms. Britain learned from this experience, slowly, and in recent years led the way in Europe for extensive privatisation of publicly owned assets. This philosophy has so far not reached some parts of Europe, particularly France where extensive areas of production remain, protected by subsidy at the expense of the French taxpayer and consumer, and even in Germany where many companies are protected from takeovers despite attempts from the EU to force liberalisation in both cases.

Returning to the question of investments, it is notable that governments similarly attempt short cuts towards improving employment by trying to influence investment decisions by means of subsidies. This leads governments to compete with each other to encourage overseas investments. In the EU development grants and other subsidies from national governments also compete, but within limits imposed, usually, by the Commission. Of course the real benefit of overseas investment is diluted to the extent that it is paid for by the taxpayer, and distorts the commercial decision being taken by the potential investor. However the creation of employment is regarded as such an important role for all governments, that attracting major investments from multi-national companies cannot be resisted. It is, after all, easier than liberalising the labour market. For Britain on the fringes of the continental market and subject to the same limitations as other parts of the EU, the prospects in such an environment would not seem positive. Moreover relying on concessions allowed under EU regional development policies will no longer offer much scope when eastern European countries become full members. So, logically it would seem that Britain cannot maintain any long term competitive advantage other than the purely cultural, in attracting future overseas investment. This is not to argue that unfettered auctioning of investment proposals would ultimately benefit anyone other than the investors themselves. It merely suggests that economic decisions taken on the basis of a "European" interest cannot be expected to operate in favour of Britain.

The factors determining overseas investment trends are clearly complex to say the least. In common with trade factors, statistics concerning investment depend on the aggregate of a very large number of free commercial entities all acting in what they perceive to be their own best interests. Investment though, despite the academic tools available for its assessment remains the most subjective of business decisions. Prevailing opinion in Britain is that stated by Mr. Hain. Britain receives more than its fair share of inward investment, largely because of its access to the European single market. Since, again, this is a critical factor in Britain's relationship with Europe the facts supporting this argument should be examined more closely.

The Office of National Statistics shows that in 1999 the total stock of direct investment in the UK amounted to £238bn, broadly supporting Mr. Hain's figure. By 2001 this had risen to £366bn. As a matter of interest 48% of this latter amount was owned by companies from the EU and this percentage has risen from 29% since 1997 when comparable records are available. It can therefore be concluded that direct investment in UK by *EU companies* is increasingly important. Of course it is possible to argue that the purchase of British companies by Europeans which this represents indicates that British companies are failing rather than thriving, but even if true sale of the company would always seem preferable to insolvency.

Next Mr. Hain boasts that Britain received a higher proportion of the total EU inward investment than a comparison of GDP would merit. Support for this assertion comes from the EU Commission in publications from Eurostat. These documents confirm the figure of 23%, (23bn Euros out of a total of 97bn Euros). However the same publication points out that both Belgium+Luxembourg, and the Netherlands each received 30%, (30bn and 28bn respectively), with Germany regularly attracting only around 8bn Euro investments. It can safely be concluded that the British minister has again quoted an accurate figure but has used it to make an unjustified and even misleading deduction.

It should also be remembered that investment flows in both directions and should be regarded as beneficial to all concerned. The EU is actually a net investor in the outside world, investing twice as much in 2001 as it received, (202bn euros as against 97bn euros). Britain is in a similar position. British statistics show that while £41bn was invested in UK in 2001, British companies invested £45bn overseas. Although the total value of investments in Britain amounted to £366bn, the value of overseas investment owned by British companies in 2001 was £619bn, of which 54% was held in the EU. The proportion in 1997 was 42%. The important result is that earnings from this investment amounted in 2001 to the remarkable sum of £45.9bn.

Although distinctly confusing, it would appear certain that Britain benefits considerably from investment flows in both directions. However, and as with trade, it is difficult to conclude as did Mr. Hain, that the balance of advantage "flows *directly* from our membership of the single market." The author would argue that there is indeed a benefit, but that it derives from the greater range of opportunities which have become available to potential investors within Europe. There is clearly a benefit in attracting external investment to Britain as opposed to one of Britain's European partners but in the single market generally potential benefits of increased choice and more open competition are sacrificed in favour of protectionist harmonisation in the interests of unity. In the case of investment this levelling of the playing field involves a gradual erosion of whatever advantages Britain may have enjoyed. However it does seem certain that for the foreseeable future but Britain will remain an important participant in this market.

One final factor in assessing investment options remains that of the single currency area. Investors are invariably attracted by certainty and the elimination of an exchange rate risk is an important element. Thus those advocating Britain's adoption of the Euro argue that future investment Britain might attract is dependant on joining the Euro zone. Returns on investments in sterling, with a floating exchange rate against the euro, are directly affected by variations in this rate. This makes favourable investment decisions less likely, and explains the historical fact that interest rates in Britain have had to be consistently higher than in more predictable areas, as a compensation for this risk. It is not a factor which potential investors in Britain can afford to ignore even though it involves them making almost impossible predictions. Supporters of British entry into the Euro therefore argue simply that this risk would be better eliminated.

Supporters of the opposite case can argue that the actual variations experienced can be either beneficial or detrimental. Only a real pessimist, lacking confidence in Britain's businesses and workforce would assume that Britain was destined to permanent inferiority, and requires bolstering from the safety of a larger currency. Certainly the people of Italy believed that they could only enjoy a successful currency if it was managed outside

Italy. Italians even tolerated a special "Euro tax" to ensure they could meet the Maastricht criteria, and avoid relegation. Conversely, Euro detractors can point to the fact that the Euro has not performed well in the currency markets since it was created, and even though a recovery did begin during 2002, the fundamental advantage justifying the abolition of national currencies, ie. stability, simply failed to materialise.

Conclusion

It is difficult to reach any reliable conclusion from this confusion of statistics. Economics as a whole remains inexact and unscientific, used by proponents to provide plausible explanations of past events, and assertive recommendations for guiding present policy, but nevertheless incapable of producing any reliable predictions. The balance between its measurable parameters, their interactions and their effects is simply unknown, even though such fundamental ignorance does not inhibit vociferous support of particular policies. However one conclusion *can* be drawn from the above account relating to just two economic parameters. Economic data in the hands of politicians is immensely dangerous. It is uniquely susceptible to selectivity and spin, and used ruthlessly for their own ends with no regard for objectivity.

Chapter 30. Economics (Stability, Growth and Euros)

Safety in Numbers

Just as in normal business activity companies find themselves in competition, so nations depending on the prosperity of their enterprises can be seen to be competing in battles for markets across the world. The analogy can be extended further to compare the growth of a mature company with the developed economies of the west. Survival of the economically fittest companies encourages co-operation, merger or even acquisitions between enterprises. Multi-national and even global companies have resulted. These normal commercial activities can be seen as in both aggressive and defensive aspects. Adoption of expensive technological advances and the promotion of worldwide marketing brands are proactive attempts to gain market strength in comparison with competitors. In addition the stronger company becomes more resistant to market turbulence or other external threats. In many respects individual countries are in the same situation and similar motives have applied to the political leaders of individual European states, particularly as they looked across the Atlantic. In co-operation, politically and economically they could at last hope to counterbalance increasing American dominance.

The creation of the common market was a first co-operative step towards what was later intended to become comprehensive economic integration. The gradual removal of artificial obstacles to trade would be soon extended to more general co-ordination in economic matters, and eventually to complete economic and monetary union. This quest for strength in numbers or stability in unity is not new in history. For example in the 19th century a Latin Monetary Union was formed with France, Belgium, Switzerland, Italy, Greece and Bulgaria. This lasted nominally until 1929 but failed earlier as a result of economic policies which began to diverge between the members after the First World War. Similarly a Scandinavian union lasted until Sweden withdrew in 1924 again following differing inflationary pressures. However a successful example is the customs union of the originally independent 39 German states of 1834, which was followed by monetary union of 1857 and which eventually led to the first and real unification of Germany in 1871.

Outside such unions currencies had once been held stable by connection to an international "gold standard". Values of currencies were backed by holdings of gold, and this financial provided discipline for national governments. After the Second World War had destroyed such discipline international stability had been supplied by a system of fixed exchange rates under the Bretton Woods agreement, but this proved incapable of surviving the turmoil of the 1970's. Europeans responded with a "snake" system of holding their exchange rates within fixed limits, but rising inflation and active speculation meant that Britain was able to join only for a short time, Denmark and Italy were also obliged to "float" their currencies and even France failed in repeated attempts to stay within appointed limits. The "snake" became little more than a Deutschmark bloc.

It was actually Valeri Giscard d'Estaing, as President of France in 1979 together with Helmut Schmidt, who created a "European Monetary System" and brought it within the institutional regime of the European Community. This involved creation of the ecu, or European Currency Unit, which became traded as a separate currency of value based on the basket of Member State currencies, and after the Maastricht Treaty and subsequent negotiations this evolved into the Euro. This in turn leads to the present continuing agony for Britain, as the country repeatedly considers whether to abandon the pound.

It should be remembered that the Germans were also attached to their own currency which had been a real success and a source of national pride. Even those who agreed with adopting the euro in principle were only convinced by the condition that the same stringent conditions imposed by the Bundesbank would be employed by the ECB in its management of the euro. Thus monetary integration with a famously lax country such as Italy with a history of huge public debt and high inflation could only be contemplated with strict entry conditions. Thereafter there had to be protection, to ensure that all members conduct their affairs "responsibly". This was the role of the "Stability and Growth Pact." This bound all members of the euro zone, to run a balanced budget, with a deficit not to exceed 3% of GDP. Failure to achieve this would eventually incur liability to a huge fine of up to 0.5% of GDP, providing a majority of finance ministers vote to impose it. The problem with this is that several members, including Germany and France are likely to be perilously close to committing the same sin.

The early years of the euro which we are seeing have resulted in serious disruption in several economies. This has by no means approximated to the disaster scenarios luridly painted by euro opponents before the currency's introduction but strains and pressures have definitely emerged. Many in Britain observed an unprecedented economic boom in

Ireland as EU aid and euro-optimism created rapid development throughout the country. Similar, and even more extreme events were occurring in Portugal with convergence through rapidly reducing interest rates feeding a consumer led boom which the government followed. A large deficit resulted, which would have caused devaluation of the old escudo. The larger euro provided protection, but now exacts its price. The economy in Portugal approaches recession, with no borrowing available to revive growth, and government spending which must be cut to reduce the budget deficit to 3% is making the recession even worse. These constraints are likely to lead to rising unemployment and voices critical of the government will certainly be raised, even though national politicians have few options.

More seriously for Europe as a whole is the fact that while the euro interest rate was probably too low for Portugal, and Ireland, it was too high for Germany and France. Paradoxically it was Germany which was the second country to experience the Commission's "excessive deficit procedure," with France next in line. The difference here though is that these larger countries are in a stronger position to bend the rules of the Stability and Growth Pact. While this might undermine the credibility of the currency there is a growing opinion that the ECB is actually fighting the wrong battle. Many economists argue that its commitment to preventing inflation is not appropriate because general inflationary pressures are low. Greater threats now come from sluggish growth throughout the euro zone. In any case, euro supporters claim that these difficulties are merely details of little significance. Deliberate exposure to these powerful economic constraints is inevitably causing temporary and actually minor inconvenience as individual economies are forced to adjust and conform. A temporary reduction in growth, or even a spurt of inflation is actually a small price to pay. Europe is rapidly approaching real economic integration. The euro is already creating a single, powerful and cohesive economy which can play its destined role in the world without internal stresses and division. The future power and influence of Europe is assured.

The Famous Five

The view in Britain is somewhat different. Just as people were told in the 1970's that Britain would join a Common Market, and to forget any political implications, many of Britain's politicians repeat that judgements regarding joining the euro should be made solely on economic grounds. Meanwhile leaders in Germany and France were proclaiming creation of the euro as a "profoundly political act" and a "victory for Europe after a century of heartbreak, war and trial-and-error." Even at the launch of euro notes on January 1st 2002 Romano Prodi was quite explicit in a BBC interview that this represented a huge development in the politics of the EU. Thus many Europeans are mystified by the British attitude that the euro is an economic issue, unable to decide whether Britain is simply obtuse, or dishonest in disguising its political objections. To them, the euro has become part of everyday life, and no longer a subject for discussion. Nevertheless the British government persists in discussing its five economic tests in exhaustive detail, diverting attention from other considerations. At time of writing a lengthy assessment of these tests is expected to be produced by the Treasury, and again expectation is that Britain should not be in a hurry to join.

The government introduced Gordon Brown's five economic tests in 1997 when they had decided not to join the euro. These would determine when it would be in Britain's best (economic) interests to join. The justification for this is again that economic interest should be the determining factor. If Britain would in the defined sense become better off, then Britain should join. The practical fact that this would involve shifting control of remaining monetary policy as well as transfer of national foreign currency reserves physically to Frankfurt; and the fact that a change in currency would cost retailers at least £2bn; would be simply the means of obtaining those benefits.

Unfortunately such a purely economic assessment could never offer certainty and will inevitably be controversial. Economists will doubtless be available to argue either way. It is also clear that many voices would be raised in loud opposition to abolishing the pound, even if the economic benefits were really proven. Therefore the tests had to be somewhat loosely drafted, to maintain future options, and to allow Tony Blair to choose to hold a referendum to accept his advice, only when he had a realistic chance of winning it. At present though Blair does acknowledge that membership of the euro has a political aspect, but he regards these as "overwhelmingly" in favour of entry. For Blair, membership represents not an irretrievable loss of sovereignty, but a serious risk of losing influence in Europe. After enlargement it will become increasingly to justify staying outside the zone, and development of "flexibility" could well leave Britain increasingly isolated. Blair then reverts to discussion of the five tests.

The first test, widely regarded as the most important concerns **convergence**. Are business cycles and structures compatible so that Britain can accept permanently and without damage, the single euro interest rate? Has Britain achieved "sustainable and durable convergence?" Since this test was failed in 1997 interest rates have become closer, and output gaps have also converged. However Britain's structure and in particular the importance of its high mortgage housing market make Britain's economy more sensitive to interest rate changes. The important point though, is that all the economic indicators examined will be subject to interpretation. For example, the fact that at some time particular indicators are close does not prove durable convergence as cycles may actually be moving in opposite directions and merely crossing over. Moreover the very fact of having a separate exchange rate for the pound is bound to create fluctuations and hence serve as a source of instability. It was once argued that the pound compared with the dollar and the euro, is a "rabbit between two elephants." Therefore it will always be possible to argue that abolishing the pound will lead to the required stability.

Brown's second test concerns **flexibility**. Is Britain's economy sufficiently flexible to cope with the shock of joining, and any subsequent economic jolts? Here the problem is that adverse changes in wage rates and reducing international competitiveness can be compensated for by an adjustment in exchange rate. With this possibility removed there will be no means of avoiding serious industrial disruption. In an alternate view the euro zone itself is showing a pronounced lack of flexibility since the extensive reforms proposed by Tony Blair at his famous Lisbon summit have failed to materialise. Instead increasing regulation is likely to reduce further whatever flexibility still remains, and Gordon Brown himself recently commented that flexibility was "too often undervalued in Europe."

The third test concerned **investment**, which we saw previously as a highly uncertain parameter. Economists can always be found who will argue that Britain's inward investment suffers from the exchange rate risk. Recently it has appeared from UN statistics that Britain's share of EU inward investment is indeed falling. This is explained, afterwards, because the improved price transparency and certainty in costing can indeed provide a boost to trade and productivity, and hence will appear more attractive to investors. The first indications that such internal trade is increasing as a proportion of countries' GDP is appearing. Therefore this test for joining the euro should appear positive. However, as mentioned previously this does disregard the fact that investment flows in both directions, and also within the areas of the EU. The actual balance of benefit will be more difficult to determine with honest confidence. This aspect though, is beyond the scope of the prescribed test.

The next test concerns the effects on Britain's financial services and in particular the **City of London**. Many commentators predicted that the City would be placed at a serious disadvantage in competition with Frankfurt. The governor of the Bank of England Eddie George, regularly comments that London has not actually suffered, except to the extent that markets generally have been seriously weak, following recent stock market plunges. So while there appears little evidence of the City losing business to Frankfurt, there is a belief that only Britain's joining of the euro would secure London's long term future as an international financial centre. The argument can be presented either way.

Finally there is a test regarding **economic growth** and employment. Here the supporters of the euro have the difficulty that the British economy had double the rate of growth of the euro zone in 2002. Furthermore the OECD forecasts British growth of 2.1% in 2003 and 2.6% in 2004. This compares favourably with the euro area forecasts of 1% and 2.4%, partly affected by the ECB's restrictive monetary policies. Similarly regarding unemployment Britain's 2003 rate is expected to be approximately 5.4% of the labour force, compared with around 8.8% in the euro zone. This is a very important figure because a Labour government in particular, having been successful in reducing unemployment would be very reluctant to contemplate measures likely to increase it.

Thus, at time of writing it would seem difficult to interpret the famous five tests as supporting British entry. An assessment required to be "clear and unambiguous" and in favour of entry would appear to be very unlikely. There are however other economic factors of relevance, many relating to the performance of the pound itself as a smaller currency British governments in particular have frequently railed against the forces of currency speculation and its tendency in common with most markets to overreact to events. Even so it does create an important mechanism for correcting, for example, adverse trade balances, and it encourages governments to promote financial discipline in their economic management. Participating in the euro provides greater protection against these forces, weathering the market storms in a larger ship, or provide a place for a smaller economy to hide.. However, a well managed economy with a reputation for rectitude and stability as nurtured in recent years by Gordon Brown (until recently), has little to fear from exposing its currency to market forces. Historically this was seen with the reputation which the Deutschmark enjoyed under management of the Bundesbank, and many Member States joining the euro hoped to gain the benefits of stability, and consistent low-inflation growth.

Europeans, viewing the predicament of sterling in past years complained that variable exchange rates disrupted trade and investment patterns, as competitive advantage shifted to the detriment of their businesses. As Britain experienced repetitive "Stop-Go" economic policies, balance of payments or sterling crises, or excessive inflation, Europeans frequently criticised the idea of competitive devaluations as a disruptive means avoiding financial responsibility. One particular aspect of the solution they suggested, was independence of the central bank from government control so that politicians were no longer able to attempt to manipulate monetary policy or interest rates for possible political advantage. It was not immediately apparent that a shift towards independence of a national bank was a mere prelude to a second shift to European control, even though this had already been agreed in the Maastricht Treaty, and this is exactly what happened. In Britain, though, with its opt out, the final step need not be taken.

In the longer term even if a decision was sometime made to join the euro there is one other factor which would be of critical importance in determining the ultimate effects. What exchange rate of sterling to the euro would be used? Economists have argued that for four years the pound has been too strong to join the euro. They pointed out that joining the ERM at too high a rate led to Britain's ejection from the system, and with this option removed a similar mistake would force Britain to endure a longer period of slow growth to allow wage levels to become competitive again. Some now suggest, almost always in hindsight, that Germany's current economic difficulties result from joining the euro at too high a level. Clearly the figure for sterling, which would need to be negotiated with all the current members, itself has an effect on the five test assessment. Although, presented as secondary to the decision in principle, it cannot really be regarded as a mere afterthought. This gives Britain even more to argue about as it considers joining, "providing the rate is right."

Will Britain Join?

The conclusion can only be that the economic case is likely to remain subjective, and subject to presentation. Intangible factors, such as the image of the Euro and its European management are certain to be just as important. Emotional factors are likely to remain important, as is a growing sense of the inevitability of the decision.

The ultimate collapse of the euro eagerly predicted by its opponents would seem unlikely especially bearing in mind the enormous political commitment to the project. It is surviving the necessary adjustments in individual economies, and it survived with a studied silence from the ECB and few political ripples a drastic initial fall in value. People in Britain know better than most, that favourable exchange rates are likely to change. On the other hand a currency increasing in value is seen as successful and enjoying a positive verdict from the markets. Voices in favour of British entry are likely to increase as the Euro recovers and appears both successful and therefore attractive, even though the result would be to eliminate another parameter of flexibility and potential advantage in favour of homogeneity. In any event the future of the currency appears increasingly assured.

This means that in Britain the debate over joining will continue until Britain joins. The Euro will become increasingly familiar, and will no longer appear something strange for the public to fear and dread, especially as potential benefits are emphasised by its supporters. For example, transparency in pricing will become very important for the business community, no longer having to convert prices and worry about potential variations. Then, for the ordinary family, there would be a definite saving and noticeable convenience in not having to change money when travelling to Europe on holiday, and with having to struggle with converting unfamiliar prices. This could be regarded as a small or even trivial benefit not even worth considering in comparison with the scale of the decision being taken. On the other hand it is a real and visible benefit which the ordinary traveller can experience. It is real money in the ordinary pocket as opposed to the theoretical "economic" benefit applicable to large companies and banks.

It is also argued that in the longer term Britain's position outside the Euro will become increasingly untenable. New members are expected to be joining the euro since there is no opt out, many by 2007. Of course, there is some doubt about this particular timetable in view of the economic adjustments in these economies. Each has a serious debate, balancing the target of full EU and hence Euro membership with the need to avoid restricting essential economic growth by premature imposition of the Maastricht criteria. The largest new members Poland, Hungary and the Czech Republic would have to adopt very restrictive measures to meet the 3% deficit target and they may prefer to delay doing so. Alternatively existing members may decline to accept this same discipline, and so agree to a relaxation of the conditions. This is just another uncertainty of the future. In the longer term they are all very likely to join, one way or another.

Therefore in a union of 25 members, growing still further, pressure to conform (or to lose influence), will become intense. Sweden is already under such pressure. Sweden did not negotiate an opt-out clause but has not been in any hurry to scrap its Krona. Now though a referendum has been scheduled for September 2003. The result is likely to be close with powerful political figures opposing the move, spreading alarm that the Swedish welfare state of which the country is so proud might be under threat. In addition with higher growth, less unemployment and stronger public finances than found in the Euro group it will not be easy to convince many Swedes of the economic benefits. If Sweden does decide to join pressure will move to Denmark, which will be more concerned with increasing isolation. Finally the pressure will appear in Britain. Would Britain really be prepared to be the only one of 25 or more members not joining the Euro?

Moreover, public opinion only needs to shift across the line of acceptance once, and momentarily on the day of a referendum, for the fateful decision to be taken. After all, an irreversible decision needs to be taken only once. There could even be further referenda, repeated until the "right" decision is obtained. This, it is said, demonstrates the ultimate inevitability of Britain's joining. Therefore, the argument proceeds, Britain would do as well to enter now rather than later. After all Britain has habitually suffered from joining European initiatives too late.

Of course, political factors will always remain important. It is widely believed that Tony Blair differs from his Chancellor on the principle of joining despite their joint position with the Five Tests. However their political opponents are always interested in imagining, encouraging, exaggerating or even creating a split between the two. For example, the British Commissioner, Chris Patten, making an outspoken attack on the Prime Minister made one telling remark. "So long as we hang back from full and unequivocal EU membership, how can we convince them [EU partners] that, for all our patronising prevarication, deep down we are mad about Europe?" He continued to deride the economic tests as an insult to the public's intelligence and a Chancellor's veto. He urged Mr. Blair to stand up to his Chancellor, exert some authority, stop Britain remaining "semi-detached," and restore Britain's influence in the important issues of the day.

On the other hand Britain's traditional reluctance would seem to be unusually appropriate at the present time. Public suspicion with the European dream was seriously enhanced as the war on Iraq approached and passed. The French position was seen by many ordinary people as a betrayal, and this was reflected in a sudden drop in support for joining the Euro. This is clear evidence that all such matters are firmly connected in the public mind, but also showing how the "economic" decision can be influenced by external factors. Nevertheless there is no doubt that the EU is about to undergo a fundamental, if nor radical, transformation as it negotiates a new constitution for itself. Britain will probably want to endorse this development but it is already clear that few of its views are likely to be adopted by the majority of Member States. In view of this particular uncertainty a commitment to joining the euro now rather than possibly in a year's time would certainly seem unwise. Euro enthusiasts in general have always argued that Britain must join the euro if it is to enjoy its rightful place in Europe. However it is not at all certain that this would still apply whatever the shape of future Europe. Integration with influence is quite different from submergence, and the directions from the near future are far from clear. Caution would, at present, appear to be sensible.

Better Off Out?

Britain's continuing reluctance to commit itself fully to European integration is nevertheless counterbalanced by a resistance to the idea of going-it-alone, strengthened by the real fear that it would have suffer insuperable difficulties and national disaster in trying to withdraw.

Advocates of British withdrawal from Europe encounter a massive resistance almost amounting to hysterical terror from all sides, in anticipation of the dire economic consequences which it is honestly believed would ensue. To succeed withdrawal would require a united Churchillian, wartime spirit impossible to develop in a country which would inevitably be fundamentally split on the issue. The idea could never take hold without some serious perceived assault on Britain, and certainly something much more emotive than a quiet humiliation at the hands of the ECJ.

This argument about inevitable damage though, is part of the assumed background to the entire European debate, nurtured by years of assertions from political leaders. The public assumes it to be the true and unchallengeable, even if some would still opt for taking this risk. Indeed, there is no doubt that a decision to leave the EU, would be truly momentous, with serious and profound effects on everything Britain has been doing for thirty years. It would create turmoil in currency markets for Sterling, and stock markets, consternation among all Britain's allies, and chaos within the legal profession. Large numbers of moderate and reasonable politicians would be honestly, and seriously horrified at even the prospect of such a decision. Even so, it is wrong that the potentially serious consequences of any choice should be used to prevent a dispassionate analysis of the issue, and equally wrong that disinformation be used to stifle honest and informed debate. There is, after all, an identifiable downside to the status quo.

In fact this claim of economic disaster is by no means indisputable. In the previous chapter it was suggested that the effects on trade and investment were not as clear cut as almost everyone believes. A similar conclusion was drawn in a more academic and wide ranging study from the Institute of Economic Affairs by economists Hindley and Howe. They pointed out that not all results of leaving the EU would be negative. Britain would experience considerable savings if it abandoned the Common Agricultural Policy, and loss of trade to Europe caused by reimposition of the EU external tariff would be roughly counterbalanced by removing the distortions from Britain's present levying of this tariff on its trade with third countries. In any case adjustments in trade patterns would *over a suitable period*, compensate for any trading difficulties. Attractiveness as a home for investment would be decreased by the threat of new tariffs and bureaucratic inconvenience from the EU, but the damage could be repaired by adopting reduced regulation. These authors at least suggest that the balance of advantage would actually be so small, at less than 1% of GDP, that even if leaving was a disadvantage it could not be imagined anything approaching economic suicide.

The answer all depends on what value you would place on a truly independent Britain.

Chapter 31. Towards 2004

The Final Step

The story of the next Intergovernmental Conference begins with the last. Several unresolved issues at Nice, sufficiently fundamental to require further treaty amendments, led to the following agenda:

- a more precise delimitation of powers between the Union and the Member States;
- the status of the Charter of Fundamental Rights of the European Union;
- simplification of the Treaties with a view to making them clearer and more readable without changing their meaning;
- the role of national Parliaments in the European system.

According to Prodi the first phase would be one of "open reflection" regarding the future of Europe including "the widest possible debate at all levels of civil society and in political and scientific circles." This would be followed by "structured reflection" which should "crystallise around an operational synthesis of representative opinions canvassed in the previous phase." After this the IGC itself would be able to reach final conclusions including complete texts of a new Treaty in 2004.

Interestingly this process is deliberately designed to be completed before the first wave of enlargement, scheduled for 2004. This was certainly seen as a final push by federalists to ensure their dream of an "ever closer union" would culminate in a political federation, before new and diverse members obtained any possibility of obstructing the process. The President of Latvia summarised the predictable attitude feared by the federal lobby. "We have had to fight too hard for our nation-state to want to dispense with it now." Despite the importance of the discussions to those countries expecting to join their representatives will not be participating, except as observers, even though they will certainly be expected to ratify the resulting decisions. This follows the EC precedent strictly adhered to since the time of Britain's application. However, the resentment that the British negotiators felt, for example at the Fisheries Policy which was being designed during their talks, pales into insignificance when compared with the constitutional nature of the 2004 Conference. In fact the impending enlargement also adds another dimension to its importance to future development of the Union. Commission President Prodi asserted that future amendments to the Treaty beyond 2004 would require a new procedure in the enlarged Communities. Ratification by individual national Parliaments or by national referenda would have to be abandoned.

In Brussels the creation of a new IGC provided a renewed opportunity to continue the construction of Europe in the path of Maastricht, Amsterdam and Nice. In the view of the Commission the unsatisfactory compromise between the federal structures of the EC, and the intergovernmental structures in the other pillars of Maastricht should now be eliminated. The Commissioner responsible for the IGC, Michel Barnier, summarised this objective with commendable honesty if not a sufficient awareness of political realities outside of Brussels.

> *"On this fundamental issue of integration, it is perhaps time to do away with the current ambiguities concerning the aims of European Union. These ambiguities, this hybrid nature of Community integration, have enabled us to make spectacular progress in the past. Europe is a federal entity: look at its currency. Europe is an open entity: look at its market. And yet there is a clear feeling that the virtues of this creative fuzziness are beginning to fade. And that, with enlargement, unless Europe is prepared to say what it is setting out to do, it will fail to recognise what it is".*

Although it may have escaped most people's attention the first phase was actually completed by the end of the Belgian Presidency in 2001, and progress summarised in document known as the "Laeken Declaration". This is a curious document defining what it regards as a truly historic mission. Its very title, "Europe at a Crossroads", indicates its purpose in determining the future direction of the entire continent, and its content includes a wide ranging description of the historical context of the forthcoming decisions. Next, it poses a very large number of fundamental questions regarding the future shape of the Union in a surprisingly open and un-dogmatic manner. Finally, it gives practical details for the next stage in the discussion process, defining the participation and the procedure for the Convention on the Future of Europe.

Most observers were not surprised that several other items were added to the original agenda, cynically noting that several could be described as either fine but empty political words or final steps in the endgame of federation. The actual list was:-

- a more precise delimitation of powers between the Union and the Member States;

- the status of the Charter of Fundamental Rights of the European Union;
- a better division of competences: more from Europe in some areas and less in areas better dealt with by Member States;
- resolving the EU's democratic deficit: how to achieve more democracy, transparency and efficiency;
- institutional changes: evolution of the Council of Ministers and the European Parliament into a bicameral Parliament; evolution of the European Commission;
- bringing the EU closer to its citizens
- defining the EU's role in an increasingly global environment;
- simplification of the EU's political instruments;
- integration of the treaties into a constitution for the EU.

This document clearly describes a considerable broadening of the aims of the IGC, such that this now becomes of fundamental importance to the future government of all Europe's citizens. Although not originally intended the process has evolved into a full constitution writing process for the EU, with profound implications for all its members. It has been likened to the 1787 conference of the "Founding Fathers" writing the US Constitution and European federalists see this as a real opportunity to create a binding European Constitution across the continent, with a fully functioning European Government. Even those determined to limit the scope of discussions realize that the intention, in a task in common with the American constitutionalists, is liable to determine the distribution of power between the EU and national governments for the foreseeable future. However there is a fundamental difference in that the American colonists started their deliberations from the people and concentrated on democratic accountability, whereas Europeans have always been inclined to build onto a central structure without regard to public opinion and loyalty. Similarly to mainstream European thought, simplification did not mean any revision of the 85,000 page acquis communitaire, but a collapse of the intergovernmental pillars of Maastricht into the main EC structure, transferring foreign policy and justice and home affairs to Community competence.

Although British ministers in particular repeatedly insist that the Union will continue to be one of independent, national sovereign states, whole areas of sovereignty will certainly be retained by the Union, and a written "constitution" will almost certainly define and almost certainly expand those areas. National constitutions will be required, either explicitly or by quiet implication, to give precedence to the new structure. In Britain where there is no written constitution but one which has evolved by convention and precedent over centuries this will be particularly difficult. Politicians will argue that this is of no real significance since the existing Treaties have already achieved the same effect using the European Court of Justice and the national courts. However this time, because of the vast expansion of EU competence, it will be more difficult to argue that national governments retain ultimate authority of any significance. In Britain's case for example, ministers' public commitments to prevent European taxation, to retain an independent foreign and defense policy and to retain border controls appear as a line in the sand. Conceding power to the EU in any other measures could be accomplished without embarrassment. In these areas a "Harold Wilson" strategy of discussing details over principles can be confidently predicted. However, having said this the British negotiating positions are much more ambitious and not solely defensive. They involve numerous initiatives aimed at improving the "democratic deficit" of the Union and introducing flexibility on the lines of Blair's Lisbon suggestions to create a dynamic European economy, and it is hoped that Blair's patient lobbying since he came to power will be rewarded with some practical successes.

So, looking back to the start of the process and to the Laeken Declaration many observers were surprised at its realistic assessment of many of the political shortcomings of the EU as perceived by its citizens. In fact this was inevitable because any future constitution could only become adopted after unanimous consent of the current members, and in many countries a referendum is required. With recent referenda won only marginally, and discontent simmering in many countries the aim of obtaining public acquiescence must be a necessary priority. One section of the declaration headed, "expectation of Europe's citizens" summarises the problem to be addressed.

> *"Citizens also feel that the Union is behaving too bureaucratically in numerous other areas. In coordinating the economic, financial and fiscal environment, the basic issue should continue to be proper operation of the internal market and the single currency, without this jeopardising Member States' individuality. National and regional differences frequently stem from history or tradition. They can be*

> enriching. In other words, what citizens understand by "good governance" is opening up fresh opportunities, not imposing further red tape. What they expect is more results, better responses to practical issues and not a European superstate or European institutions inveigling their way into every nook and cranny of life."

This was indeed music to the ears of generations of British politicians, and not least to Tony Blair who, despite his new and "positive" attitude to Europe still retains reservations that most of his predecessors would have supported. Certainly, the possibility that powers could be repatriated to national level was rarely contemplated in European circles and could be seen as a vindication of Blair's conviction that Europe was after all moving his way. Unfortunately for this proposition, it quickly became clear that very few members of the Convention were in favour of any repatriation at all, since this concept is regarded as a retreat if not a defeat for the European ideal. The fact is that this opening document contained something for everyone, and was designed to engage debate rather than indicate direction. For example, the Belgians, ever federalist in Europe despite the fragility of their domestic federation, thought that appearance in the document of a commitment to a European constitution and of a directly elected President was a major achievement.

It appears that the European tradition of horse-trading has simply been opened up to include areas previously held as taboo by different parties for different reasons. Unpalatable proposals can still be traded away. Thus the scope of the subjects raised cannot really be regarded as any indication of the final result. Neither can the extensive consultation exercises being conducted provide any guarantee that the numerous voices and bodies offering their opinions and the vast number of papers being presented for consideration will have a real effect on the political process. After all in 2004 the final decisions will be taken by the Council in the usual manner. It seems certain that the final compromises achieved will combine victories and defeats for all participants, and will then be subjected nationally to the presentational skills of the government responsible. There is though, one final guarantee in that whatever the result the politicians produce, this time it must overcome the various degrees of suspicion and dissatisfaction held at popular level across the continent, and in every nation if it is really to succeed.

Convention on the Future of Europe

Before the middle of 2003 the Convention for the Future of Europe is required to present its report, recommending final options for debate and decision by the Council. The appointed Chairman is Valeri Giscard D'Estaing, the former French President who was forced on EU leaders by President Chirac, despite criticism that he was personally haughty, devious and elitist, and despite objections that he was too in tune with the "Community method." Two deputies were appointed to assist him: Giuliano Amato, a former Italian prime minister, and Jean-Luc Dehaene, a former prime minister of Belgium. The Council indeed selected suitably experienced and eminent politicians to lead them to the next stage. Perhaps it was mere coincidence that all three have a reputation for supporting federalist measures, having recently supported Jacques Delors in a "wake up call" to Europe calling for "a continuous transition towards greater European integration", notably in economic and social policy.

The Convention itself comprises 105 delegates representing each national government, each national parliament, and the Community Institutions, as well as observers from candidate countries for entry. Delegates are split into eleven working groups tasked with reviewing and deciding one of the policy areas such as subsidiarity, or social affairs. although not addressing any of the fundamental constitutional questions. In due course each presented its considered recommendations. Activities are co-ordinated by a Praesidium comprising the Chairman Giscard D'Estaing and his deputies, representatives of the three governments holding the presidency during the convention, two representatives of the national parliaments, the European Parliament and the European Commission. Numerous working papers and reports are published and discussed at monthly plenary sessions of the Convention. In Britain both the House of Commons and the House of Lords takes considerable interest in the proceedings and regularly publishes Committee reports after questioning the British government and Parliamentary representatives.

The Convention opened in March 2002 with Giscard d'Estaing commenting that this was to be the most fundamental review of European co-operation since the conference of Messina in 1955 and emphasising that the long term implications over a 25 or 50 year timescale would be an essential feature of their deliberations. By October he was ready to launch its first major report. It comprised a skeleton for a new constitution listing just a heading for each article, and followed by proposed flesh for each item where the working groups had reached some form of consensus. Numerous proposals likely to generate heat rather than substance were reported. For example, should the new Union be a "United States of Europe", "United Europe" etc.? Should citizens enjoy joint national and European nationality? Many of the more controversial suggestions were also dismissed as "Giscard's discards", recognising how the process of negotiation is likely to proceed. Finally, many commentators concentrated on how the Convention was being used to make advances on the general outstanding issues of the day, under the umbrella of institutional reform. For example, the working group on economic issues had decided that a minimum rate of corporation tax was essential "to let the internal market operate effectively and stop unfair tax competition." However it also identified the principle that while monetary policy was a matter of EU competence, economic policy should remain primarily a national concern.

The Convention Chairman admitted that difficult decisions would be faced by all parties, but hoped to design a final document which would be able to resist brick-by-brick removals as individual members objected to individual articles. Examples included of course, British and Irish resistance regarding taxation; or the German refusal to give up a veto on immigration issues. Strengthening the suggestion that the final document would have to be indivisible he included both a carrot and a stick. Firstly the possible mechanism to deal with particularly sensitive issues such as tax or foreign policy by a system of "super" majority voting which would prevent a single country from blocking an initiative but might enable perhaps one large one with some support to do so. The stick was that since previous treaties were to be repealed, failure to ratify the entire replacement would amount to leaving the Union.

Among one of the most important of the numerous submissions was that from the European Commission entitled "Peace, Freedom, Solidarity". Drafted in secrecy, under a codename "Operation Penelope", many Commissioners, eg. Mr. Patten and Mr. Kinnock, were not aware of it until it was virtually finished. They may have been angry that Mr. Prodi was pushing forward his own integrationist policies in the guise of a formal Commission proposal but they were unable to stop it. National governments were also taken by surprised as they saw its draft EU constitution which would enable efficient operation of an enlarged Europe of 25, 30 or even 35 states. It proposed the abolishing of the national veto in every area of policy including foreign policy, including the setting of "European taxes", and future constitutional amendments. The only exception would be the admission of new member states. Foreign Policy would be under the control of a new Secretary based in Brussels who would represent the EU at the United Nations and turn the EU into a world power as a counterweight to the USA. It would have an independent defence policy with powers to intervene with force in the domestic affairs of member states in cases of "serious internal disturbances affecting the maintenance of law and order." The Charter of Fundamental Rights, would be fully incorporated as a legally-binding text under the jurisdiction of a new "Supreme Court". Finally in order to prevent repetition of Ireland's near destruction of the Nice Treaty Member States not accepting the constitution would achieve a "special status" somewhere between associate and outcast. Naturally the entire document was dismissed as fanciful.

The entire negotiating process is likely to become a fascinating display of the ebb and flow of political forces throughout Europe, but unfortunately with few people noticing. Even those items reaching public awareness create confusion with distortion and exaggeration appearing from all sides of any issue. Informed public debate is impossible. For example a new draft of the first part of the "Constitution" published in February 2003 caused contrived outrage among British Eurosceptics for its inclusion of the word "federal" and its claimed massive extension of European power over national states. As usual, closer examination revealed something slightly different. Soothing words over the word federal appeared, explaining that the actual meaning of the word, as understood in Europe, did not justify the traditional British terror. It was merely a shorthand for defined layers of government power more akin to decentralisation. Who could doubt that there are some decisions which really are better taken at a central, (not higher) European level?

Similarly, a claimed takeover of economic policy was described as actually an honest and open statement of the agreement by all members to co-ordinate their economic policies, which had been agreed at Maastricht, and didn't represent any new development to be feared. Of course this spirit of openness does not make unpalatable policy decisions more acceptable, but on the positive side, there is a clear intention from the Convention that definitions of such competences will be clearly stated. Exposure will certainly improve the quality of the debate, and may succeed in legitimising its conclusions in a way Maastricht never achieved. Naturally some parties will want to extend their limits and others will want to reduce them. Nevertheless the final outcome is intended, by some, to define the boundaries permanently, and not just until the next time, and eliminate continuous creeping and surreptitious extension of EU power as seen over the previous thirty years.

In the area of Foreign Policy the document also revealed an interesting manoeuvre from the Praesidium. The article involved called for Member States to be formally prevented from conducting any foreign policy contrary to a common position of the Union. Peter Hain, the former Europe Minister, who remained as government representative at the Convention after being replaced as Minister for Europe, explained that foreign policy would indeed be much more effective if it could be magnified by European solidarity. However, he complained that the article worded by the Praesidium bore no resemblance to the recommendations presented by the working party on foreign policy of which he was member. Elsewhere documents "were being falsified to suggest uncontested support for federalist proposals," ignoring dissenting views from British, Irish, and Scandinavian members.

Controversy also appeared in areas designated as "shared competence" applying to a long list of areas ranging from health to justice. The draft stated that "[Only] where the Union has not exercised or ceases to exercise its competence in an area of shared competence, the member states may exercise theirs." In a similar way a clause that giving the Union power to coordinate and establish broad guidelines for member states' economic policies was read as including a plot to harmonise taxes. A leading Liberal Democrat MEP commented, that the Minister had little chance against the highly experienced teams from France and Germany. "Peter Hain has got an awful lot to learn about the workings of the EU."

Later, in April 2003, Giscard d'Estaing himself produced his proposals on institutional reform. Naturally any such proposal would be controversial, but his proposal to create a President of the Council with a five year tenure, with his own staff to guide the future strategy of the Union provoked energetic denunciation from both the Commission and the Parliament. They were objecting to this shift in the balance of power and complaining that it would duplicate bureaucracies, and provide unequal treatment of Member States. He also proposed a European Congress, acting like a second Parliamentary chamber, and made up largely of members from national Parliaments. Fundamental changes certainly seem on the agenda, but it is not possible to predict which of them will reach the document representing Giscard d'Estaing's final recommendation ⌁, and which of these will survive the IGC.

What is also interesting is to contrast this frenetic activity with the views of the British Parliamentary representative to the Convention, Mr Heathcoat-Amory.

> *"There is no European electorate, there is no European public opinion, there is no European press scrutiny, there are no European political parties, there is no European demos, and it may arise one day, but it cannot be created out of the air by politicians, or by laws, or by waving a European Union flag. Therefore, in my view, the conditions for a quasi-federal democracy are absent in our continent, and we therefore have to reinvigorate our democracy by bringing decision-making back to Member State level."*

So the tortuous jostling for position, for influence and for acceptance of favoured policies will remain a feature of this Convention and the subsequent Conference, fascinating because of the large numbers of bodies involved at least nominally in the process. It is a unique example of widespread consultation subjected to active filtering as ideas permeate through established institutions and well organised lobbying bodies; through working groups appointed from the Convention membership; through a Praesidium with objectives of its own; and finally to government leaders in the form of the European Council with their various agendas and domestic positions. This will inevitably lead to another round of "consultation" or "selling" as the public, sitting mainly oblivious to all the forces determining their political destiny will finally be either heard or ignored. Meanwhile Jack Straw reassures the British people and asks them not to worry. Forget about the word "constitution" he says. Even golf clubs have constitutions. It doesn't mean anything.

Conclusion: The Europe of our Children and Grandchildren

This book opened with a summary of the different constitutional traditions brought by the different peoples of Europe. It argued that the constitution may not sound very interesting, but that it remains essential in protecting the everyday lives of the people. It sits unnoticed in the background of society but is nevertheless too important to be either neglected, or left to politicians.

Britain has a democracy which is far from perfect but which has gradually adapted and served tolerably well for many, many years. Over the long term it is important to consider what mechanism should provide the future guarantee of British freedom and prosperity. In theory there is a choice. Britain can still decide that its best option is to trust its system of Parliamentary democracy protected by the descendants of Queen Elizabeth. It could even reject the concept of monarchy if republicans were able to devise acceptable protection. On the other hand, it could also decide to become part of the United States of Europe.

This book has described many of the events leading to the Europe of today, and the approaching steps about to be considered towards the Europe of tomorrow. It has described both the disgraceful motives of politicians stealthily trading pieces of national sovereignty for temporary benefits, and the high minded ideals of the many sincerely committed to the future peace and prosperity of the continent.

It has described how the law of the European Union has developed a life of its own; how this has quietly grown into a potential threat to democracy throughout Europe; and how it is ensuring a continent free of discrimination and with entrenched protection of human and social rights.

However, beyond the pros and cons of the single currency it described, beyond the benefits and disadvantages of harmonisation, and beyond the legislative procedures and questions of institutional balance among the EU structures and between nation states, all described earlier, lies the same fundamental question still facing Britain after half a century of prevarication.

The British people remain resistant to the idea of becoming embedded within Europe and suspicious of European interference with the British way of life. Even so the decision will soon be taken in which direction the country will go, for the foreseeable future.

Britain remains willing to co-operate on individual items when it appears in her interest to do so, and has been prepared to be swept along in directions contrary to her perceived interests for purposes of retaining influence in Europe. Now though, it is becoming clear that real and fundamental decisions are being made about the future shape and direction of the continent. For many years Britain has remained uncertain whether to be independent in the world or to be an integral part of Europe. This is the essence of the British contradiction, and its enduring dilemma. This book suggests that the people cannot permanently pretend to be both, even though this illusion best serves their politicians. History should not be allowed to repeat itself as when entry into the "ever closer union" was itself accomplished against a background of fierce argument regarding the price of butter. This time the facts and implications should be faced, honestly.

Of course pragmatism remains an important part of the issue. The future depends to many on exactly what kind of Europe is required for our children and grandchildren. Pondering this question from its constitutional aspect, most people would insist that we bequeath the next generations some secure form of democratic government. In frustration, people are frequently attracted to the idea of a benevolent dictator but the problem is that dictators do not remain benevolent. On the other hand the early American Vice-President John Adams once remarked that "unbridled majorities are as tyrannical and cruel as unlimited despots." This is significant in the light of earlier accounts in this book describing the fundamental and persistent divergence between British and European thinking. It implies that in future Britain is likely to remain on the minority side of most arguments.

This, in turn reveals the basic weakness in considering what type of Europe Britain would like. The reality is that Britain and its people will be given no such choice. The story of Europe has been one of relentless advance towards federation which will not be stopped. They, in Europe, simply do not want it to be stopped. Historically, this book shows how as options have arisen in the past, British politicians have themselves decided what they think would be best and simply presented to the public whatever information was available to support that conclusion. Rarely were issues honestly explained. Rarely was it defined what prices would really be exacted for what benefits. Now, as plans for the future emerge some details will be open for discussion, but the overall directions will not be altered by any amount of British persuasion.

The future Europe will almost certainly be built in the same way as the present one. Guiding principles will largely be European and distinctly at variance with opinions regarding the role of governments, freedom of individuals which most British people hold even though they rarely consider such values. Europe will develop in directions which the British would not themselves choose. Will they nevertheless decide to go along the same route in a real spirit of European harmony and solidarity, or will they be persuaded to accept "the inevitable" in poorly informed trust of their leaders? One way or another, a constitutional *package* is soon to be produced, and Britain will have to decide whether to accept it or whether to reject it and to face the daunting prospects of either option.

The traditional decisions of British politicians ultimately to accept the terms on offer, belatedly, grudgingly and without admitting them to the people have not served Britain well. The problem is that the British people are never asked to think about such fundamental questions. Politicians have actually denied them the opportunity of doing so. Distracted by details, and tricked into discussion of incremental decisions, Britain has been led blindly, well along the path of European integration. So far has this progressed that a reversal even of a part of this process would probably prove impossible to achieve except by withdrawing from the EU, involving a truly momentous decision. Instead of this Britain, often motivated by such a fear of isolation, has been moving inexorably in the European direction.

But it should be realised that at the destination of this journey ultimate responsibility for protecting and guaranteeing the freedom of the British people is granted to the European Court of Justice, while Britain's usually cherished institutions fade into subservience. While European peace, security and prosperity is a likely result, this will forever be dependent on obedience to European governance.

In the final analysis the question is, whether it is really in the best interests of the British people to sacrifice their historical constitution in the interests of and for the benefits of European unity?

What do you think?

ACKNOWLEDGEMENTS

It was Sir Isaac Newton who wrote in 1675, thinking of illustrious predecessors such as Galileo and Kepler, that if he had seen further than certain other men it was only by standing on the shoulders of giants. My own experience as author is nowhere near such an exalted level, and I have not seen further than many others have looked, but it remains similar in that I have looked over the shoulders of many highly skilled and knowledgeable authors whose work I have read over many years.

Of most value to this present work was the extensive political study of the same subject by Hugo Young entitled "This Blessed Plot". This is a highly readable, entertaining and thoroughly researched account of British politicians' role in Europe which I would thoroughly recommend to anyone interested in more detail than I have included in this book.

Secondly I would like to thank my tutors, Semple Piggot Rochez, who helped me through the London University LL.B. via their impressive internet course, and who encouraged my interest in constitutional law. They introducing me to numerous expert authors such as Prof J.H.H. Weiler and his colleagues, whose work provided me with a much greater understanding of the legal issues. Of particular interest was his book "The Constitution of Europe" containing the intriguing article "Do the New Clothes have an Emperor". Aidan O'Neill who wrote an excellent account of pre-Maastricht "Decisions of the ECJ", is also thanked especially for his welcome emphasis on Scottish aspects of the law.

In specific areas some other authors provided invaluable guidance. The report by Sir Con O'Neill on Britain's negotiations to join the Common Market is a truly fascinating account of real politics; and the work by the American Anthony King, "Britain says Yes" provided a remarkable insight into the winning of a referendum. Memoirs by several of the politicians mentioned in the text were also invaluable.

Finally, thanks are due to numerous friends and family members who have corrected the text and generally argued. Despite this assistance any mistakes which remain are entirely my own responsibility. Readers are encouraged to offer any comments either constructive or critical via the book's website, where any corrections and updates will be posted prior to updating the book itself.

David Winn   May 2003

APPENDIX 1:
ORGANISATION OF THE EUROPEAN COMMISSION

POLICIES OF THE EUROPEAN UNION

<u>Directorates General</u>
    <u>Areas of Competence</u>

Agriculture

Directorate A.I:	International affairs I, in particular WTO negotiations
Directorate A.II:	International affairs II, in particular enlargement
Directorate B:	Relations with other institutions; Communication and Quality
Directorate C:	Markets in Crop Products
Directorate D:	Markets in Livestock Products; Specialised Crops and Wine
Directorate E:	Rural Development Programmes
Directorate F:	Horizontal aspects of Rural Development; Sapard
Directorate G:	Economic Analyses and Evaluation
Directorate H:	Agricultural Legislation
Directorate I:	Resource Management
Directorate J:	Audit of Agricultural Expenditure

Competition

Directorate A:	Policy, Legislation, International Affairs,
Directorate B:	Mergers
Directorate C:	Post, Telecommunications, Media & Music Publishing, Consumer Electronics
Directorate D:	Financial Services, Transport, Distributive Trades
Directorate E:	Cartels, Basic Industries, Energy Water & Steel
Directorate F:	Consumer Goods (Textiles, cosmetics), Mechanical/Electrical Goods, Vehicles, Food & Pharmaceuticals
Directorate G:	State Aid (Regional, horizontal and Business Taxation)
Directorate H:	Sectoral State Aid (Metals, Mining, Vehicles; Other manufacturing sectors, Public undertakings)

Economic & Financial Affairs

Directorate A:	Economic Studies and Research
Directorate B:	Economies of each Member State
Directorate C:	Economy of the Euro Zone
Directorate D:	International (Enlargement; G7; Regional Policies)
Directorate E:	Evaluation of Financial Markets; Competitiveness; Structural Funds; CAP; Environment, Transport & Energy; Capital Movement.
Directorate L:	Financial Operations with European Investment Bank
Directorate R:	Resources, and Institutional Relations

Education and Culture

Directorate A:	Lifelong Learning; Socrates, Erasmus and Tempus Programmes
Directorate B:	Vocational Training Policies; Languages
Directorate C:	Culture; Media; Multi-Media; Sport
Directorate D:	Youth, Civil Society & Communication
Directorate E:	Resources

Employment and Social Affairs

Directorate A:	Employment Policy, Analysis, Strategy & Services
Directorates B & C:	Monitoring of National Employment Policies and Social Inclusion
Directorate D:	Social Dialogue; Labour Laws; Anti-Discrimination; Health, Safety & Hygiene.
Directorate E:	Social Protection and Inclusion; Free Movement; Integration of the Disabled.
Directorate F:	Internal Resources
Directorate G:	International Issues; Enlargement; Sex Equality.

Energy and Transport

Directorate A:	Internal Resources; International Relations.
Directorate B:	Trans-European Energy & Transport Networks.
Directorate C:	Electricity, Gas, Coal & Oil
Directorate D:	New and Renewable Energy Sources; Regulatory Policy; Clean Transport
Directorate E:	Inland Transport (Roads, Waterways, Rail); Safety; Navigation
Directorate F:	Air Transport (Regulation, Traffic Management, Security & Safety; International Agreements)
Directorate G:	Maritime Transport; Ports; Safety.
Directorate H:	Euratom; Nuclear Safety; Non-Proliferation
Directorate I:	Nuclear Inspections; Reprocessing and Enrichment Plants

Enterprise

Directorate R:	Internal Resources, Management & Strategy
Directorate A:	Enterprise Policy, Competitiveness and External Aspects
Directorate B:	Promotion of Entrepreneurship and Small & Medium-Size Enterprises
Directorate C:	Innovation & Communication
Directorate D:	Service Industries, Tourism; Textiles, Fashion and Design.
Directorate E:	Environmental Aspects; Metals, Chemicals, Forestry & Transport Industries
Directorate F:	Single Market Management; Consumer Goods Legislation; Pharmaceutical, Food & Automotive Industries.
Directorate G:	Single Market Regulation; Standardisation; Engineering, Medical, Scientific & Construction Industries

Environment
Directorate A:	Production, Consumption & Waste
Directorate B:	Water, Sea, & Soil; Forests & Agriculture; Health & Urban; Bio-Diversity
Directorate C:	Air, Noise & Transport; Climate Change; Biotechnology & Pesticides.
Directorate D:	LIFE Programme; Civil Protection; Legal Implementation & Enforcement.
Directorate E:	International Affairs; Trade & Environment; Global Development & Biodiversity.
Directorate F:	Internal Resources Directorate G: Sustainable Development.

Fisheries
Directorate A:	Conservation Policy; Fleet Management; Environmental Health
Directorate B:	External Relations; Bilateral Agreements; Organisation of Markets and Trade.
Directorate C:	Structural Policy; Aquaculture; Monitoring of each Member State
Directorate D:	Horizontal Policy; Internal Co-ordination; Legal Controls.

Health and Consumer Protection
Directorate A:	Resources; Internal Relations; Legal Affairs.
Directorate B:	Consumer Affairs; Product Safety; Financial Services
Directorate G:	Public Health; Cancer, Drug Dependence & Pollution Related Diseases; Communicable & Emerging Diseases.
Directorate C:	Scientific Opinion
Directorate D:	Food Safety; Food Law; Animal Nutrition; Biological, Chemical & Physical Risks.
Directorate E:	Food Safety; Plant & Animal Health
Directorate F:	Food & Veterinary Office; Food of Mammal, Bird, Fish & Plant Origin; Import Controls

Information Society
Directorate R:	Resources & Support
Directorate A:	Information Society Strategy
Directorate B:	Regulatory Framework; Communications; Internet
Directorate C:	Electronics Components & Systems: eHealth; eGovernment
Directorate D:	Communications Networks; Security & Software; eBusiness; eTen
Directorate E:	Interfaces & Cognition; Learning; Preservation and Enhancement of Cultural Heritage
Directorate F:	Emerging Technologies; New Working Environments; Elderly & Disabled Persons

Internal Market
Directorate A:	Administrative Support & Communication
Directorate B:	Internal Market Strategy, Analysis and Legal Affairs
Directorate C:	Free Movement of Goods; Regulated Professions; Postal Services

Directorate D:	Public Procurement Policy; Surveillance of each Member State.	
Directorate E:	Industrial Property; Intellectual Property; Media and Data Protection	
Directorate F:	Financial Services Policy; Banking and Financial Conglomerates; Insurance; Retail and Payment Systems.	
Directorate G:	Financial Markets; Company Law; Financial Crime; Accounting & Auditing.	

Joint Research Centre

Directorate of Science Strategy
Directorate of Resources
Institute of Reference Materials and Measurements
Institute of Transuranic Elements
Institute for Energy
Institute for the Protection and Security of the Citizen
Institute for the Environment and Sustainability
Institute for Health and Consumer Protection
Institute for Prospective Technological Studies

Justice and Home Affairs

Directorate A:	Free Movement of Persons (Visas, borders, Schengen area); Immigration & Asylum; Judicial Co-operation (Civil); Drug Abuse Prevention; Citizenship, Fundamental Rights, Racism & Xenophobia.
Directorate B:	Police & Customs Co-operation; Organised Crime; Judicial Co-operation (Criminal); external Relations; Management of Title VI Programmes
Directorate C:	Resources & Communications

Regional Policy

Directorate A:	Conception, Impact, Co-ordination and Evaluation of Regional Policy.
Directorate B:	Community Initiatives and Innovative Action
Directorate C, D & E:	Regional Operations in each Member State
Directorate F:	ISPA and Expansion Measures
Directorate G:	Resources and Management

Research

Directorate A:	Co-ordination of Community Activities
Directorate B:	Structuring European Research; Strengthening Co-operation
Directorate C:	Science & Society; Ethics, Young People, Women.
Directorate D:	Human Factors and Mobility in Science; Fellowships
Directorate E:	Biotechnology and Genomics; Agriculture & Food.
Directorate F:	Health; Major Diseases, Poverty Diseases.
Directorate G:	Industrial Technology; Materials, Nanotechnology, Coal & Steel.
Directorate H:	Space & Transport; (Surface, Aeronautics, Space)
Directorate I:	Environment; Sustainable Development, Water Cycle, Biodiversity, Marine Ecosystems, Urban Sustainability

Directorate J:	Energy; (Production, Distribution, New/Renewable, Nuclear Fission & Fusion)
Directorate K:	Knowledge Based Economy; (Foresight, Competitiveness, Social & Human Sciences)
Directorate L:	Resources

Taxation and Customs Union

Directorate A: Strategy, Internal, International, Legal Affairs. Directorate B: Customs Policy; Legislation, Modernisation, Tariffs.
Directorate C: Tax Policy; Direct, VAT/Turnover Tax, Excise Duties; Transport, Environment and Energy Taxes.
Directorate D: International Training, Management & Co-operation

EXTERNAL RELATIONS OF THE EU Development

Directorate A: Strategy, International Co-operation Directorate B: Political and Sectoral Development Directorate C: Regional; (East Africa, Indian / Pacific Ocean) Directorate D: Regional; (West Africa, Caribbean)

Enlargement EuropeAid - Co-operation Office

Directorate A:	Europe, Caucasus, Central Asia
Directorate B:	Southern Mediterranean, Middle East
Directorate C:	Africa, Caribbean, Pacific
Directorate D:	Asia
Directorate E:	Latin America
Directorate F:	Horizontal Operations; Human Rights and Democracy
Directorate G:	Operational Support Directorate H: General Affairs

External Relations

Directorate A:	Common Foreign & Security Policy
Directorate B:	Multilateral Relations; Human Rights; UN, Law of the Sea, Council of Europe
Directorate C:	North America; East Asia, Australasia, EFTA.
Directorate D:	Western Balkans
Directorate E:	Eastern Europe, Caucasus, Central Asia
Directorate F:	Middle East, South Mediterranean
Directorate G:	Latin America, Asia
Directorate H:	Asia
Directorate I:	Resources
Directorate K:	External Staff and Delegations

Humanitarian Aid Office - ECHO

ECHO 1:	Africa Caribbean, Pacific
ECHO 2:	Eastern Europe, Mediterranean, Middle East
ECHO 3:	Asia, Central & Latin America
ECHO 4:	General Policy; Crises
ECHO 5:	Resources

Trade

Directorate A:	Resources and Analysis
Directorate B:	Trade Defence Instruments and Investigation
Directorate C:	Free Trade Agreements; Agricultural, Fisheries and Sanitary Measures
Directorate D:	WTO; OECD; Dispute Settlement
Directorate E:	Sectoral Trade Agreements; (Textiles, Footwear, Heavy Industry)
Directorate F:	Sustainable Development; New Technologies, Intellectual Property; Standards

GENERAL SERVICES

European Anti-Fraud Office
Eurostat
Press & Communication
Publications Office S
ecretariat General

INTERNAL SERVICES

Budget Office
Financial Control
Policy Advisers
Internal Audit Service
Joint Interpreting & Conference Services
Legal Services
Personnel & Administration
Translation Services

INDEX

Acheson, Dean	50. 104	Caetano	26
Acquis Communitaire	123, 129, 136,	Callaghan, James	171, 180, 187
Act of Parliament	10	Carl Gustav XVI	29
Act of Union 1707	7	Carrington, Peter	199
Adams, John	1	Cash, William	206, 247
Albert II	23	Charles I	5
Alfonso III	24	Charles II	5
Algeria	78	Chirac, Jacques	22
Amery, Julian	54	Churchill, Hague Congress	41
Arsenal Football Club	304	Churchill, Winston	39
Asquith	31	Churchill, Zurich Address	40
Attlee, Clement	45	CILFIT Case	196
Attlee, Clement	46	Clarke, Kenneth	265, 268
Austria	337	Cockfield, Arthur	203
		Colonels, of Greece	27
Baltic States	34	Committee of the Regions (CoR)	88
Bank of England	285	Common Fisheries Policy	130, 157, 221
Barber, Anthony	139	Common Foreign & Security Policy	369
Baudouin, King	23	Commonwealth Sugar	154
Beatrix, Queen	23	Company Law	330
Beivin, Ernest	45	Constantine I	26
Benn, Tony	176	Constitution, Austria	20
Beyen, J.W.	67	Constitution, Belgium	23
Bill of Rights	5	Constitution, Denmark	28
Black Wednesday	245	Constitution, Finland	27
Bretherton, Russel	70	Constitution, France	22
Britain in Europe	185	Constitution, Germany	19
Brown, George	138	Constitution, Ireland	32
Brown, Gordon	285	Constitution, Italy	22
Bruges	213	Constitution, Luxembourg	24
Bruning	18	Constitution, Netherlands	23
Brussels, Treaty of	46	Constitution, Portugal	26
BSE	266	Constitution, Spain	25
BSE	274	Constitution, Sweden	29
Budget	353	Constitution, Switzerland	35
Bulmer v Bollinger	190, 194	Convention on the Future of Europe	412
Butler, R. A.	68	Cook, Robin	285
		Corruption	313

Costa v ENEL	143, 162, 309
Council of Europe	42
Council of European Union	83
Court of Auditors	90
Court of First Instance	87
Cresson, Edith	313
Currency Stability	398
Cyprus	34
De Gaulle, General	79, 112
De Valera, Eamonn	31
Declaration of Indulgence	7
Dehaene, Jean-Luc	264, 412
Delors, Jacques	202, 211, 215, 413
Denning, Lord	1, 197
Dicey, A.V.	1, 9
Diplock	15
Direct Effect	117
Directives	99
Discrimination	225
Disraeli	63
Dollfuss	20
Douglas-Home, Alec	107
Duke v GEC Reliance	225
Dulles, John	64
Duncan-Smith, Ian	274
Eccles, David	54
Economic & Social Committee (ECOSOC)	87
ECSC (European Coal & Steel Community)	52
ECSC (European Coal & Steel Community)	56
EDC (European Defence Community)	60
Eden, Anthony	54, 59, 61, 79
Eisenhower, Dwight	65
Empty Chair	113
EMU	397
Enabling Act	18
Enforcement, Commission	100
Enforcement, Commission	219
Enlargement	356
EPC (European Political Community)	60
Equal Treatment Directive	122
ERTA Case	256, 306, 325
European Arrest Warrant	377
European Central Bank (ECB)	90
European Commission	84
European Communities Act 1972	173
European Council	83
European Court of Justice	85, 117
European Free Trade Assocn (EFTA)	80, 135
European Investment Bank (EIB)	91
European Parliament	83
European Scrutiny Committee	382
European Security & Defence Policy (ESDP)	368
European Standing Committees	381
Exchange Rate Mechanism (ERM)	197, 213, 215, 217, 239
Factortame Case	229, 271, 309
Five Economic Tests	399
Flexibility	340
Foot and Mouth Disease	279
Foot, Michael	170, 280
Foster v British Gas	123
Fouchet Plan	112
Franco	25
Francovich Case	125
Fuller, Thomas	1
Gaitskell, Hugh	104
Garland v British Rail	224
General de Gaulle	21
George I & II, Hellenes	26
Giscard d'Estaing, Valeri	21, 181, 333, 363, 412
Goldsmith, James	268

Gustav V & VI	29	Judicial Obedience	14
		Judicial Reasoning	13
Habsburg Monarchy	20	Juliana, Queen	23
Haider, Jorg	337	Justice & Home Affairs	373
Hain, Peter	388, 391		
Håkon VII	30	Karamanlis	27
Hallstein, Walter	113	Keynes, John Maynard	44
Harald V	30	King, Anthony	179
Harmel, Pierre	140	Kinnock, Neil	242, 280, 305, 318
Hattersley, Roy	170, 178	Kohl, Helmut	200
Healey, Dennis	170, 187		
Heath, Edward	53, 96, 131, 166	Laeken Declaration	409
Helsinki Summit	295	Lamont, Norman	244, 260
Henn & Darby Case	194	Lawson, Nigel	212
Henri, Grand Duke	24	LeCourt, Robert	259
Henry VIII	6	Leopold, King	23
Heseltine, Michael	218, 268	Les Verts Case	101
Hindenburg	18	Levi Strauss v Tesco	302
Hitler	18	Lisbon Summit	299, 352
Hogg, Quintin	54	Litster v Forth Dry Dock	224
Howe, Geoffrey	198, 212, 215	Literal Interpretation	14
Human Rights	312	Lloyd, Selwyn	66
Hurd, Douglas	216, 243, 260, 260	Louis XIV, XVI	5
		Luxembourg Accord	113
Implied Powers	58		
Implied Repeal	10	Macmillan, Harold	51, 63, 69, 79, 92
Indirect Effect	122	Mad Cow Disease	266
Intellectual Property	302	Macarthys v Smith	223
Intention of Parliament	14	Major, John	216, 238
International Treaties	160	Makarios, Archbishop	35
Interntaionale Hendelsgesellschaft Case		Malta	34
	233, 331	Mandelson, Peter	280
		Margrethe II	28
James I	5	Marleasing Case	125, 225
James II	5, 6	Marshall v Soton AHA	123
Jay, Douglas	176	Marshall Plan	45
Jenkins, Roy	170, 177, 178, 190	Messina	67
Juan Carlos, King	25	Metaxas, General	26
Judge Jeffreys	6	Metric Martyrs	307
Judicial Abuse	6	Mintoff, Don	34

Mischief Rule	14	Quisling	30
Mitterand, Francois	22, 200		
Molotov	45	Redwood, John	260, 265
Monarchy	3	Referendum Party	268
Monnet, Jean	49, 67	Regulations	99
Moro, Aldo	23	Robinson, John	114
Mussolini	20, 22	Rogers, William	170
		Roosevelt, Theodore	1
Napoleon	17	Royal Power	4
Nasser, Colonel	64	Rule of Law	1
National Referendum Campaign	185	Rutili Case	228
NATO	341, 368		
New Labour	282	Salazar, Antonio	25
New Zealand Lamb	154	Santer, Jacques	264, 291, 314
Nice Treaty	339	Schmidt, Helmut	181
		Schumann Plan	43, 49
Ombudsman	90	Schumann Plan	49
O'Neill, Con	107, 109, 147	Scottish Parliament	384
Open Skies	305	Scrutiny Reserve Resolution	383
Operation Resurrection	78	Secondary legislation	99
Overseas Investment	394	Sforza, Count	53
Owen, David	199	Simmenthal Case	145, 230
		Single European Act	205, 207
Papandreou	27	Smith, John	282
Parliamentary Supremacy	7, 9	Soames, Christopher	114, 198
Patten, Christopher	371, 405	Social Chapter	272, 285
Pearson, Lester	66	Social Democratic Party	280
Pickstone v Freeman	225	Social Legislation	348
Pleven Plan	59	Sovereignty	93
Pompidou, Georges	21, 127, 177	Sovereignty, Pooling	96
Portillo, Michael	265	Spaak, Paul-Henri	42, 46, 67
Powell, Enoch	168	Stability and Growth Pact	399
Precedent	13	Star Chamber	6
Pregnancy	225	Stewart, Michael	115
Preliminary Reference	101	Strasbourg Assembly, 1949	42
Primary legislation	98	Subsidiarity	332
Primo de Rivera	24	Suez Crisis	65
Prodi, Romano	316	Sunday Trading	234
Proportionality	232	Supremacy	57, 143
Purposive Interpretation	87, 223		

Tax	294	Victor Emmanuel III	22
Tescos	303	Vitorino, Antonio	374, 376
Thatcher, Margaret	186, 198, 211	Von Colson Case	124
Thousand Years of History	16	Von Papen	18
Tizard, Henry	44	Webb v EMO Air Cargo	225
Torfaen Council v B & Q	234	Weiler, J H H	57, 259
Trade Statistics	389	Weimar Constitution	17
Treaty Making Power	160	WEU (Western European Union)	61
Treaty of Amsterdam	287	William III and Mary II	5, 7
Treaty of Rome	73	Williams, Shirley	178
Turkey	363	Wilson, Harold	106, 107, 169, 177
		Working Time Directive	271
Van Duyn v Home Office	193, 228		
Van Gend Case	117, 121	Young, Hugo	183
Veto, De Gaulle	97	Younger, Kenneth	52